Windows NT Network Management

Reducing Total Cost of Ownership

Other Books by New Riders Press

Windows NT DNS
Michael Masterson, Herman Kneif, Scott Vinick, & Eric Roul
ISBN: 1-56205-943-2

Windows NT Registry
Sandra Osborne
ISBN: 1-56205-941-6

Windows NT Performance
Monitoring, Benchmarking, and Tuning
Mark Edmead & Paul Hinsburg
ISBN: 1-56205-942-4

Windows NT TCP/IP
Karanjit Siyan
ISBN 1-56205-887-8

Windows NT Terminal Server & Citrix
MetaFrame
Ted Harwood
ISBN: 1-56205-944-0

Implementing Exchange Server
Doug Hauger, Marywynne Leon, & William C. Wade III
ISBN: 1-56205-931-9

SQL Server Administration
Sean Baird & Chris Miller
ISBN: 1-56205-955-6

Cisco Router Configuration &
Troubleshooting
Mark Tripod
ISBN: 0-7357-0024-9

Windows NT Network Management

Reducing Total Cost of Ownership

201 West 103rd Street,
Indianapolis, Indiana 46290

Anil Desai

Windows NT Network Management Reducing Total Cost of Ownership

Copyright © 1999 by New Riders Publishing

All rights reserved. No part of this book shall be repro-
duced, stored in a retrieval system, or transmitted by any
means, electronic, mechanical, photocopying, recording, or
otherwise, without written permission from the publisher.
No patent liability is assumed with respect to the use of the
information contained herein. Although every precaution
has been taken in the preparation of this book, the publisher
and author assume no responsibility for errors or omissions.
Neither is any liability assumed for damages resulting from
the use of the information contained herein.

International Standard Book Number: 1-56205-946-7

Library of Congress Catalog Card Number: 98-89435

Printed in the United States of America

First Printing: *March 1999*

03　02　01　00　99　　　7　6　5　4　3　2　1

Interpretation of the printing code: The rightmost double-
digit number is the year of the book's printing; the rightmost single-digit number is the number of the book's
printing. For example, the printing code 99-1 shows that
the first printing of the book occurred in 1999.

Publisher
David Dwyer

Executive Editors
Ann Trump Daniel
Al Valvano

Acquisitions Editor
Suzanne Toppy

Development Editor
Kitty Wilson Jarrett

Managing Editor
Patrick Kanouse

Project Editor
Jen Nuckles

Copy Editor
June Waldman

Indexer
Cheryl Landis

Technical Editors
Raymond Goss
Brent Jones
Andrew Lam
Andie O'Brien

Proofreader
Megan Wade

Production
Darin Crone

Contents

Introduction   xv
Who This Book Is For   xv
How This Book Is Organized   xvi
Conventions Used   xxiii

I   An Introduction to TCO   1

1   Measuring Total Cost of Ownership   3
Defining TCO   3
The TCO Reduction Process   5
IT Organization Structure   10
Information Technologies   15

2   Total Cost of Ownership Studies and Tools   19
Who Should You Believe?   20
TCO Studies   21
TCO Assessment Tools   25

3   General Best Practices for Reducing TCO   33
Managing IT's Business Role   33
Managing the Help Desk   36
Establishing Goals and Metrics   38
Managing Assets and Technology   41
Managing Employees   45

II   Network Administration   51

4   Policies and Procedures   53
The Importance of Policies   53
Network Policies   55
Communications Policies   59
IT Resource Management   62
More Best Practices   66

5 Network Management   69

Using Administrative Tools   69

User Management   73

File System Management   77

Command-Line Management Tools   78

Service Management   82

License Management   83

More Network Management Features   85

Case Study: Getting Network Information   87

6 TCP/IP Management   89

An Overview of TCP/IP   90

TCP/IP Name Resolution   92

TCP/IP Tools and Troubleshooting   96

Implementing DHCP   102

TCP/IP Security   107

Case Study: Improving the Management of an IP-Based Network   110

7 Security   113

Planning for Security   114

Windows NT Security Basics   116

Managing User Permissions   117

Windows NT Auditing   121

Network-Level Security   124

Additional Security Measures   127

Case Study: Tightening Security Policies   129

8 Data Protection   133

The Basics of Backing Up   134

Using Windows NT Backup   139

Fault-Tolerance: RAID   141

More Data Protection Options   144

Recovering Lost Data   147

Case Study: Data Protection   149

9 Performance Monitoring 153

Performance Monitoring Methodology 154

The Windows NT Performance Monitor 155

The Windows NT Task Manager 162

The Windows NT Network Monitor 166

The Windows 95/98 System Monitor 168

Case Study: Troubleshooting Server Performance 169

10 Performance Optimization 173

The Goal: Moving the Bottleneck 174

Hardware Basics 174

Optimizing Memory Settings 177

Optimizing Network Performance 182

Hardware Tuning 184

More Performance Optimization Tips 187

Case Study: Increasing Memory Performance 188

III Advanced Network Administration 191

11 Remote Management 193

Server Management 193

Workstation and User Management 200

Web-Based Management 202

More Remote Management Techniques 207

Thin Clients and Windows NT Terminal Server 210

Case Study: Remote Troubleshooting 212

12 Remote Access Service 215

Windows NT RAS Basics 216

Server Configuration 216

Setting Up Your Modems 217

Client Configuration 223

Other New Features in Windows NT RAS 224

Case Study: Making Applications Available Remotely 227

13 Virtual Private Networking   231

Virtual Private Networking Basics   232

Server Configuration and Client Setup   234

Internet Reliability and Service Levels   240

The Routing and Remote Access Server Update   241

Alternatives to a Windows NT VPN   241

Case Study: Improving Remote Access   244

14 Automated Software Installations   249

When to Automate   250

Automating a Windows NT Workstation Installation   250

Installing Applications with SysDiff   256

More Automation Options   261

Other Automated Installation Methods   262

Case Study: Automating Installations Based on User Requirements   265

15 Web-Based Technologies   269

Web–Based Solutions   270

Web–Based Publishing Tools   276

Building a Windows NT Web Platform   282

Other Web-Enabling Technologies   285

Case Study: Making Information Access Easier   288

16 Web Applications   291

Outlook Web Access   292

Web Database Publishing   295

Streaming Media Content   303

More Web-Based Applications   304

Case Studies   305

17 Implementing a Secure FTP Site   309

What Is FTP?   310

Configuring the FTP Service   311

Managing Security   314

Accessing the FTP Site   318

Case Study: Using FTP for Cross-Platform, Secure File Sharing   321

18 Enforcing System Policies 323

The Importance of Enforcing Policies 324

Managing User Profiles 324

System Policies 332

The Windows NT Zero Administration Kit 338

Other Concerns 340

Case Study: Managing Profiles and Policies Based on User Requirements 342

19 Scripting 345

Scripting Basics 346

VBScript Language Basics 352

Running WSH Scripts 353

WSH Scripting Applications 356

More Scripting Tools 360

Case Study: Automating Routine Tasks 361

IV The Future of TCO 363

20 Windows 2000 TCO Features   365

Windows 2000 Packaging 366

Simplifying Administration 367

Client Management 368

Storage Management 369

Active Directory Services 372

Network Support 374

Additional Enhancements 376

Preparing for Windows 2000 379

21 The Future of TCO Management 381

Technology Advances 382

IT Industry Advances 386

Business Advances 389

Social Changes 392

The Future of Microsoft Windows 393

V   Appendixes   395

A   Windows Updates   397
Versions Used in This Book   398
Windows NT Service Packs   398
The Routing and Remote Access Update for NT Server   398
Windows NT Option Packs   398
Security-Related Hotfixes, Patches, and Bulletins   400
Windows 95/98 Updates   401
Downloading Updates   401

B   Resources for More Information   403
Microsoft Resources   403
Internet Resources   407

C   What's on the CD   413
Multimedia Demonstrations   414
Macmillan Knowledge Base   418

Index   421

About the Author

Anil Desai is currently working as a consultant and technical trainer in Austin, Texas. He specializes in Windows NT consulting, implementation, and troubleshooting. Anil's technical qualifications include being a Microsoft Certified Systems Engineer and an Oracle Certified Database Administrator. He has written numerous technical papers on topics relating to best practices for using Windows NT and continues to present them at national conferences. Anil is also the co-author of *MCSE Fast Track: SQL Server 7.0 Administration Exam Guide* (New Riders Press).

In his free time, Anil enjoys cycling in and around Austin, playing the electric guitar, and playing computer games. He welcomes your questions and comments at Akdesai@austin.rr.com.

About the Reviewers

Raymond Goss is a computer telephony systems architect for MCI Worldcom. He has been using and programming on Windows NT since 1993. His current focus is on network routing of phone calls, email, voice over IP, and other communication requests for large call centers. He received a degree in material science and engineering from the University of Pennsylvania.

Brent Jones is a senior systems analyst with Sprint Paranet, specializing in the areas of UNIX administration and management, heterogeneous systems integration, and improving UNIX and NT interoperability. He also has an interest in database administration and has worked extensively with Oracle databases for the past two years. He is an alumnus of the University of Texas at Austin, with a bachelor's degree in computer science, and is currently a resident of Austin, Texas.

Andrew Lam is a technical analyst working for Sprint Paranet in Austin, Texas (www.sprintparanet.com). He is working toward becoming a Microsoft Certified Systems Engineer. He graduated from ITT Technical Institute with an associate's degree in electronic engineering. He has worked as an NT administrator at Motorola in Austin, Texas.

Andie O'Brien is an NT and SMS administrator for Akzo Nobel, Inc., in Chicago. She is a Microsoft Certified Systems Engineer in NT 4.0 as well as a Certified Network Engineer in NetWare. She has previously done consulting work around the country. She is pleased to be able to combine her technical skills with her bachelor's degree in English.

For Monica

Acknowledgments

It would be easy for me to take credit for all the material in this book, but it's only fair to acknowledge everyone who helped to make this book a reality. As I read over the final manuscript, I noticed how well things seemed to flow together. This was not due to a stroke of genius—it took a lot of hard work from a lot of people. First, I'd like to thank **Kitty Jarrett** for all her hard work in editing every chapter of this book. Several months ago, in relating a story to me, she mentioned that "No one buys a book because of the development editor." That's a shame, because I can't overemphasize how much of a difference she made by editing and coordinating the seemingly endless steps of the publication process. Thanks must go to **Ann Daniel** for giving me the opportunity to write this book and to **Suzanne Toppy** for her help in overseeing the process to completion.

All the technical chapters you are about to read have been thoroughly reviewed by several IT professionals. I'd like to thank **Andrew Lam**, **Brent Jones**, **Raymond Goss**, and **Andie O'Brien** for their insights. Each reviewer brought a different perspective to the material. They made sure that if something wasn't covered, it was because it was outside the scope of the chapter. They also caught places where I needed notes and pointed out areas that needed improvement. I'd also like to thank **Jack Belbot** for creating the excellent front end for the information included on the CD-ROM.

There are many others who worked behind the scenes to bring the book to completion. Their names are mentioned on the copyright page, and I am grateful for all their hard work. With the help of this team, the book you are holding contains polished and technically accurate content that I hope you find useful in your career.

Your Feedback Is Valuable

As the reader of this book, *you* are our most important critic and commentator. We value your opinion and want to know what we're doing right, what we could do better, what areas you'd like to see us publish in, and any other words of wisdom you're willing to pass our way.

As the executive editor for the Networking team at New Riders Press, I welcome your comments. You can fax, email, or write me directly to let me know what you did or didn't like about this book—as well as what we can do to make our books stronger.

Please note that I cannot help you with technical problems related to the topic of this book, and that due to the high volume of mail I receive, I might not be able to reply to every message.

When you write, please be sure to include this book's title and author, as well as your name and phone or fax number. I will carefully review your comments and share them with the author and editors who worked on the book.

Fax:	317-581-4663
Email:	newriders@mcp.com
Mail:	Al Valvano
	Executive Editor
	New Riders Press
	201 West 103rd Street
	Indianapolis, IN 46290 USA

Introduction

Welcome to *Windows NT Network Management: Reducing Total Cost of Ownership.*
Perhaps you're thinking about purchasing the book, or you've already bought it and
want an overview of the content. In either case, this introduction gives you a brief
idea of the thoughts and goals that made the book a reality. The goal of this book is
to provide real-world solutions that you can apply in your own environment to reduce
costs and complexity while increasing operating efficiency. I joked with an editor a
while ago that a critical reader would say that there's one sure-fire way to save
a little money—not buying this book. However, in order to save money, you know
you'll have to spend some first (the basic idea of investing). So how do I justify this
investment?

Several months ago, I was looking through a bookshelf at a local bookstore and saw
what many of you are probably looking at right now—a sea of technical books.
Subjects ranged from details on implementing Active Server Pages to working with
Microsoft Word. At the other end of the spectrum (not in the technical section at all)
were a few books on reducing costs and efficiently managing technology in organizations. Recently, many independent research groups have published total cost of ownership (TCO) studies that outline how other organizations have saved money by
implementing certain unspecified best practices. Although these resources generally
deliver what they promise—technical or management information—they often fall
short of displaying the whole picture. The missing link seemed to be something that
bridged this gap. What about readers who are currently working in an IT organization
and want to know how specific solutions will fit into their corporate structure? They
want answers to questions such as, How much can I reduce my own TCO? What are
some specific ways to do this? How do certain technical ideas fit into my company's
business plan?

Who This Book Is For

In the following chapters, you'll find information about how you can maximize the
efficiency of the hardware and software you already own. In fact, in most cases you
will be able to avoid making additional investments by better managing your existing
ones. The goal of this book is to provide IT professionals with concrete ideas for
improving their own environments. I explain how you can implement some of the
many different technologies available on the market today and give examples and case
studies that illustrate how they may best fit into your organization. Few readers will
find all of the ideas helpful and applicable to their environments. This is good, though,
because part of your job is to assess and recommend ideas for your own environment.
However, I expect that even fewer readers will find nothing here that can help them.
The goal, then, is to make you—the IT professional—more proactive and to move you
into a problem-solving role.

This book was not designed to prepare you for taking Microsoft Certified Professional (MCP) certification exams. However, this material will be very helpful for readers seeking that certification. The best way to learn some of the intricacies of a network operating system is to perform useful, real-world tasks with it. Some of you may remember trying to set Audit permissions on an NT Server share without first enabling Auditing in User Manager for Domains. These are very useful lessons, and nobody should think less of you for making the mistake the first time. By the same token, I suspect that it would be very difficult to even *think* about implementing some of these solutions without learning something new about Windows NT and the functionality it supports.

How This Book Is Organized

As I mentioned earlier, this book contains information related to technical implementations and management considerations. It is broken into five parts. In Part I, "An Introduction to TCO," we discuss the meaning of TCO, including the factors that make up this somewhat mysterious money pit. After you have a good handle on how to measure and manage TCO, you'll be ready for Part II, "Network Administration," in which you learn best practices for maintaining your network. Part III, "Advanced Network Administration and Implementation," takes these ideas further by covering newer technologies that can be used to increase efficiencies and reduce costs. Parts II and III home in on the actual practices you can employ in your own environment to control the cost impact of these factors. You will find many ideas to help you tame the challenges of managing your own network environment. Whether you're supporting 5 nodes or 5,000, simple administration tools and techniques can help increase efficiency. Finally, Part IV, "The Future of TCO," looks ahead to technologies that will help reduce TCO in the future. Part V, "Appendixes," provides valuable information about Windows updates and sources for further information.

I am hoping that you will read the book from cover to cover, but it's more realistic to assume that you'll search for specific items of interest. Much of the information relates to both IT management and IT personnel. Here are some general recommendations on where to start:

- If you're a semi-technical IT manager and are looking for new ways to control costs and increase the efficiency of your network management, start at Chapter 1, "Measuring Total Cost of Ownership." You'll probably find Part I to be of most value as a general overview. To find specific solutions, review the introduction and conclusion of each technical chapter in Parts II and III to get an idea of what changes can be implemented in your own environment. Pass these ideas along to your technical staff to evaluate if they're the right solutions for you.

- If you're an experienced Windows NT systems administrator looking for technical information about specific solutions, you may want to jump ahead to Part II. That's where the technical information about Windows NT starts. However, I also strongly urge you to read about TCO in Part I to see how these solutions fit into the big picture for your organization. This information will greatly help you get buy-in from managers so that you can realize your ideas.

■ If you're a newcomer to Windows NT and want to learn more, there's no better place to start than with Chapter 5, "Network Management." There you learn about the basic administration tools included with the Windows NT operating system. If that information is a little over your head, you can find help by turning to Appendix B, "Resources for More Information." Then continue with the chapters in Parts II and III and wrap up by reading Part I for an overview of business applications for TCO.

Throughout this book, you'll find solid discussions of Windows NT– and TCO-related best practices that can be applied in your environment. In many cases, the technical tools and techniques in this book give you enough information to implement specific solutions. However, one of the problems with covering so many topics is that some of the depth must be sacrificed (unless, of course, you want to carry a book that only Fred Flintstone would approve of). Therefore, if you need details on implementing a specific solution, you may need to refer to some of the resources cited within the chapters. For example, in Chapter 14, "Automated Software Installations," I describe various techniques for using freely available tools for automating an otherwise tedious process. I provide a basic walkthrough of the steps and include enough information for you to effectively use them in your own environment. However, if you need more details on troubleshooting a specific error message or you encounter other problems, you need to refer to one or more of the numerous resources cited in the chapter. By covering information at this level, I can more easily address a broad range of topics without wallowing in too many details.

Software developers have noticed the need for supporting the software they develop. After all, a mysterious black box that contains the secrets of the universe is useless if you don't know how to open it. For those of us who are used to working in Windows NT environments, simply knowing that a solution exists is enough information for finding out how to do it. In many cases, the technical tools and techniques in this book give you enough information to implement specific solutions.

Because of the complexities of systems administration, no section of this book really stands completely by itself. The topics in each section are interrelated. For example, in Chapter 17, "Implementing a Secure FTP Site," I show you how to set up a secure solution for sharing files. However, portions of this topic go hand in hand with learning how to use the command line. From command-line basics, you may want to learn how to use the Windows Scripting Host (described in Chapter 19, "Scripting"). You'll also want to reference information about setting Windows NT File System (NTFS) permissions in Chapter 5. So the goal of the chapters is not to give you one isolated topic that can be used apart from all the others. Instead, I provide ideas that will *add* to your list of tools. And, as always, you'll be referred to sources outside the confines of this book for more information. The result, as you'll see in every chapter, is to increase the efficiency and decrease the costs associated with implementing, supporting, and managing any Windows NT–based network environment.

How Each Chapter Is Organized

One of the ideas that I mention repeatedly throughout this book is the importance of organization. Therefore, it's only fair that I explain the organization of the chapters:

- *Introduction*—This section points out the background behind a certain technical issue. Specifically, it discusses the problems that the chapter intends to solve and gives an overview of the solution.

- *The technical stuff*—You may not see this heading anywhere in the book, but this is the real substance of most chapters. Here you find information on implementing a new solution or using various network management techniques to improve your environment. Although it is part of my goal to walk you through the implementation of a solution, I simply don't have enough space to discuss all the details. Wherever appropriate, sidebars refer you to an external source for further information on specific details or to one of the many useful multimedia demonstrations on the CD-ROM (see Appendix B and Appendix C, "What's on the CD," for a complete reference).

- *Case studies*—Appearing at the end of most chapters, the "Case Study" section focuses on a specific task or problem faced by XYZ Corp. Before you try to look up their stock symbol, I should tell you that this is a fictitious company (although some of the examples are based on real stories). The solution to each case study represents one possible way of solving the problem and provides a high-level technical overview of the steps involved. For details, you need to have read the information earlier in the chapter or, on occasion, refer to other sources.

- *The bottom line*—This is what it's all about! I recap how the solutions we discussed will help reduce your TCO. Although I'd love to tell you that this solution will reduce your TCO by 31.7% in the first year and pay for itself in 723 days, it's much more plausible to be vague. I mention potential benefits such as a reduction in personnel or time savings. Ultimately, it will be up to you to find out if and how these tools and techniques can benefit your environment.

- *For more information*—Throughout the text, I refer to product documentation, Internet resources, and a host of other tools and utilities. The reference icon in the margin of pertinent paragraphs directs you to a particular item in the "For More Information" section of the chapter.

- *Further reading*—Many other resources provide detailed information on the topic of each chapter. In the "Further Reading" sections, I mention papers and other books that offer extended coverage.

Implementing the Ideas

A common complaint of IT implementers is, "We'd like to do that, but management won't let us." If you're working in an IT organization of any size, you've probably seen that the challenge of getting support from management can be far greater than the challenge of implementing a technical solution. You're not alone in feeling that many great ideas get passed up for not-so-great ones. If managers often seem to be an obstacle, it is partially because it is part of their job to serve as a gatekeeper between ideas and implementations. Indeed, if they gave every person with a "great idea for redesigning the entire network" free reign, chaos would ensue. However, it is unfortunate how easily just a few people can stomp on an excellent and low-cost solution. Consequently, your job includes the goal of selling your solutions to others in the organization. Here are a few techniques you can use to get buy-in for your ideas:

- *Explain the problem*—Although it may not seem necessary, specify why you think there is a problem. Perhaps management is not aware that your end users require some functionality or that a great deal of your time is spent solving problems based on a single cause. If possible, include hard numbers on costs that you think are incurred by the problem. Use this to get others' attention.

- *Explain your solution*—Go into the details of how you plan to solve the problem. For management, it is probably appropriate to ignore technical details. Describe how your solution addresses the problem as you see it and the potential benefits. Be prepared for alternative suggestions and justify why yours is better.

- *Outline costs (including time)*—Estimate the costs of any new hardware, software, or networking items you'll need to purchase. Also, give a best estimate on how long it will take you to implement your idea and how other projects may be affected.

- *Specify benefits of implementing the solution*—For accountants and managers who see things in the light of cost savings, outline how you think your idea will fit into the grand design of your organization. Suppose you're trying to get buy-in on a $15,000 help desk system. If you're supporting 400 users, a one-time cost of $37.50 per user might sound much better than the initial purchase price. Also, a potential reduction in the size of the help desk staff could represent a substantial savings, making the solution pay for itself quite quickly. Part I provides more details on addressing these benefits.

For many, this is far too much work for implementing what may seem like a simple idea. For example, suppose a network administrator wants to implement the Dynamic Host Configuration Protocol (DHCP) (described in Chapter 6, "TCP/IP Management") to make addressing easier on a network segment. His manager, however, says that users are already upset that the IT department is making too many changes, and she turns down the idea. There are several ways to approach this situation. Of course, the first is to give up. There's also a good chance that this approach will be the easiest. But if you really believe in the idea, go through the preceding steps. Explain that managing IP addresses takes a significant chunk of your time—time that could be better spent on other projects (such as rolling out new software or answering help desk calls). Explain that implementing DHCP will be completely transparent to most of your users. Furthermore, mention that you can still allocate static addresses using DHCP but that now you can do so more efficiently from a central point of administration than by visiting individual machines. Emphasize that setting up DHCP on the server takes only a few minutes and that clients can be configured whenever IT visits the desktop for a routine troubleshooting call. Finally, be sure to mention the amount of time you expect to salvage by ditching your semiaccurate Microsoft Access database of IP addresses and concentrating on more challenging tasks.

The question remains: Why should you go through this trouble? First, the proposed solution attracted your attention for some reason—perhaps it makes your job easier, enhances the end-user's experience, or is better for your company in some way. Second, it's a way for you to work with upper management on getting things done. If that doesn't make you feel better, at least consider that you've tried your best to improve the situation. Better yet, document your suggestion—if the solution is ever implemented, you want to get the credit. Finally, finding new solutions is probably one of the things that attracted you to IT in the first place. It's also one of the things that will help you move up (within your company or at another one). Implementing DHCP may not seem like a big deal now, but just mention that you "helped make the process of creating and maintaining network addresses much easier" at your next review! Finally, if your company is too stubborn to use your strengths, there are many others out there that will!

Few things work completely on the first try. Although this may sound pessimistic, it's also one reason IT professionals have jobs. Figuring out what went wrong, and how to fix it, can often be the most challenging part of our jobs. If a given tool or technique doesn't do everything you want, be sure to use your resources. Investigate alternatives, find add-ons, and use information from the Internet. Chances are, you'll find something that will at least help, if not solve, your problems.

Reader Assumptions

Many IT solutions are based on the applications of some basic ideas and concepts. The technical walkthroughs and examples in this book assume that the reader is familiar with basic network administration skills such as

- Using the Windows interface, including scrollbars, drop-down boxes, and check boxes
- Navigating the file system, including copying and moving files
- Using standard command-line functions, including changing directories and copying and moving files
- Installing common applications

- Adding and modifying user accounts
- Differentiating between a workgroup and a Windows NT domain
- Handling addressing and connectivity requirements
- Working with hard disks, CPUs, and memory
- Making basic network configuration changes (such as TCP/IP addressing)

If you need more information on some of these topics, don't worry. You can find excellent sources for learning these skills in other places. Several resources are outlined in Appendix B, and you'll find the contents of the CD-ROM to be invaluable (see Appendix C for details).

Best Practices Summary

If you're unfamiliar with some of the topics in this book, you can use the following table to get an idea of some of the best practices you'll learn in each chapter.

Chapter Number	Title	Best Practices Discussed
1	Measuring Total Cost of Ownership	Define TCO and how it can be calculated for your own environment
2	Total Cost of Ownership Studies and Tools	Learn about TCO-related tools that can assist you in reducing TCO and studies that demonstrate TCO issues based on industry research
3	General Best Practices for Reducing TCO	Utilize general best practices for reducing TCO in your own environment
4	Policies and Procedures	Develop and implement policies and procedures for better managing your network
5	Network Management	Use Windows NT's Administrative Tools and other utilities to efficiently manage your networked environment
6	TCP/IP Management	Use Windows tools to simplify the implementation, management, and support of the TCP/IP protocol in your own environment
7	Security	Prevent unauthorized network and systems access by implementing and enforcing a strong security policy
8	Data Protection	Develop and implement a comprehensive backup and restore plan to protect your organization against data loss

continues

Chapter Number	Title	Best Practices Discussed
9	Performance Monitoring	Measure the performance of your hardware, software, and network investments and identify bottlenecks
10	Performance Optimization	Apply performance information to alleviate bottlenecks and to maximize the value of your investments
11	Remote Management	Save time and increase efficiency by managing your hardware, software, and network resources from a central location
12	Remote Access Service	Allow traveling and other remote users to transparently access network resources
13	Virtual Private Networking	Leverage the availability of the Internet to decrease remote access costs and increase information accessibility
14	Automated Software Installations	Efficiently deploy operating systems and applications while ensuring consistency and manageability
15	Web-Based Technologies	Utilize new technologies in Web-based intranet/Internet information dissemination
16	Web Applications	Create data-driven Web applications for making information more easily available
17	Implementing a Secure FTP Site	Use the FTP standard to easily share files between heterogeneous operating systems on an intranet or the Internet
18	Enforcing System Policies	Use built-in Windows NT tools to limit end-user configuration options and settings
19	Scripting	Automate common tasks and increase efficiency by creating scripts
20	Windows 2000 TCO Features	Learn how Windows 2000 addresses TCO issues and about new features that can help lower operating costs and increase efficiency in your environment
21	The Future of TCO Management	Predict how organizations will continue to address TCO issues in the future by using TCO analysis, measurement, and reduction methods
Appendix A	Windows Updates	Learn about important Windows 95/98 and Windows NT operating system and application updates

Chapter Number	Title	Best Practices Discussed
Appendix B	Resources for More Information	Use a variety of to find more information on specific tools and technologies
Appendix C	What's on the CD	Learn about the multimedia tutorials included on the accompanying CD-ROM

Conventions Used

Throughout this book, I've used several means to help you find the information you need:

- *Sidebars*—These sections introduce information that is relevant to the content covered but may not flow well with the discussion. Use this information to find tips and notes about the tools and technologies described. "On the CD-ROM" sidebars inform you of multimedia demonstrations that are available on the CD-ROM. For a quick tutorial on how to use or implement a solution, see the demonstrations. For details, see Appendix C.

- *For More Information references*—Throughout Parts II and III, I point you to resources for exploring a given topic in more detail. The number in the margin of the page tells you which resource I've cited. Reference details are listed in the "For More Information" section at the end of each chapter.

- *Web references*—Web links are based on standard URLs. You can type them as listed into any current browser to find more information.

- *Microsoft Knowledge Base articles*—Microsoft uses the designation Q followed by a six-digit number to uniquely identify each of its technical support documents. This information can be used to easily find what you're looking for either in Microsoft TechNet or at `support.microsoft.com`. See Appendix B for more information.

The chapters in Parts II and III of this book assume that your operating system is installed in the following directories:

- Windows 95/98: `c:\windows`
- Windows NT: `c:\winnt`

To provide information on a consistent basis regarding interface and products enhancements, this book assumes you are using the following:

- Windows NT Server or Windows NT Workstation with Service Pack 4. For chapters that reference it, Windows NT Option Pack (including IIS 4.0 and related components).

- Windows 95/98 with the latest Service Pack/Service Release.

Now that we've got all of the basic information out of the way, let's move on to the real content of the book!

I

An Introduction to TCO

1 Measuring Total Cost of Ownership

2 Total Cost of Ownership Studies and Tools

3 General Best Practices for Reducing TCO

1

Measuring Total Cost of Ownership

I F YOU'VE TAKEN THE TIME TO FLIP THROUGH this book or have read the back cover, you know that most of the information in this book is technical. The underlying goal of each tool, technique, and best practice presented is to lower an organization's total cost of ownership (TCO). Before we can do that, however, we need to define what this enigmatic value really is and how it can be calculated.

As promised, we begin with a description of what TCO represents and how it can be measured. Just as important as the study of TCO is the application of the information you've obtained. The emphasis in this chapter is on defining what makes up TCO and general methods for applying its usefulness. In Chapter 2, "Total Cost of Ownership Studies and Tools," we look at ways to collect and analyze information and compare your business with others in the industry. The remainder of this book focuses on methods for improving efficiency and reducing overall TCO in a Windows NT–based network environment. With that high-level overview, let's delve into the meaning of TCO!

Defining TCO

Most readers will have heard the term TCO before seeing the cover of this book. However, relatively few would find TCO easy to define—and with good reason. The idea is fairly new in the industry and is deliberately vague. Although TCO can pertain to any aspect of a business, this book focuses on costs related to information technology (IT). In this book, we define TCO as the costs related to acquiring, maintaining, and supporting an organization's assets—that is, its information, hardware, software, network devices, and labor. This measurement includes many factors such as the effects on productivity for those involved and the costs associated with supporting new technologies. Let's begin the discussion by looking at another calculation.

A useful measurement for organizations is return on investment (ROI). This value calculates the cost of implementing a solution against the time it takes to recover the cost. ROI values are often presented as a function of time (for example, it will take 1 year to recover the money spent in this investment) or as a percentage (for example, the ROI of implementing Product A instead of Product B can be as high as 32%).

To consider the value of this information, let's use a common example: Suppose you are shopping to replace an air-conditioning unit in your house and a salesperson tells you that the unit will pay for itself in 3 years. What she means is that in this time period, you will save an amount of money on your electrical bill equal to the purchase price of the unit as compared to another unit or an existing unit. Similarly, IT planners use these calculations to determine, for example, whether to perform an email platform migration.

One problem with the traditional calculation of ROI is that it generally takes into account only the up-front costs (the price of the air conditioner plus installation or the cost of hardware, software, and labor to implement a new messaging solution). What it does *not* include are costs such as maintenance and support and the effects on the end user—for example, an expensive service contract for the air conditioner or specialized technicians to support the features of the new email package. This expense would add to the original purchase cost and should be factored into the ROI value. Table 1.1 presents some basic numbers that you might want to take into consideration when deciding on any kind of upgrade.

Table 1.1 **Simple TCO Calculations**

Cost Element	Air-Conditioner Replacement	Email Migration
Evaluation	N/A (time only)	$3,000 (consulting)
Initial purchase	$750	$20,000 (software and hardware)
Implementation	$100 (delivery and installation)	$12,000 (installation and configuration time)
Management	N/A (assuming no problems occur)	$10,000/year (system administration time)
Support costs	$50/year (maintenance contract)	$20,000/year (end-user support time)
Total first-year costs (including one-time costs)	$900	$65,000
Total recurring cost	$50	$30,000
TCO (3 years)	$1,050	$155,000

▶ For More
Information
1

TCO is a model that attempts to assess *all* the costs associated with owning and maintaining assets in an environment. TCO is usually mentioned in absolute terms (for example, dollars per year) or in relative terms (for example, Product A presents a 28% lower overall TCO than Product B). Those who have never taken a holistic look at this type of information might be surprised to find that supporting an item such as a desktop computer can incur costs of several times the initial purchase price of the device. For example, Deloitte & Touche Consulting Group, in its study titled "Technical Workstation Total Cost of Ownership Study: A Cost Comparison of Microsoft Windows NT Workstation and UNIX," surveyed engineering-related users of UNIX and Windows NT Workstation machines. One important finding was that the average 3-year cost of purchasing and supporting a Windows NT engineering workstation is $62,000. From this estimate, it can clearly be seen that the initial capital cost—the money required to purchase the hardware and software—becomes a very small part of the overall cost of the machine. The details of this study, along with several others, are presented in Chapter 2.

TCO considerations are not just for large corporations. Even smaller companies can use this view to find out where money is going and what changes could improve operations. We also see that TCO is not a fixed value that can be easily controlled. Changes in TCO can occur as a result of business decisions but are also likely due to changing external conditions. For example, a few hot summers may really change the numbers related to the air-conditioner upgrade.

With this basic working understanding of what TCO is, let's look at how it can be measured.

The TCO Reduction Process

Organizing the study and application of TCO information is a vital first step when undertaking this type of project. A successful TCO reduction process includes organized evaluation, analysis, and reevaluation. Before you can hope to make any changes, you must know where you're starting. Figure 1.1 shows some basic steps to perform in the continuous cycle of a TCO reduction plan:

- *Measurement*—Taking an inventory of all of your current costs. This may be related to capital expenditures (purchasing of hardware and software), labor costs, and management overhead.

- *Evaluation*—Considering the meaning of your findings and analyzing its impact on your business.

- *Planning*—Using your findings to pinpoint areas in which TCO reduction is practical and developing a method for addressing these problems.

- *Implementation*—Putting your TCO reduction plan into practice.

- *Review*—Evaluating the effects of your TCO reduction attempts and finding more areas for improvement.

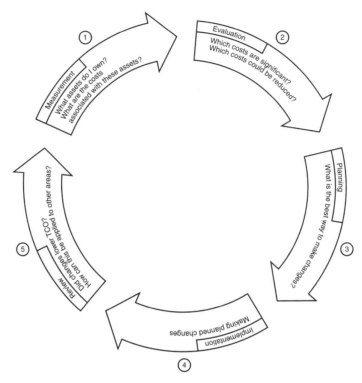

Figure 1.1   An overview of the TCO reduction process.

Before beginning with the measurement phase of a TCO study, let's look briefly at some of the factors that contribute to this value.

Total costs depend on the environment in which the study is done. For example, the major costs of networking computers in my home office are the cost of the devices and my time in setting them up. In a larger corporate environment, however, I would need support from network and systems administrators to get my machines online.

Evaluating Case Studies

When evaluating information provided in studies, it's important to be sure to look at details and not just the bottom line. Consider the source of the information—is this truly an independent research firm or was it commissioned for marketing purposes? Also, take the time to look at the details. Does the methodology make sense? Are these numbers applicable to your own environment? With these questions in mind, you may come to different conclusions than the researchers that compiled the study.

When evaluating TCO for an organization of any size, you need to consider the following major types of costs:

- *Hardware*—Costs associated with purchasing new hardware devices such as desktop computers, servers, and networking devices.
- *Software*—Money paid for developing, testing, deploying, and maintaining business software solutions.
- *Data transport*—Costs for maintaining network connectivity between computers and fees for leased services such as wide area network connections and Internet access.
- *Downtime*—Loss of productivity due to the inability of users to perform business functions because of unavailable resources.
- *Training*—Time and material costs associated with teaching users and IT professionals how to best use their resources. Also includes potential lost productivity due to time spent in training.
- *Support*—Costs associated with maintaining the help desk and making any necessary changes to other IT-related assets. Support costs may also include leasing fees and third-party support contracts.
- *Management*—Managing IT-related resources such as servers, data backup and restore, and labor for systems support and implementation. Additionally, general overhead for managing IT staff should be considered.

Organizing the types of information you need to collect is a formidable task in itself. For example, support related to hardware devices is often difficult to isolate from costs related to software support. In Chapter 2, we look at details including the actual numbers you need and organized ways of collecting this information. For now, let's begin by looking at ways to collect data.

Measurement

Before you can get an accurate picture of your current environment, you need to measure what you have. Trying to obtain all the information can be a daunting task. In smaller environments, it might be manageable with only one or a few dedicated people. In larger businesses, however, you need the cooperation of managers from all departments. A TCO study does not have to involve a complete re-engineering of a global corporation, though. In fact, it might be more easily managed by viewing sections of your organization separately. You might begin, for example, by examining help desk practices to see where time and resources are being spent.

For More
Information

Because concrete numbers are necessary to justify any type of cost savings, it's important to look at existing budget information. Asking certain questions can help to isolate the tangible facts from popular perception. For example, how much money was spent on hardware last year? If training was done externally, how much did we pay to train vendors? What about software costs? How many calls did the help desk receive regarding a specific piece of software or hardware? Answers to many of these questions can be found in corporate purchasing logs and in annual reports to management. The difficult part is obtaining and compiling all this data into a usable format, but new software tools are making this process easier. We discuss these in Chapter 2. Additionally, consultants can help you measure the information you need.

Evaluation

After you have collected the information you need, it's time to review and analyze it. When looking at cost-related data, consider the source of the cost. People tend to think in terms of concrete objects. For example, I might say that my car cost me more than $800 in maintenance in the past year. This statement obscures several variables. First, the costs were actually incurred by the service performed on the car. The assumption is that the problem was related to the failure of a component of the vehicle. But the real source of my costs may have been the expensive mechanic I hired to fix it. In this case, the problem is not the car at all, but rather my support personnel. And, coincidentally, this is a much easier problem to fix!

This analogy can be adapted to typical IT environments. You might be tempted to think that if desktop computers are very expensive to maintain, perhaps we should look at other solutions such as thin clients. Thin-client computers are diskless workstations that rely on a central server for processing and data storage and are therefore potentially less expensive to purchase. Again, we make an assumption. This time it is that the device itself is the source of the costs. However, suppose the real issue is that those users do not know how to properly operate their computers or that productivity losses are actually due to an unreliable router. In this case, the replacement would have little impact in reducing costs.

Because so many different cost estimates and conflicting figures are involved, how can an organization estimate TCO? Perhaps the absolute values are not as important as the relative ones. Just as no two networks are exactly alike, it is important to consider the current state of an organization's environment and associated costs. For example, saving $1,000 per year per workstation may not be as important as reducing the number of calls to the help desk through better training.

Assessing whether costs are reasonable is often difficult in an absolute sense. That is, how will you know if spending $6,500 per year per desktop computer is reasonable? A logical way to answer this would be to find out how similar companies compare to your own. To answer these questions, you need research from the industry as a whole. In Chapter 2, we look at some of the studies that make measurements of these values. After you have an accurate idea of where money is being spent in your environment, it's time to move on to thinking about making improvements.

Planning

Before beginning the planning stage of the TCO reduction process, you should have a good idea of what areas in your environment stand to improve most. If the majority of your resources are spent in supporting database replication, perhaps a third-party package or training for database administrators would be useful. Similarly, if your cost per help desk call is much higher than the industry average, you need to find out whether end-user training or the help desk staff could stand to improve most. For forward-thinking IT managers and planners, this experience can be challenging but also enjoyable.

Begin by looking at some of the changes that might save you money. Compare various areas of your business to see whether you can use that information to help in reducing costs. For example, if support related to desktop PCs is lower for marketing users than for users with similar functions in the sales department, this is an excellent area for investigation. As you compare operations in both departments, be sure to note any differences. Then, ask those involved how they feel about your findings. Perhaps all that is required is a few hours of training for a select group of users. Or, maybe the support staff should be reallocated to better meet demands.

Beware of making drastic changes, as it can be very easy to go too far in cost-cutting strategies. As with any business decision, you need to consider the pros and cons of your actions. For example, suppose your IT personnel present a significant drain on the company budget. If reducing the size of the IT staff looks like an attractive way to save money in the short run, consider the cost of users becoming their own resident experts. In the big picture, this approach may increase costs and decrease productivity for the organization overall. The best solution is to find a balance between costs and maintaining a reasonable number of IT support personnel. The challenge of determining the best way to address problems is best met by those familiar with a specific environment. The success of actual TCO reduction methods relies heavily on the quality of your decisions in this step.

Implementation

By measuring, assessing, and planning for TCO, you've discovered areas for improvement. Now it's time to put your findings to use. The information you have painstakingly collected and analyzed likely gave you some important insights. In the planning stage, you should have isolated certain areas that could benefit from cost reduction. In larger environments, a good way of reducing costs is to delegate ownership of one part of the problem to specific individuals. For example, if users in the accounting department often call the help desk for assistance with a proprietary database application, give someone the task of isolating the cause of the problems. In this example, the cause may be end-user error, the application itself, or the knowledge of support personnel.

Finding Better Solutions

Parts II, "Network Administration," and III, "Advanced Network Administration and Implementation," of this book are dedicated to teaching you about some new technology that may be used to solve a business problem and lower overall TCO. Sometimes just knowing that a solution exists (for example, ideas presented in Chapter 14, "Automated Software Installations") can be a big part of the solution. Be sure to take the time to evaluate your options and seek better solutions for existing problems. Remember, your organization is not the only one facing the challenges of managing IT!

If you are working in a complex environment where management is distributed, you may find it difficult to implement large-scale solutions by yourself. Having seen many environments where a single person is able to hold the IT sector together, I firmly believe that one person can make a difference. That's the good news. The other side of the coin is that it can be extremely difficult to effect any kind of change within an organization that likes to preserve the status quo. I could fill a book on that subject alone, but it's important to keep your goals in mind. Chances are, if you believe your idea will help you, your peers, your business, and/or your customers, someone else will listen. Getting to your destination may require many small steps, but if you're successful, the effort can be personally rewarding.

After you have implemented changes, it's time to take a look at the results of your work.

Review

You're never really done with the TCO process. To determine whether your TCO reduction attempts were successful, plan to reevaluate the costs you want to control. This step is often much easier than redoing a full-scale measurement and inventory, as you are looking only at changes in your environment since the initial study. You also have the buy-in from people who are willing to provide the necessary information and can see the value of the process. But be careful that a cost decrease in one department does not cause a reciprocal increase in another. If changes do not have a positive impact at all, the most important step is to learn what has gone wrong. Then, you can return to the planning stage for a new course of action. If things have gone well, however, you can begin to focus on improving other problem areas. With each iteration of this ongoing process, you end up with a more manageable and less costly enviroment.

IT Organization Structure

So far, we've taken a look at what TCO is and a general process for managing it. Before moving on to more specifics, it's important to look at the roles involved in a typical IT organization. In this section, we look at specific positions and functions; note, however, that the actual job descriptions and titles in your situation are probably not identical to the ones I am using here. Small organizations usually allocate these responsibilities to one or a few individuals. Larger organizations have multiple people who fill each role and many whose responsibilities cross these imaginary boundaries. This section begins by looking at some typical IT functions. Then, we look at goals for a typical IT department and at some of the challenges that must be overcome to reach these goals.

IT Functions and Goals

The purpose of IT is to provide the technology to help business processes. This tie-in with the business model gives IT departments an important and powerful position in the overall company structure. If technology is a means to an end, there is a point where the costs required to implement and support a technical solution outweigh the benefits. Before considering a TCO reduction plan, it's important to determine the purpose of IT and how it impacts the organization as a whole. There are several different components of businesses' information systems that fall under the responsibility of most IT organizations:

- *Business*—All IT functions must be in line with the strategic business directives of an organization. IT must work within budgets and deliver the desired service levels as efficiently as possible.

- *User support*—In general, a large portion of employees in any organization depend on the provisions developed by their IT departments. In this area, IT educates and trains users and provides troubleshooting for any problems. Additionally, feedback from these users drives future developments in IT technology.

- *Hardware management*—IT is responsible for setting up, configuring, and rolling out new computers. This task involves managing configurations, responding to user demands, and keeping up with technology refresh cycles.

- *Software development and support*—Among the most visible products of an IT department are often the applications it develops. Often, these applications query data from a remote server and present it to the user for viewing or modification.

- *Networking and communications*—In addition to assigning resources (such as network addresses) to users, IT must manage and optimize the current networking environment. This function often involves upgrading hardware, reconfiguring networks, and optimizing current settings.

To illustrate these ideas, let's look at an issue that's a concern for many companies right now: remote access (see Chapter 12, "Remote Access Service," for technical details). In this scenario, IT is responsible for addressing the hardware, software, and network needs for supporting remote dial-in via analog modems. Furthermore, there will be a need to support new technologies, as they become more easily available. Finally, and most importantly, all of these tasks must be accomplished in accordance with the strategic business goals of the organization and within an acceptable budget. If a solution fails to address all of these goals, it is likely to be unpopular and will soon be changed.

The Many Hats of IT Personnel

A typical IT organization has several people who fill specific roles. In smaller organizations, one person may handle everything, whereas large organizations may have several specialists at each level and a few people whose duties overlap. Each person is responsible for contributing to TCO in some way. For example, labor costs for support personnel and hardware costs for systems impose costs. Before developing a TCO reduction plan, it's a good idea to have an organized overview of how your personnel resources fit into the big picture. Figure 1.2 shows the typical IT personnel roles and responsibilities in a medium-sized or large-sized business. These roles and responsibilities include the following:

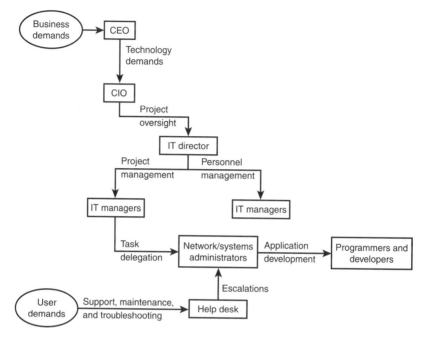

Figure 1.2   Typical IT personnel roles and responsibilities.

- *Help desk technicians/support personnel*—This role is usually the first line of support for all IT problems reported by end users. A user typically calls, sends an email message, or otherwise submits problem information. This information should then be entered into some type of database. Basic assistance and common troubleshooting are often handled at this level. If the problem cannot be resolved immediately, the issue is assigned to another person or group (such as email administrators) and the appropriate individuals are notified. In small organizations, a few people "own" the issue and see it through to completion. In larger organizations, the goal of the help desk is to answer all calls as quickly as possible and to escalate any issues that cannot be handled within 5 minutes.

- *Systems administrator*—This role is where the terms get somewhat hazy. For the sake of this book, a systems administrator is primarily responsible for the maintenance of one or several network servers. This person handles the day-to-day administration of adding users and groups and also handles all network-related troubleshooting. The more challenging parts of the job include implementing new technologies.

- *Network administrator*—Primarily responsible for connectivity issues and network hardware, a network administrator handles cabling and associated network devices. Typical tasks include maintaining routers, pulling cable connections and troubleshooting performance problems.

- *Developers/Programmers*—In some organizations, these people belong to IT. In others, they're found in various departments and labeled as engineers. Although they may be fairly technical, these power users require some end-user support themselves. They may also have special requirements such as the setting up of special test environments and the providing of network resources.

- *IT Manager*—This person is responsible for coordinating the personnel who make up an IT workgroup. This function includes the allocation of personnel resources. IT managers may or may not be technically inclined because their primary function is managing people.

- *IT Director*—In medium- to large-sized businesses, the IT director is charged with the execution of various strategic plans for IT. This person has oversight over multiple projects and is the person from whom IT managers receive direction.

- *Chief Information Officer (CIO)*—In large organizations, this individual is responsible for the overall strategic direction of IT. The CIO makes and/or approves the big decisions, develops budgets, and is ultimately responsible for the success or failure of strategies that affect the entire corporation. A key strength for individuals in this position is to be able to understand business requirements and find the appropriate technical solution. The CIO must then effectively communicate this information to others in the organization and gain the necessary buy-in to move forward with these plans.

- *Chief Executive Officer (CEO)*—Although the CEO is not an employee of the IT department, this person plays a key role in deciding what IT does and does not do. The CEO is ultimately responsible for determining what role IT plays in the business direction. And let's not forget who ultimately holds the purse strings! It's very important for the CEO to realize the true role and importance of IT in the overall business picture. With this understanding, IT can be seen as a strategic business partner instead of a cost center.

Again, few people fit into any of these categories exactly. It is natural for job functions to overlap and responsibilities to coincide. However, it is also important to maintain some segmentation and division of responsibilities within the organizations. Overall, however, these people represent the cogs that keep the IT machine moving.

Consulting and Outsourcing

IT groups are not restricted to doing all the work themselves. You may be able to reduce overall TCO by focusing on tasks you are good at and leaving other responsibilities to outside professionals. Hiring consultants and contractors is always an option for technical staff. Many companies experiment with outsourcing certain tasks. The idea has been to allow companies to focus on what they do best and let others manage the rest. The benefits of outsourcing include:

- *Flexibility in number of staff*—Contractors can be brought in for short periods of time, especially for short-term projects. After a project is complete, an employer may choose to discontinue a contract.

- *Cost efficiencies*—Despite the fact that hourly rates may be very high, there is little administrative overhead involved with paying benefits and typical human resources inefficiencies.

- *Avoiding office politics*—Consultants and outsourced staff members are usually not involved with competing for promotions or budget items and can be more objective in making some decisions than internal staff members.

There are, however, several potential drawbacks of outsourcing. First, contract-based staff and consultants might require a higher level of pay. Although these costs are often defrayed by the fact that you do not have to pay benefits, a company must accurately plan for how much outside help it will need. Second, it is likely that contract workers will not be familiar with the needs of the business and technical goals of the organization as a whole. This can be a benefit in the sense that new ideas might be presented, but these workers also require more from management to define and monitor tasks. Managers must recognize that knowledge from temporary workers should be frequently transferred to permanent employees to ensure the success of projects. Finally, companies must be just as careful in selecting contractors as in selecting employees. A contract firm may recommend a potential hire with insufficient skills. In this case, it is the hiring party's obligation to test these claims before investing in personnel resources.

The specific benefits of consulting must be looked at from within the organization as whole. For most organizations, consulting and outsourcing can be a valuable practice. However, the real challenge is in determining where this solution is appropriate.

Education and Training

Most people recognize that keeping pace with an industry that is as rapidly changing as IT is of paramount importance. An important factor in reducing TCO is making sure that support personnel and end users alike are able to fully utilize the potential of their resources. IT staffers get information and stay current with new technologies in many ways:

- *Traditional education*—For many IT staffers, the main benefit of obtaining a 2- or 4-year college degree is learning some of the basics that will be built upon in business. Most programs require a very broad base of education. Traditional programs are often criticized for not teaching current skills and not giving information that is applicable to the vast majority of businesses today. However, some programs are beginning to address this issue.

▶ For More Information
3, 4

- *Technical classes*—A variety of national training providers offer intensive and focused instructor-led classes on mastering specific tools and technologies. The benefit is that students can ask questions and learn from interacting with peers. However, this is often the most expensive option and can involve travel costs.

- *Computer-based training*—Though it is somewhat of a new field, many companies have realized the benefits of computer-based training. Being self-paced gives this approach the flexibility that many people desire. Computer-based training can be cost-effective and very convenient. However, it also requires significant motivation to complete the subjects. Also, students may lack a test environment (present in most classrooms) in which to practice new skills.

For More
Information
5

- *Internet-based learning*—Perhaps the newest and most revolutionary (at least in concept) method of learning is via the Internet. Combining the advantages of computer-based training with the interactivity of classes, this solution can provide the best of both worlds. Examples include the Ziff-Davis University Web site and numerous other resources for technical professionals.

- *Other self-study materials*—This term is a catchall for non-instructor-led training. It includes exam preparation materials, books, and on-the-job training.

For More
Information
6

Companies can utilize a combination of training methods to make sure that their employees are up-to-date on new technologies. This approach often is much less expensive than hiring in new people with specific skill sets and gives current employees an opportunity to learn new techniques.

Information Technologies

Several technical innovations have shaped the current environment for IT organizations. In this section, we look at some of the major advances and the role of innovations such as the Internet and Microsoft's Windows NT. It is important to understand these ideas before developing a plan to reduce TCO.

Client/Server Architecture

The invention and usage of modern personal computers have evolved into the ideas of client/server computing. In the beginning of computing, mainframes ran the entire show. Dumb terminals served as simple input and output devices that relied on a large, central machine for all data processing. The introduction of the personal computer moved the environment the other way—that is, all computing responsibilities were placed on individual, freestanding computers. This technology introduced the problems of managing heterogeneous systems and acquiring and managing many different computers. To partially address these issues, file/print server computers that centrally stored and managed files were implemented. As applications evolved, it became practical for a company's information to be stored in central databases. Database servers would store and provide data to client computers that could then analyze the information.

Today, distributed computing is truly a hybrid of these models. Nowadays, multitier applications that rely on the computing power of multiple servers and the client are most commonly deployed. Also, many major vendors are working to increase manageability for all types of network devices and provide features such as centralized remote management and common application interfaces. Although the overall goal has remained the same—to get information to end users who need it—the methods have changed.

The Role of the Internet

The rise in popularity of the Internet has brought with it expectations on the availability and accessibility of information. People dislike having to mail a letter to a customer service department or to wait in line to fill out paper-based forms. It has been said that true freedom of the press belongs to those who own presses. Though this statement may still be accurate, almost anyone now has the ability to have his or her voice heard. There's no guarantee that anyone will care to read or hear the words, but technology has provided a way to make them available.

Thanks to the Internet, computer and network users believe that information should be easily accessible. And anyone who has spent hours on the phone waiting for technical support and then waiting for hotfixes and drivers on floppy disks to arrive in the mail would certainly agree. A case in point: Old-timers at the network administration game will remember the days when obtaining a patch or driver for an operating system involved calling the technical support department of a company, waiting on hold, ordering a disk, and then hoping that it would arrive within a reasonable amount of time. High tech, at the time, was the availability of a standard dial-up bulletin board system (BBS). Though these avenues may still be available, by far the most popular method of obtaining information and files is via the Internet. In fact, today it's frustrating if we can't find the information we need on a company's Web site. We expect businesses to make information easy to find and readily available. These demands on accessibility are transferred to IT departments who also must make company resources easily available.

Windows NT and the Marketplace

Windows NT has very rapidly become the dominant network operating system (NOS) in the marketplace. Many organizations of all sizes have already implemented large-scale Windows NT deployments or are planning to adopt the operating system into their environments. Few large environments are homogenous, and it is often inevitable that a company must support more than one basic NOS. There is no point in arguing which system is the best because this is largely a matter of opinion (strong opinions, in the case of most technical people). The bottom line is that it is unlikely that there will ever be a single standard NOS that will satisfy all users and applications. Instead, a combination of technologies will most often be the best solution.

Windows NT's strengths lie in its usability, flexibility, and performance. First, if you ask someone to describe Windows NT, you'll almost surely get a reference to its graphical user interface (GUI). Windows NT stands out from some of its other counterparts—namely, Novell's NetWare and all flavors of UNIX—with its familiar

For More
Information
7
Windows 95–style interface. Today, of course, all these NOSs include graphical utilities. Microsoft's premier NOS also offers widespread support for thousands of applications currently available for Windows-based computers. Based on these strengths, Windows NT will continue to be a powerful and flexible solution in the marketplace.

What are Windows NT's weaknesses? First, it is relatively new to the marketplace. Although this may not be considered a weakness in itself, it means that the product has not yet gone through the same tests of time that various flavors of UNIX have survived. Though getting accurate statistics is difficult, a common complaint about Windows NT is that it is not stable or scalable enough for mission-critical applications. Whether these problems are valid, however, is a question that will be answered in time. Furthermore, the decisions must be made on a case-by-case basis, depending on the business needs of an organization. Microsoft is not waiting for the current version of Windows NT to win over everyone. Instead, the company is working hard to make the next version of its flagship NOS faster and stronger than its predecessors. Only time will tell the future of Windows NT. One thing is for sure, though: It's popular today, and it has many benefits over its competitors!

Evaluating Products

Currently, there are a lot of strategies designed to help you save costs. Vendors often claim that their products, though they require an initial investment, will result in significant savings over their life cycles. The examples are similar to those used in the air-conditioner upgrade example at the beginning of this chapter. Although the numbers quoted for various cost savings based on products vary widely, the operating system marketplace is one that is getting a lot of attention. Microsoft, specifically, is asserting that moving corporate desktops and workstations from UNIX to Windows NT can result in large cost savings through increased productivity and reductions in management and support. Microsoft has a lot of data from third parties to support this claim.

What it really comes down to, however, is that no matter which technology you choose, making better use of what you have can almost always reduce costs. Many companies have large installed bases of Windows-based clients. The majority of the desktop market share belongs to Microsoft. A well-managed Windows-based PC may be less expensive than switching to any other type of operating system. Most of the information in this book focuses on what you can do to improve operations in your Windows NT–based environment. As you read that information, be sure to think about ways you can apply tools and techniques to make you life easier and reduce costs!

The Bottom Line

TCO is difficult to quantify. Through the use of structured methodologies and precise calculations, however, useful information can be discovered and applied to increase overall network efficiency and reduce operating costs. The overall process involves measurement, evaluation, planning, implementation, and review. Resources from throughout the company are usually required, and the various members of the IT department are responsible for seeing that it is done. In the end, however, the hard work pays for itself in a leaner, meaner, and more cost-efficient environment.

Now that you have a good idea of what makes up TCO, let's move on to some ways to calculate it in Chapter 2.

For More Information

1. "Technical Workstation Total Cost of Ownership Study: A Cost Comparison of Microsoft Windows NT Workstation and UNIX," Deloitte & Touche Consulting Group, 1997

2. Chapter 2 of this book: "Total Cost of Ownership Studies and Tools"

3. Productivity Point Web site: `www.productivitypoint.com/`

4. Infotec Systems Web site: `www.infotec.com`

5. Ziff-Davis University (ZDU) Web site: `www.zdu.com`

6. Microsoft Training and Certification Web site: `www.microsoft.com/train_cert`

7. Chapter 20 of this book: "Windows 2000 TCO Features"

Further Reading

For more information on defining and calculating TCO, see

- "The Microsoft TCO Model: Applying the Microsoft Solutions Framework to Reduce TCO," Microsoft TechNet
- "Microsoft Windows TCO Resource Guide," Microsoft TechNet

Total Cost of Ownership Studies and Tools

2

To truly understand the meaning of total cost of ownership, you need to look at some concrete numbers and findings. TCO studies can be used for learning by example. That is, information found in some of the studies can be applied to the way you do business in your own environment. The rest of the chapters in this book include hypothetical case studies to illustrate specific technical points.

In this chapter, I provide some basic information obtained from TCO studies performed by various research firms. In most cases, I present a brief abstract of the information available and omit many of the details such as methodology, procedures, and exact numbers. As product vendors and other users may dispute the validity of some of the results in these studies, you will want to reference the entire work for information on how each study was performed. Also, be careful when considering the extrapolation of results. For example, if one environment found that implementing "Bob's Excellent Word Processor" reduced overall costs when compared to implementing "Jane's Almost-as-Excellent Word Processor," these results may not indicate that your organization will experience the same savings.

In this chapter, I provide information about several different research topics and tools related to TCO. I do not attempt to vouch for the validity or usefulness of any of this information and have attempted to provide only factual information. After we look at some of the published research results, we look at tools for assessing, measuring, and analyzing TCO-related information.

With all of the disclaimers aside, let's look at some of the current TCO research and how it may apply to your own environment.

Who Should You Believe?

It's important to be careful to scrutinize assessment methodology. In most cases, legitimate researchers take the necessary steps to warn readers of reaching misleading conclusions from the research. To evaluate whether you are receiving accurate information, consider the following:

- Who is the source? If a product vendor performs the review or study, be sure that it measures statistics that are valuable to you.

- Listen to both sides of the story: Begin by examining why the study was performed. If it was commissioned by one party, be sure to check competitors' information for rebuttals. If one company claims that its products can lower your TCO, be sure to check out what its competitors say. In many cases, there will be responses to the results of specific studies.

- Do researchers have a vested interest in the results? If Company A hires a research firm to perform a study, you should be sure that results were verified for accuracy and that interpretations are valid.

- Is the comparison valid and does the performance methodology make sense? For example, comparing the performance of two different server types running different applications will undoubtedly yield inconsistent information. Be sure that studies are comparing equivalent products and functions in a rational way.

With all of the marketing information and fluff presented, you might wonder if the information is even worth considering. The fact remains that few organizations provide this information for purely academic reasons or out of their benevolence for the IT industry. At the very least, however, you will learn about various product features and the strengths of competing products. You also get an idea of how to budget for these costs based on the experiences of other companies. To answer the question that is the title of this section, you should not trust *any* individual or single group as a final authority on TCO. Instead, you need to assimilate information from various sources and decide which findings are most relevant to your own environment. Overall, when used properly, TCO studies and assessment tools can be a very vital part of any TCO reduction strategy.

Getting the Whole Story

The full details for all of the studies are available from the group that performed the research. In this chapter, I provide summaries of findings for studies. Be sure to check the "For More Information" references to get more information.

TCO Studies

Examples of TCO-related studies in the IT industry can be very useful. Many TCO studies have already been performed for specific companies or as a survey across many different IT organizations representative of some section of the industry. Most of the research focuses on one or more competing products or technologies and aims to answer specific questions about how they compare. In this section, we look at some of the major studies related to Windows NT–based environments and the conclusions they reach.

Better Management for Windows

For More Information
1

Many TCO studies focus on comparing two different products in similar environments. If you're trying to decide which platform to use, this approach can be very helpful. However, what if you want to optimize operations in your existing environment? It may seem obvious that organizations that manage their existing operating systems well will have a lower overall TCO. In a Microsoft TechNet article titled "Well-Managed Windows-Based Solutions Offer the Lowest TCO," Microsoft claims that better management of Windows can significantly reduce support and management costs. This claim is based on data drawn from a study performed by the GartnerGroup titled "TCO: New Technologies, New Benchmarks." The chart in Figure 2.1 compares various implementations of Windows-based technologies and their relative costs of ownership as determined in this study.

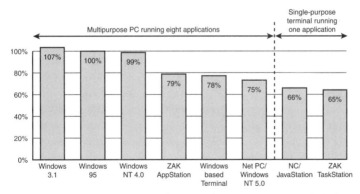

Figure 2.1   Relative TCO values of using different Windows-based platforms. (Source: "TCO: New Technologies, New Benchmarks," GartnerGroup)

These numbers clearly show that different versions of Windows-based operating systems can affect the costs associated with supporting them. Using the correct tools for the job (such as terminal servers for task-based users) and enforcing system usage policies can significantly reduce costs. The logical next question is, How can I apply these practices in my own environment? In Part II, "Network Administration," and Part III, "Advanced Network Administration and Implementation," we look at specific ways in which TCO can be reduced in a Windows NT–based environment. For now, however, know that managing your current assets can often be at least as important as upgrading them.

Windows NT Server Versus UNIX Servers

Microsoft's strategy for Windows NT Server has focused on moving the operating system into large-scale, mission-critical applications, which have been traditionally dominated by UNIX-based servers. Microsoft and Compaq Computer Corp. commissioned the Business Research Group to conduct a study comparing these total costs. Specifically, the study compared the cost of purchasing and maintaining Windows NT Server running on Intel-based servers against the same for Solaris running on SPARC servers. The study was based on a survey of 400 companies that employ at least 500 people each and use both technologies in client/server environments. The intent of the study was to compare real-world usage and operating costs. The conclusion states that Windows NT servers present an overall 36% or more lower total cost of ownership when compared to UNIX servers.

▷ For More
Information
2, 3, 4

Microsoft comments on the results of this study in an article titled "Windows NT Server: Delivering Value to the Enterprise." It is important to note that the exact functions performed on both systems varied for the respondents. As cited in the research, many organizations place much greater demands on their Solaris-based servers. For example, more UNIX users run transactional operations. In general, Solaris databases are almost 50% larger than those running on Windows NT. Finally, on average, the Solaris servers support many more concurrent connections than does Windows NT. These differences make it difficult for any party to claim that Windows NT presents a lower TCO than UNIX-based solutions in all areas. However, it can accurately be stated that for the group polled, costs associated with the tasks performed by UNIX machines were higher than those for Windows NT machines.

Windows NT Workstations Versus UNIX Workstations

▷ For More
Information
5

Although many technical professionals choose UNIX workstations, Windows NT Workstation can be a cost-effective and high-performance solution for company workstations (see Figure 2.2). To test this, Deloitte & Touche Consulting Services performed a study titled "Technical Workstation Total Cost of Ownership Study—A Cost Comparison of Microsoft Windows NT Workstation and UNIX." The tasks measured on technical workstations included mechanical design automation, geographic information systems, and digital content creation. These applications were the most common workstation tasks, and the most popular software packages designed for each function are now available for the Windows NT platform at prices identical to those for UNIX machines. The study compared the cost of using, managing, and supporting Windows NT platforms versus UNIX platforms for the same tasks. Other issues measured included ease of use, functionality, and application support.

Based on conclusions reached in the study, the costs of using Windows NT Workstation was, on average, 36% less than the cost of using UNIX computers for the same tasks with the same performance. One reason for the lower cost is that UNIX-based users often required PCs running Windows for performing nonengineering tasks such as email and word processing functions. This situation also placed additional burdens on the IT department that had to support multiple platforms for the same user. The study also found that hardware, software, and management costs were lower overall for Windows NT users. Details of the research study can be found in the white paper.

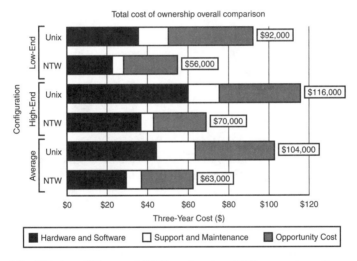

Figure 2.2   Windows NT versus UNIX workstations TCO comparison. (Source: "Well-Managed Windows-Based Solutions Offer the Lowest TCO," Microsoft TechNet)

Evaluating Network Computers and Thin Clients

▶ For More
Information
6, 7, 8

Several companies, such as Oracle, Inc., Citrix Systems, and Boundless Technologies, Inc., have claimed that replacing single-task workstations and terminal emulators with network computers (NCs) can significantly reduce TCO. These machines are called thin clients because they lack features found in traditional desktop PCs. Thin clients are diskless workstations that obtain storage space and processing time from a central terminal server. The original promise of NCs was that they would be much cheaper to purchase and that all administration could be performed from a single point. Anticipated cost reductions in using these devices are shown in Figure 2.1. However, trends such as the rapid decrease in client computer costs and centralized management through system policies have addressed many of these needs already. We look at some of the technical issues involved with managing thin clients and network computers in Chapter 11, "Remote Management."

▶ For More
Information
9, 10

In an article titled "The 'Network Computer'—The Hype and the Hope," Microsoft discusses some of the issues against the deployment of NCs. Despite some of the potential problems mentioned, however, Microsoft has recently made available the Terminal Server Edition of Windows NT Server. This product allows multiple thin clients to connect over a network or other connection and run a session on the server. Overall, most analysts agree that thin clients may be a good replacement for single-task users and traditional terminal applications. Whether they will eventually make inroads to replacing traditional PCs is still a matter of much debate. More information on thin client issues is available from several manufacturers and vendors.

Product-Specific and Company Studies

Several companies, including Microsoft, are now including TCO statements as part of their product marketing campaigns. Many vendors choose to have a third party perform an analysis of their product versus those of their competitors. However, it is important to note that these evaluations are not always as independent as they may seem. Research organizations may be asked to focus on the specific strengths of one product in comparison to the weaknesses of others. Also, questionable conclusions may be drawn from the hard data. To accurately evaluate this type of information, it's important to hear all sides of the story and try to compare facts such as product features and tangible costs.

▶ For More
Information
11, 12, 13

Other types of studies focus on specific companies and how they have solved a specific business problem or improved their processes. This research often documents the products used and how they were employed in a specific environment. When reading the results, be sure to keep in mind that many variables must be considered before generalizing the results. For example, if Company A saved 30% in data processing costs by moving from a mainframe to a Windows NT–based environment, that does not guarantee that your company will see the same benefits. Actual study information is available from several sources.

Evaluating Study Conclusions

Trying to apply TCO information gained from representative case studies is a difficult process. For example, suppose your organization is involved in selling clothing at retail outlets. Does this mean that other studies involving retailers would be most useful to you? Perhaps, but not necessarily. If your company supports purchasing via the Internet, you may want to look at information related to companies that support this type of business. Also, labor costs and technology availability vary widely if parts of your operations are located in different areas of the world. Although it's unlikely that you'll find a single study that is very similar to your own environment, you can clearly gain valuable TCO-related insights from collecting information from multiple resources.

TCO Assessment Tools

After examining some of the studies that have already been performed, beginning a complete TCO assessment for your business probably seems like a lot of work. Realizing this, software products and services to assist you are available from various vendors. In this section, we look at several tools and methodologies available for assessing and lowering your own TCO.

GartnerGroup's Chart of Accounts

Finding out what information to measure is often the first step in performing a TCO assessment. To help answer this question, GartnerGroup has created its Total Cost of Ownership Distributed Computing Chart of Accounts. The goal is to provide organizations with the types of information required in a typical TCO assessment. The model divides expenditures into two major groups. Direct (budgeted) costs include the more tangible costs of hardware, software, and labor related to IT functions. Indirect (unbudgeted) costs are based on the level of support provided by IT. This group includes costs related to users attempting to solve their own problems instead of relying on IT organizations and costs incurred by hardware, software, or network-related downtime.

The model breaks down typical costs into five main categories:

- *Hardware and software*—Including purchase and leasing costs of hardware and software for new computers and costs associated with upgrading older ones
- *Management*—Labor and other costs related to managing networks, systems, and data storage
- *Support*—Costs for help desk staff, end-user training, support-related travel, and management overhead
- *Development*—Costs associated with developing and deploying applications
- *Communication*—Data transport and other communicators costs

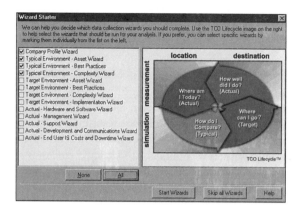

Figure 2.3   Selecting areas from GartnerGroup's TCO life cycle in TCO Manager.

▶ For More
Information
14

Within each of these categories is a list of the areas that must be examined to obtain a complete cost analysis. The full Chart of Accounts is available free from the GartnerGroup. The complete document includes details on how to evaluate and assign numbers to the various categories and subcategories specified in the Chart of Accounts.

GartnerGroup's TCO Manager

TCO Manager has been designed to allow IT professionals to collect, compare, and analyze TCO information from their own environments. The software package uses graphical wizards for obtaining and analyzing information. IT managers begin by selecting the areas on which to focus research. Choices include measuring complexity, tracking assets, and determining best practices. GartnerGroup defines the TCO life cycle according to four stages, shown in Figure 2.3.

Based on the areas on which you choose to focus, various wizards walk you through the data-collection steps. To complete all the information, you need to have certain information. For example, the Asset Wizard asks you to estimate the number of server and client computers in your environment. Fortunately, the program provides help screens for most of the data it requests and allows you to select defaults if you don't have the requested information. You can also save information at any time and return to it for later analysis. Other wizards are more subjective, such as the "Typical Environment—Best Practices" questions. This section asks you to rate the level of your own environment on areas such as standardizing platforms, restricting user access to certain resources, and implementing data-protection strategies. All this information pertains to the "typical" part of the TCO life cycle, which measures how your business compares to similar businesses.

Evaluating TCO Manager

A multimedia demonstration and evaluation version of GartnerGroup's TCO Manager application can be ordered from the company's Web site.

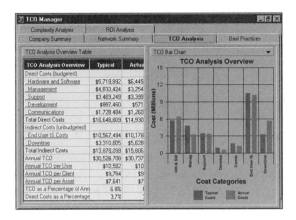

Figure 2.4 TCO manager typical versus actual analysis overview.

After you've gone through the steps of basic data collection, it's time to enter actual information. In this step, you need to enter information about the headcount of the IT staff, average salaries, and actual asset inventory data. Other information involves details from the Help Desk, such as number of calls, average wait time per call, and so on. Finally, to assess some of the indirect costs associated with IT, you can enter information such as the average annual salary of employees and estimated amount of time spent in self-support. This data can be obtained most easily by using a survey that is sent to users that IT supports. With this information, you are ready to perform a typical versus actual comparison, as shown in Figure 2.4. The values displayed compare costs for organizations similar to yours with your actual calculated costs.

The value of these comparisons is only as accurate as the data with which it is compared. GartnerGroup's GartnerMeasurement division compiles and maintains a database of TCO for hundreds of businesses in various industries. GartnerGroup's analysis team maintains accuracy. To keep the data current, older information is discarded, and new information is frequently added.

Using the information previously obtained, TCO Manager can create a TCO audit that compares the information you entered with industry averages. It can then show which areas could use help and can assist in planning goals for target improvement areas. Additionally, you can enter information about future plans to determine target values. TCO Manager then calculates cost savings based on certain implementations. The final charts you view compare typical, actual, and target TCO-related expenses. To keep the information current, you can enter updated information, as it becomes available. Figure 2.5 shows a view that you can use to handle actual versus target TCO for your environment.

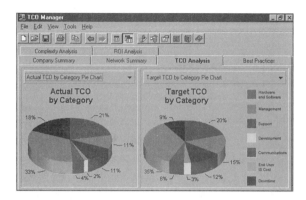

Figure 2.5 Actual versus target TCO values.

GartnerGroup offers a service that performs an on-site analysis of a company's IT environment. TCO Assessment is designed to help companies interpret information obtained using TCO Manager and to analyze their impact on an organization's TCO. It includes on-site assessments and validation of the data collected. Factors evaluated include current and target costs, ways to reduce the complexity of the current environment, and future technology investments and business directions.

GartnerGroup's TCO Analyst has been created as a tool for IT vendors to assess their own products with respect to TCO. This information can then be used as a sales and marketing tool and for product improvements. Information about prospective clients' environments and the impact of the product can also be predicted.

Interpose's Desktop TCO & ROI Calculator

▶ For More
Information
15

Interpose, Inc. (now part of GartnerGroup) developed the Desktop TCO & ROI Calculator to help organizations assess the financial impact of their usage of client operating systems and software. The free tool allows IT managers to determine potential benefits of using Microsoft products and technologies, including:

- Microsoft Windows 95
- Microsoft Windows NT Workstation 4.0
- Microsoft Office 97
- Microsoft Zero Administrator Kit for Windows (described in Chapter 18, "Enforcing System Policies")
- Microsoft Systems Management Server

The Desktop TCO & ROI Calculator is most useful for IT managers who are considering upgrading machines to 32-bit operating systems and applications. Users can create a new analysis using an Input Wizard (as shown in Figure 2.6). Information such as the current percentage of machines running specific operating systems, hardware and software costs, and support statistics must be entered.

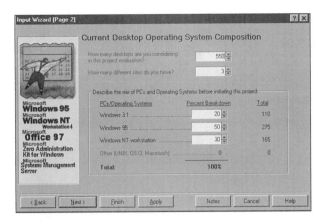

Figure 2.6   Using the Input Wizard to start a new TCO analysis.

For More
Information
16   This information can then be used to provide an analysis of current costs and costs after upgrading to newer software. All comparisons and estimates are based on findings from Interpose studies in which many companies were asked about their operating costs. If you're planning specific implementations, such as only upgrading to Microsoft Office 97, you can choose to open premade analyses. In both cases, you can view the results of the information in chart and table formats for analysis. Figure 2.7 shows an example of a cost comparison.

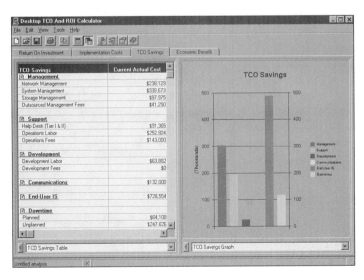

Figure 2.7   Viewing TCO savings information.

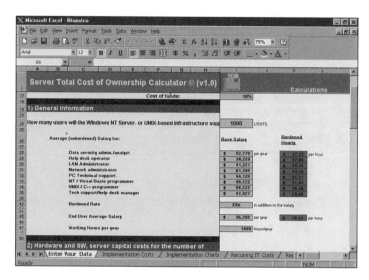

Figure 2.8   Entering your own data into the Server TCO Calculator spreadsheet.

Microsoft's Server TCO Calculator 1.0

▶ For More
Information
17
Microsoft has designed the Server TCO Calculator 1.0 to allow users to perform TCO calculations based on their own numbers. The free download includes a Microsoft Excel 97 spreadsheet that IT managers can use to input numbers and measure TCO. Facts and statistics are based on a study performed by the Business Research Group (BRG)/Cahners-Instat Group. The files also include a PowerPoint presentation discussing results obtained by this firm in a comparison of Windows NT versus UNIX servers. Figure 2.8 shows a sample of the data-entry portion of the spreadsheet.

The accuracy of the data output largely depends on the accuracy of the information you have obtained. The formulas used in the spreadsheet are based on findings of studies performed on server purchase, support, and maintenance costs. Based on the numbers you enter, calculations and graphs are generated showing relative TCOs. Figure 2.9 shows sample results using the default data provided.

On the CD-ROM

Demonstration 2.1, "Server TCO Calculator," shows you how to enter and analyze your own information using the Server TCO Calculator spreadsheet.

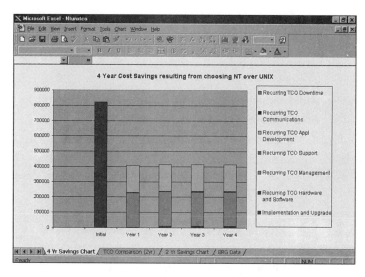

Figure 2.9   Viewing a chart of savings information.

The Bottom Line

You can use TCO research and case studies for assessing some of the cost-related issues with owning hardware, software, and networking devices. Although you need to do thorough research to find factual information, industry averages and survey results can be very insightful. An excellent way to measure and analyze your TCO is by using software tools available from various vendors. After you obtain this information, you need to compare it with other businesses like yours in the industry. Then, you can put this information to work by focusing on areas for improvement. Finally, you can use the same methodologies to reevaluate your situation. The overall result will be reduced operating costs, increased efficiencies, and a better bottom line.

For More Information

1. "Well-Managed Windows-Based Solutions Offer the Lowest TCO," Microsoft TechNet

2. "Windows NT Server: Delivering Value to the Enterprise," Microsoft TechNet

3. "Comparing Microsoft Windows NT and UNIX Remote Management," Windows NT Server Product Facts, Microsoft TechNet

4. "Comparing Microsoft Windows NT and UNIX System Management," Windows NT Server Product Facts, Microsoft TechNet

5. "Technical Workstation Total Cost of Ownership Study," Microsoft TechNet

6. Oracle Corporation: www.oracle.com

7. Boundless Technologies, Inc.: `www.boundless.com`

8. Citrix Systems, Inc: `www.citrix.com`

9. Windows NT Server Terminal Server Edition:
   `www.microsoft.com/ntserver/terminalserver/`

10. "The 'Network Computer'—the Hype and the Hope," Microsoft TechNet

11. Total Cost of Ownership, Case Studies, Microsoft TechNet

12. "The Total Economic Impact of Microsoft Office 97 Migration," Microsoft
    TechNet

13. "An ROI Analysis of Enterprise-Scale Use of Microsoft System Management
    Server," Microsoft TechNet

14. GartnerGroup Interactive IT Manager home page: `www.gartner.com/itmanager`

15. Microsoft Desktop TCO & ROI Calculator: `www.microsoft.com/`
    `ntworkstation/basics/features/lowesttco/tcocalculator.asp`

16. "The Microsoft and Interpose Total Cost of Ownership (TCO) Model,"
    Microsoft TechNet

17. Cahner's Instat Group Web page: `www.cahnersinstat.com`

Further Reading

For more information on total cost of ownership studies and assessment tools, see

- Microsoft TechNet Total Cost of Ownership Web site: `www.microsoft.com/`
  `technet/tco`

- "Managing Total Cost of Ownership in the Enterprise," Microsoft Windows NT
  Server Product Facts, Microsoft TechNet

- GartnerGroup Interactive home page: `www.gartner.com`

- Microsoft Management home page: `www.microsoft.com/management/`

- Forrester Research home page: `www.forrester.com`

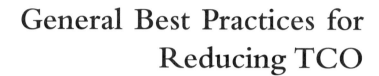

3

General Best Practices for Reducing TCO

MOST OF THE INFORMATION IN THIS BOOK pertains to specific tools and techniques that you can use to improve operations in your Windows NT–based environment. Before answering the *how* question, however, it's important to understand *why* and *what* changes might be beneficial. In this chapter, we look at several ways your organization can reduce overall costs and better manage its assets. In most cases, I also refer to technical chapters that contain useful information for implementing the suggestions. Specifically, we look at defining and managing IT's role in business and managing the help desk, assets, employees, and policies. As you read these sections, be sure to keep your organization's challenges in mind. I can't guarantee that all of these "best practices" will be suitable for your own environment, but I do hope that they will give you some useful ideas!

Managing IT's Business Role

The main function of any division of a company is to bring the group closer to its goal. In this section, we look at where information technology (IT) fits into the picture. Then, we see ways that IT staff members can better address business challenges by first defining them and then setting concrete goals.

IT as a Business Partner

The end users that IT supports are the direct profit-generating portions of any business. In many organizations, IT has been seen in a supporting role. IT professionals manage the tools and technologies that are used for taking care of the "real" business. As such, IT is generally seen as a cost center. For many companies, this view has changed in recent years.

Forward-thinking businesses now see IT more as a business partner, instead of a necessary evil or a stepping stone. Indeed, business mergers and acquisitions rely heavily on IT for successful execution, and all company employees benefit from improvements in the efficiency of their resources. Entire businesses, such as online retailers, are being built around Web-based technologies. Clearly, none of these accomplishments would be possible without the technology upon which they rely. With this new emphasis on strategic planning and sharing of successes and failures, the role of IT should be seen as vital to the success of any business. Therefore, companies should seek out knowledgeable professionals with the creativity to find the best solutions for common business problems.

Defining Business Cases and Goals

Before embarking on a technical project, it's important to consider the business problem a solution is designed to address. It is often easy for IT personnel to think of their jobs in a largely reactive way. That is, when problems occur or changes are to be made, help desk and support personnel go to work. When working on maintaining servers and troubleshooting end-user problems, it's difficult to keep the big picture in sight. For this situation, a systems administrator may try to reduce the amount of time for problem resolutions or work toward increasing server uptime. Similarly, help desk staffers in large organizations respond to problems as they are reported. In this case, there may be no clear result in sight because no matter how hard one technician works, more problems always arise. It is important—both for business reasons and for job satisfaction—to set clear goals and make sure that all employees know them. In the case of the help desk (which we discuss in the next section), this might mean obtaining a certain satisfaction level in an end-user survey. Attaching tangible goals to these support-related tasks makes the job seem more worthwhile for all of those involved.

Goals for projects are often clearly stated, but it is important to set realistic milestones. In setting goals for certain tasks, IT planners and implementers must first consider how the results will affect the business as a whole. Even seemingly simple tasks such as dividing a network or installing a new database server can assist entire departments in reaching their goals. Making large projects manageable is an important first step. For example, a 200-server email migration should be broken down into phases. At the completion of each phase, all of those involved will get a sense of accomplishment from their hard work. By ensuring that everyone is aware of the end goal and their own role in it, you can help them feel like a significant part of the team. After an implementation is complete, it is important to assess the project and make sure that everyone involved agrees that the problem has been addressed as well as possible. With this focused view in mind, IT staff members can positively impact the way their companies do business.

Getting Buy-in from Other Departments

IT departments cannot function independently of the departments and users they support. The first step in this process is to closely examine the business goals of users that IT staff supports. Then, IT should define its role in assisting others. After considering these business reasons and establishing goals, the IT staff must consider how changes affect others. For example, if the accounting department has five servers, IT staff members should be familiar with the content of each database. Perhaps a more efficient usage of space or application redesign may improve performance and reduce management for both departments.

Before expecting management or other individuals to accept and encourage the use of specific technologies, it is important that they understand it. To this end, it's always a good idea to demonstrate how other departments or areas of the company are employing techniques to help cut costs and make information access easier. Abstract concepts, like the importance of implementing Dynamic Host Configuration Protocol (DHCP; described in Chapter 6, "TCP/IP Management") can be better explained by stating that another department's IT staff was reduced by more efficient network management.

Actions such as license and asset management help get buy-in from finance and accounting departments, but it is also vital to explain to other managers exactly how IT is helping them. The chief financial officer probably doesn't care whether your server is a 486 or a Dual-Pentium-II machine. But if you explain that she can receive her daily reports by 8:00 a.m. instead of sometime in the afternoon, the benefits of the particular server become much clearer to her. By taking the time to get the support of other departments and users, IT will be better able to meet business challenges.

Seeking Out and Applying Feedback

It is often much easier to compile statistics than it is to find out what people *really* think about service. For example, IT may have an average problem resolution time of 2 hours, but do end users know this? A good way to find out is to randomly call users who have reported problems to IT. Ask questions such as, Was the problem resolved in a timely manner? and Were you kept informed of the status of the issue? This information provides an overall impression of the situation.

A more scientific method would be to design a survey for some or all users to rate the IT staff. Quantitative questions might ask the users to rate various aspects of support on a scale of 1 to 10. The results could then be compiled and analyzed.

It's often much easier to ask for criticism and evaluation than it is to really consider the feedback you receive. Chances are you'll hear at least a few comments that are not favorable. Granted, it would be very difficult to satisfy a user who has had two hard disk failures in a single month. However, it is important to improve operations (or at least perceptions) in some ways. As an example, suppose many users believe that IT is not doing an adequate job of training end users. Perhaps such training is not even an IT function, but is a part of human resources. In this case, making the policies known (or changing the policies) helps make users more appreciative of the IT department and makes everyone's job easier.

Managing the Help Desk

▶ For More
Information
1
One of the most vital areas of IT operations is the help desk. It is also one of the areas of highest profile. Most users rarely talk to network and systems engineers but call the help desk for troubleshooting or instructional assistance. Keep in mind that end users usually call when they have problems. This can make it difficult for help desk staffers to feel satisfied with their jobs. In this section, we look at some of the issues involved with managing IT support and some best practices for streamlining operations.

Helping the Help Desk

Supporting and managing computers, like many other technologies, requires support from experts. One of the fundamental purposes of an IT staff is to provide end-user usage and troubleshooting assistance. All IT personnel spend a portion of their time solving basic problems and helping others use their business tools properly. To provide better service, there are many different implementations that help desk management may want to consider.

Another challenge of IT is that users often do not call the help desk to report problems. By adhering to certain service levels, users become more confident in the services offered by their support staff. Instead of asking someone in a neighboring cubicle to help with a problem, the issue can be reported to the appropriate people and resolved as quickly as possible. A well-managed help desk can help to streamline calls and control the costs of routine troubleshooting. It can also provide management and help desk personnel with useful reports and metrics for assessing and improving day-to-day support operations. Before looking at ways to address these goals, let's look at some best practices for managing the help desk:

- *Establish support policies*—Whether you already have a help desk in place or are planning to form one from scratch, it's a worthwhile investment in time to determine the exact role of the help desk. Will it only be responsible for setting up new computers and handling network-level problems? Or will it also handle software usage questions and training issues? What types of issues are outsourced? For example, remote access issues may be handled by your Internet service provider (in the case of a virtual private network) and physical network issues (moves, adds, and changes) might be outsourced to a cabling contractor.

- *Set a guideline for the amount of time a first-line technician may spend on an issue*—In many cases technicians who may not be the best qualified to find the resolution spend a long time trying to search around for it. This effort wastes time for the end user and for the technician and increases overall problem response time. A typical guideline might state that if a first-level technician is unable to diagnose and solve a problem within a specified amount of time, he or she should escalate the call to a second-level support engineer.

- *Assign ownership of each issue to only one individual at any given time*—It is the responsibility of this person to either resolve the problem or assign it to someone who can. This approach prevents issues from falling through the cracks.

- *Review common issues and resolutions*—Set aside some time for first-level technicians to look over the resolutions to escalated calls. If the solution was a simple one, the escalation may be avoided in the future.

- *Train your end users*—If you're receiving several calls a week to the help desk regarding usage of Microsoft Office 97, it might be worthwhile to hold a quick Microsoft Office training class during lunch. Invite questions and discuss the most commonly encountered issues. If you give a technical staff member the opportunity to do some teaching, you are likely to reduce calls to your help desk, and you'll learn more about the needs of your user community.

- *Support specialization and cross training*—Allow help desk team members to specialize in specific areas. For example, if the entire human resources department uses a single proprietary application, it would be a worthwhile investment to make one or two people technical experts on this subject. Also, be sure that help desk technicians have the opportunity to train each other.

- *Communicate*—The help desk should be the first to know about any problem on the network. A large help desk may receive multiple calls about not being able to log in. In a well-managed environment, all except the first user will be told that a server is down and will be given an expected time for restoring of service.

- *Keep users updated*—If a router goes down or other network problems occur, help desk staff should make it a priority to inform users. One way to distribute this information is with an automated voice-mail message or on the company's intranet. Updates on status help avoid calls and help users make alternative plans if needed. It's also important to take the time to follow up with certain users to make sure that issues are resolved. Even if you use an automated system for tracking and resolving problems, it's always good to perform spot checks. You'll probably find that customers are pleased with the service they received but are glad that you asked.

- *Promote from within*—Those who work well in a support role deserve to be rewarded. Promoting from within an organization can boost morale and give technicians a goal to work toward. Few help desk staffers hope to be answering technical support calls several years after they're hired. It is management's responsibility to move them into more challenging positions. Promoting from within is often better than hiring an outsider because those who have worked with a company are more familiar with common issues and business practices. IT workers who are technically qualified and motivated *will* move on to greater responsibilities, so try to make sure that they do so *within* your organization!

■ *Reevaluate*—You should never consider a help desk implementation complete. The help desk evolves as business, hardware, software, and network needs change. It is important to seek out the opinions of your customers. Although in some companies the results might be quite harsh, you must be able to make this constructive. It is often possible to change people's opinions just by asking questions. Distributing a survey shows that an IT organization cares about how it is perceived and is willing to make changes. This need not be an enterprisewide initiative. Instead, you might start with a simple suggestion and feedback box. To invite responses, a monthly drawing from the respondents should provide adequate incentive for most to voice their opinions. Finally, it's important not to fall into the most common trap of all—soliciting feedback but never analyzing and acting on it.

Now that we've looked at some of the goals of the help desk, let's look at some best practices for reaching them. There are several common ways in which an IT organization can better manage its resources and provide service to its customers. Next, we look at goals and metrics, service-level agreements, and support policies. With these general policies and practices in place, the help desk will have the tools, information, and support to better assist end users with problems.

Establishing Goals and Metrics

Setting goals and metrics to measure success can greatly improve the performance of a help desk. These goals and metrics may start out as very vague service targets, but can evolve to become very precise statistical information. It is important that these goals be attainable. For example, a goal of zero sick days per month is not very useful. Table 3.1 provides a sample of some typical help desk metrics and goals.

Helping the Help Desk

Because of the actual function of the help desk, few users call in unless they have a problem or need some assistance. Inevitably, some of these calls are from frustrated users. To counteract these negative calls, help desk staffers and management must work as a team to support each other. For example, first-level technicians who know that their decisions will be supported by supervisors and second-level technicians should feel more empowered to get their job done. Also, by placing more emphasis on customer satisfaction than on call statistics, they will feel like they are making a positive difference. It may take some creativity, but don't forget that the help desk sometimes needs support for itself!

Table 3.1 **Sample Help Desk Metrics and Goals**

Task	Metric	Goal
Customer satisfaction	Rating of 4 (good) or 5 (excellent) on surveys	> 80%
Issues resolved on initial call	Number of calls resolved in first call/total number of calls	> 60%
Average total call resolution time	Total time spent on calls/number of calls received	< 12 minutes/call
Percentage of calls open > 2 days	Number of calls open > 2 days/total number of calls	< 5%

Recording metrics and graphing them over time can provide a simple but valuable feedback mechanism for help desk staffers. To help empower employees, make specific individuals responsible for attaining certain goals. Also, be sure to reward them for these accomplishments. Of course, it's important to keep in mind the human factor—no one wants to hear that they are not meeting expected performance levels week after week. If your staff regularly falls short of current goals, it might be a good idea to change the goals to make them easier to achieve and then gradually build them up. The overall purpose is to work toward improvement while still maintaining job satisfaction.

Help Desk Procedures

A vital part of any help desk organization is to have some process for resolving issues. One efficient way to organize your help desk is to establish a hierarchy of responsibilities. For example, first-level technicians may be instructed to solve only simple problems and usage issues with which they are familiar. Second-level technicians may be dedicated to solving server and network problems. Other personnel may be regarded as specialists on certain applications or procedures. Because of the nature of technical problems, many companies have front-line support personnel answer all calls. This approach usually results in more efficient routing of calls to the appropriate personnel. However, an automated phone system (though it may seem annoying to most) can also aid users in contacting the appropriate person. Figure 3.1 shows an example of a typical process flow for a first-level technician. It is important to emphasize to first-level technicians that their job is as important as those of others and that they are ultimately responsible for seeing to the resolution of issues.

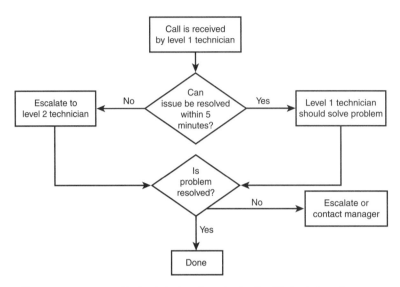

Figure 3.1   A typical help desk flowchart for levels of help desk technicians.

Policies, procedures, and service-level agreements are extremely important for help desk operations. An example of a policy is for first-level technicians to escalate all calls that they cannot resolve within 10 minutes. This plan prevents "busy signals" caused by all first-level support personnel working on a task that might be resolved much more quickly by a specialist in that area. Chapter 4, "Policies and Procedures," provides some recommendations for developing support policies and service-level agreements. Finally, for operations to run as smoothly as possible, it's important for each member of the help desk team to know exactly what his or her role is in the established process.

Tools and Technologies

Recording help desk problems, resolutions, and statistics can be instrumental in streamlining policies and procedures. For example, managers can easily find out which issues require the most time to resolve and when the most calls are being reported. Maintaining help desk information can be made much easier with an organized tracking database and other software tools. The use of a well-maintained help desk database can often provide IT staffers and end users with quick solutions to common problems. Statistics compiled from this information can be used to justify additional training or additional staffing if required.

▶ For More
Information
2

Many of the ideas presented in this book can help with the technical aspects of setting up a help desk. For example, in Chapter 16, "Web Applications," we create a database-driven Web page from which users can query and input information. This sample can easily be extended to create a system that allows end users to directly enter in trouble tickets and assign the tickets to appropriate personnel. The processes of troubleshooting and problem resolutions can also be performed more efficiently utilizing software such as remote diagnostics. In Chapter 11, "Remote Management," we cover several ways to reduce time and costs by managing and troubleshooting your network assets.

Managing Assets and Technology

It's very difficult to measure and attempt to improve your TCO without first knowing what you own. On its most basic level, asset management involves the development of a basic network inventory. All available hardware, software, and network devices should be included. However, there are many other concerns, such as keeping up with technology. In this section, we look at some areas to measure and the potential uses of this information.

Taking Inventory of Your Network

Managing a networked environment is very difficult if you don't know what types of devices you're supporting. Though you can use various software packages to find network information after deployment, the easiest method is to keep complete records when rolling out a PC. This is just the initial step, of course. Along with configuration information and user specifics, it's important to maintain the documentation and update it over time. For example, a typical PC configuration worksheet might include information on the hardware, installed applications, and network. Preferably, this information will be stored electronically, such as in spreadsheets or in a simple database. However, it may be more efficient to simply attach a sheet of paper near each machine.

For More
Information
3, 4, 5

Several software packages are available for managing large networks. For example, Microsoft's Systems Management Server and Hewlett Packard's OpenView programs can be used to automatically discover devices on your network. Other products, such as diagramming software from Visio, can be used to develop network maps and diagrams. A drawback to many of these solutions is that they can be very expensive to implement and seem to be targeted toward larger companies. In the future, however, we'll surely see more tools for managing smaller environments.

The systems and network management personnel who take the time to catalog the actual components of TCO will probably see that many of the costs incurred can be avoided. For example, an initial increase in investment for more manageable PCs may result in fewer user-related problems and hardware replacements.

Creating a Configuration Worksheet

A good configuration worksheet includes the information about the basic hardware and software installed on a workstation. An example is:

Item	Example
Manufacturer	Cool Computers
Model	Screamin' Deamon
Serial number	12345
CPU	AMD K6-III 400MHz
RAM	96 MB SDRAM
Hard disk	6.0 GB IDE
Network address	TCP/IP: 192.168.0.201
Operating system	Windows NT Workstation 4.0 (Service Pack 4)
Software installed	Microsoft Office 97 Std.; Internet Explorer 4.0; Accounting application
Notes	Accounting workstation for Jane Doe

Managing Licenses

For More
Information
6, 7

Keeping track of software licenses is very difficult because computer programs are not tangible like other assets. That is, a single CD-ROM can be used to install hundreds of copies of a program. However, this does not make the action legal. Companies and their employees are legally responsible for verifying that software is licensed before it is installed (except in cases where trial versions are being used). Many product vendors have complex licensing schemes that must be understood completely.

One of the most important areas involving license management has to do with educating your users about installing software on their own systems. If you don't prevent local software installation, instruct users to call IT before they install any programs on their system. IT should be able to verify whether a license is available for this user. If one is not available, the user should go through the proper procedure for requesting and ordering a new product license. In general, it is usually considered legal for users to install software from another source as long as it has been purchased. For example, if a user needs Office 97, as long as you have ordered the software, you can use another CD-ROM to install the product immediately. The best way to ensure compliance with such policies is to make the procedure quick and easy. Forcing users to wait a week or more to install software that they already have a copy of is frustrating for everyone. To solve this problem, many companies, including Microsoft, make evaluation versions of their products available on the Internet and on other media. Also, flexible site licensing and upgrade procedures are available from several vendors and resellers. If your organization is lacking licenses for what you are already using, confronting management with the additional unexpected costs is not likely to be well received. However, it is much better to take the time to enforce license management before you are audited than to try to make excuses for it afterward.

There are several benefits to managing licenses properly. Many large vendors offer certain benefits for large customers, and the only way to know if you qualify for discounts is to count the licenses you currently own. This information helps you answer several questions:

- Are we eligible for a discount?
- Can we negotiate a better deal with our vendor?
- How much would it cost to switch to a competing product and can our existing software be considered for a competitive upgrade program?
- Is a site license available for a certain piece of software, and would it save us money?

Evaluating Hardware

For More
Information
8, 9

Even for IT organizations, "the right tool for the right job" are good words to live by. In typical environments, servers are rarely used to their true potential. Performance monitoring and optimization are very important methods for determining whether hardware, software, and network upgrades are really necessary. When determining the kinds of client-side hardware to deploy, you need to consider the purpose of these devices. Table 3.2 shows some common computer usage recommendations.

Table 3.2 **Computer Usage Recommendations**

Platform	Description	User Types	Notes
Workstations	High-power desktop computers	Engineers	More expensive than traditional desktop PCs
Corporate PCs	Desktop PC with management functions	Knowledge workers	Includes manageability hardware and software
Desktop computers	Standard personal computers optimized for affordability and functionality	Home/ small- business users	Often includes multimedia options plus entertainment hardware and software
Network PCs	Scaled-down personal computers designed for network operations	Single-task workers	Dependent on network resources
Network computers (NCs)	Low-powered, diskless workstations	Single-task workers (terminal replacements)	Dependent on terminal servers (see Chapter 11)

Desktop computers are a good fit for home users, whereas business users require more or less functionality based on their job functions. Despite what you might read in marketing brochures, older computers might still be quite useful. Even an old Pentium or 486 machine could well serve as a backup domain controller in a Windows NT environment, for example. Although it may be difficult, try to ignore the marketing hype that suggests you need a dual-processor workstation with a half-gigabyte of RAM to run Microsoft Word properly.

On the other hand, the costs required to replace and update computers may be minimal compared to the increase in productivity that is realized. If power users are able to run several applications at once and complete processing-intensive tasks much more quickly, they clearly will be more productive. A major problem in many companies is managing the politics of handling technology. Users can, and often do, find ways to justify upgrades that are not done for business purposes. Also, departments with better funding often choose to get the most powerful machines whether or not it is practical. Determining the validity of these types of requests is very difficult because IT cannot always claim to be the sole expert on what is needed to perform job functions. A potential problem with this practice (other than higher purchase cost) is that IT support personnel will have to manage more complicated configurations. Ultimately, managers will make decisions about appropriate requirements, ideally basing their decisions on some unbiased input from IT professionals. We talk about some of the specific upgrades you can make to your system in later chapters.

Keeping Up-to-Date on Technology

Keeping pace with technology advances is particularly difficult for IT departments. It seems that as soon as one product is rolled out, another one is waiting to replace it. In many cases, this cycle is unavoidable—it is just the nature of invention. However, the implementation of a technology refresh cycle can save a lot of money over the long run. For example, companies might choose to refresh 30% of their hardware devices every year. What is the business justification for this? First, if employees are unable to do their jobs efficiently on older hardware, it's often worth the additional outlay of capital to keep people productive. Second, older machines can cost many times their worth in support headaches and troubleshooting of outdated components.

Business leases have become popular options in some industries because they offer a method for companies to automatically dispose of hardware as its usefulness decreases. Managing leases can be difficult, and all assets must be closely evaluated before an agreement is made. In managing technology refresh procedures in large organizations, the distribution of items such as laptops must be dealt with fairly and quickly. By planning for hardware, software, and network upgrades instead of haphazardly deploying devices, companies can more accurately budget and plan for keeping pace with technology.

Managing Employees

Without an IT staff, there would probably be no reason to even consider any of the ideas in this book. As businesses become increasingly reliant on technology and communications, the importance of people to manage IT increases. Hiring managers and departments often report problems finding and keeping qualified IT professionals. In a worker's market, organizations must constantly struggle to remain competitive in compensation and other benefits of employment. Those businesses that only talk about implementing such methods constantly find themselves looking for new people, often at a very high cost. There are many ways to keep employees happy. In this section, we look at a few ideas that may seem like common sense but are worth mentioning. A good goal is that if an employee decides to leave the company, the departure should not come as a surprise to management.

Effective Management Techniques

▶ For More
Information
10
Keeping qualified employees happy is a challenge that all managers face. So what is it that IT people are looking for in a job? One would immediately guess that salary plays a big role—and it does. However, many other factors are at least as important. Cited time and again as factors that make a good workplace are independence, the ability to move upward, and recognition for their contributions. Although it might seem obvious, here are a few factors that can positively motivate IT staff:

- *Empowerment*—Although it may sound like a frequently overused corporate buzzword that has lost its meaning, empowerment has to do with giving employees the freedom to do their jobs in their own way. For an IT staffer, empowerment may mean a few hours a week to research a topic of interest or ownership over the support and maintenance of a few servers.

- *Sharing information*—IT workers who really enjoy their jobs also truly enjoy learning. An important part of working in any business setting is the ability to communicate information clearly. You can combine these two potential strengths and allow your IT staffers to teach each other. Set aside an hour or two per week (or perhaps a lunch) for a database administrator to explain to other IT staffers what his or her job really involves. Perhaps a developer writing client/server applications can apply something a network technician explains about routing issues. The sharing of information benefits both the speaker and the audience and can be the key to fostering teamwork.

- *Evaluating management*—Find out what employees think about their managers on a regular basis—perhaps via interviews or anonymous surveys. Granted, a well-liked manager might not be a good one, but a manager is often an employee's only window to his or her future within an organization. Employees often cite disliked management as a reason for leaving their jobs.

- *Performance-based compensation*—If managers and business leaders pay an individual a basic salary with fixed benefits, budgeting salaries and calculating standard raises are quite easy. However, in the IT industry standard compensation packages do not keep many employees for long. An organization that lacks flexibility, opportunity, and incentive soon finds itself trying to bring in new people to fill the voids opened by those who left. Worse yet, those who stay might not be as performance driven as those who leave. Many organizations have implemented some form of profit-sharing, based on how the company performs as a whole. Profit-sharing is a good benefit when things are going well, but it can have many drawbacks. First of all, many individuals may be doing an excellent job regardless of whether the company as a whole meets its goals. For them, individual recognition and compensation would be a good reward. It is also fairer to accurately measure individual contributions over which employees have more control. Rewards may be a monetary bonus, but can also be as simple as an award or a day off from work.

- *Stability*—In large organizations, it seems customary to "restructure" an organization after profits are low. Although this action may appease shareholders, change for the sake of change can be a detriment to everyone in the long run. Take the time to consider the short- and long-term effects of making shifts in management approach and reorganizing departments. You may find that this energy could be better spent in another area. On the other hand, change and reevaluation for companies that are growing and changing can be a good thing if implemented correctly.

- *Investments in employees*—A common phrase for investors is "You've got to spend money to make money." In many ways, businesses realize that they must spend money on human resources and research and development. However, it's easy to overlook investing in your people. Sending employees to training and helping them increase and maximize their abilities is important to the business. Of course, as in every investment, there is a risk. Companies often fear that employees will leave and take their new skills to a competitor. Companies also tend to neglect employees who may not be seen as people who directly generate revenue. This view is clearly short sighted. For example, imagine an organization with an IT help desk (the members of which may be seen as a burden on the budget). In addition to maintaining adequate staffing, it's important to recognize the true value of individual skill sets. Becoming a Microsoft Certified Systems Engineer (MCSE) is definitely a plus, but be sure to take into account the knowledge that employees have about the culture, goals, and practices of your company. Spending a little more to keep existing employees could be an excellent investment when compared to the costs of hiring and training a new employee. Companies that overlook the growth of their employees may find it too late to make such an investment in the future.

- *Assessing the real cost of hiring employees*—In many cases, managers refuse to give a percentage raise to an employee who may be deserving because they look at the market and see that they can hire other people with that same skill set for less money. However, it's important to take into account the one-time human resources cost for bringing a new employee on board. Combine that expense with the fact that existing employees will have a much better knowledge of your business and the specifics of your environment, and the choice may be much easier.

The list of factors that help satisfy employees could be endless. Notice that many of the items I've mentioned do not require an increase in spending. They just require creativity and some management efforts. As IT becomes increasingly important for many organizations, addressing these concerns should be at the forefront of decision making.

Goals and Rewards

It's easy to forget that it's not the technology and the intellectual property that keep your business running—it's the people! Although most of the fruits of employee labor go to company investors and shareholders, keeping workers happy is the key to long-term growth. Unfortunately, it's also one of the biggest challenges that all types of organizations face. If giving a pat on the back or a small monetary bonus keeps an employee working in your organization for an extra week, the investment may be well worth it.

Managers often assume that they know what employees want. Typically, it is understood that an increase in salary and promotions are desirable. However, it is becoming increasingly common for employees to claim other desires from their jobs, including

- *Feeling of accomplishment*—All workers want to see the results of their work. For managers, this might be as simple as showing increases in sales or results from customer satisfaction surveys. Often, this information is kept within management and not shared with workers. Also, employees should be kept updated about information regarding their organization as a whole. In too many companies, employees find out about important events through newspapers, television, and radio!

- *Individual recognition*—No one wants to feel like a small gear in a very large machine. Making sure that individual accomplishments are recognized is important. The recognition may be a certificate, a plaque, or something as simple as a public statement of appreciation. It should be easy for a manager to determine individual employees' strengths and reward them for these skills. The investment may be very small, but the payback—in satisfied employees—can be tremendous.

- *Team dynamics*—Employees who enjoy interacting with coworkers will clearly be more productive. Creating such an environment has to do with developing trust and communication between team members. Providing team-oriented goals and encouraging events such as team lunches can help foster a productive workplace.

Although it might seem that employees would leave your company for another job based strictly on salary, this might not be the case. If you lose an employee, it may be for a reason other than money alone.

Encouraging Communication and Development

As discussed earlier in the chapter, it's important to actively seek out the opinions of other employees. How you ask questions can often be just as important as what you ask. If you're surveying a very large population, it may be practical to seek only statistics. If you really want to conduct a useful survey, make sure you understand that you should never ask questions without truly wanting to know the answers. Although many organizations seem to go to great lengths to conduct employee surveys, many fall short in actually interpreting and acting on the results. When given an open and anonymous forum, employees are sure to offer some criticism. It is very important to admit to receiving this. However, it is just as important to recognize that you won't be able to address all of the company's problems overnight. Perhaps the most important part of communication is to acknowledge that you understand that problems exist and state what you will do to fix them. Then comes the hardest part—living up to the promises or explaining why it is not possible! Openly addressing concerns, questions, and problems can greatly help managers keep in touch with their employees.

Training is vital to keeping your IT staff up-to-date on current technologies. If the cost of training—both for classes and for lost work time—seems high, consider the cost of replacing an unsatisfied employee entirely. No matter how skilled a person is, you need them to learn the specifics of your environment. Also, it's important to make the most of your training dollars. For example, people who go to a training class on a specific product should be asked to give a brief summary of what they learned. In many ways, this information can be used to gauge the value of the training. It can be done during a company-paid lunch or a short break from work and gives everyone the opportunity to present and learn new skills while breaking the monotony of a typical day.

For More Information 11

Learning new skills for the sake of learning itself does not satisfy most people. Attending a class on creating Web databases might be informative but is unlikely to have any long-term benefit unless the skills are employed. However, it is good to set aside some time for your staff to work on noncritical projects. For example, you might have someone make IP address information or an automatically updated IT phone list available via the Web. This project not only helps move your IT organization forward but also reduces some of the monotony of a typical job. Be sure to reward employees in some way for successful tasks and include it as part of their review.

The Bottom Line

In this chapter, we have looked at several best practices for managing IT, including issues with the help desk, keeping current with technology, and ensuring employees are happy. Best practices are much more easily talked about than implemented. They require determination, practice, and commitment to be done right. It may seem as if there is little time for implementing new practices when you're constantly fighting fires in your environment. However, finding the time to do so will clearly streamline operations and prevent problems from occurring in the long run. Best practices will reduce TCO by organizing, standardizing, and better managing every aspect of your organization.

Although planning and best practices are vital for any organization, those of us who implement solutions keep the wheels turning (and, in many cases, make them move faster). Now that you've seen some benefits of better managing your environment, it's time to look at some good ways of doing so. The technical chapters in Part II, "Network Administration," and Part III, "Advanced Network Administration and Implementation," provide many tools and techniques that can be applied in your environment. In most cases, you'll learn ways to reduce your overall TCO by implementing some fairly simple changes.

For More Information

1. "Microsoft Sourcebook for the Help Desk, Second Edition," Microsoft Corporation, 1997

2. "Enhancing Your Help-Desk Performance with Microsoft Systems Management Server," Microsoft TechNet

3. Visio Corporation Web site: `www.visio.com`

4. HP OpenView Web site: `openview.hp.com`

5. Microsoft Systems Management Server Web site: `www.microsoft.com/smsmgmt`

6. Chapter 5 of this book: "Network Management"

7. Microsoft Protection Against Piracy Web site: `www.microsoft.com/piracy`

8. Chapter 9 of this book: "Performance Monitoring"

9. Chapter 10 of this book: "Performance Optimization"

10. The Computer Jobs Store: `www.computerjobs.com`

11. Chapter 16 of this book: "Web Applications"

Further Reading

For more information on best practices for managing your network environment, see the following resources:

- Microsoft's Management Web site: `www.microsoft.com/management`

- Managing IT, Microsoft TechNet: `www.microsoft.com/technet/`

- Sprint Paranet's Network Operations Management (NOMAN): `www.sprintparanet.com/our_services/noman.html`

Finally, no discussion involving management would be complete without a little humor. On the Dilbert Zone Web site (`www.dilbert.com`), Scott Adams presents a sarcastic but humorous view of life for one engineer in corporate America. You can learn a lot by counterexample!

II

Network Administration

4   Policies and Procedures

5   Network Management

6   TCP/IP Management

7   Security

8   Data Protection

9   Performance Monitoring

10 Performance Optimization

Policies and Procedures

A TECHNICAL SOLUTION IS NOT THE ONLY way to increase the manageability of your network. Careful implementation of policies and procedures can streamline IT operations and determine a defined service level. After these policies are in place, it is important for users to understand them and agree that they are appropriate. In this section, we look at some benefits of having policies in place, methods for creating network and communications policies, and information on managing IT-related resources. Having well-defined IT guidelines can help streamline support operations and provide a better experience for end users.

The Importance of Policies

In a typical company, many departments have found ways to communicate policies. For example, due in large part to our litigious society, many businesses provide employees with information on acceptable conduct. New employees often must verify that they have received and read this information by signing a document. Although it may seem odd for an IT staff to adopt these same rules, it is vital in corporations of any size for everyone to understand the roles and limitations of the organization. For example, few people would think twice before calling IT to fix a computer that is not functioning properly. However, is it appropriate to request assistance for applications that are not necessarily business focused? Also, what level of support can employees expect? Some of these matters can be addressed on a case-by-case basis, but it is much better to have set policies so there is no question. In the end, however, IT is likely to solve most problems as they come up.

Defining IT's Business Function

Few employees would ask a member of their accounting department to loan them some money. This is clearly outside the function of these individuals. However, users are often unclear as to what level of support to expect from the IT department. Should IT staffers be able to teach users how to use applications? Or, are they primarily available for troubleshooting and network changes? A well-managed help desk should know what issues it is responsible for handling and which issues to refer elsewhere. Later in this chapter, we look at some examples of good policies.

Many companies have developed internal charge backs for IT support services. Much like charging departments for phone services and office supplies, this is one way to ensure that all employees understand the cost of IT support services and use them wisely. For example, nontechnical managers commonly expect servers to have 100% uptime but are unwilling to pay for redundancy or clustering solutions to ensure this. A charge-back system allows an IT department to internally bill its end users based on the services they use. This model can reduce problems caused by departments competing for IT personnel's time. It can also make IT look like less of a cost center to the company as a whole, because the department can fund itself through service. However, it's important to realize that the IT department must remain competitive in order for this system to work. For example, if a department can get better service by outsourcing tasks, this could defeat the purpose of having an IT department altogether. Also, coordination between department heads, contractors, and other staff is of vital importance when managing this kind of system.

Regardless of the roles and responsibilities handled by IT organizations, defining a policy and making it known to users can go a long way toward providing good service. It also helps lessen some of the burden on IT and gives users an idea of what to expect when problems do arise.

Improving Communications

To many employees, the help desk *is* the IT department. Much like a repair shop, IT is rarely called unless something has gone wrong or a new technology must be implemented for business reasons. Support and troubleshooting are vital functions, but IT staffers should also seek out the opinions of the employees it supports. End users can provide information about whether they feel support personnel are doing an adequate job and can point out areas for improvement. Conversely, supported users should feel free to contact the IT department about general concerns. In this way, the role of IT can be seen more as a business partner than a dedicated repair staff.

All the chapters in Part II, "Network Administration," and Part III, "Advanced Network Administration and Implementation," focus on making information more accessible. However, the message is just as important as the means of communication. It's important for IT staffers to consider the users they support when making decisions. End users are much more likely to adhere to specific policies if they understand the reasons for their implementation. For example, the following email message probably won't be well received:

Effective immediately, no users will be allowed to send email attachments larger than 2.0MB on the network.

It would be better received accompanied by an explanation, as follows:

The IT department has recently noticed a delay in service for email traveling over our Internet links. In many cases, these problems seem to be caused by a few users sending very large files attached to email messages. Because this affects the ability of all users to do business, we have placed a limitation of 2.0MB on Internet-bound email messages. Special accommodations will be made if business reasons require you to regularly send larger messages. Please contact IT with any questions and/or comments you may have.

This second example explains the problem, the cause, and the steps taken to resolve the immediate problem. It also welcomes questions and/or comments from those who feel that the policy should change. In many environments, technical people are known for not taking the time to explain policies and to be more sensitive to technical issues than people issues. Although it's likely that some users will still complain that the policy is unfair, they will at least understand the reasons for its implementation. A potential benefit is that dissenting users will attempt to work with IT toward a resolution, instead of trying to circumvent the policies.

Network Policies

A clearly defined set of policies for IT resource usage can go a long way in telling users what to expect. This works in both directions. First, it is very important to communicate to users what is expected from them. Statements outlining disk quotas, server storage areas, Internet usage policies, and so on are all very important pieces of information.

The other side of this equation—one that is often overlooked—is notifying users of what to expect from the IT staff. Good policies answer the following questions:

- What is the best way to report a problem or request a change from IT?
- How/when will IT inform me if network services become unavailable for a specific amount of time?
- How will IT deal with unplanned downtime?
- Is my server-based data being backed up regularly? May I request my local workstation to be backed up?

- What is the expected turnaround time of a help desk ticket on an issue I call in? How are calls prioritized?

- How can I check on the status of an overdue request?

- What are the support boundaries for the IT department? (In addition to troubleshooting and systems management, decide whether help desk staff should be responsible for teaching users how to use applications.)

- How long will typical calls take to address?

- Which types of issues take priority? (It's good to have a set priority for expected events such as moves, adds, and changes versus troubleshooting problems that prevent multiple users from working.)

- How can a user check on the status of a help request? If the request is not fulfilled on time, what's the next step?

Addressing these issues in advance not only states the service level attempted by IT, but also sets concrete goals for IT personnel. Many organizations have found that providing help desk personnel with daily and weekly statistics helps keep the group focused, motivated, and goal oriented. It also offers management an excellent way to judge performance. After policies have been developed, they must be documented and distributed to end users. Collecting and distributing this type of information via a Web-based solution can be an easy and efficient procedure. For more details, see Chapter 15, "Web-Based Technologies," and Chapter 16, "Web Applications."

Keeping Users Informed

▶ For More
Information
1

In even the best-managed network, unexpected problems arise. There are many ways to immediately notify users of issues that affect them. Windows NT Server, for example, allows the sending of broadcast messages to all users who are connected to a specific machine.

Maintaining Effective Policies

One reason employees often criticize policies is that they tend to be extremely complex and are often outdated. When you simply amend existing policies as new ones are developed, it's easy to see how this condition can develop. It's important to take the time to look over policies and rewrite them periodically. Most employees are aware of what is appropriate and what is not. For them, most of the information is common sense. Perhaps a 70-page Code of Conduct manual could be reduced to a few manageable guidelines.

Sending messages at regular intervals prior to planned network unavailability can be very helpful. For example, an administrator may send a message 1 hour prior to a server restart, with reminders 30, 15, and 5 minutes before the event. Well-written messages include when the system will be unavailable, for how long, services that will be affected, who to contact with questions/issues, and, if appropriate, the reason for the downtime. For example:

> *Server1 will be temporarily unavailable from 12:00 noon to 1:00 p.m. for the installation of additional storage space. All files on Server1 will be unavailable during this period. If you have any questions, please call ext. 5555.*

An intranet is an excellent place for disseminating this type of information. We look at the technical details of implementing Web-based content in Chapters 15 and 16. For now, however, if your company does not yet have an efficient method for communications, consider implementing an intranet. As always, it is important that any changes to existing policy be clearly highlighted and that all information is kept up-to-date.

By keeping users informed, you can avoid surprises and prevent many calls to the help desk. You will also give those that are affected by IT's actions an opportunity to make alternative plans. These simple practices can help improve the perception of IT in users' eyes and can provide a good customer service experience.

Service-Level Agreements

In Chapter 3, "General Best Practices for Reducing TCO," we describe service-level agreements (SLAs) related to help desk practices. An SLA provides a goal for the level of support end users will receive from their IT organization. An example might be that typical move/add/change requests are taken care of within 24 hours. The idea behind the SLA is that users should be given accurate expectations on problem resolutions. SLAs can help enforce compliance with other IT policies. For example, all assistance with tested and supported applications may receive priority and a 4-hour response time. Help with unsupported applications will be provided as quickly as possible, but there is no guarantee on turnaround time.

SLAs also give IT management an easier way to discuss issues with other departments. For example, if accounting managers say that a 3-hour problem-resolution time is unacceptable, they may be willing to pay for additional staff to reduce the time. Even if they choose not to do so, the support level will be seen as a cooperative choice made between the departments and not one arbitrarily defined by IT.

Evaluating SLAs

Although they may sound like guarantees of quality, be sure to consider penalties if an SLA is not met. This is especially important when dealing with external vendors and contractors. For example, Internet service providers may "guarantee" 99% annual uptime for an additional cost. Many of the guarantees, however, only specify that if the provider does not meet this level, service is free for one day. Clearly, this type of agreement offers very little to the buyer in compensation and reassurance. Be sure to clarify terms and penalties before entering into an SLA.

Standardizing Hardware and Software

Systems administrators who work in heterogeneous environments can attest to the fact that it's much easier to manage several similar servers than it is to work with very different platforms. One of the basic steps in reducing environment complexity is the creation of standards. Standards are so important that we often take them for granted. For example, when we're looking for a common household item such as batteries, we can find out whether the device uses AA, C, or D cells. Imagine the hassle if you would need to specify the manufacturer and model of each item to receive the battery. Also, imagine how expensive these parts would be if each one had to be custom-made. It wouldn't take long to realize that having common device types and power sources can make support and maintenance much easier.

Consistency is also important when you consider your client hardware and software. IT departments should work toward creating approved hardware, software, and network buying lists. The enforcement policy could state that the IT department does not support or give lower priority to any items not on the list or specifically approved otherwise. A policy might specify several choices for desktop systems, a standard notebook configuration, and a list of supported applications. The benefits of standardization include

- *Providing better support to end users*—When IT and help desk staff can focus on working with similar applications and troubleshooting, they quickly develop a knowledge base for handling specific problems. This information can be used to quickly and efficiently troubleshoot user problems.

- *Reducing costs*—By having standardized platforms, you'll be able to swap parts and/or perform upgrades more efficiently. It may even be worthwhile to have a spare machine available to minimize downtime. Larger companies will be able to obtain preferred customer discounts from vendors. Support contracts may be better negotiated, and a technology refresh cycle might be easier to implement.

- *Making good purchasing decisions*—IT personnel are often more qualified to make decisions on which hardware and software will fit best in the environments they support. To avoid misleading information from product vendors, actual features can be compared and tested for compatibility, performance, and value.

Regarding software, an approved application list should be developed and distributed. If users require additional software, they should contact IT first regarding an evaluation of the product. This allows an organization to keep track of licenses and to maintain a list of all applications installed on users' systems. Problems such as software incompatibilities can be detected in a test lab environment without affecting critical business functions. If users do not go through this process, they should know that they will receive limited or no support from IT other than reinstalling their systems.

There are, however, some trade-offs in adhering to standards. For example, computer CPUs could be made much faster than current Intel processors and clones if they were redesigned from the ground up. However, a major factor in the success of current and future Intel chips is that they must support previous CPU instructions. Intel's Pentium II chip, for example, allows you to run programs that were designed to run on the Intel 386 or later processors. Another modern example is often seen in Web-based standards. The Hypertext Markup Language (HTML) is based on standards ratified by the World Wide Web Consortium (W3C). However, browsers from the leading vendors—Microsoft and Netscape—support different functionality. This makes it very difficult for Web developers to write Web pages that work well on both platforms. Determining the proper items to standardize and making sound choices on which standards to support can help to drastically increase supportability and reduce TCO.

Planning for Technology Refreshes

One problem with implementing and supporting technology is that hardware, software, and networking devices quickly become outdated. The problem is bad enough when it comes to updating skills for support personnel. However, as computers become no longer suitable for common business functions, it's important to upgrade them. Although this does require an initial capital outlay, the increases in productivity can easily justify the expense.

In Chapter 3, we discuss the importance of planning to regularly replace outdated equipment. A good general policy is to make sure that users are aware of the technology refresh plan. They should also know that hardware and software upgrades may be provided outside of these guidelines, based on business needs. By anticipating and planning for changes, you'll be able to better budget time, money, and other resources for maintaining a useful work environment.

Communications Policies

One of the most vital functions of any IT department is making sure that the information that users need is easily available. That requirement usually includes access to the public Internet and support for global messaging. However, with this new functionality comes the need to define and enforce acceptable usage policies. There are several reasons for this. First, businesses could experience a loss of productivity if users frequently spend time checking stock quotes or sports news on the Web. Also, recent lawsuits have shown that companies could be held responsible for employee access to offensive, illegal, or otherwise inappropriate content from work. In this section, we look at some ideas to consider when defining an acceptable usage policy for network communications.

Internet Usage Policies

Although many organizations were once fearful of the Internet, most now recognize that the benefits of information access far outweigh potential losses in productivity. Through the wealth of information available on the World Wide Web and the convenience and timeliness of email, individuals are often much more effective at doing their jobs. The Internet is a public network, and accordingly, its content is not regulated. This moves the burden of ensuring that data received is appropriate for viewing from business sites. It is vital that companies develop fair and sensible policies to regulate the use of public Internet sites. Users should understand that their actions may be monitored and that their computers and network access are intended for business purposes only. On the other hand, it makes sense to allow users to access the Internet for personal reasons after hours or during lunch. Few corporations will be negatively affected if an employee searches for information for a child's book report.

▶ For More
Information
2, 3

In many cases, making a policy known deters users from abusing their access to the Internet. However, depending on the environment, other measures may be necessary. Perhaps a more feasible way of enforcing Internet usage policies includes auditing information that is accessed by certain users. Through the use of a proxy server or firewall, companies can record which information was sent to and from users' internal computers. Cross-referencing this log with a list of known sites with inappropriate content is a quick way to find users who are not following the policy. Software packages for enforcing content access restrictions are available, but these are generally designed for home users and maintaining this software can be quite a burden for IT. The bottom line is that employees must ultimately be held responsible for the content they access. If employees choose to ignore the policies, then at least the company can claim to have taken reasonable measures to prevent it and the individual can be held responsible. Finally, consider making technical implementations lighthearted because users are often suspicious of management monitoring their activities. For example, whenever someone visits resources that are off-limits, you might have an animated picture of your CEO instructing the user to get back to work. If done properly, this will be much better received than a traditional "Access denied" message while still serving the same purpose.

Email Policies

It's important to make it clear that IT owns and operates all aspects of the organization's communications infrastructure. Some companies even go so far as to tell all users to assume that management at any time may read anyone's email. Though this policy may be too strict for most environments, it does emphasize the fact that network resources are to be used for business purposes only. Realistically, IT should give guidelines for acceptable messaging. Also, giving sound business reasons for these decisions is just as important. Some examples include

- *Email security*—Users should not allow others to use their email account and are ultimately responsible for all information sent from it.

- *Appropriate content*—In general, users use messaging resources like any other means of communications such as telephones. However, some companies may want to prevent the sending of any nonbusiness email such as jokes or personal messages. These types of items can use up tremendous amounts of network resources and can result in a loss of productivity. Whatever is deemed acceptable, the policy (and its reasons for implementation) should be made known to all users.

■ *Privacy*—In most cases, users' email will be kept confidential. However, in certain circumstances, such as the termination of an employee or unexpected absence from work, administrators may be required to give another individual access to this information.

■ *Attachments*—Sending files attached to email messages can be very useful. This practice can, however, cause delays in message transfers for many users. If there is a restriction on the size of email attachments, users should be aware of it. IT should also work with individuals to find solutions for transferring data if business needs demand it. For example, if a manager must distribute a large spreadsheet to many users every morning, it might be better to place the files centrally on an FTP server (see Chapter 17, "Implementing a Secure FTP Site," for details).

For More Information 4, 5

■ *Virus prevention*—Although the overwhelming majority of virus warnings and threats are bogus and otherwise harmless, preventing viruses on a network should be a real concern for IT. There are several software solutions available, and employees and/or the IT staff should be responsible for performing regular virus scans. Users should also be instructed about forwarding likely hoaxes and chain letters only to the IT department.

■ *Alternative communications*—In some cases, it is easier and more productive to discuss something quickly over the phone instead of sending numerous replies back and forth on an issue. A good guideline is if the issue is not resolved after three replies, use the phone or a face-to-face meeting.

■ *Using email etiquette*—Email messages have the tendency to sound much colder than speaking in person or on the phone. Users should keep this in mind when communicating with others. People can misunderstand actions such as receiving blind carbon copies or messages that are typed in all capital letters.

■ *Using mailing lists*—If your company has email distribution lists in place, they should either have restricted access or be regulated by IT. This policy can avoid, for example, the sending of a message with inappropriate content to `allusers@company.com`.

■ *Enforcing policies*—If it's necessary, you can implement messaging filters that routinely scan messages for certain criteria. A good example would be to scan messages for viruses in file attachments. Beware, however, that some solutions may be worse than the problem they attempt to prevent. For example, suppose a company implemented a filter that automatically discarded all email that contained the string "XXX." Clearly, this could decrease some of the excessive traffic generated by unsolicited and inappropriate messages. In this case, however, suppose marketing editors use the symbol "xxx" to denote a placeholder in edited materials. The filter would cause many problems for these users and could give others the wrong impression. To avoid such problems, be sure to advertise any filtering policies before implementing them. Also, actively seek out feedback on the policy. Remember, if the solution is worse than the problem, it's better to rethink your plan.

It is up to management to decide which policies are most appropriate for a given environment. Companies can ensure that messaging resources are used for safe and productive purposes with these types of policies in place. Despite the implementation of any level of policies, however, there is always the potential for employees to circumvent policies. In this case, it should be clear that the company has taken reasonable precautions and cannot be held responsible for all actions of its users.

IT Resource Management

For the benefit of IT staff and end users alike, it's important to develop, maintain, and support workflow policies. For example, suppose a router problem is detected at 3:00 a.m. All IT personnel should know who to contact and how to do so.

Service-related organizations often suffer from perception problems. For example, people hate waiting in line to pay for groceries when a checker must manually find the price of an item. This is seen as a relatively inefficient process that could be avoided. The same may be true for a network configuration change request. However, if users understand the actual processes being carried out, they will be more understanding. For example, setting up a new networked workstation may involve steps to be carried out by general management, human resources departments, physical cabling crews, network engineers, PC configuration personnel, and systems administrators. In light of all this, waiting 24 hours for a new workstation installation may not seem unreasonable.

Security Policies

▶ For More Information 6

IT staff often view security as a technical issue. They provide firewalls, devise complex authentication mechanisms, and keep security databases updated. The best of these practices, however, does not protect your network from someone who finds a password taped to the side of a monitor or under a keyboard. Many security analysts agree, however, that managing security is at least as dependent on policy as it is on technology. In Chapter 7, "Security," we discuss some technical ways to enforce the security of your environment. Here, we look at general policies.

▶ For More Information 7

Preventing unauthorized access to data always includes a trade-off between security and convenience. If policies are too strict, legitimate users (the vast majority of people in your company) will find it difficult to get their jobs done. With this in mind, the main goal of security should be to give users only the appropriate permissions for performing business-related tasks. Some good general policies include

- *Educate users*—The importance of securing network resources can hardly be overstated. Make sure that they realize that a password can give any network user access to their email, applications, and locally stored data.

- *Hold end users responsible*—The ultimate responsibility for protecting passwords and other company resources lies in the hands of the users themselves. Be sure that employees know that it is up to them to protect company data.

- *Give users only necessary permissions*—Just as you wouldn't grant administrator access to a novice user, be sure that all personnel have permissions to view and modify only the information they require.

- *Review security permissions*—It's easy for systems administrators to make slight mistakes that may give users inappropriate permissions. Be sure to frequently review access to particularly sensitive information and make changes as necessary.

- *Assign only one user per account*—Network environments often use one administrator account, and several people know the password. Even as a consultant, I am often greeted at the door with the administrator password for a server.

- *Perform external security audits*—External consultants can be called on to perform a security evaluation. This can help ensure that security settings are appropriate and that no single user has too much control over the system.

- *Enable auditing*—Modern network operating systems allow you to make a note of every time specific resources are accessed. You can extend this to physical resources, for example, noting when servers and other computers are physically accessed and what changes were made. However, reviewing the data you collect is as important as recording the information.

For More
Information
8

Security analysts claim that at least 80% of unauthorized access to company data comes from internal sources. Many of these people are casual snoopers who stumble upon information to which they should not have access. But with the general policies listed here in place, you can move on the technical aspects of securing company resources.

Change and Configuration Management

With today's pace of business expansions, the only constant is change. If your organization is not continually evolving, chances are good that it will fall behind its competitors. Few networking environments are free from the problems associated with users installing applications at will on any machines. This not only causes license management and support headaches, but can also be counterproductive and costly. How quickly and efficiently you can adapt to changes is crucial.

IT software, hardware, and network devices change frequently throughout the days and years of a company's operations. When people move out of a specific job function, they may take with them valuable information about a system. All of a sudden "Jane's server" becomes "the Web server," and no one has any idea how to administer it. Also, it is quite easy to forget any changes that were made on a specific piece of equipment until problems crop up. To avoid these potential problems, it is extremely important that any and all changes be documented completely.

It may seem difficult to take the time to develop a change management procedure, but a simple sheet like the one shown in Figure 4.1 may be sufficient.

Date	Action Performed	Performed By
1/11/99	Installed Windows NT Server 4.0 and Option Pack 1 with all default options	John Smith, Systems Admin (ext. 1234)
1/15/99	Implemented daily incremental and weekly full backups using NT Backup	Jane Doe, Network Operations Specialist (ext. 555)
2/1/99	Installed network version of Microsoft Office 97 for Developers group	John Smith, Systems Admin (ext. 1234)

Figure 4.1   A sample configuration management worksheet.

Developing and maintaining documentation can seem time-consuming and tedious. If you can get in the habit of doing this regularly, you'll realize that you have plenty of time to document most changes while waiting for application installations and server restarts. The information can be invaluable in troubleshooting problems and in keeping an accurate hardware and software inventory.

Knowledge and Information Management

One of the most important assets your company has is its knowledge. Though employees may come and go, it is the responsibility of all business units to ensure that information is kept within the company and transferred onward. The IT organization can be instrumental in this procedure. Consider some of the information stored in very large databases managed throughout the company. Look for ways that this information could be better used. Could data from a sales-related database be useful to marketing department users for demographic information? The goal should be to make the information easily accessible and useful.

Protecting company information is also very important. Before implementing a backup policy, take the time to understand the business reasons for doing so. The most obvious reason is that the theft or misuse of information can be very costly. However, it's more likely (and perhaps just as costly) that you will lose data due to user errors, hardware failures, natural disasters, or other unforeseen circumstances. No matter what the cause, it's important to secure your data against unauthorized access and loss. In Chapter 8, "Data Protection," we look at several considerations to make when implementing a backup policy. It is important to make end users aware of data protection guidelines before they need their data to be restored. Included in this policy should be information regarding how frequently data is backed up and for how long it is archived.

Controlling Resource Usage

Server and network resources can be very costly to purchase and maintain. Earlier in this chapter, we discussed the possibility of implementing departmental charge backs. This mechanism allows those who use resources to pay for what they need. End users should be made aware that storing hundreds of megabytes of downloaded files is inappropriate and wastes space on servers. Ideally, IT could prepare a report of disk space usage by user account. In many cases, users may be unaware of the size of their email files or download directories stored on the server. On the other hand, modern computers come with plenty of local storage space, and noncritical data can be stored on cheap desktop hard drives. If appropriate, make sure that users understand that this information will not be backed up regularly.

Consolidating multiple servers into fewer, more powerful machines can help lower costs. Managing multiple machines that serve similar purposes can be quite demanding for IT personnel. Resources required include labor costs, backup and data management costs, and the hardware cost itself. Also, centralized management and remote troubleshooting can increase efficiency. Parts II and III are devoted to solving such technical problems.

More Best Practices

In addition to those already mentioned in this chapter, IT organizations of all sizes can benefit from more best practices. Whether you're working alone or as part of a large IT department, competently managing a seemingly chaotic network can make everyone's job easier. In this section, we briefly look at some ideas for being responsible and planning for the worst.

Environmental Responsibility

A friend once told me a story of a Fortune 500 company where executives and managers would routinely print out 40 to 50 email messages (one per page) each morning. Of these, about 80% would be discarded immediately as junk mail. This wasteful practice is not only costly to the company but also negatively affects the environment. Until legislation providing severe penalties for wasting resources is passed, it is up to everyone to help conserve them wherever possible. In several chapters in this book, you'll see ways for using electronic methods of transmitting information. For example, in Chapters 15 and 16 we look at ways of publishing information on an intranet or on the Internet. This practice can reduce costs associated with distributing paper-based forms or full-color marketing materials that quickly become outdated. Even if you don't consider paper and printing costs as a major expense, it's worthwhile in the long run to do things more efficiently. Better yet, many cities have programs that obtain and remove recycled paper for free. Overall, keeping the environment and natural resources in mind can be a winning situation for everyone.

Expecting the Unexpected

Unplanned downtime is a possibility in even the best-managed environments. Power failures, network outages, and other unforeseen problems can cause loss of service for many network users. Although you can't plan when these problems will occur, it's important to know what to do when they happen. A good solution is to develop contingency plans and procedures for situations in which loss of services or loss of data occurs. There's nothing worse than having to develop these procedures when they're needed. If your environment allows, be sure to regularly test the plan and keep it updated. The next time the power goes out and IT staff start scrambling, you'll be glad you did!

The Bottom Line

Hopefully, many of the ideas I've presented in this chapter seem like common sense. However, few network and systems administrators take the time and effort to implement them all. The main concern for IT organizations is to focus on keeping systems running and moving ahead with other technical goals. Establishing policies and procedures can go a long way toward preventing future problems. With documentation of policies and procedures, IT staff can increase the quality of their customer service. Use such practices as standardization, communications policies, and resource management to better handle change in your own environment. The benefit is a reduction in TCO by increasing manageability and decreasing support costs.

For More Information

1. Chapter 11 of this book: "Remote Management"
2. SafeSurf home page: `www.safesurf.com`
3. The Learning Company Cyber Patrol home page: `www.cyberpatrol.com`
4. McAfee Online: `www.mcafee.com`
5. Symantec, Inc. Norton Anti-Virus home page: `www.symantec.com/nav/`
6. NT Security.net Web page: `www.ntsecurity.net`
7. Chapter 18 of this book: "Enforcing System Policies"
8. Chapter 7 of this book: "Security"

Further Reading

For more information on general policies and procedures for network management, perform a Web search for phrases such as "IT network policies," using any of the popular Internet search engines. You'll find information from many different organizations, including universities, government offices, and Internet service providers. It's unlikely that any one of these specific policies will be immediately adoptable, but you'll get many great ideas and samples of effective policies and procedures.

Network Management

F OR THE NETWORK ADMINISTRATOR, the network is the highway that allows the interchange of data throughout an organization. Without it, IT would be managing a large collection of disparate, standalone systems that did little sharing of information. Managing a network is the heart of a system or network administrator's job. In many ways every chapter and topic in this book is devoted to managing one aspect or another of working in complex networking environments. In this chapter, however, we begin by looking at some of the tools and techniques available for managing your Windows NT–based networks. If you're a veteran Windows NT administrator, much of this content will be a review. I also point out chapters to which you can refer for more information.

Using Administrative Tools

Windows NT includes several tools for managing the various aspects of a network operating system. You can access the programs by clicking on Start, Programs, Administrative Tools. Although you probably use most of them on a daily basis, a brief look at the purpose and features of each tool follows.

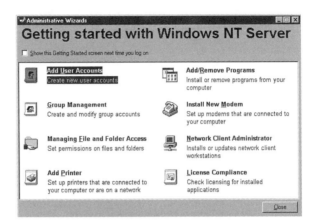

Figure 5.1 The Windows NT administrative wizards.

Administrative Wizards

Windows NT 4.0 includes administrative wizards for handling common user-management functions such as adding users and groups (see Figure 5.1). Although this isn't the most efficient way to manage network administration functions, Windows NT 4.0 provides step-by-step wizards that walk the user through common tasks. For example, clicking on the Add User Accounts option walks you through the basics of creating a user—creating an account name, a password, and group membership. It's important to note that all of the functionality provided by the administrative wizards (and much more) can be accessed by using other system tools.

Server Manager

▶ For More
Information
1

Server Manager allows you to view the current connections and files in use on a server. This information can be valuable in deciding when is the best time to restart the server. With Server Manager, you can send broadcast messages to all users connected to a machine, view information on current shares, view information on files in use, and disconnect specific users. In Chapter 11, "Remote Management," we look at how Server Manager can make remote management of servers and workstations much easier.

Event Viewer

The Windows NT Event Viewer provides a way to view messages sent by the operating system and applications. There are three Event logs:

- *System log*—Displays operating system notices and information about services, such as programs that executed during startup or drivers that failed to load.
- *Application log*—Records events reported by applications. Any Windows NT program can generate entries in the Event log if it is designed to do so. For example, Microsoft's SQL Server writes database alerts here.

- *Security log*—Used for viewing information on events that are audited (described later). Only a member of the Administrators group may view this log.

Each recorded event can be one of three types. A blue information icon represents status information, a yellow exclamation point signifies a warning, and a red stop sign specifies an error. The Event log can contain a large amount of information. In most cases, you cannot control what is recorded, but you can alter what you view by setting filters to display only specific information. To set a filter:

1. Click on View, Filter Events.

2. In the Filter dialog box, select the date and time for the starting and ending point of events you want to use (see Figure 5.2). Next, choose the types of information to view. For the Source setting, you can choose any service or device driver. The Category list displays options based on the Source setting. Finally, you can filter by user, computer, and/or event ID.

3. To apply the filter, click OK. No records are deleted, but the listing of events is restricted to those that match the filter.

4. To return to viewing all information, click on View, All Events.

The default option for the Event Viewer settings is to overwrite all events that are older than 7 days. On a server that generates many Event log messages, this setting may cause the log to become full and stop recording events. It's a good idea to set log settings to Overwrite Events as Needed. To do so, click on Log, Log Settings and make the necessary changes (see Figure 5.3), once for each log.

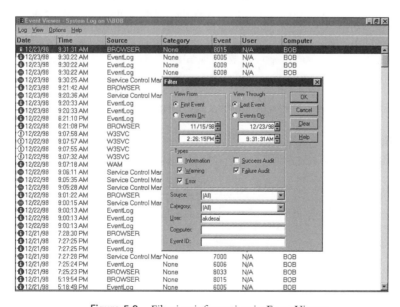

Figure 5.2   Filtering information in Event Viewer.

Figure 5.3 Modifying the Event log settings in Event Viewer.

▶ For More
Information
2

If you're trying to troubleshoot a driver or service-related problem, the System Event log is a good first place to check. There you'll find information on any errors encountered by the operating system during startup or normal operations. The Event Viewer can also be particularly useful in viewing status information for remote machines. To select a source other than the local computer, click on Log, Select Computer and find the name of the Windows NT machine of interest. Finally, you can save information from Event Viewer for later analysis or for viewing on another computer by clicking on File, Save As. .evt files are specific to Event Viewer, but you can also save them as standard or comma-delimited text files for importing into other applications.

Performance Monitor

▶ For More
Information
3, 4

The Windows NT Performance Monitor can be used to view performance statistics. Windows NT automatically monitors most of this information while it is self-tuning the operating system. Performance Monitor is a very comprehensive and user-friendly way to establish performance baselines, monitor specific system components, and view information from remote computers. You can use this data to find performance bottlenecks and to plan for hardware upgrades and replacements. Chapter 9, "Performance Monitoring," covers the details of finding bottlenecks, and Chapter 10, "Performance Optimization," describes how to apply this information.

Network Client Administrator

▶ For More
Information
1, 2

The Network Client Administrator utility copies Windows NT Server Administrator tools to a local share. Windows NT Workstation and Windows 95/98 users can use these tools to view and modify Windows NT Server configuration options. It can also create boot disks and install shares for MS-DOS and Windows 3.x operating systems. We discuss the specific usage of this tool in Chapter 14, "Automated Software Installations;" for now you just need to know that it is available.

On the CD-ROM

Demonstration 5.1, "Administrative Wizards," walks you through some of the common tasks that can be easily performed with this utility.

Demonstration 5.2, "Server Manager," covers information on viewing shares, currently connected users, and files in use.

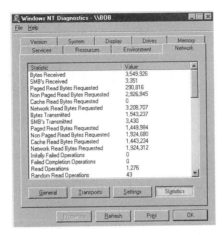

Figure 5.4   Viewing network statistics for the local computer by using Windows NT Diagnostics.

Windows NT Diagnostics

For More Information 3
If you're looking for information about the performance or configuration of a specific Windows NT computer, the best place to start is with the Windows NT Diagnostics applet. You can use this tool to view information about the operating system version, memory statistics, services, storage devices, network configuration and statistics, and system resource usage. The tool does not provide real-time information (for that you need Performance Monitor) or allow you to change settings, but it is a good way to get an overview of how the hardware and software are configured, as shown in Figure 5.4. Optionally, you can choose to save or print information for your own records.

User Management

One of the most basic functions of a network operating system is to manage user accounts and their permissions. Windows NT network administrators already know that the User Manager utility is the key to adding, modifying, and deleting user accounts. There are, however, several User Manager tips and tricks for working with accounts.

General best practices for handling user management include the following:

- Placing users in groups and assigning permissions to groups
- Using environment variables to automatically create home directories
- Disabling user accounts whenever possible and placing account expirations
- Using special accounts for applications and services that require them

On the CD-ROM

Demonstration 5.3, "Event Viewer," shows you how to view and filter events that occur on your server or workstation.

Demonstration 5.4, "Windows NT Diagnostics," shows you the types of information that you'll be able to find using this utility.

Windows NT Domains

▶ For More
Information
5

A Windows NT domain is created when you have at least one Windows NT server created as a primary domain controller (PDC). In a domain-based environment, users log in to the domain instead of logging in to individual machines. One or more back-up domain controllers (BDCs) can also be configured to allow users to log in when the PDC is unavailable. User account information is stored on the PDC, and the security database is replicated to all domain controllers. This allows all domain controllers to distribute the load of processing logins in large environments. There are several benefits of setting up a Windows NT domain, including centralized account management and management of resources. In a workgroup, resources (directories, files, and printers) must be password protected, which introduces the challenge of assigning and remembering passwords. In a domain, all resources use a single set of accounts for assigning permissions (see Figure 5.5).

▶ For More
Information
6, 7

Larger environments may choose to have multiple domains to ease administration and improve performance. There are several domain models from which to choose. More information on domains and configuration guidelines is available from Microsoft. Information can be shared across domains using a system of one-way trusts.

To share information across multiple domains, you need to place domain users in global groups. Then, in the resource domain, add the global groups to local groups and assign permissions. In this way, users never need to have multiple accounts in different domains and can avoid reentering password information.

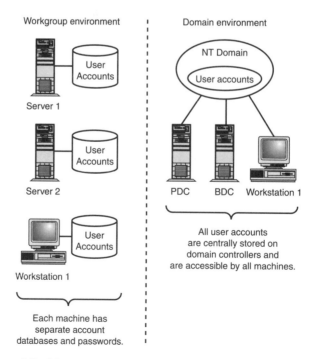

Figure 5.5 User accounts in workgroup and domain-based environments.

Assigning Permissions to Groups

Assigning and maintaining proper user permissions can be quite time-consuming. A good practice when assigning permissions is to create groups based on job functions. Then, assign file system and other permissions to these groups, not to individual users. In fact, a good rule of thumb is to rarely give access permissions to individual users. One exception to this rule may be in the case of home directories where only a single user should be able to store information.

For example, suppose you've given read/write access to specific files to Jane, who is now the supervisor of the accounting department. When Jane leaves the company, you have a few options. The first is to rename the user account to give the appropriate permissions to Jane's replacement. This approach works if the new person's job functions are identical to Jane's and if only one user requires these permissions. However, a better option is to create a group called Accounting Supervisors and assign all appropriate permissions to that group. If another accounting supervisor is hired, you need only place that user in this group to give all appropriate file permissions. Also, if someone is filling this job function temporarily, you can easily add and remove that person from the group.

Creating User Templates

If multiple users have similar group memberships and permissions, you should create a single user account with the default setup and then copy this account for subsequent users. You can use environment variables to automatically create a home directory and set permissions for a user's home directory. Follow these steps:

1. In User Manager for Domains, double-click on an existing user account.

2. Click on Profile. In the Home Directory section, choose a drive letter to which you want to map a home directory and type in the universal naming convention (UNC) path for the server share. UNC paths take the format of \\servername\ sharename. You can use the environment variable %USERNAME% to automatically connect the user to a share based on the account name (as shown in Figure 5.6).

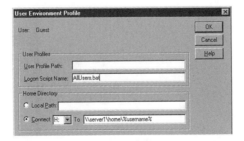

Figure 5.6   Setting a home directory for users.

▶ For More
Information
8   Now any new account you create by copying this template uses the actual login name for the full path of the home directory. Note that the home directory must be shared with the appropriate name and permissions, or this will fail.

Disabling Versus Deleting User Accounts

Each user account on a Windows NT machine has a specific security identifier (SID). This SID is unique for each Windows NT object. Objects include files, folders, users, groups, and machines. When any of these items are created, an appropriate SID is generated. The SID is tied directly to the object, not to its name. So why does all this matter? If you change a username, all security permissions for this user remain intact because the SID remains the same. However, if you delete a user and then re-create one with the same name, you have created a new SID. In this case, it is necessary to reassign all permissions and user rights to the new user account. Also, you have no way of knowing that a previous account for this user ever existed. Therefore, a good rule of thumb is to disable user accounts instead of deleting them.

Setting Logon Restrictions

Although the overwhelming majority of networked environments are loosely managed, Windows NT Server offers many options for securing accounts and network access. Logon hour restrictions are one such option (see Figure 5.7). If you've set logon hours for a user account, you also have the option of kicking the user out at the end of this period. This is particularly useful when you have multiple shifts of workers, or you want to enforce a no overtime policy. Restrictions may also be placed on the workstations a user may log on to. This approach can be useful if certain groups of users are permitted to share computers.

▶ For More
Information
9, 10   Finally, remote access permissions may be granted or denied for specific users. It is always a good idea to deny remote dial-in permissions for all users except those using this feature. A main reason for this restriction is that it makes password-guessing hack attempts much less likely.

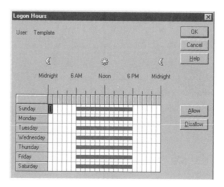

Figure 5.7   Setting logon hour restrictions in User Manager.

Using Special Accounts

By default, a Windows NT domain controller includes several special groups:

- *Administrators*—Users in this group have permissions to all files and operating system–level functions.

- *Server operators*—Users in this group have permissions to basic server management functions, such as managing file and directory permissions and services.

- *Backup operators*—These users can bypass file security for reading information to store on tape or other devices. However, members cannot view or restore this information without appropriate file permissions.

- *Account managers*—These users can modify the Windows NT account database, including adding, removing, and modifying accounts and account policies.

> For More
> Information
> 11

File System Management

> For More
> Information
> 12

The Windows NT File System (NTFS) is a secure data storage system. It supports file- and directory-level security for local and networked users on a Windows NT machine. Compared to the file allocation table (FAT), NTFS uses space more efficiently for hard disks larger than approximately 400MB. In most cases, you'll want to place all operating system and user files on NTFS partitions. A possible drawback is that only Windows NT supports NTFS, and other operating systems can only access this data over the network. For this reason, NTFS may not be a good choice if you're considering a dual-boot environment with these operating systems.

To convert a FAT partition to NTFS, you need to go to a command prompt and type Convert x: /fs:ntfs (where x: is the letter of the drive you want to convert). Depending on the types of files stored on that partition, you might have to restart the system for the conversion to begin.

Although disk space has become very inexpensive, you can always utilize the capability to compress data stored on an NTFS volume. Unlike FAT, NTFS supports per directory and even per file compression as a built-in portion of the operating system. In general, good candidates for compression are archive directories and other seldom-accessed files. Although it does incur a performance penalty, the difference is barely noticeable on modern machines with a moderate level of server activity. On the other hand, it is not advisable to compress frequently used data such as operating system files or applications. To compress a file or folder, right-click on it, select Properties, and enable the Compress attribute (see Figure 5.8).

Disk Administrator

> For More
> Information
> 13

The Windows NT Disk Administrator (see Figure 5.9) can be used to view information on the physical and logical partitions available on a Windows NT machine. You can also use Disk Administrator to modify drive letter assignments and to configure advanced features such as disk striping (with and without parity) and disk mirroring.

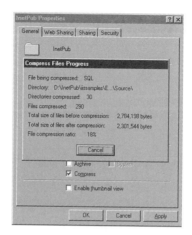

Figure 5.8 Compressing a folder on an NTFS partition.

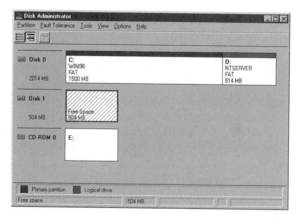

Figure 5.9 Using Disk Administrator to view partition information.

Command–Line Management Tools

Although the Windows NT graphical user interface (GUI) is great for performing specific tasks and displaying information, it is somewhat limited. Before the GUI made *point and click* a common phrase, relatively cryptic text commands were used. The basis of many operating systems is working from a text-based command line. In Windows NT 4.0, most operating system functions can be performed through the GUI. There are several useful command-line utilities that can make working in a Windows NT–based network environment more efficient.

Why Use the Command Line?

Those of us who remember the days of DOS realize that certain operations were much easier to perform from a command prompt. For example, suppose you want to copy all the executable files from one directory to another. In Windows Explorer, you might choose to sort the file list by type, highlight the required files, and then drag and drop them to the desired destination. Depending on how you choose to do this, the process may require several mouse clicks. From a command line, however, you can just change to the appropriate directory and type the following:

```
copy *.exe c:\destination
```

Those that are unfamiliar with command-line operations may point out that there is no room for error and there's no Undo feature at the command line. Nevertheless, you'll see several areas where this method is useful.

Accessing a Command Prompt

For More
Information
14

In Windows NT, there is a difference between the command line and a DOS session. The former is simply an interface that allows you to access a text-based alternative interface. To access a command prompt in Windows NT, click on Start, Run and type cmd. A DOS session, on the other hand, is opened if you're trying to run an MS-DOS program or utility. You can open an MS-DOS session manually by double-clicking on any MS-DOS program, or by clicking Start, Run and typing command. This opens a virtual DOS machine (shown as NTVDM in Task Manager) and sets aside a specific, isolated memory area in which the program will run. For all the utilities mentioned in this chapter, you'll want to start with the command prompt. The following sections assume that you have a basic understanding of DOS. Specifically, you need to know how to change directories, move, copy, and rename files.

Using the *NET* Commands

In Windows NT 4.0, you can use the NET commands to give specific information that is otherwise available only through the GUI. Table 5.1 lists the basic NET commands and briefly describes their functions. For example, to view a list of all the current drive mappings on a computer, you can simply type NET VIEW *computername*.

For help with the multiple levels of NET commands, just place a /? at the end of the command. For example, to see the parameters specific to NET PRINT, type NET PRINT /?. Provided you have the appropriate user permissions, you can start and stop services and view user and group information.

> ### Case Sensitivity and the Command Line
> Command-line interactions are not case sensitive. That is, the commands Ping, ping, and PING are identical. In the following sections, I use mixed cases only for clarity and for convenience. (Most users type commands in all lowercase characters.) NTFS preserves case information but also is not case sensitive.

Table 5.1   **Useful *NET* Commands**

Command	Example	Purpose
NET ACCOUNTS	NET ACCOUNTS	View current account policy settings
NET CONFIG	NET CONFIG SERVER	View basic network configuration statistics
NET GROUP	NET GROUP	View domain groups (on a domain controller)
NET PRINT	NET PRINT \\printserver\printer1	View or change printer mappings
NET SEND	NET SEND server1 "Test Message"	Send a message to another computer or send a broadcast
NET SHARE	NET SHARE	View shares on the local computer
NET START	NET START Messenger	Start a service
NET STATISTICS	NET STATISTICS SERVER	View network traffic statistics
NET STOP	NET STOP Messenger	Stop a service
NET USE	NET USE x: \\server1\admin	Map network shares to a drive letter
NET USER	NET USER	View local user accounts
NET VIEW	NET VIEW	View computers available on the network

The best way to learn about the NET commands is to try them out. Most of them provide output similar to what you find in other Windows NT administrative tools. However, the NET commands can provide all the information in a single location and can redirect output to the printer or a standard text file.

Creating Batch Files

Any number of DOS-based commands can be placed in a single text file called a *batch file*. To create a batch file, you can use any standard text editor (such as the MS-DOS EDIT command). The following example is a batch file I use to back up my Windows 98 Registry. Type the following lines into a text file and save it as Regback.bat:

```
Attrib -h -r -s c:\windows\system.dat
Attrib -h -r -s c:\windows\user.dat
Copy c:\windows\system.dat c:\backup
Copy c:\windows\user.dat c:\backup
```

Batch files are limited in that they don't support looping structures and complex input and output commands. Microsoft has released the Windows Scripting Host to fill in these gaps. For more information on advanced scripting, see Chapter 19, "Scripting."

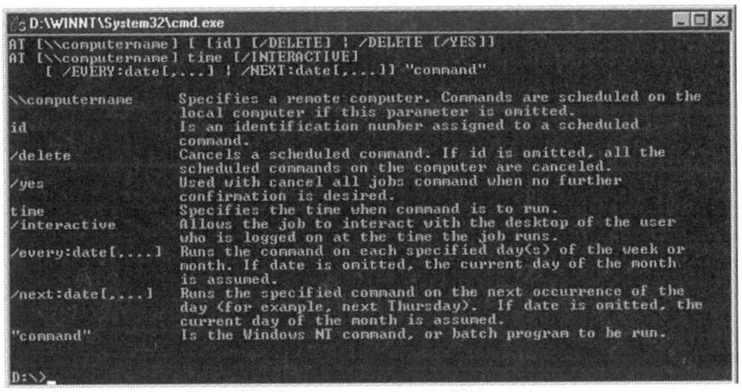

Figure 5.10   AT command-line options.

Scheduling Tasks

A command-line utility called AT is included as part of Windows NT Workstation and Server operating systems. A member of the Administrators group can use this program to schedule various tasks that you want to perform regularly. For information on the syntax of this command, type AT /? at the command prompt. The results are shown in Figure 5.10.

For example, the following command executes a batch file every Monday, Wednesday, and Friday at 10:00 p.m.:

```
AT 22:00 /every:m,w,f "c:\scripts\backup.bat"
```

You could also have designated the start time as 10:00pm. To view currently scheduled jobs, type AT with no command parameters at the command line. In order for the AT command to run, you need to make sure that the Schedule service is running. The Startup value for this service is usually set to Automatic to ensure that scheduled jobs will run even if you have to restart the computer.

A useful program that's available as part of the Windows NT Resource Kit is the WinAT command. This program provides a graphical alternative to using the cumbersome command-line options. Figure 5.11 shows the WinAT interface.

For security, you can assign a specific account under which the command will be executed, or you may opt to use the Local System account. The former allows you to perform functions based on the rights of a specific user. The Local System account, by default, has administrator access to the computer but cannot access network resources.

> For More
> Information
> 15

Internet Explorer 4.0 for Windows 95/98 and Windows NT 4.0 includes its own task scheduler application. Double-clicking on My Computer and then on Scheduled Tasks can run this program. Windows 98 includes its own task scheduling program that is much more user friendly. It can be accessed by clicking on Start, Programs, Accessories, System Tools, Scheduled Tasks.

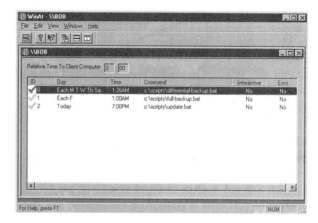

Figure 5.11   Viewing and changing scheduled jobs by using WinAT.

Service Management

Windows NT allows the programs to execute without regard to user logins. For example, I could write a program that automatically sends an email message every hour regardless of whether a user is currently logged in to the machine. Such programs are called *services,* and they can be viewed and modified by clicking on Control Panel, Services. An example of a service is the Schedule Service (mentioned earlier in this chapter) that must always be running to execute a command file. Figure 5.12 shows the Startup options for the Schedule service.

Figure 5.12   Viewing properties of the Schedule service.

Before You Modify Services...

If you're unsure of the exact purpose of a Windows NT service, do not modify its settings. The operating system requires certain services to function properly.

Services have three possible states:

- *Started*—The service is currently running on the system.

- *Stopped*—The service is not running on the system.

- *Paused*—This option is available only for certain services, and its exact meaning is based on the service itself. For example, when paused, the Microsoft SQL Server (MSSQL) service does not accept any new database connections but does not disconnect active users.

Additionally, services have startup values:

- *Automatic*—The service starts automatically when Windows NT starts.

- *Manual*—The service does not run automatically at startup but can be started manually by a program or another user.

- *Disabled*—The service can only be started by a member of the Administrators group.

Finally, all services assume the role of a specific user when they are running on the system. The available options for the Log On As setting are

- *System account*—This setting uses a built-in Windows NT account that has access to all local settings on the computer. It does not, however, have access to network resources or computers. Certain services must use this account to function correctly. Allow Service to Interact with Desktop can be used for services that must request and respond to input from the current user of the workstation or server.

For More
Information
16

- *Specific account*—If a specific user account is chosen, the user's password must be specific. The service runs within the security context of this user and is able to access network resources if the account has those permissions.

For More
Information
17

The Windows NT Resource Kit includes a method for running simple programs as a service under Windows NT. You can use the `srvany.exe` file to make sure that certain programs run at startup and/or without regard for user logins. For more information on the utility, see the Windows NT Resource Kit documentation. If you're designing a program that requires this functionality, however, it's a better idea to write the application to run as a service.

License Management

For More
Information
18

Although it may not be the foremost concern of network and systems administrations, it is very important to manage the licenses that you own for server and client computers. One important reason for this is to ensure that your site is legally compliant. Often, companies haphazardly roll out new machines without purchasing sufficient client-access licenses for all the software that is to be installed on that machine. Managing licenses can be especially confusing, and it's often a topic that can silence a room full of IT managers. In this section, we look at some built-in ways for managing licenses in Windows NT.

It's important to know what licenses you have purchased and how many of each you own. In the event of an audit from a regulatory agency, your organization will be required to show proof of the licenses it owns for each of the clients and servers you are operating. Audits are not regularly scheduled and are currently performed only when piracy is suspected. For small companies, it may be sufficient to maintain purchase records, receipts, and certificates from retail boxes. Larger corporations may want to consider creating databases and centralizing license management for the entire company. License management issues should not be taken lightly. The current regulations make a systems or network administrator responsible for knowingly installing unlicensed software. Employees may also be legally responsible if they do not attempt to manage licenses well. In many cases, companies sue for damages or loss of revenues and fines that may also be incurred.

Understanding Windows NT Server Client Access Licenses

Owning a Windows-based client operating system does not automatically include the right to connect to a Windows NT Server. To legally allow clients to access the resources of a server, you must purchase client access licenses.

Windows NT Server licenses are purchased by the unit (or in multipacks) and can be used in two different ways. Per-connection licensing allows a specific number of simultaneous connections to a single server. Per-seat licensing, on the other hand, requires that client operating systems be licensed for accessing the server. Microsoft provides a formula for determining which method would be better for you. Microsoft allows a one-time conversion of per-server licenses to per-seat licenses. This will most likely be done if you're expanding from a single-server environment to one that involves multiple servers that are accessed by many users.

The number of licenses installed on your server is determined during installation. You have the option of specifying per-server or per-seat licensing, along with the number of licenses that you have purchased. For example, if you have purchased 10 client access licenses, you must choose one of the two licensing models and then specify that you have 10 of that type. To view current license settings, click on Licensing in the Control Panel (see Figure 5.13).

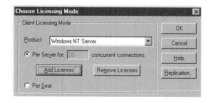

Figure 5.13   Viewing licensing information in the Control Panel.

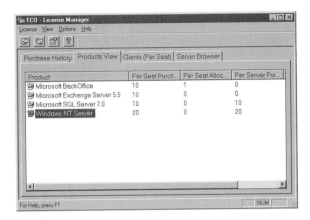

Figure 5.14   Using License Manager to view license information.

Using the Windows NT License Manager

For More
Information
19

Windows NT includes the License Management Service, which can be used for viewing licensing information across all the servers on your network. The heart of this system is the Windows NT License Logging Service. This service records information about which users are accessing a system and records potential violations when the number of installed licenses is exceeded. Figure 5.14 shows the main screen of the License Manager application.

To view information generated by the License Logging Service, you can use the System log of the Event Viewer application (described earlier in this chapter). You can also use the auditing capability of Windows NT to see who is accessing certain files and applications. This information can then be used to see which users are logging in to which servers for making licensing and access permission decisions.

More Network Management Features

Several other features of the Windows NT operating system can be used to automate and improve network functions. The remainder of this book looks at most of those features. In this section, I've included some other best practices that don't fit well elsewhere.

Directory Replication

For More
Information
20

An often-overlooked feature of Windows NT is directory replication. This functionality was designed to keep directories synchronized between servers. Windows NT Server computers can serve as replication importers and/or exporters, but Windows NT Workstation computers may only import data. There are several scenarios in which replication is helpful. The most obvious is for replicating login scripts between domain controllers. Because a BDC can authenticate users, it is important that the login scripts for these users are consistent with that on the PDC. Suppose you have three servers supporting a total of 100 users. All user-based information is stored on the servers. You want to make sure that all directories are consistent across the different machines because users may choose to access any of the three. Replication would be an ideal solution for keeping files consistent. Figure 5.15 shows replication setup options in Server Manager. More information on setting up replication is available from Microsoft.

Login Scripts

Login scripts can be used to enforce a similar environment for multiple users. The main function of a login script is to map local device and drive letters to home directories and network printers. In this way, all users can refer to their home directories as, for example, the H: drive and public directories as, for example, the P: drive. The following listing is a simple login script that can map several drives and a network printer for users:

```
NET USE H: /DELETE
NET USE P: /DELETE
NET USE X: /DELETE
NET USE LPT1: /DELETE
NET USE H: \\server1\home
NET USE P: \\server1\public
NET USE X: \\server1\CD-ROM
NET USE LPT1: \\server1\Marketing-Printer
```

▶ For More
Information
21

The script begins by deleting any existing drive mappings. It then employs the NET USE command to add mappings sequentially. The login script should be stored in the winnt\system32\repl\imports\scripts directory by default. This enables it to be automatically replicated to other domain controllers, if available.

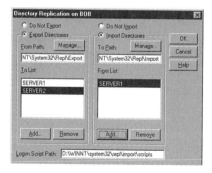

Figure 5.15 Viewing replication configuration in Server Manager.

Case Study: Getting Network Information

A network administrator at XYZ Corp. is asked to create a new server that will support 25 users. Management wants to keep network administration to a minimum and would like all users to experience a common environment.

Solution

First, the administrator creates a typical user account template for department users. This template uses an environment variable to set the user's home directory. She then creates a share for each user home directory. She uses this template to create each required user account. Next, to ease administration, she collaborates with managers in determining how to handle groups most efficiently. All users are placed in groups (although some groups currently contain only a single user). Finally, to provide a common work environment, she creates a login script that automatically maps several network drives and the department printer. Although we haven't covered it yet, Chapter 18, "Enforcing System Policies," shows how she could use system policies and profiles to further configure user environments.

This is an efficient and manageable solution. Group-based management allows administrators to easily add and remove employee permissions based on job functions without worrying about file system and other permissions. Additionally, any changes to drive mappings can easily be made from within a single login script. Using typical Windows NT tools, administrators can also monitor server performance and usage.

The Bottom Line

Basic network management utilities can greatly increase the efficiency of daily network operations. Most system administrators are familiar with the basics of User Manager and other server tools but may be unaware of the benefits of other options such as command-line utilities. In this chapter, we covered several ways to increase functionality and efficiency in daily administrative tasks. More efficient network management helps to reduce your TCO by freeing personnel to handle more important matters. Also, by maintaining a fully working environment, you'll have more time to implement the other ideas in this book!

For More Information

1. Chapter 11 of this book: "Remote Management"
2. "Reading a File Saved with the Event Viewer of Another Computer," Q165959, Microsoft Knowledge Base
3. Chapter 9 of this book: "Performance Monitoring"
4. Chapter 10 of this book: "Performance Optimization"
5. Chapter 14 of this book: "Automated Software Installations"

6. Chapter 1, "Managing Windows NT Server Domains," Concepts and Planning Guide, Windows NT Server Manuals

7. Chapter 2, "Network Security and Domain Planning," Networking Guide, Windows NT Server Manuals

8. "Environment Variables in Windows NT," Q100843, Microsoft Knowledge Base

9. Chapter 7 of this book: "Security"

10. Chapter 12 of this book: "Remote Access Service"

11. Chapter 2, "Working with User and Group Accounts," Concepts and Planning Guide, Windows NT Server Manuals

12. "Overview of FAT, HPFS, and NTFS File Systems," Q100108, Microsoft Knowledge Base

13. Chapter 8 of this book: "Data Protection"

14. Chapter 6, "MS-DOS 6 Command Reference," MS-DOS Resource Kit

15. "How to Schedule a Program Using Task Scheduler," Q178706, Microsoft Knowledge Base

16. "System and User Account Difference with AT Command," Q158825, Microsoft Knowledge Base

17. "Troubleshooting SrvAny Using Cmd.exe," Q152460, Microsoft Knowledge Base

18. Microsoft Piracy Home Page: www.microsoft.com/piracy

19. Chapter 12, "Licensing and License Manager," Concepts and Planning Guide, Windows NT Server Manuals

20. "Configuring Windows NT for Replication," Q101602, Microsoft Knowledge Base

21. Chapter 3, "Managing User Work Environments," Concepts and Planning Guide, Windows NT Server Manuals

Further Reading

For more information on network management in general, see

- Microsoft TechNet online: www.microsoft.com/technet
- Microsoft Windows NT Server 4.0 Resource Kit
- Microsoft Windows NT Workstation 4.0 Resource Kit
- "Administration of Windows NT," Windows NT Server Technical Notes, Microsoft TechNet
- Windows NT Magazine home page: www.winntmag.com

6

TCP/IP Management

Largely because of the popularity of the Internet and applications that use it, more and more companies are selecting Transmission Control Protocol/Internet Protocol (TCP/IP) as their primary networking protocol. Although it was originally designed to be used over the noisy lines characteristic of data transfers several years ago, TCP/IP has proven to be robust and has widespread support from all major operating systems. However, it is not the simplest protocol to manage.

Choosing which network protocols are appropriate for your own environment depends largely on the applications and services you support. For example, the NetWare Link (NWLink) protocol is appropriate for environments that support Novell NetWare. Most users who work in a Windows NT–based environment choose the NetBEUI protocol for file and print services. Table 6.1 gives an overview of the advantages and disadvantages of protocols supported by Windows NT.

This chapter begins with an overview of TCP/IP; then we look at the tools and techniques available in Windows NT to help manage TCP/IP in your own environment. The goal is to reduce the total cost of owning your network by increasing efficiency and automation.

Table 6.1   **A Comparison of Windows NT Protocols**

Protocol	Advantages	Disadvantages	Suggested Usage
IPX/SPX	Supports NetWare; Automatic addressing	Does not support Internet applications	Medium-size environments supporting Novell NetWare
NetBEUI	Fast and efficient for LANs	Not routable; not widely supported	File and print services in small- to medium-size Windows NT environments
NETBIOS over TCP/IP	Efficient and routable	Not widely supported across operating systems	Windows NT–based LAN communications (file and print services)
TCP/IP	Widely supported; broad addressing capabilities; Internet support	Difficult to manage; Less efficient for file and print services	Medium to large environments supporting; Internet applications; wide area networking

An Overview of TCP/IP

▶ For More Information 1

TCP/IP is the standard method of data transfer over the Internet. Many popular protocols such as Hypertext Transfer Protocol (HTTP, used by the World Wide Web), File Transfer Protocol (FTP), and Simple Mail Transfer Protocol (SMTP, used for email) rely on TCP/IP for functionality. All flavors of UNIX use TCP/IP natively for network connectivity. Although not always the case, TCP/IP is now a popular protocol for Windows NT–based networks. It is based on an open standard managed by the Internet Engineering Task Force (IETF). This organization manages new functionality for the TCP/IP specification through requests for comments (RFCs). The RFCs are not light reading, but they are freely available on the Web. Table 6.2 lists common RFC numbers for IP-based protocols. Some protocols, such as User Datagram Protocol (UDP), are connectionless. That is, they send IP packets to a client without confirmation that the packets are received. Others, such as TCP, form a logical connection between machines that ensures that data is received.

Table 6.2   **Common IP–Based Protocols**

Protocol	Full Name	RFC	Description
FTP	File Transfer Protocol	959	Efficient for file transfers
ICMP	Internet Control Messaging Protocol	792	Used for troubleshooting and testing (e.g., ping)
IP	Internet Protocol	768	Routing and addressing of IP packets
PPP	Point-to-Point Protocol	1548	Used for serial IP-based communications
Telnet	Telnet	854	Remote terminal emulation
UDP	User Datagram Protocol	768	Connectionless data transfers

Table 6.3   **The Relationship Between the OSI and TCP/IP Models**

OSI Model Layer	TCP/IP Model Layer	TCP/IP Layer Purpose
Application	Application	Communicates between the protocol stack and the application
Presentation		
Session		
Transport	Transport	Manages connections between network nodes
Network	Internet	Places data in IP packets
Data link		
Physical	Network interface	Physically transmits packets on the network media

The Open Systems Interconnection (OSI) model provides a method for organizing the many functions of the network protocols. The overall goal of the protocol stack is to transfer data to and from the physical layer (the network cable) to the applications that require it. The TCP/IP model provides this same functionality but names the layers differently. Table 6.3 shows the relationship between the OSI model and the TCP/IP model and gives the purpose of each layer.

TCP/IP was designed to support large and complex environments. Each machine on a TCP/IP-based network requires a unique IP address. Each address is made up of four binary octets; they are most often represented in dotted-decimal form, with each of the digits being an integer between 0 and 255. For example, `10.5.5.1` and `250.5.5.6` are IP addresses. A *subnet mask* is a value that is used to identify when machines are local to a given subnet and which addresses are remote (that is, must be accessed via a router). This value indicates which portion of the IP address refers to the machine address and which portion is the subnet designation. A router that connects remote networks is referred to as a *gateway* and also has at least two IP addresses. Figure 6.1 shows a TCP/IP network with multiple subnets connected by routers. More information on subnetting and choosing valid TCP/IP addressing schemes is available from multiple sources.

For More Information 2   In network diagrams, an icon of a cloud often represents the Internet. The cloud suggests the difficulty of predicting the exact path that a packet will take when traveling from one machine to another on large TCP/IP networks. It is beyond the scope of this book to explain the intricacies of TCP/IP fully, but if you're running the protocol in your environment, you probably know enough to continue with this chapter. If you need further information, you can always consult one of the numerous resources available for learning about TCP/IP.

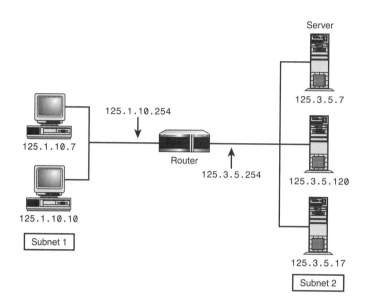

Figure 6.1 A TCP/IP network with multiple subnets.

TCP/IP Name Resolution

▷ For More
Information
3

To make managing unique IP addresses easier, methods were developed for associating a hierarchical name with an IP address. For example, you could register the domain name xyzcorp.com with the Internet Network Information Center (InterNIC), which would uniquely associate that name with a single IP address. You could then have this address hosted on either your own server or with an Internet service provider. You could also choose to make any sublevel names for machines from this top-level domain name. For example, sales.xyzcorp.com and engineering.xyzcorp.com are valid. Before users can access these machines, however, some method of resolving their names to IP addresses is required.

Static *HOSTS* Files

Originally, UNIX-based operating systems used static text files to store IP address–to–machine name mappings. The files had entries similar to the following (the names are not case sensitive):

```
150.1.6.28          server1.mycompany.com
150.1.6.29          workstation1.mycompany.com
150.1.6.30          workstation2.mycompany.com
```

Each computer uses its own HOSTS file, and any changes must be made on all systems. As you can imagine, this process can get quite difficult to manage for large networks with thousands of machines. The Windows NT HOSTS file is located in the winnt\system32\drivers\etc directory. By default, no HOSTS file is present, and a user must create one or use the HOSTS.SAM template provided by Microsoft. Windows 95/98 users can find the HOSTS file in the Windows directory. You can add static name mappings to this text file; however, the next few sections describe much better ways of managing the same information automatically.

DNS

For More
Information
4

The Domain Name System (DNS) uses a distributed database to resolve host names to IP addresses. DNS is similar in function to Windows Internet Naming Service (WINS) but is supported on many more platforms, including the Internet. DNS servers can be implemented on a variety of operating systems, including most flavors of UNIX and Windows NT Server. In most implementations, DNS is a static, manually updated database of mappings. Every time the IP address for a machine changes or a new machine is added to the database, the static tables must be updated manually. The benefit is that all information is stored only once on a single server. Also, all servers in the world work together to resolve names via a hierarchical naming system. If one machine does not have a mapping for a specific machine, it can transfer the request to another name server for more information. Figure 6.2 shows multiple DNS servers working together to resolve a name.

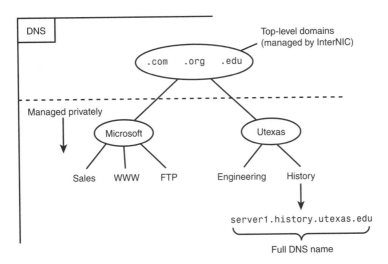

Figure 6.2   The hierarchical relationship between DNS servers.

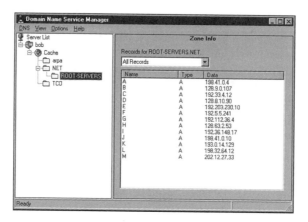

Figure 6.3   The Windows NT DNS Manager.

▶ For More
Information
5, 6
    A major benefit of using Microsoft's DNS is that it can automatically resolve host names on a network using WINS. That is, you do not have to type in all the machine names that are available on each of your subnets, because Microsoft's DNS automatically gets this information from the WINS database. Figure 6.3 shows the Windows NT DNS Manager main interface. You can also use this application to manage remote DNS servers from a single location.

▶ For More
Information
7
    The details of DNS are fairly complicated, and more information is available from various sources.

WINS

In Windows 95/98 and Windows NT environments, each computer has a NetBIOS name. This name is up to 15 characters long and must be unique within a subnet. WINS is specific to Windows NT–based networks. It was designed to ease the browsing of network machines by automatically maintaining a dynamic database of machine names and IP addresses. WINS is easy to install, configure, and maintain because the service pretty much runs itself. To set up WINS, you need Windows NT Server installed as a standalone server or a domain controller. To install WINS, complete the following steps:

1. Click on Control Panel, Network.

2. On the Protocols tab, click Add and choose Windows Internet Naming Service.

3. Click OK to accept the selection and then restart the system when prompted.

The Future of DNS

If you're planning an upgrade to future versions of Windows NT, DNS will play a much greater role in network management. DNS replaces other methods of name resolution for use in the Windows 2000 Active Directory. See Chapter 20, "Windows 2000 TCO Features," for more information.

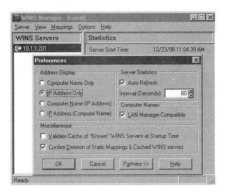

Figure 6.4   Setting WINS Server options.

Following a restart, the WINS Manager icon is available in the Administrative Tools program group. All current Microsoft operating systems are capable of using WINS. For WINS to work, though, the clients must specify the IP address of at least one WINS server in the TCP/IP properties. When WINS-enabled computers attempt to access one another, they first query the WINS server for an IP address. If they cannot find one, they then try to send a broadcast on the network. Broadcasts can create a lot of network traffic because every computer on a given network subnet receives and processes the request. Figure 6.4 shows basic settings options available in the WINS Manager.

For More Information 9, 10, 11   One of the best things about WINS is that it requires very little configuration. In most cases, the default options are best. However, you can change the intervals between name registrations. Figure 6.5 shows the default configuration settings for a WINS server. Multiple WINS servers can function on the same network to provide redundancy and load balancing. WINS servers can either be push partners (in which replication occurs after a specific number of changes) or pull partners (in which replication occurs at specific times). More information on configuring replication scenarios is available from Microsoft.

For More Information 8

WINS Settings on WINS Servers

The WINS Server must point to itself as both a primary and secondary WINS server. Otherwise, known problems, such as database inconsistencies and incorrect name mappings, will occur.

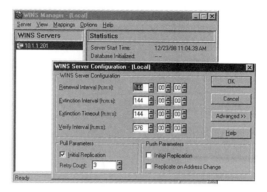

Figure 6.5   Configuration options for the WINS server.

TCP/IP Tools and Troubleshooting

For machines to be connected on a TCP/IP-based network, they must know each other's IP addresses. As long as you have network-level connectivity between machines, you should always be able to connect by typing the IP address of the remote device. In this section, we look at ways of troubleshooting problems with TCP/IP connectivity.

TCP/IP Command-Line Tools

Windows NT provides several command-line utilities that can be used to quickly and efficiently diagnose TCP/IP problems and verify connectivity. In this section, we look at the most important ones.

ipconfig

You can obtain IP address information by navigation through the Windows GUI, but it's much easier to get all the information in a single place. For just the basics, type ipconfig at a command prompt. If TCP/IP is installed, this command lists the computer's IP address, subnet mask, and default gateway. You no longer need to click through multiple dialog boxes to find an IP address, routing information, or WINS server addresses. If you need more information, use the more capable ipconfig /all command. Figure 6.6 shows the output you receive from ipconfig /all. You get complete TCP/IP configuration information for all adapters available on your system. ipconfig /all provides more information than can fit on a single screen. If you're not ready to take a speed-reading course, type ipconfig /all |more to pause after each display of text.

On the CD-ROM

Demonstration 6.1, "Viewing TCP/IP Information," shows the types of information you'll be able to obtain using the ipconfig and winipcfg commands.

```
D:\WINNT\System32\cmd.exe

Microsoft(R) Windows NT(TM)
(C) Copyright 1985-1996 Microsoft Corp.

D:\>ipconfig /all

Windows NT IP Configuration

        Host Name . . . . . . . . . : bob
        DNS Servers . . . . . . . . : 10.1.1.1
        Node Type . . . . . . . . . : Hybrid
        NetBIOS Scope ID. . . . . . :
        IP Routing Enabled. . . . . : Yes
        WINS Proxy Enabled. . . . . : No
        NetBIOS Resolution Uses DNS : No

Ethernet adapter elnk31:

        Description . . . . . . . . : ELNK3 Ethernet Adapter
        Physical Address. . . . . . : 00-A0-24-24-E4-CF
        DHCP Enabled. . . . . . . . : No
        IP Address. . . . . . . . . : 10.1.1.201
        Subnet Mask . . . . . . . . : 255.255.255.0
        Default Gateway . . . . . . : 10.1.1.1

D:\>
```

Figure 6.6   The output from running `ipconfig /all` from the command line.

Windows 98 machines can use either the command-line–based `ipconfig` command or the `winipcfg` command. Windows 95 computers can only use `winipcfg`. Both methods provide the same useful information but in different formats. To run the command, click on Start, Run and type `winipcfg`. You'll see information similar to that shown in Figure 6.7.

Figure 6.7   The `winipcfg` utility on Windows 95 and 98 computers.

Documenting Your Network Settings

To save the results of the command to a text file, use the redirect operation invoked by the greater than (>) character. For example, `ipconfig /all > textfile.txt` saves the output of this command to a text file. You can view this information with any text editor or word processor. Redirect works for almost all command-line utilities that output text. To send this information directly to a local printer, you can type `ipconfig /all > lpt1`. This technique is particularly useful if you need to document network resources for servers or workstations or are planning to make a network change.

ping

The ping utility can be used as a basic TCP/IP diagnostic method. ping verifies network connectivity by sending an Internet Control Messaging Protocol (ICMP) packet to a device on the network. Unless you explicitly prevent this step, most devices return some information. The command can use either an IP address or a machine name as the destination. For example, the results of the command ping 199.164.131.66 on my LAN resulted in the following response:

```
Reply from 199.164.131.66: bytes=32 time=243ms TTL=243
Reply from 199.164.131.66: bytes=32 time=815ms TTL=243
Reply from 199.164.131.66: bytes=32 time=957ms TTL=243
Reply from 199.164.131.66: bytes=32 time=1268ms TTL=243

Ping statistics for 199.164.131.66:
    Packets: Sent = 4, Received = 4, Lost = 0 (0% loss),
Approximate round trip times in milli-seconds:
    Minimum = 243ms, Maximum =  1268ms, Average =  820ms
```

The reply time measures the time required for a response in milliseconds (thousandths of a second). You can use this value as a rough estimate of network congestion and server workload. Longer response times indicate that the server may be overloaded or the presence of a lot of network traffic. On a LAN, response times should usually be less than 1,000ms unless network traffic is high. Slower connections (such as WAN connections) typically have higher response times. By default, the ping utility times out if no response is received within a specified amount of time. This and other options can be modified by using command-line switches. Type ping -? to get a list of options (see Figure 6.8). The ping -a command is particularly useful for resolving an IP address to a host name. Also, you can verify that TCP/IP is working by using the command ping localhost or ping 127.0.0.1 (both are loop-back addresses that point to the local machine). We cover more troubleshooting in a later section.

Figure 6.8   The command-line switches for the ping command.

On the CD-ROM

Demonstration 6.2, "TCP/IP Diagnostic Tools," walks you through using the ping, tracert, and netstat commands for verifying TCP/IP connectivity and obtaining statistics information.

tracert

The TraceRoute (tracert) utility shows the path of a packet as it travels over the network. This utility instructs all routers along the way to pass back response information. You can use the feedback provided by tracert to find out which hops along your network are taking the most time. This data can also be useful for measuring performance for Internet sites. However, you should use the information as a general guideline rather than as raw performance data because many variables can affect the length of the hops. Nevertheless, if you're unable to connect to a remote machine, tracert is a great way to see which device is not working, because the requests will time out and eventually abort at this step.

Following is a capture from a tracert command that I ran while connected to my ISP. The command traces the hops used to reach rs.internic.net via my 44KBps analog modem connection:

```
C:\tracert rs.internic.net

Tracing route to rs.internic.net [198.41.0.13]
over a maximum of 30 hops:
  1    105 ms   103 ms    110 ms   tnt16.hou3.da.uu.net [206.115.152.77]
  2    105 ms    98 ms    100 ms   207.76.52.186
  3     99 ms    92 ms     99 ms
➥452.ATM3-0.XR2.HOU4.Alter.Net [137.39.82.138]
  4    105 ms   100 ms    100 ms
➥292.ATM2-0.TR2.HOU4.ALTER.NET [146.188.240.186]
  5    133 ms   120 ms    120 ms
➥112.ATM7-0.TR2.DCA1.ALTER.NET [146.188.136.201]
  6    131 ms   126 ms    128 ms
➥298.ATM6-0.XR2.DCA1.ALTER.NET [146.188.161.153]
  7    131 ms   133 ms    127 ms
➥194.ATM1-0-0.GW2.DCA1.ALTER.NET [146.188.161.37]
  8    139 ms   137 ms    137 ms
➥Internic1-gw.customer.ALTER.NET [157.130.32.242]
  9    149 ms   141 ms    128 ms   rs.internic.net [198.41.0.13]
Trace complete.
```

For More Information 12 Of course, if you try the same command, you will get different results because of your network topology. In fact, if I try the same command several times, the packets take different paths each time. What is really happening is that each router along the way forwards the packet to the next known router with the least workload. To get a list of options for using the tracert command, type tracert -? at the command prompt.

nslookup

For More Information 13 The Name Server Lookup (nslookup) command-line utility provides information about the DNS server that is used to resolve a specific host name. If you have trouble connecting to a host by name but not by IP address, this command can be very useful. More information about using nslookup is available from Microsoft.

nbtstat

The NetBIOS Over TCP/IP Statistics (nbtstat) utility shows you the names in your network cache. These entries are the names of the machines you have recently connected to and are stored in memory for quicker retrieval. If the IP addresses shown are incorrect or outdated for some systems, you probably have a name resolution problem. The following is the result of an nbtstat -r command run on a small network (note that the -r and -R switches have different functions):

```
NetBIOS Names Resolution and Registration Statistics
----------------------------------------------------
Resolved By Broadcast    = 1
Resolved By Name Server  = 0
Registered By Broadcast  = 14
Registered By Name Server = 0
NetBIOS Names Resolved By Broadcast
----------------------------------------------------
        FROGGY
```

Notice that the results show how names were resolved. If name resolution methods (described later in the chapter) are working properly, the number of broadcasts is minimal. To refresh the name cache (for example, after updating the LMHOSTS file), you can use the nbtstat -R command.

netstat

The netstat utility can be used from the command line to show the computers and devices to which the local machine can connect. It can show information on a per-adapter and per-protocol basis and is useful in troubleshooting connectivity issues. When configuring a firewall (described later in this chapter), you can use netstat to determine which TCP/IP ports your applications are using. netstat also provides Ethernet transfer statistics such as packets sent and received by a specific adapter.

TCP/IP Command Compatibility

Trying to remember which commands run on which operating systems can be quite confusing. Table 6.4 gives a breakdown of what's available on Windows NT 4.0, Windows 95, and Windows 98.

Table 6.4 **TCP/IP Commands Available on Windows Platforms**

Command	Windows NT 4.0	Windows 98	Windows 95
NBTSTAT	Yes	Yes	No
NET	Yes	Yes	Yes
NETSTAT	Yes	Yes	Yes
NSLOOKUP	Yes	No	No
PING	Yes	Yes	Yes
TRACERT	Yes	Yes	Yes

TCP/IP-Based Troubleshooting

Using the tools described so far, you can usually determine the cause of a specific network problem. Although you may not be able to fix it with these commands, you should at least know where to look. The first step is to run ipconfig to make sure that the local machine's IP configuration is correct. If you're having trouble connecting to a specific device on the network, a good first step is to try to ping it by machine name. If the result is destination host unreachable, but a valid IP address is returned, your problem is most likely a routing issue. If you receive a failed response message, a problem with the destination device is probably preventing it from responding to the command. If you receive a host name unknown message, your computer has no way of converting the given name to an IP address. Several basic problems, including DNS configuration issues, HOST file data, and WINS problems, can be responsible for this condition.

If you are unable to connect to a machine using its friendly name, you can try pinging it by using the IP address. If this approach doesn't work, you can be fairly sure that the problem is related to some kind of network or destination device failure or that a firewall (or some other device) is preventing the passage of ICMP packets along the way.

Finally, if you are receiving ping times that seem too high, try using the tracert command to find the bottleneck. If you're on a small network, chances are you won't get too much helpful information—either the slow link is on the way to your router or on the other side of it. Figure 6.9 provides a flowchart of this process.

For More
Information
14, 15

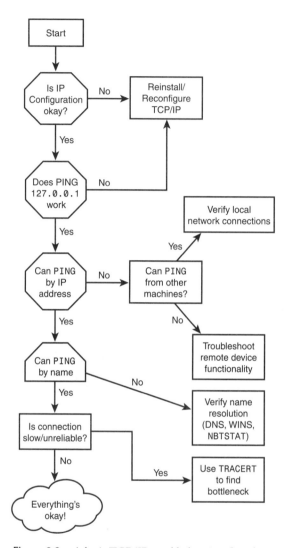

Figure 6.9 A basic TCP/IP troubleshooting flowchart.

Implementing DHCP

▶ For More
Information
16
Managing network addresses and client workstations can be one of the most time-consuming, yet necessary, of all regular IT functions. TCP/IP requires all machines to have unique IP addresses and to specify a valid subnet mask and default gateway. Furthermore, these addresses must be assigned using a given set of rules. It is beyond the scope of this chapter to fully explain IP addressing. More information is available from many different sources.

The Dynamic Host Configuration Protocol (DHCP) was created to ease the allocation of network addresses on TCP/IP networks. The protocol is based on an Internet standard and allows network administrators to specify a centralized database that all machines query when they are first booted on the network. To set up a computer to use DHCP, you can modify the TCP/IP protocol settings to enable this option.

Using DHCP for Dynamic Address Allocation

When a client initializes its network protocols (usually during start up), it sends out a broadcast requesting an IP address. A DHCP server receives this broadcast and sends back an IP address assignment based on those available in its current database. The client machine then has a "lease" on this address. If more than one DHCP server responds, the client uses the IP provided by the first machine to respond. DHCP servers each have a *scope* that contains a unique set of IP addresses from which they may assign a lease. These scopes specify the amount of time a client may keep an IP address before renewing it. Additionally, DHCP servers can send information regarding a large number of different parameters, including subnet masks, default gateways, WINS server addresses, and DNS server addresses. Using DHCP makes sense on a network of any size because it enables administrators to change and track settings from a centralized location.

IP address leases may have a limited duration or may last indefinitely. If the DHCP server specifies that the lease period is 3 days (the default), for example, the computer must renew its lease within this time period. (Lease renewals are attempted several times during the lease period.) If the DHCP server does not specify the lease period, the computer is likely to be assigned a different IP address on its next start up. This process is invisible to the user. In the normal order of events, a client requests a lease renewal; provided that the lease hasn't expired, the client can keep its IP address indefinitely. DHCP can increase network traffic, but this feature is significant only for extremely large subnets. In most cases, the increase is more than compensated for by the reduction in broadcasts made by clients.

On the CD-ROM

Demonstration 6.3, "DHCP," shows how to set up and configure the DHCP service on a Windows NT Server computer. It includes a walk-through of defining a scope, activating the scope, and specifying scope options.

DHCP Lease Considerations

Choose the Infinite Lease Duration option with care. If enabled, clients will be told that their IP addresses are effectively assigned forever and that they need not check back with the DHCP server. If you ever change your scopes or subnets, you'll need to manually reconfigure the clients to renew their IP addresses.

Installing the DHCP Service

DHCP is available on the Windows NT Server operating system. To install the service, follow these steps:

1. Click on Control Panel, Network.

2. On the Services tab, click on Add. Highlight Microsoft DHCP Server and click OK.

3. Click OK and restart the computer.

You are warned that the DHCP server itself may not use DHCP—it must have a static address defined. If you have not already given this server a static address, you need to do so now. Following a restart, the DHCP Manager applet appears in the Administrative Tools program group.

Configuring DHCP Scopes

▷ For More
Information
17

After you have installed the DHCP service, you must set up and activate a DHCP *scope*, which is a range of addresses that are assigned to the DHCP server.

1. Click on Start, Programs, Administrative Tools, DHCP Manager.

2. Highlight the local server and click on Create, Scope. The dialog box shown in Figure 6.10 opens.

3. Enter a start address, an end address, and a subnet mask for the range of IP addresses that DHCP may assign. If you want to exclude specific IP addresses (or groups of IP addresses) from the scope, enter those in the Exclusion Range options and click on Add.

4. Finally, if you want to reduce network traffic and have plenty of IP addresses available, you might want to increase the lease duration. Otherwise, the default of 3 days is adequate for most scenarios.

5. Enter a name for the scope, along with an optional description. Click OK to accept the changes. If you're ready for this server to start assigning addresses, choose to activate the scope when prompted. You can activate the scope at a later time by highlighting it and then clicking on Scope, Activate.

Finally, you must instruct your clients to use DHCP to obtain their IP addresses. When you are working with servers, you want the IP addresses to always remain the same. To keep the servers' addresses from changing, you can add static IP addresses for these machines or you can create an IP Address Reservation within DHCP Manager. The latter option allows you to continue to use DHCP while ensuring that the address never changes.

Table 6.5 **Primary and Backup DHCP Server Configuration**

Server Role	Range Starting Address	Range Ending Address	Subnet Mask
Primary DHCP	192.168.0.1	192.168.0.200	255.255.255.0
Backup DHCP	192.168.0.201	192.168.0.245	255.255.255.0

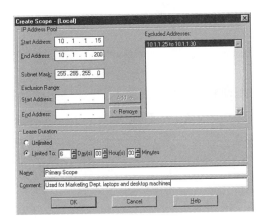

Figure 6.10 Creating a DHCP scope with DHCP Manager.

A recommended approach to networking is to have multiple DHCP servers available on a network. The benefit is that even if one DHCP server is down, clients can still receive IP assignments. However, the scopes of addresses on the respective servers must not overlap because DHCP servers do not communicate, and if one makes an assignment from within a scope, the other server may not know about this assignment. Table 6.5 shows an example of divided scopes that allow for fault tolerance and prevent overlaps.

Defining Scope Options

For More Information 18

An advantage of using DHCP is that you can use this protocol to assign various other parameters. For example, DNS server addresses, default gateway information, WINS server addresses, and even time-server options can be automatically sent to clients. You can set these parameters by highlighting the scope and clicking on DHCP Options, Scope (see Figure 6.11).

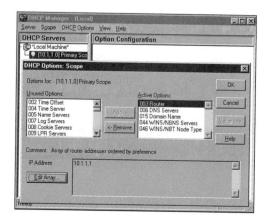

Figure 6.11   Assigning DHCP scope options.

Options can be set in multiple categories. IP parameters are used in the following order of precedence:

- *Client options*—Statically assigned in client configuration
- *Scope options*—Defined for the selected DHCP scope
- *Global options*—Defined for all DHCP scopes; takes effect when no scope settings are present for a selection
- *Default options*—Application defaults; used when no other settings are specified

The DHCP Relay Agent

By default, DHCP broadcasts may not cross over all types of routers. If you have machines across routers that require information from a single DHCP server, you can enable DHCP forwarding (sometimes called BOOTP forwarding) on the router. Alternatively, if you have a Windows NT Server on each subnet, you can set up the DHCP Relay Agent. This service automatically receives any DHCP information from a server that you specify and echoes the broadcasts on another subnet. It also communicates back to the main server any DHCP assignment information. Enabling the DHCP Relay Agent helps by centralizing the administration of DHCP servers. However, this approach presents the potential problems of increasing traffic across routers and of working with large subnetted environments. To install the service, go to Control Panel, Network, Services, Add and select DHCP Relay Agent. You are prompted to enter the name of at least one DHCP server in the TCP/IP Properties dialog box (see Figure 6.12). Following a restart of the server, the agent is active.

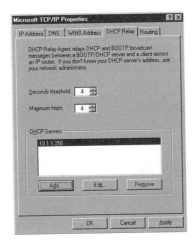

Figure 6.12   Configuring DHCP Relay properties.

TCP/IP Security

In addition to the basic troubleshooting and configuration tools mentioned thus far, many other tools and techniques enable you to make your TCP/IP-based network more secure. The default option for all Windows-based TCP/IP computers is to allow all types of traffic using this protocol. For this reason, you may need to restrict certain types of network traffic. In this section, we look at some methods for managing networks—from a home-based network to an international WAN.

Firewalls

It's difficult to talk about the Internet and TCP/IP without discussing firewalls. The purpose of a firewall is to protect a company's internal network from remote network traffic. In most cases, the *remote network* means the Internet and *allowed traffic* means Web-based and email packets. Firewalls basically offer three types of security measures:

- *Network address translation (NAT)*—Uses a static table to hide internal TCP/IP addresses from machines on another network (such as the Internet).
- *Packet filtering*—The acceptance or rejection of IP packets based on certain criteria, such as source or destination address, packet type, or packet contents.
- *Authentication*—To obtain information from remote networks or the Internet, clients may have to use a username and password. This technique assures access to authorized users only.

▶ For More
Information
19   Firewall security can be implemented in hardware (for example, in router configurations or on dedicated machines) or in software (TCP/IP security applications and
network protocol configuration). Based on firewall security, certain protocols and
troubleshooting tools mentioned in this chapter may fail to give expected results.
For example, a `ping` command may give a `destination network unreachable` error if
ICMP packets are not allowed to cross onto the remote network. Firewalls are covered
in more detail in Chapter 7, "Security."

Windows NT Packet Filtering

Windows NT includes the capability to perform basic packet-filtering functions
on LAN and WAN adapters. Though it is not as thorough as a complete firewall,
Windows NT can protect your network from various types of attacks. For example,
a typical *denial of service* attack (one that overloads a server or otherwise prevents
resource access) is done by sending a large number of `ping` requests in a short amount
of time. The hacker hopes that this overload brings down the server by generating too
much work, but even in the best case, this type of attack causes a nuisance by decreasing performance. To prevent `ping`-based traffic from entering the network, follow
these steps:

1. Click on Control Panel, Network.

2. Select Protocols, TCP/IP Protocols, Properties, Advanced.

3. You now have the opportunity to check the Enable Security box. Do so and
   then click on Advanced to modify the settings.

4. The TCP/IP Security dialog box (shown in Figure 6.13) appears, allowing you
   to modify the types of data that can be sent and received on the specified network adapter. Choose the appropriate adapter from the drop-down list. Before
   setting filtering options, be sure that you understand the ramifications of these
   options—you may not be able to connect to network resources if they are set
   incorrectly.

5. For the TCP, UDP, and IP settings, choose whether you want to allow all packet
   types or only specific selections.

▶ For More
Information
20   Windows NT's packet filtering is not intended to be a full firewall, and only a limited number of ports can be restricted or accepted. When communicating using IP,
machines use the first available IP port by default. Standard TCP/IP ports have also
been defined to allow certain applications to always use the same values. A complete
list of standard TCP/IP ports is available, as is complete information regarding port
assignments.

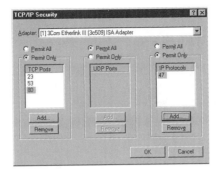

Figure 6.13   Specifying ports for packet filtering.

Proxy Servers

For More
Information
21

Internet access has become indispensable for many business users. In the early days of the Internet, all machines that participated on the network had registered IP addresses. That is, each had a unique IP address that was assigned to it by an authority and was directly available to all computers worldwide. Today, most network administrators choose to use a proxy server to obtain Internet data. When Internet clients request data, they actually send the request to a proxy server. This machine then obtains the data for the user and sends it back over the LAN (see Figure 6.14). The client's IP address is never actually exposed to the Internet. Modern proxy servers add to this functionality by performing some firewall functions (usually packet filtering) and by caching frequently accessed Web pages for faster retrieval.

Proxy servers restrict some Internet functionality, however. For example, UDP packets (which do not establish connections before data is sent) may be discarded by the proxy server. This type of data is frequently used by multimedia applications. Also, outgoing data may be restricted, preventing external access to Web and FTP servers. This situation can cause problems if users are running public servers on their client machines. Various proxy configurations can overcome these problems, and product vendors often provide specific information.

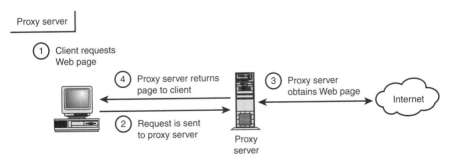

Figure 6.14   Obtaining a Web page through a proxy server.

Future Versions of IP

▶ For More
Information
1

The IETF continues to work on future updates of the TCP/IP protocol standard. IP Security (IPSec) is currently the proposed standard for encrypting all IP-based data intended for travel on the Internet. It is expected to be part of the upcoming IP version 6 (IPv6) protocol (the current version of IP is version 4). IPv6 will expand the functionality of this protocol in several ways, including increasing the number of available IP addresses, securing transmissions, and improving performance. However, many debates over the details of the protocol standard may delay general acceptance of IPv6 for several years.

Case Study: Improving the Management of an IP-Based Network

An organization has 125 workstations located on three subnets. The company will use arbitrary IP addresses for the internal network. Five main file/print servers require static addresses. Additionally, consultants will be using laptops on a separate subnet designed specifically for this group. All other clients will use dynamic mappings for their IP information. Finally, there is a business reason to provide all users with Internet access without compromising the security of the internal network.

Solution

These requirements can be easily met by using a variety of TCP/IP tools. First, to accommodate IP addressing constraints, the DHCP service is installed on a Windows NT server. A scope including DNS and WINS server addresses is created. A backup DHCP server is created with a small subset of IP addresses. All clients are configured to use DHCP. Because the servers require static IP addresses, the administrator chooses to create DHCP address reservations. Consultants will use DHCP to easily configure laptop machines. The fact that they are on a separate subnet will help in isolating this traffic and provide for implementing network-level security.

Internet access will be provided through a proxy server. All client computers are directed to use the proxy server for Internet communications. A firewall is placed between the company's LAN and the Internet. Only traffic from trusted remote connections and the Proxy Server are allowed to pass. This secure and low-maintenance configuration easily meets the above requirements and leaves the IT staff free to work on other projects!

The Bottom Line

The intricacies of managing TCP/IP come with the territory if you want to provide the many benefits of Internet access to your environment. By using various automated methods of TCP/IP network management, you can ease the allocation and administration of devices on a Windows NT–based network. This most fundamental purpose of

IT organizations can be designed to be almost entirely automated and self-sufficient. The ideas presented in this chapter can lower your TCO by making network management easier and more efficient. The time and costs incurred by providing basic network connectivity can be spent moving ahead with more business-related projects. Just the job satisfaction benefits of not having to memorize IP addresses, DNS server addresses, and router information will be helpful!

For More Information

1. IETF (`www.ietf.org`)
2. "Understanding TCP/IP Addressing and Subnetting Basics," Q164015, Microsoft Knowledge Base
3. Internet Network Information Center (InterNIC) Web site (`www.internic.net/`)
4. "Description of Domain Name System (DNS)," Q174224, Microsoft Knowledge Base
5. "Interoperability of WINS and Microsoft DNS," Q164176, Microsoft Knowledge Base
6. "How WINS Lookup Works from Windows NT DNS," Q173161, Microsoft Knowledge Base
7. "How to Install and Configure Microsoft DNS Server," Q172953, Microsoft Knowledge Base
8. "WINS Server Sporadically Loses Name Resolution," Q150520, Microsoft Knowledge Base
9. "Explanation of Advanced Options in WINS Manager," Q167806, Microsoft Knowledge Base
10. "Recommended Practices for WINS," Q185786, Microsoft Knowledge Base
11. Chapter 8, "Managing Microsoft WINS Servers," Networking Guide, Windows NT Server 4.0 Resource Kit
12. "Using TRACERT to Troubleshoot TCP/IP Problems in Windows NT," Q162326, Microsoft Knowledge Base
13. Chapter 9, "Managing Microsoft DNS Server," Networking Guide, Windows NT Server 4.0 Resource Kit
14. "How to Troubleshoot Basic TCP/IP Problems in Windows NT 4.0," Q169790, Microsoft Knowledge Base
15. Chapter 12, "Troubleshooting Tools and Strategies," Networking Guide, Windows NT Server 4.0 Resource Kit
16. Chapter 7, "Managing Microsoft DHCP Services," Networking Guide, Windows NT Server 4.0 Resource Kit

17. "Creating DHCP Scopes Using DHCP Manager," Q150565, Microsoft Knowledge Base

18. "Methods of Setting DHCP Options," Q187742, Microsoft Knowledge Base

19. Chapter 3, "Server Security on the Internet," Internet Guide, Windows NT Server 4.0 Resource Kit

20. Appendix B, "Port Reference for Microsoft TCP/IP," Networking Guide, Windows NT Server 4.0 Resource Kit

21. Microsoft Proxy Server 2.0 Reviewers Guide, Microsoft TechNet

Further Reading

For more information on Windows NT TCP/IP management in general, see

- "Windows NT 4.0 FAQs: Connecting to the Internet Questions," Microsoft TechNet

- "DHCP/WINS Release Notes for Windows NT 4.0 SP4 Update," Q184693, Microsoft Knowledge Base

7

Security

A FUNDAMENTAL REQUIREMENT OF NETWORK operating systems is their management of security—only authorized users must be able to access specific data and functions. However, somewhere between theory and practice, the ideals of implementing a secure environment are lost. Establishing and enforcing a security policy clearly takes time and effort and requires cooperation from all those involved. It also involves regular maintenance and auditing. Usually, the most a systems or network administrator can hope for is to make unauthorized access to data more difficult. If it were possible to absolutely eliminate the chances of an intrusion attempt, the resource would be very difficult for legitimate users to use. For example, the easiest way for me to prevent a network-based attack on a server would be to unplug it from the network entirely! Of course, this step would defeat the purpose of the device itself.

Finally, it's very important to recognize that implementing security is often a trade-off between convenience and protection. If I eliminate the use of passwords and allow all users access to all information, I've greatly enhanced the convenience but have opened the gate for unauthorized use of my system. Figure 7.1 shows this inverse relationship between security and usability.

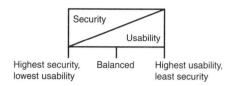

Figure 7.1   Balancing security and usability.

It is often important to solve an IT problem when it occurs. For example, a virtual private network may be implemented in response to a need for cheaper and faster methods of remote access. In the case of security, however, it may be too late to implement security measures after problems begin to surface. For this reason, setting up and managing user rights and permissions proactively is especially important. Though this approach might require an initial investment of time and effort, it will pay off. Measuring the actual value of security is difficult because it prevents something that may or may not happen. To estimate its importance, consider the cost of losing sensitive data or having it fall into the wrong hands. The best way to preemptively lower your TCO is to take small steps that may prevent data loss and misuse of information. In this chapter, we look at the tools, practices, and configuration options that can be used to limit access to network resources.

Planning for Security

Before implementing any security measures, it's important to answer a few questions regarding needs that are specific to your environment. In many cases, organizations create security policies without paying attention to what the policies really mean and how they affect the business environment. In this section, we look at some questions to answer before implementing a policy.

Determining Security Requirements

Implementing security requires time and resources. As with any investment, you should first consider your goal. For example, if the purpose of a group of users is to perform basic data entry of customer information, simply setting default permissions for all users may be appropriate. Because their job functions do not require further access, the biggest problem to worry about is incorrect data entry. However, if sensitive financial information is being stored, giving each user appropriate access only to the files he or she requires to perform the job is important. Another good idea is to enforce some level of accountability for all users. Finally, assess the impact this policy will have on convenience. A security policy that makes it difficult for employees to perform their jobs may not be worthwhile.

Measuring Security Risks

An accurate perception of security is often difficult to obtain. Studies have shown that the overwhelming majority of security violations occur from within an organization rather than from outside it. Focusing on securing internal resources is just as useful (if not more so) than protecting against outside intruders. Often, security risks are overstated. Popular technical media expose some shortcoming in a networking protocol and give the impression that no computer is safe. Although the threat may be real, it's relevance is often exaggerated. A common example is a legitimate virus warning that would affect few (if any) systems. At the same time, you should never underestimate the potential for security violations; the best approach is to consider what is possible instead of what is probable. For example, many organizations keep controls in their human resources department for handling salary information. However, they overlook the fact that a junior database administrator may have unrestricted access to this information.

Security Standards

For More
Information
1
The network operating systems world has few security standards. One of these is the C2 level of security defined by the United States National Security Agency (NSA). Described within these guidelines are issues regarding the ownership of files, auditing, and sharing of resources. It is beyond the scope of this chapter to describe the various requirements in detail, but different levels of C2 certifications are spelled out in the Red Book, Orange Book, Blue Book, and so on. Windows NT 3.51 is C2 Orange Book certified, and Windows NT 4.0 is currently undergoing the evaluation process. Orange Book certification applies only to the product functioning in non-networked environments. Of course, a given installation of Windows NT Server or Workstation is secure only if certain options are implemented and others are disabled. For those who wish to meet some of the stringent guidelines set forth in the C2 documentation, Microsoft has made available the C2 Configuration Manager program. Shown in Figure 7.2, the program queries the status of the current configuration and can fix options to increase security.

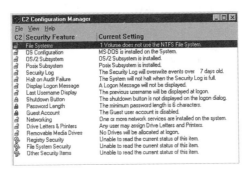

Figure 7.2 The Windows NT C2 Configuration Manager.

Thinking Like an Intruder

It's wise to know the ways and tactics of one's enemies. When designing security policies, you should always think about which gaps are being left open and how they may be exploited. Also, it's tempting to implement "security through obscurity." For example, you might set up a server with an IP address that is unlisted in DNS and other name resolution services. The administrator may think that this server is fairly secure because few people know that the machine exists. However, potential intruders can use several tools to find it:

- *Network analyzers*—Also called *sniffers*, these devices monitor all raw data packets that are traveling on your network. This data includes password information (hopefully encrypted) and all data transfers.

- *Password-breaking tools*—These include utilities such as password breakers that use a dictionary of common passwords to break into accounts.

- *Impersonation*—Perhaps the best way to get passwords is to call users and say that you're calling from the IT department and need their password to make changes to their email accounts.

Windows NT Security Basics

Windows NT Workstation and Server were designed to be secure operating systems. They offer the same security functionality as all major network operating systems. Windows NT domain security allows for the creation of network accounts on secure servers. These are the only accounts that can be granted network access. To log on to resources located on any computer within a Windows NT domain, the user must first have a domain account. Remember that users in the Administrators group have a great deal of power and flexibility. For example, they can add other users to the Administrators group and change the password of any existing account (and thus be able to use it for logon purposes). In this section, we see how the pieces of the Windows NT architecture can fit together to form a secure solution.

The Windows NT File System

The Windows NT File System (NTFS) has been created to be a secure method to store data on fixed and removable disks. For this security to be useful, appropriate permissions must be set. NTFS requires users to first authenticate with a trusted Windows NT computer and also be granted specified usage permissions to files before they can be accessed. File-system permissions are cumulative with the exception of the No Access option. That is, if a user is a member of a group that has read-only permissions and also belongs to a group that has write-only permissions, the user is effectively able to read and write to files.

▶ For More
Information
2
For networked environments, Windows NT allows the setting of share-level and file-system-level permissions. Although you can implement both types of permissions, many administrators choose to allow all users to have full control using share-level permissions. They can then place more granular security permissions using NTFS security. This approach makes managing permissions more efficient because they are only managed in one place.

▶ For More
Information
3, 4
The File Allocation Table (FAT) file system was not designed to be secure and therefore can only use share-level permissions. Although this system may be okay for network users, any user who can log on locally will be able to access all files on a FAT partition. Finally, FAT partitions have a larger cluster size. Consequently, files occupy more slack on the partition, thus taking up otherwise usable space.

Educating End Users

In many network environments, the knowledge of a simple password can circumvent any level of security. Perhaps one of the most important security measures an administrator can take is to educate users about potential security risks. Tell them never to share their password with other users and that IT staff members will never ask them for this information because an administrator can always change a password if needed. A good way to enforce this measure is to recommend that they choose an embarrassing or very personal password. Finally, to keep users from using scraps of paper stuck to the bottom of their keyboard, notify them that they will be held responsible if anyone else uses their account without permissions unless adequate security measures are taken. Also, make sure that users have a good basic understanding of NTFS permissions—file and directory permissions may change if these objects are moved or copied to different locations.

In many ways, maintaining a secure environment is more dependent on personnel and policy issues than on technology. It's much more likely that a secretarial user will accidentally delete a file or incorrectly make changes than that an intruder will maliciously corrupt data. Although the first scenario doesn't get as much media attention as the second, the potential for accidents and the potential for intrusion are equally important reasons for having an adequate security policy. Data entry clerks simply should not have the permissions to drop a table in a database whether they know how to do it or not.

Managing User Permissions

▶ For More
Information
5
To manage your network properly, you need to give all users (including administrators) sufficient permissions to carry out their tasks. It is also important to restrict access to tools that they do not use or should not have access to. In this section, we look at some of the Windows NT features for restricting access. User rights can restrict the functions that users with above-normal user permissions can perform.

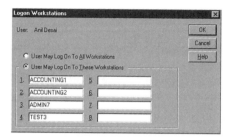

Figure 7.3 Setting workstation logon restrictions in User Manager.

For example, in the Windows NT User Manager, an administrator can restrict the workstations to which a user may log on. This step may be useful if you have a set group of users who share machines, and you do not want these people to log on to other computers. Figure 7.3 shows an example of such restrictions.

To prevent the loss of data, all network operating systems feature a user account or group from which all rights are inherited. In Windows NT, the Administrators group serves this purpose. Managing permissions for administrator accounts is particularly important. Organizations commonly set up a single user account for all network and systems administrators and give several people the password for this account. However, this system has several major security problems. First, if more than one user can log on to the system as the administrator, it is difficult to determine accountability. For this reason, all users should be given separate accounts. Second, potential intruders trying to guess passwords often assume that this account exists; therefore, the default administrator account should be renamed. In addition, all logon attempts (successes and failures) should be audited to maintain accountability.

Managing User Accounts

The 32-bit Windows client operating systems (Windows 95/98 and Windows NT) support the implementation of certain policies and profiles that, when used properly, allow users enough freedom to do their jobs without allowing them to delete files to which they should not have access. Users who are network/systems administrators should have two user accounts. The first should be their main user account under which they log on for all normal tasks. A second administrator account should be used only when necessary. For example, a network administrator named Jane Doe would have two user accounts: JDoe and JDoe-Admin.

On the CD-ROM

Demonstration 7.1, "User Manager," shows how to apply basic security settings for user accounts in User Manager.

Tightening Account Policies

The Windows NT default account policies are created for convenience. For example, the settings allow a user to use a blank password or choose a password of any length. With these settings, intrusion attempts are likely to be successful; therefore, such policies should be changed in all but the least secure environments. Figure 7.4 and Table 7.1 show the various options available when you click on Account, Policy from within User Manager.

Table 7.1 **Windows NT Account Policy Options**

Feature	Recommended Setting	Benefits
Minimum password length	6–8 characters	Makes passwords more difficult to guess
Password expiration	30–90 days	Forces users to generate a new password after a certain number of days
Password uniqueness	5 passwords	Prevents users from reusing the same passwords
Account lockout	After 5 attempts; Reset after 30 minutes	Prevents password-guessing hack attempts
Minimum password age	3 days (allow changes immediately if Password Uniqueness is enforced)	Prevents users from immediately changing their passwords back to the original setting
Lockout duration	30 minutes	Prevents password-guessing hack attempts by forcing users to wait until retrying
Forcibly disconnect remote users from server when logon hours expire	Enabled if using logon hour restrictions	Enforces shift-work or no-overtime policies
Users must log on to change their password	Disabled (to prevent administrative work)	Prevents users from renewing a password if it has already expired

On the CD-ROM

Demonstration 7.2, "Account Policies," walks you through the various screens used for setting password and account policies.

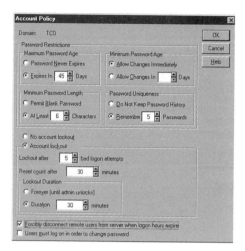

Figure 7.4 Account policy options available in User Manager.

Note that in Windows NT, accounts are locked out automatically by the operating system. Administrators cannot lock an account manually, but they can unlock accounts or disable them.

Enforcing the Use of Stronger Passwords

In several ways, the idea of network security goes hand in hand with the ideas in Chapter 4, "Policies and Procedures." No matter how strong your router security or how restrictive your Internet firewall, the weakest point in your defenses is in the password policy. A very easy way for anyone to gain access to a system is to call users and simply ask for their password information by claiming to be from the IT department. Instruct users *never* to give out their password. Even if network administrators must access the system as a particular user, they have specific methods of gaining access to a resource that do not require them to ask the user for this information. One good way to enforce strong password policies is to instruct users to choose potentially embarrassing passwords—this will make them think twice before divulging the information.

Case Sensitivity
Windows NT and Windows 95/98 usernames are not case sensitive. However, Windows NT passwords are case sensitive. Windows 95/98 does not support case-sensitive passwords, but the authenticating server retains the case information. This is important if the user also uses a Windows NT computer, where case sensitivity is enforced.

For More
Information
6
Using the Password Filter DLL file, you can force the use of stronger passwords. In this case, a password is required to include at least one character from among three of the following categories:

- Lowercase characters

- Uppercase characters

- Numbers

- Symbols (such as ! @ # $ % ^ & *)

How do stronger passwords increase security? A typical hack method for cracking passwords is to use a dictionary of common passwords. The common passwords include first and last names, common English words, dates, and so on. It is important that IT find a way to hold users responsible for hacks under their accounts. As an analogy, if an employee carelessly left a key near the company safe, he or she would be accountable for anyone's entry into that area. By the same token, users should take precautions to avoid passwords falling into the wrong hands. Although the `passfilt.dll` file is included with Windows NT Service Packs, it is not enabled by default. The functionality for enforcing stronger passwords can be put in place by making simple changes to the Windows NT Registry as explained in the Windows NT Resource Kit. To access this functionality, a developer can access the code in this file to require stronger passwords for the operating system and for applications.

Windows NT Auditing

You might implement auditing on an NT Server for many reasons. First, you need to be able to verify that only authorized people can access the information on your network. One of the best ways to track this information is to audit logon and logoff attempts. A large number of failed logon attempts should alert you to the fact that a user may be trying to guess a password.

Implementing Auditing

One of the best security measures is the audit log. Though it technically won't prevent unauthorized access, auditing a system can be used to determine what happened in cases of illegal activity and can also serve as a deterrent. In this section, we look at how to generate an audit trail for specific objects and how to manage the audit information once it's available.

Passfilt.dll Limitations

The changes enforced by the `passfilt.dll` file apply only to password changes over the network. These policies are not enforced if the password is changed from within User Manager.

Enabling Auditing

On a Windows NT Workstation or Server, two major steps activate auditing. First, the auditing feature must be enabled for the object type you want to examine. Enabling the auditing feature makes the second step—actually setting specifics on which actions to audit—possible. To enable the auditing function, you must have the Access the Audit Information user permission. Permissions are described in detail later in this chapter.

To turn on auditing:

1. Click on Start, Programs, Administrative Tools, User Manager for Domains.

2. Click on Policies, Auditing and turn on the various available auditing options. Figure 7.5 shows a dialog box displaying the available choices.

3. When you have selected the appropriate options, click on OK to activate your selections.

Choosing What to Audit

You can enable some auditing options simply by placing a check mark in the appropriate box. For example, to store logon information, nothing more needs to be done. For other options, such as file accesses, you must also tell Windows NT which files to audit and what type of information to log. For each type of event, you can choose to audit successes, failures, or both. You should always record any changes to the audit log itself to prevent users from turning off the audit log, performing some actions, and then restarting the log. Additionally, a good general guideline is to always audit at least logon failures. Figure 7.6 shows the screen that allows you to set audit permissions on an NTFS directory.

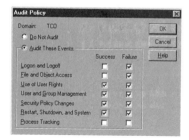

Figure 7.5 Auditing options available in User Manager.

On the CD-ROM

Demonstration 7.3, "Auditing," shows how to enable auditing options using User Manager.

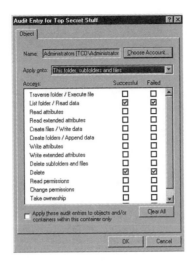

Figure 7.6 Setting audit permissions on a directory.

Viewing the Audit Log

After you tell your NT machine to capture the information you're interested in, you can use the Event Viewer to view the data. Assuming that you enabled the File and Object auditing option, you can set auditing on a directory. In the following example, we audit all accesses by certain users to a directory on a local hard drive:

1. Click on Start, Programs, Administrative Tools, Event Viewer.

2. To view the Security log, click on Log, Security.

3. Choose to audit logon failures and all accesses by any employees.

Viewing Event Log Information

For More Information 7, 8

Now that you've captured the data you need, let's analyze it. If you're searching for specific information, such as failed logon attempts from a single machine, you can apply a filter. The filter affects only the displaying of data in the Event Viewer—it does not delete any data. Figure 7.7 shows the type of information available in the security event log.

Choosing What to Audit

Audit only information that you feel will be useful. If you audit all successful accesses to a specific share, your event log will grow out of control. Also, auditing decreases system performance. Remember that enabling any security option requires some trade-off.

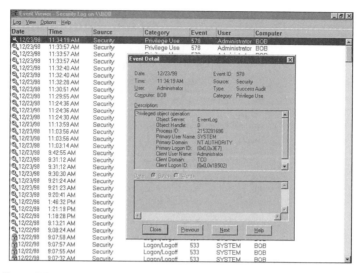

Figure 7.7 A successful logon event documented in the Security event log.

In the following example, we search for failed logon attempts on the local server. This example assumes that you have enabled the Logon and Logoff option in the Audit Policy dialog box:

1. Click on Start, Programs, Administrative Tools, Event Viewer. Click on Log, Security.

2. Click on View, Filter Events. In the dialog box, leave the default options for the View From and View Through options.

3. Select Success Audit and Failure Audit from the Types selection. For the Source, choose Security. The Category can then be set to Logon/Logoff.

4. You can optionally filter information by user, computer, or Event ID. In this example, we leave the settings blank. To enable the filter, click OK.

The Security event log now shows only logon and logoff events. In this way, you can isolate the information you want. All the events from the event log are still available and can be accessed by clicking View, All Events.

Network-Level Security

The purpose of networking computers is to share data. But by their very nature, networked environments present the risks of illegal access of a system and unauthorized access. However, security restrictions should be put in place so that only certain users can access certain resources. In this section, we look at ways to protect your network from external and internal attacks.

Firewalls

For More
Information
9
The exact definition of a firewall is somewhat vague. Its purpose is quite clear—to prevent unauthorized access to resources. At its most basic level, a firewall provides packet-filtering capabilities. Instead of allowing any and all packets to traverse the network, the packet filter performs some type of check to make sure that this data should be allowed to pass. This feature is especially important because many networks have recently been opened up to the Internet, where essentially any user in the world would be able to attempt access.

Although firewalls are most commonly used to filter Internet traffic, they may also be used to enforce security between networks. The check may be based on the source and destination address of the sending computer or may restrict traffic to certain packet types (for example, allowing only FTP or HTTP connections). Figure 7.8 shows a firewall that accepts all TCP/IP packets originating from a remote branch office and rejects all packets from all other users (including those from the Internet). This is a fairly lax configuration, and security can be increased by restricting data based on TCP/IP ports. In this example, Internet users access a Web server located outside the firewall.

Performing network address translation (NAT) is a firewall's second function. NAT may be done to allow users to have Internet access without giving out the internal addressing scheme. NAT tables hold a relationship between legal Internet IP addresses and those on your own network. Finally, a firewall may implement authentication services. These techniques range from simple password-based logons to more complex methods that utilize digital cipher cards.

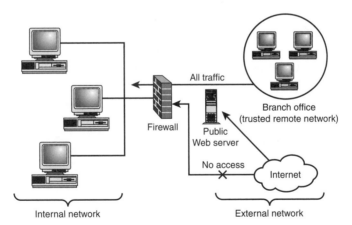

Figure 7.8   A typical firewall configuration.

▶ For More
Information
10, 11
    We see the trade-off between security and functionality again in firewalls. Firewalls are generally implemented with one of two methodologies: accept all (for maximum application compatibility) or deny all (for maximum security). In either case, only the exceptions to the rule are specified. It's important to note that specific applications require certain TCP/IP ports to be open for communications. One example is Windows NT trust relationships, which require certain types of NetBIOS traffic. For this reason, you must always test your firewall policies with business applications before deploying them in the real world. Physically, a firewall may be a piece of software, a router with specialized functionality, or a standalone server optimized to look at packets. The solutions vary in security, price, and performance. Microsoft's Proxy Server product has been designed to provide basic firewall functionality. More information can be found from Microsoft and from various companies' Web sites.

TCP/IP Security

TCP/IP, mainly due to its ubiquity on the worldwide Internet, has been the target of many hacking attempts. However, there are several ways to reduce the likelihood of successful attack attempts. First and foremost, network administrators need to pay attention to security alerts and apply the appropriate security measures to prevent these problems from occurring in their environments. For example, any issues with a large number of failed logon attempts should be investigated. Most commonly, this involves calling a user to resolve the problem. However, in the rare case that this is unknown to the user, it will be worth the extra effort.

▶ For More
Information
2
    Windows NT Server does not include full firewall functionality (as described previously in the chapter), but it does provide several ways in which the server can be made more secure. First, packet filtering for TCP/IP data can be enabled. This feature is available on a per adapter basis. Therefore, if you have a server with an ISDN connection to the Internet and network access to a LAN, you can allow the server to recognize only certain types of Internet packets while allowing all data to be transmitted to and from the LAN.

Internet Information Server

▶ For More
Information
12
Microsoft's Internet Information Server (IIS) was designed to make a Windows NT Server computer more accessible via intranets and the global Internet. In Chapter 15, "Web-Based Technologies," and Chapter 16, "Web Applications," we see how IIS can be used to help in remote administration and FTP services, as well as in publishing Web-based information. Although the use of this service may be indispensable, adding a Web server can cause many problems for systems administrators. You can secure an IIS installation in several ways. Each method involves the correct combination of IIS permissions, Web application permissions, and NTFS permissions. Figure 7.9 shows the relationship of these components.

On the CD-ROM

Demonstration 7.4, "Packet Filtering," shows how to increase TCP/IP security by enabling packet filtering options.

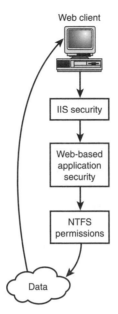

Figure 7.9   Internet Information Server security permissions.

Additional Security Measures

In addition to the utilities included with Windows NT, several steps are required for a good level of security. Monitoring and maintaining security configurations is as important as implementing them in the first place. In this section, we look at ways to restrict access to sensitive computers and ways to regularly maintain and audit security.

Enabling Physical Security

Unless your server is physically secured, all the configuration options in the world cannot prevent someone from carrying it out of the building. To prevent this misfortune, restrict physical access to your computers as much as possible. If possible, place servers in designated areas to which only authorized network and systems administrators have access. Also be sure that servers are physically accessed only when necessary. Most common functions on a Windows NT computer can be performed from a remote workstation. For more information, see Chapter 11, "Remote Management." By employing remote administration techniques, you can not only cut down on time wasted traveling back and forth from the server room but also place more restrictive physical access on the server itself.

External Security Audits

Although it may not sound like the most direct way to handle security, having an external organization perform a security audit might be very useful. Managing security and user permissions can often be a touchy subject for everyone involved. Employees may feel that they are not trusted if you limit their user access rights. An independent consultant or contractor can be asked to document the current security configuration, along with possible security problems. This person may then make recommendations on current security policies—both technical and procedural. The security audit can help ensure that no single user has complete control over company resources and that security permissions are neither too liberal nor too restrictive.

The Security Configuration Manager

▶ For More
Information
13, 14

New with Windows NT Service Pack 4 is a tool called the Security Configuration Manager. The purpose of this utility is to provide a single point of centralized administration for Windows NT's security features. System administrators can create various security configurations and enforce them on a per machine basis. These templates provide an easy way to enforce similar security policies on multiple systems. The Security Configuration Manager can also notify users and system administrators when security policies change. Figure 7.10 shows the main interface of the GUI version of the utility.

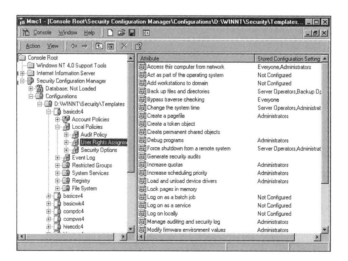

Figure 7.10 The Windows NT Security Configuration Manager interface.

Enforcing User Policies

In many cases, it is important to notify users that they must be authorized to access resources. In Chapter 18, "Enforcing System Policies," we look at some easy ways to restrict the functionality available to network users. For example, you can have Windows NT present a logon banner with a warning message that clearly spells out policies regarding the usage of network resources.

General Security Best Practices

Always lock the workstation when leaving it unattended. This precaution prevents users from walking up to your computer and casually viewing any onscreen information or using your user permissions. To lock a Windows NT computer, press Ctrl+Alt+Del and click on Lock Workstation. Unfortunately, Windows 95/98 computers only offer screensaver passwords, which are easy to circumvent.

Also, be sure to manage cached passwords very carefully. In the case of a Windows 95/98 computer, for example, a user who can log on to your machine may have access to any Web-based and network-based information for which you have a cached password.

The People Factor

Explaining why you want to restrict user permissions is often difficult because people may believe that you are reducing their empowerment to do their jobs. However, if you explain that such restrictions benefit both parties, users are more likely to accept the security measures. You can use this analogy to show them that the restrictions are logical, not personal: If I have the key to a safe and something is stolen from it, I am automatically a potential suspect. Cooperation, communication, and understanding between departments and all personnel are vital for enforcing security policy.

Case Study: Tightening Security Policies

XYZ Corp. has recently begun to have intermittent server failures and loss of data. The exact cause for each incident is unknown, but management suspects that one of the current employees is responsible. The current server configuration consists of a single administrator account. Five IT staff members know the password for this account, and all five require use of the account to perform their jobs.

Solution

For More Information 15

The IT manager decides to set up separate accounts for each user with administrative access. The users will each have a regular account and an Administrator account. They are instructed to use the Administrator accounts only when necessary. The password of the original Administrator account is changed and is given only to the IT manager.

The IT manager instructs an administrator to set up auditing and regularly reviews the audit log. Additionally, server auditing is set up to track any systemwide changes. Because IT staff members work on shifts, logon hour restrictions are set for specific users. Workstation logon restrictions are enforced so that only workstations in the IT department can access servers. Password policies are implemented, and account lockouts are enabled. Finally, remote administration software is enabled to restrict the IP addresses from which administrators may log on.

This setup enables managers to track when users log on as administrators and also to know which individual performed a given action. Problems may truly be simple mistakes or coincidental; the server logs show when changes were made and, in most cases, the effects of these changes. If the problems have been caused by malicious intent, on the other hand, management has a way of uniquely identifying those responsible. Everyone affected should be notified of changes during the implementation of these security features, and the reasons for each change should be fully explained.

The Bottom Line

The connection between ensuring the security of Windows NT-based systems and reducing operating costs is not obvious. Indeed, careful planning and implementation time are prerequisites to implementing an effective security plan. However, securing your network resources can save time and costs by preventing unauthorized usage of your system. The costs of unauthorized users accessing information may be as little as an employee playing unauthorized network games. However, it could be much more serious, such as a malicious employee obtaining confidential salary records. Security can also prevent accidental problems that occur when users inadvertently make a system setting change or delete a file to which they should not have access. Taking the time to audit security permissions is a great way to prevent problems and can significantly protect your total cost of ownership. As the old saying goes, an ounce of prevention is worth a pound of cure.

For More Information

1. "C2 Security Overview," Windows NT Server Technical Notes, Microsoft TechNet

2. Chapter 5 of this book: "Network Management"

3. Chapter 4, "Managing Shared Resources and Resource Security," Windows NT Server Concepts and Planning Manual

4. Chapter 17, "Disk and File System Basics," Windows NT Workstation Resource Kit 4.0

5. "How to Activate Security Event Logging in Windows NT 4.0," Q157238, Microsoft Knowledge Base

6. "How to Enable Strong Password Functionality in Windows NT," Q161990, Microsoft Knowledge Base

7. Chapter 9, "Monitoring Events," Windows NT Server Resource Kit 4.0 Networking Guide

8. "Auditing User Authentication," Q174073, Microsoft Knowledge Base

9. Chapter 3, "Server Security on the Internet," Windows NT Server 4.0 Resource Kit Internet Guide

10. Firewall company Web sites:

    CheckPoint Software Technologies (`www.checkpoint.com`)

    Cisco Systems PIX Firewall (`www.cisco.com/pix`)

    BorderWare Firewall Server (`www.borderware.de`)

    CyberGuard Corporation (`www.cyberguardcorp.com`)

    Raptor Systems, Inc. (`www.raptor.com`)

11. "How to Configure a Firewall for Windows NT and Trusts," Q179442, Microsoft Knowledge Base

12. Chapter 8, "Security," Internet Information Server Resource Kit

13. "List of Bugs Fixed in Windows NT 4.0 Service Packs," Q150734, Microsoft Knowledge Base

14. "How to Obtain the Latest Windows NT 4.0 Service Pack," Q152734, Microsoft Knowledge Base

15. Chapter 11 of this book: "Remote Management"

Further Reading

For more information on Windows NT security in general, see

- NT Security Web site (`www.ntsecurity.net`)
- Chapter 6, "Windows NT Security," Microsoft Windows NT Workstation 4.0 Resource Kit
- Microsoft's Security Advisor Web site (`www.microsoft.com/security`)
- Chapter 14, "Security," Windows 95 Resource Kit
- Chapter 2, "Network Security and Domain Planning," Windows NT Server Resource Kit 4.0 Networking Guide

8

Data Protection

SYSTEM ADMINISTRATORS UNDERSTAND THE IMPORTANCE of backing up data. When questioned about it, most people concede that an organization's information *is* the company. Among the many reasons to back up your data regularly are the following:

- To maintain historical copies of files for tracking changes and reverting to old versions
- To protect against accidental deletion of files
- To protect against data loss from malicious employees or intruders
- To protect against physical hardware failures

However, somewhere between theory and implementation, the requirements for setting up and maintaining reliable data protection methods are overlooked. Often, backup policies and testing of backups are just as important as storing the data itself. Windows NT includes tools and features that can help guarantee that your data will survive even in worst-case scenarios. If TCO is your concern, imagine the cost of losing a month or more of data because of a disk failure or a malicious hack attempt. Backups can also make the problems of day-to-day computing a little less serious. For example, it is much more likely that a user will accidentally delete a file than that a natural disaster will wipe out your data.

Windows NT includes two backup features: (1) NT Backup for backing up data to compatible tape devices and (2) the emergency rescue disk for backing up security and Registry information. Although the utilities are simple enough, the programs themselves are just one part of a complete backup and restore solution. This chapter focuses on several methods for protecting your company's most important asset—its data. It then talks about the other half of the equation—restoring the data.

The Basics of Backing Up

Before you design and implement a backup procedure, it's important first to understand the basics of how Windows NT manages files, directories, and security. In this section, we look at reasons to choose the NT File System (NTFS) and the steps involved in planning a backup solution. The specific steps include choosing backup hardware, documenting backups, and determining a backup schedule.

NTFS: The FAT-Free Alternative

NTFS was created to allow for security and recoverability in the Windows NT operating system. Both of these features are unavailable in the File Allocation Table (FAT) file system supported by MS-DOS, Windows 3.x, and Windows 95/98 operating systems. NTFS uses transaction logging for all disk functions. Basically, *transaction logging* means that before any disk operation is attempted, a log of that action is created. The transaction is then attempted. If, for any reason, the command cannot be completed, it is rolled back and no data is written to the disk. The operation can then be retried. Relational databases operate in much the same way to protect the integrity of their data—you would never want half of an operation to complete. Imagine the fun you'd have if your system updated a customer's street address, but didn't update the zip code.

If NTFS is secure, you may be wondering how a backup program can access all files on your hard drives without having the permissions of all users on your network. Windows NT handles this problem by allowing you to assign the user right Bypass File Security for Backing Up Files. With this granted, the account is allowed to back up any and all files on a system. The account can be used to restore files unless Windows NT Backup (described later in this chapter) permissions specify that only file owners or administrators may restore data. These features allow you to easily back up files without compromising security.

Establishing Backup Policies

▷ For More Information 1

Before implementing a backup solution designed to protect an entire network, it is important to establish a set of policies and procedures. Unfortunately, it often impractical to back up all the data on all machines using your network. Fortunately, doing so is often unnecessary. Unlike user data, you can easily restore operating system and program files by reinstalling from the original media. Some important questions to answer before implementing a backup solution are

- For how long after a file is modified will a user be able to request that it be retrieved?

- Which storage areas will be backed up? If only files stored on servers will be backed up, then users must be notified. If workstation files will be backed up, then users must be told exactly what data will be saved (all directories, or specific data directories only?).

- What is the maximum storage capacity of the backup hardware and media?

- Can backups be done during normal business hours, or must they be performed when there is a reduced load on the network resources?

- Which backups will be stored onsite and which will be moved offsite? Onsite data is useful for quickly performing restores, but offsite tapes offer greater data protection against the physical loss of data in case of a natural disaster or theft.

Based on your answers, you must first estimate the amount of data you expect to back up. The media and hardware you select must meet this standard. Be sure to plan for the future in your estimates. Second, it's important to consider how long a typical backup and/or restore might take. A tape backup unit may meet your other requirements, but if a full backup takes 10 hours, this procedure might not be practical on a busy server. Recovery times are important, as well. Finally, and most importantly, the solution must fit your IT budget.

Choosing Backup Hardware

In the past, a backup device was almost always a tape drive. Magnetic media is reliable and inexpensive. It also has a longer shelf life than some of the alternatives have. However, recent advances in technology have increased solutions for backing up. Table 8.1 shows various backup types and their characteristics. Note that the capacities indicated are for uncompressed data.

Drives also support a variety of hardware interfaces, ranging in performance from parallel port to IDE to SCSI. Although they're the slowest method, parallel ports allow you to move tape drives between systems. The IDE interface supports internal drives only and is the standard in most desktop systems. SCSI devices are the best choice for mainstream servers and support both internal and external devices. Other technologies, such as Fiber Channel buses and automatic media changers, are available for even higher storage requirements.

Measuring Real-World Tape Capacities

Always determine whether storage capacities for selected tape devices and media are based on compressed or actual data capacities. Most vendors advertise devices and media that store 4GB of data as "4GB (uncompressed)/8GB (compressed)." The assumed compression ratio of 2:1 is wishful thinking in most real-world scenarios. When you are choosing a system, consider the type of data you will be backing up. Text and data files generally compress well, but program files and other binary files normally do not achieve a 2:1 compression ratio.

Table 8.1 **General Characteristics of Common Backup Hardware**

Drive Type	Capacity	Speed	Best Use	Comments
CD-ROM writers	650MB	Slow (~900KBps)	Frequently accessed archives; software distribution	Media can be written to only once
CD-RW (CD-rewritable)	650MB	Slow (~900KBps)	Frequently accessed archives	Rewritable media; Incompatible with some CD-ROM drives
Quarter-inch cartridges (QIC)	Up to 4GB	Medium (~1MBps)	Workstation backups	Inexpensive drives and media
4mm cartridge	Up to 4GB	Slow (~800KBps)	Workstation backups	
8mm digital tape	Up to 7GB	Medium (~1MBps)	Server and workstation backups	Media is inexpensive
Advanced intelligent tape (AIT)	Up to 25GB	Fast (6MBps)	Workgroup/ enterprise backups	
Digital linear tape (DLT)	Up to 70GB	Fast (3MBps)	Enterprise backups	

Determining a Backup Schedule

In many cases, doing a single full backup and then backing up selective files is an adequate backup strategy. For example, if you have 10GB of data to back up but only a small portion of it changes, the most efficient plan is to have a full backup and then subsequent backups of only the files that changed. The main types of backups that can be performed are

- *Full (normal) backup*—Stores all files on the selected partitions.
- *Differential backup*—Stores all files since the last full backup.
- *Incremental backup*—Stores all files since the last full or incremental backup.
- *Daily backup*—Stores all files that were modified on a single day.
- *Archive (copy) backup*—Stores all selected files regardless of other backups performed and does not mark the files as having been backed up.

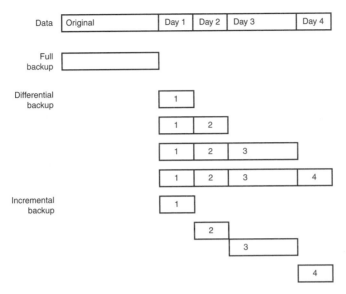

Figure 8.1   Full, incremental, and differential backup types.

Figure 8.1 illustrates the differences between three backup types. Differential and incremental backups use the archive bit, which is stored for every file in the file system (whether NTFS or FAT). Full and incremental jobs always reset the archive bits for any files that they back up. Differential backups do not reset the archive bit. You should not mix full and incremental backups because it is easy to confuse exactly which data is stored. For example, if you perform a full backup, followed by an incremental and then a differential, the latter operation will not include all files stored since the last full backup. Instead, it will contain only files changed since the last incremental operation and all three backups will be required to do a full restore. Incremental backups are often faster than differential backups, but it takes longer to restore incrementally because all tapes in the series must be loaded sequentially. Differential backups store more data on each backup, but restores require only the full backup and the last differential backup.

In determining a backup schedule, it's important to answer several questions:

For More
Information
2, 3

- How much data do you need to back up?

- How much tape/other storage space is available?

- Should operating systems and applications be backed up, or should only user data be stored?

- Will any data on users' local machines be backed up, or must users store all data on the servers?

■ How much data changes daily? weekly? monthly?

■ What are the business requirements regarding time for a complete restore?

Using this information, you can define an appropriate schedule for backing up files. Figure 8.2 shows a method that includes reusing tapes and storing information offsite.

Cataloging and Documenting Backups

You should always have an organized cataloging system for specifying the information stored on tapes. Be sure to keep log files regarding backup failures or any files that are not backed up. Cataloging and organizing backup media may seem fairly simple at first, but there are many reasons to come up with a good system initially. First, if only a date is used on backup tapes, you may be unsure whether the media contains full backups or only incremental backups. Also, for performing a restore operation, you need to find all necessary tapes. If a set of tape numbers is used, the contents must be described in detail elsewhere, such as in a log book or in a simple database. Figure 8.3 shows an example of a tape-labeling scheme.

Week \ Day	M	T	W	TH	F	SAT	SUN	Tape #
1	1 Increment	2 Increment	3 Increment	4 Increment	5 Increment	6 Increment	7 Full	
2	1 Increment	2 Increment	3 Increment	4 Increment	5 Increment	6 Increment	8 Full	Offsite
3	1 Increment	2 Increment	3 Increment	4 Increment	5 Increment	6 Increment	9 Full	
4	1 Increment	2 Increment	3 Increment	4 Increment	5 Increment	6 Increment	10 Full	11 Monthly archive copy

Figure 8.2   A typical monthly backup schedule.

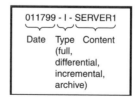

Figure 8.3   A typical tape-labeling scheme.

A good cataloging system meets the following criteria:

- Allows tapes to be reused (if this procedure is in accordance with the backup policy)
- Specifies whether tapes are taken offsite
- Describes the type of backup (full, incremental, differential, or copy) and clearly indicates the contents of the media

Alternatively, you may choose to use a sequential logging scheme in which you number (or otherwise uniquely identify) all tapes and keep a separate log that describes their contents.

Using Windows NT Backup

Windows NT Backup was created to be a simple disk-to-tape storage utility. It provides all the functions necessary to back up and restore data on your server. To use Windows NT Backup, you must first install and configure any tape devices you have available. Then, click on NTBackup in the Administrative Tools program group. Figure 8.4 shows the main screen of the NTBackup utility.

Selecting Files to Back Up

Windows NT Backup can copy all local files, including the Windows Registry, to tape. The user running the Backup operation must have read access to the files or must have the user right to bypass file system security. You can optionally back up remote network drives through drive mappings. Note that Windows NT Backup cannot back up the Registry of a remote machine.

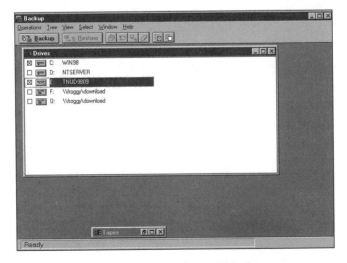

Figure 8.4   The main Windows NT Backup screen.

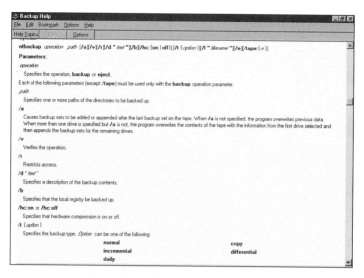

Figure 8.5   The NT Backup Help file.

Using Windows NT Backup from the Command Line

▷ For More
Information
1

Windows NT Backup jobs can be run from the command line and can be included in batch files. The Backup Help file in Figure 8.5 describes basic options that can be used from the command line. For a complete listing of the various options available, see the Windows NT Backup Help file.

An example of running Windows NT Backup from the command line is

```
Ntbackup backup c:\ /t normal /b /d "Full backup of Server1"
➥/v /l "c:\backup.log"
```

This command tells NT Backup to do the following:

- Back up all files on the C: drive (`c:\`).

- Perform a normal backup operation (`/t normal`).

- Back up the Windows NT Registry (`/b`).

- Add a description to the backup set (`/d "Full backup of Server1"`).

- Verify the backup (`/v`).

- Write a backup log to a text file on the C: drive (`/l "c:\backup.log"`).

▸ For More
Information
1, 4, 5 You can call this command from within a batch file when, for example, you want to map network drives before running the backup command. This also makes it easy to schedule the backup program to run via the AT command within Windows NT. More information on using the AT command, as well as the WinAT graphical interface, is available in Chapter 5, "Network Management."

Fault–Tolerance: RAID

Besides storing data files on tapes, you can replicate the data on multiple hard disks to protect against a disk failure. The Redundant Array of Independent Disks (RAID) specification was developed to allow several devices to function as a single logical device. One of the least reliable (yet most relied on) components in modern computers is the hard disk drive. Ironically, it is the information stored on these devices that is most difficult to retrieve in the case of a failure. Even with exemplary system backups, retrieving data can be time-consuming. For many businesses, this time is worth money. One way to protect against hard drive failures is to configure drives in groups that can continue to function despite the failure of one member.

Using the Windows NT Disk Administrator

The key to managing your hardware storage devices is to understand the Disk Administrator program. To run this application, click on the Disk Administrator icon in the Administrative Tools program group. In Figure 8.6, you can see the type of information the program generates.

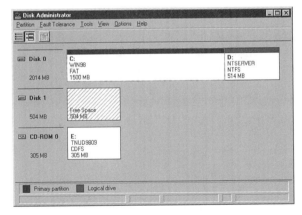

Figure 8.6 The main screen of the Disk Administrator application.

On the CD–ROM

Demonstration 8.1, "Disk Administrator," demonstrates how to view logical and physical disk information and perform basic disk management tasks.

▶ For More
Information
6
The graphical display of the Disk Administrator shows you the relationship between the physical drives and logical partitions on your system. Figure 8.6 shows a configuration of three logical devices located on two physical drives. A many-to-many correspondence exists between disks and partitions in Windows NT. For example, several disks can make up a single partition (as is the case with disk striping, described later in the chapter). Or, you can have one physical disk with multiple partitions. Additionally, in Windows NT you can assign specific drive letters to each partition. To make the assignments, right-click on the desired partition and choose Change Drive Letter.

RAID Levels

RAID specifies different arrangements of physical and logical hard disks. Levels of RAID can provide fault tolerance, improve performance, or do both. Figure 8.7 shows a graphical depiction of RAID disk layouts. Windows NT supports the following levels of RAID:

■ *RAID 0: Disk striping*—Optimizes performance by spreading data across several physical disks, but does not offer any fault tolerance. Also aids in manageability by creating one large volume from at least two smaller disks.

■ *RAID 1: Disk mirroring*—All data is stored on two physical drives that are always kept synchronized. This level performs fault tolerance and slightly increases performance but reduces usable storage space by 50%.

■ *RAID 5: Disk striping with parity*—Uses one disk in the array as a "parity" drive. RAID 5 can survive a failure in any disk without data loss or interruption of service (although performance decreases).

▶ For More
Information
7, 8
Table 8.2 shows how RAID levels affect performance and disk space. One limitation is that Windows NT Boot and System Partitions can only use RAID Level 1 (disk mirroring) for protection. Implementing RAID Level 5 (disk striping with parity) does come at a price: Server processing and memory are used for calculating, reading, and writing the additional information required. However, having multiple physical disks working at the same time decreases data access times, and performance degradation with modern processors is negligible.

How Disk Administrator Tracks Disks

The first time you use Disk Administrator, you are told that the program needs to add information to the drive. Windows NT uses this safe process to uniquely identify each disk in your system (because drive labels, locations, and boot status can all be changed).

Potential Problems When Changing Drive Letters

Changing drive letters may have effects outside Windows NT. If you are running other operating systems on a machine, changing drive letters from their defaults is not recommended. Also, certain applications look for media by using specific drive letters. For example, if you change the letter of your CD-ROM drive, your programs may not be able to access required data from the CD.

Table 8.2 **RAID Levels**

RAID Level	Performance Effect	Loss of Disk Space	Fault Tolerant?
0	Increase	0%	No
1	Increase (slight)	50%	Yes
5	Faster reads, slower writes	Up to 33%[1]	Yes

[1] *This value is equal to the size of one of the drives in the array.*

Many third-party server and peripheral manufacturers sell hardware-based RAID controllers. Hardware-based RAID is often faster than its software counterpart (because disk I/O is performed on the controller itself) and offers several other bene-fits, such as

- Hot-swappable drives, which offer the capability to change drives while the server is running

- Hot spares, which are spare drives that automatically take over for failed drives

- Dynamic array configuration, in which drives can be added to and removed from a stripe set without the loss of any data

All this activity occurs independently of the operating system—Windows NT sees this entire set of disks as a single logical volume. The drawbacks are increased initial cost and reliance on a single-vendor product.

Nevertheless, implementing RAID is not a substitute for maintaining regular back-ups. Although RAID-based fault tolerance protects against physical disk failures, it does not protect against the accidental deletion of files or a natural disaster.

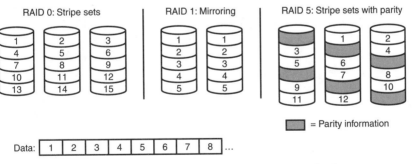

Figure 8.7 A visual depiction of the various RAID levels.

More Data Protection Options

In addition to standard backup practices, several other alternatives for ensuring the protection of your data are available. This section covers the creation of an emergency repair disk and provides an overview of clustering technology and backup up for special applications such as Exchange Server and SQL Server.

Emergency Repair Disks

Although complete backups protect your Windows NT installations even in a worst-case scenario, it is often unnecessary to resort to formatting the hard drive, reinstalling the operating system, and then restoring from tape. The problem may be a corrupt Registry or another minor problem such as a corrupt boot file. Windows NT enables you to back up the essentials of your system configuration to an emergency repair disk (ERD) and use it for restoring sometime in the future. On a Windows NT computer, the emergency essentials include portions of the Registry, the Security database (including all user accounts and groups), and hard disk information. You can use the Repair Disk utility (RDISK) to back up this data to a floppy. To use RDISK, click on Start, Run and type RDISK. Figure 8.8 shows the main screen.

The data copied to the floppy is taken from the Winnt\Repair folder on your hard drive. The files in this directory are automatically refreshed every time you click on the Update Repair Info button. Note that clicking on the Update Repair Info button does not back up to your floppy disk—you are prompted to do this after the update is finished. Maintaining regular updates of the data stored on the ERD is a very important part of your data protection plan. Also, as the program warns, you should store these disks in a secure location because they include security and account information. Just like a backup, the ERD is only current up to the point of the last successful update. Also, note that restoring these files resets your system to its configuration at the time of the backup. This is especially important when you have changed your disk configuration via Disk Administrator or if you have added Service Packs or other operating system updates. The data stored on an ERD is specific to the computer on which it was created, and you should never mix ERDs and machines. In the "Recovering Lost Data" section, we talk about how you can use an ERD to solve simple problems.

▶ For More
Information
9

Using rdisk to Back Up Security Information

By default, the rdisk utility does not back up the Security Accounts Manager (SAM) database. The SAM contains all locally stored user and group account information. The omission is deliberate because the SAM database can be very large for environments with many users. However, you can use the rdisk /s command to update this information in the winnt\repair directory and then back up to a floppy.

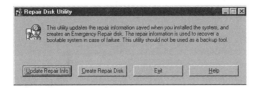

Figure 8.8 The main screen of the Repair Disk utility.

Clustering

Clustering is a technology that allows the use of multiple servers to act as one logical unit. The goals are high availability (greater uptime) through fault-tolerance and load balancing (sharing resource access load across multiple machines). In its simplest configuration, clustering can create a hot standby server that accepts connections only when the primary server fails. Figure 8.9 shows an example of what occurs in a standard fail-over cluster. A fail-over occurs when a member of the cluster notices that another member is unavailable and assumes the functions of that machine. Originally, Server 1 is active and is providing resources to the clients. Meanwhile, Server 2 is replicating all data in a shared disk configuration. When Server 1 fails, Server 2 becomes active and immediately assumes the function of Server 1, unknown to clients.

An in-depth discussion of clustering and the many intricacies of its implementation is beyond the scope of this book. Microsoft's Cluster Services (MSCS) is included as part of Windows NT Server, Enterprise Edition. Certain clustering functionality is restricted to "cluster-aware" applications. All these products have different limitations, and setting up a reliable cluster is not something you should expect to do overnight. Detailed information on clustering with MSCS is available from Microsoft.

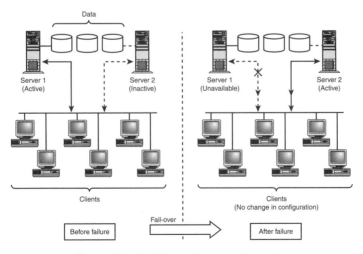

Figure 8.9 A fail-over cluster configuration.

Microsoft Exchange Server

When you install Microsoft's Exchange Server on your computer, the installation program automatically updates the Windows NT Backup program. Additional options are available to back up the Exchange Server information stores (the files to which Exchange stores all the public and private email that is sent through your server). Saving this information within a backup set allows you to rebuild an Exchange Server should a loss of data occur. For more information on backing up Microsoft Exchange, see the article "Microsoft Exchange 5.5: Backup and Restore Basics" from Microsoft TechNet or Exchange Server Documentation.

Microsoft SQL Server

Microsoft SQL Server, like most database applications, presents a special challenge for backup software. The problem is backing up files that are always open or are currently being written to. Using the Database Maintenance Wizard, SQL Server can perform backups while leaving databases open for access by users. A common method is to regularly offload data to dump devices and then to back up these dump devices to tape. For more information on performing live backups, see the SQL Server documentation.

Third-Party Backup Software

▶ For More Information
12, 13

Windows NT Backup was created to perform the basic functionality of a backup tool. However, it omits many desirable features, such as scheduling, notification of complete backups, and multiple-server administration. Although a correctly managed, basic Windows NT Backup solution gets the job done, commercial programs offer enhanced features and greater integration of various backup methods. Many third-party programs support multiple platforms and allow administration from a single point for all backup servers. Such programs can also automatically notify administrators of failed backups or other problems. Additions to these packages can be used for rapid tape recovery by booting to a floppy and directly restoring the disk contents. You may also have the option of backing up data over your network or over the Internet. For more information, look for various vendors' Web sites.

Uninterruptible Power Supplies

Finally, using an uninterruptible power supply (UPS) can protect against data loss due to loss of power by giving a system enough time to properly save data. UPS devices can use the Windows NT UPS service to automatically execute a batch file if the power goes out and/or perform an automatic shutdown of the system. For more information, see documentation from UPS device vendors.

▶ For More Information
10, 11

Performing a Remote Exchange Server Backup

If you want to back up a Microsoft Exchange Server computer from a machine that does not have Exchange Server installed, you need to copy the files specific to NTBackup between the machines.

Recovering Lost Data

You've gone to great lengths to make sure that your data is safely stored on another type of medium. Recovery can be a perplexing situation if you don't understand how all the pieces of the puzzle fit together. How and what you recover largely depends on why you need to recover the information. In this section, we look at methods and procedures for recovering data.

Testing Backups

For More Information 14

Although testing the quality of your backups might sound like common sense, many administrators neglect to do so. You're sure that *something* is being written to the tape, but are you sure that it can be retrieved? NT Backup allows you to perform a verify backup process that compares the files on tape to the files currently on your hard drive. Although you can be reasonably sure that this means your backup is usable, the best test is to do a complete restore on a test machine. It's quite possible that certain database files will be in an inconsistent state or files that were in use during backups may be missing. You may choose to get the experience by running the restore yourself, or you can assign the task to a help desk technician.

A major benefit of performing a trial restore is that you can document the *exact* procedure required and you can time the process. With this information, when a server goes down, you can ease some of the panic by giving a reasonable estimate of when service will be restored. Table 8.3 shows a sample of the steps involved in a full server recovery. Of course, be sure that the restored machine is not online in a production environment, as network address and machine name conflicts may occur.

Table 8.3 **Restore Procedure Documentation**

Step	Operation	Time Taken (Minutes: Seconds)	Total Time
1	Replace failed hardware or entire machine	25:00	25:00
2	Reinstall Windows NT operating system	25:00	50:00
3	Install tape backup drivers and reboot	10:00	60:00
4	Perform full restore of failed partition(s)	120:00	180:00
5	Reboot system and verify that it is working	15:00	195:00
6	Bring system online and notify users	15:00	210:00

▶ For More
Information
15
Note that many of these steps could be speeded up. For example, if a hot standby server (that is, an existing server with a similar configuration) is available, it may not be necessary to repair the hardware fault and reinstall the operating system. In the example in Table 8.3, having a hot standby server would have saved more than an hour! Documentation is available on restoring from several special cases.

Fixing Corrupt Boot Files

▶ For More
Information
16
You may be faced with a situation in which you receive errors on startup that prevent you from entering Windows NT. In the case of corrupt boot files (that is, the data appears to be available on the drive, but Windows NT will not start), you may be able to verify the Windows NT installation. To do so, boot the system from the three boot-up floppy disks (you can create them from another computer by using the `WINNT /ox` command). At the initial prompt, choose the option to repair an existing installation. The following options are then available:

- *Inspect Registry Files*—Selecting this option gives you the choice of restoring specific portions of the Registry. Note that this option *overwrites* your current Registry with the one stored on your ERD. Depending on the age of your ERD and the system changes that have occurred since you first set it up, you may lose configuration information.

- *Inspect Startup Environment*—This option verifies that the files needed to start up Windows NT are available on the hard disk. If they are not, it will copy those files from the installation media.

- *Verify Windows NT System Files*—If you're receiving error messages such as `Missing NTLDR` or `Can't find NTOSKRNL.exe` on bootup, select this option to replace these essential files.

- *Inspect Boot Sector*—This option makes sure that the system is set up to boot into Windows NT and rewrites the boot sector if necessary. Use this option when you are receiving a `Missing Operating System` or an `Invalid System Disk` error.

Complete System Restoration

If you've lost all the data on a disk (for example, in the case of a failed non–fault-tolerant drive), you need to start from scratch. You should start by reinstalling the Windows NT operating system; then reinstall the drivers for your backup device and start a full restore, using your backup device and Windows NT Backup. Be sure to tell Windows NT to replace the existing system Registry so that all of your settings are restored. Assuming that the restore is successful, you will be able to reboot the computer and be back in business!

Case Study: Data Protection

An IT organization, XYZ Corp., supports approximately 100 users, each of whom has a home directory stored on a Windows NT Server. Currently, the volume of data in all the home directories is 3GB. A local 4GB (uncompressed) DAT tape drive is being used. User data must be backed up at least nightly, and data must be restorable up to any day within the past three months. Additionally, a full backup must be taken offsite for security every week. Finally, the engineering server cannot afford any downtime due to disk failures.

Solution

XYZ Corp. has decided to implement the backup schedule shown in Table 8.4.

Tapes 2–8 are reused for incremental backups each week. All network administrators have been notified of tape change schedules and tape-cataloging schemes, and at least one person is in charge of taking tapes offsite. To prevent downtime due to disk failures on the Engineering server, fault tolerance is set up. The five hard drives in this server are configured using RAID 1 (disk mirroring) for the system partition and RAID 5 (disk striping with parity) for data drives. Figure 8.10 illustrates this configuration.

Table 8.4 **XYZ Corp.'s Backup Schedule**

Operation	**Mon**	**Tues**	**Wed**	**Thurs**	**Fri**	**Sat**	**Sun**
Full backup							Tape 1
Incremental backup	Tape 2	Tape 3	Tape 4	Tape 5	Tape 6	Tape 7	
Copy (full backup)							Tape 8 (offsite)

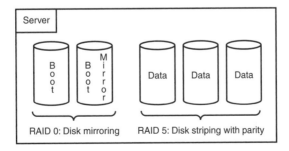

Figure 8.10 Complete fault tolerance for a Windows NT server.

The Bottom Line

For reducing TCO, data protection is of paramount importance. Although an initial outlay of expenses incurred in terms of time and hardware resources is necessary, this strategy may save an organization much greater costs in the future. Although performing efficient and effective storage and retrieval is much more easily said than done, a vital function of IT departments is to plan, organize, maintain, and keep backups. This level of data protection not only lets you sleep more easily at night but also may save your business from potential ruin. There's no better way to protect your greatest asset than to make provisions for its backup and recovery.

For More Information

1. Chapter 5 of this book: "Network Management"

2. "Backup Strategy," Microsoft TechNet

3. "Description of Full, Incremental, and Differential Backups," Q136621, Microsoft Knowledge Base

4. "Windows NT Backup Command Prompt Parameters," Windows NT Server Manuals: Concepts and Planning

5. "Implementing Scheduled Backups with Windows NT Backup," Q103474, Microsoft Knowledge Base

6. "Disk Administrator Overview," Windows NT Server Manuals: Concepts and Planning

7. "Understanding RAID," Windows NT Server Manuals: Concepts and Planning

8. "Overview of Redundant Arrays of Inexpensive Disks (RAID)," Q100110, Microsoft Knowledge Base

9. "RDISK /S and RDISK /S- Options in Windows NT," Q122857, Microsoft Knowledge Base

10. "Microsoft Exchange 5.5: Backup and Restore Basics," Microsoft TechNet Exchange Server Documentation

11. "NT Backup Cannot Back Up Microsoft Exchange Server," Q141839, Microsoft Knowledge Base

12. Seagate Software's Backup Exec product information (www.seagatesoftware.com)

13. Cheyenne's ArcServe product information (www.cheyenne.com)

14. "Restoring a Backup of Windows NT to Another Computer," Q130928, Microsoft Knowledge Base

15. "Recovering a Mirror Set or Stripe Set With Parity," Windows NT Server 4.0 Resource Kit

16. "Using an Emergency Repair Disk Created by Windows NT," Q103280, Microsoft Knowledge Base

Further Reading

For more information on data protection in general, see

■ Part 4, "Maintaining Your SQL Server Installation," Microsoft BackOffice Resource Kit

■ "Microsoft Cluster Server," Windows NT Server Manuals, Microsoft TechNet

■ "Troubleshooting Tape Backup Issues in Windows NT," Q162972, Microsoft Knowledge Base

9

Performance Monitoring

AN OLD ADAGE SAYS, "IF YOU can't measure it, you can't manage it." Even if you can measure something, how can you tell if your changes are making a difference if you don't have baseline information? It's important to monitor a server's or workstation's performance to maximize your investment in these tools. If a user complains that her computer is too slow, you often need more information to fix the problem. For example, if the problem is loading Web pages on a computer using an analog modem, the modem is probably limiting the system's performance. However, if the computer is an older model, certain operations may wait for the CPU to finish processing. In this case, a complete system upgrade may be the best solution.

The usefulness of performance monitoring goes far beyond handling user expectations. A network and systems administrator can use information obtained by analyzing the operations of existing hardware, software, and networking devices to predict the timing of upgrades, justify the cost of replacing and upgrading devices, and assist in troubleshooting. Performance monitoring ultimately reduces TCO and is a vital part of managing any IT environment.

Performance monitoring helps answer important questions about your current environment. For example, you may want to know which activity specifically uses the most resources in your environment. If you determine that it is loading Web pages, then upgrading the RAM or the CPU speed of client machines may not help much.

Here the performance bottleneck is likely to be the remote access device. With modern desktop computers and analog modems, the latter is often the point of slowest data throughput.

The details of performance monitoring—which tools to use and which information to track—are largely based on the specifics of your environment. For example, suppose the user complaining of a slow computer is connected to a network with Internet access. The administrator might want to check basic network utilization statistics—perhaps the new marketing database application is causing a lot of collisions on this subnet, thereby reducing overall performance. On the other hand, if this machine is a home computer using a modem to dial up an Internet service provider, the best place to check would be the modem itself.

In this chapter, we look at some good ways to monitor performance levels. Windows NT includes tools that are designed to profile hardware, software, and network metrics. After reading this chapter, you should have a better idea of what's going on in your own environment.

Performance Monitoring Methodology

▶ For More
Information
1

To monitor performance, you need to have a baseline of information. This baseline should be compiled over time and should be used for measuring any significant changes to your system. A nagging question that may have occurred to you is, By measuring performance, am I not actually decreasing it? And the definitive answer is, Sometimes. In some cases, performance monitoring may present a significant drain on resources. For example, the Windows NT Performance Monitor application itself uses CPU time, memory, and display resources. On modern systems, however, this drain is negligible. In this chapter, I note where significant performance reductions may occur. Whether you are running the Performance Monitor application or not, Windows NT automatically keeps track of performance data for tuning itself. Therefore, it does not matter if you measure 100 different parameters or only 1. The impact of running Performance Monitor also remains constant for most types of monitoring, so you need not worry about it as long as you consistently use the same tool to measure performance.

When you're monitoring performance, it is always a good idea to make only one change at a time. This way, you can measure the effects of modifying a single parameter. Also, if performance decreases or other problems come up, you'll know what to change to return to the original configuration. Documenting performance values is just as important as making changes.

Windows NT includes several tools that can aid in the evaluation of performance. This chapter covers three of them:

- Performance Monitor
- Task Manager
- Network Monitor

The Windows NT Performance Monitor

The Windows NT Performance Monitor is installed by default with all Windows NT installations. You open Performance Monitor by clicking Start, Programs, Administrative Tools, Performance Monitor. The program starts with the default, blank Chart view, which is one of the four Performance Monitor views.

We discuss these four modes and their typical uses later in this chapter. For now, you can switch between them by clicking on the View menu and then choosing one view at a time. The settings for each view are independent of the values examined in other views, so you can specify different counters for each at any time.

The Performance Monitor includes many counters and objects with which you can monitor certain aspects of system performance. *Counters* are general aspects of the system that can be monitored (for example, memory, processor). *Objects* are the actual details you wish to track for the selected object (for example, bytes committed, processor utilization). To add a counter to the default view, click on the Add button and view the various options. In the Add dialog box, you can click on the Explain button for more information about each option (see Figure 9.1). Table 9.1 lists some of the most useful measurements. Some counters include instances if multiple items are available. For example, on a dual-processor server, you can choose to monitor data for one or both processors. Note that the guidelines in the Usefulness column should be taken as generalizations for sustained levels. For example, pages/sec often goes above the recommended value for short periods of time.

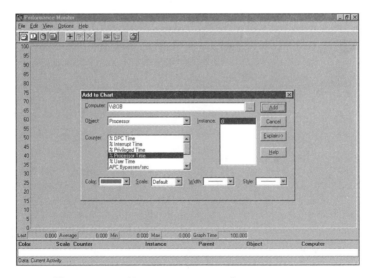

Figure 9.1   Adding a counter to Performance Monitor.

Table 9.1   **Useful Performance Monitor Counters and Objects**

Counter	Object	Meaning	Usefulness
Memory	Pages/sec	The number of times/ seconds the memory subsystem had to get information from the hard disk	If sustained greater than five, you may want to consider a RAM upgrade.
Logical Disk	% Free Space	Percentage of free space per volume or per all volumes	A value of less than 10% indicates that additional storage space is needed.
Physical Disk	Avg. Disk Queue Length	The number of tasks that had to wait for disk-based data	If high, disk performance may not be sufficient.
Server	Bytes Total/sec	The amount of data transferred by this server	High values indicate many and/or large file transfers to and from the server.
Server	Server Sessions	Number of active processes on this server	Indicates current activity; use to compare loads on different machines.
Network Segment	% Network Utilization	Percentage of total network bandwidth in use	If sustained greater than 40%, it may be decreasing performance.
Redirector	Reads/writes denied/sec	Rejected requests for data transfer	Large file transfers may be occurring to/from this server.

▶ For More Information 2

The objects and counters that are available are based on the services and applications installed on the local machine. For example, if you have the Remote Access Service (RAS) installed, the RAS Port and RAS Total counters are available. These counters help you determine the current status of your remote access users.

▶ For More Information 3

Microsoft ships Windows NT with basic performance counters enabled. For most systems administrators, these defaults are sufficient. If you require more specific information, however, you can also enable other counters and objects. For example, to measure disk performance, you need to specifically turn on disk performance logging. To do so, you must go to a command prompt and type `diskperf -ye` (the y flag activates disk performance monitoring, and the e flag specifies performance monitoring for stripe set volumes). This change takes effect the next time you restart the system. Why isn't this option enabled by default? Well, keeping track of disk performance information creates a slight decrease in performance (Microsoft estimates less than 5% in most cases). Whether this slowdown is worth the additional information depends on your environment and the use of the server. To monitor various network performance values, you also need to add the Simple Network Management Protocol (SNMP) service and the Network Monitor Agent in the Network Control Panel applet.

For More
Information
4

Figure 9.2 shows a Performance Monitor chart while performing a large file copy over the network. This example includes the counters and objects in Table 9.2. Note that certain instances are system specific. For example, the instance for % Network Utilization is a 3Com Etherlink III network interface card. Although the type of information captured is the same, the specific names of instances will be based on the network adapter or adapters present in your system. Similarly, if you are monitoring a multiprocessor system, instances will be available for viewing statistics on one or all of the processors.

Table 9.2 **Performance Monitor Values Measured During a Large File Copy**

Object	Counter	Instance
Processor	% Processor Time	0
LogicalDisk	Free Megabytes	Total
Memory	Pages/sec	N/A
Server	Bytes Total/sec	N/A
Network Segment	% Network Utilization	El3c5741

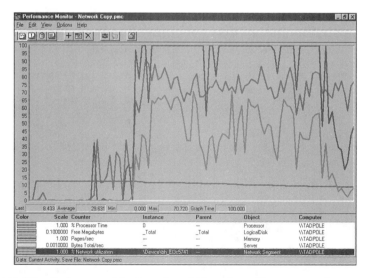

Figure 9.2   Performance Monitor values during a large file copy over the network.

Chart view is only one way of viewing the information you are interested in monitoring. Performance Monitor offers four views from which you can choose, depending on the type of data you want to collect and how you want to analyze and display this information:

- *Chart*—Graphs real-time system parameters over time
- *Alert*—Provides notification when certain criteria are met or exceeded
- *Log*—Records performance information for detecting trends over time
- *Report*—Displays real-time data in column format

Chart View

Chart view shows performance information in a graphical format. Figure 9.3 shows a typical chart generated by Windows NT's Performance Monitor. The x-axis of the graph (horizontal) represents time. The y-axis (vertical) represents the measured performance values. To add information to a chart, click on Edit, Add to Chart. You can then choose an object, a counter, and an instance to monitor. Additionally, you can select color, scale, width, and style for the chart item. The scale is a multiplier that can alter the range of values displayed on the y-axis of the graph. For most scenarios, the default values are appropriate, but you can select the multiplier based on what you are monitoring. For example, the default for the number interrupts/sec counter (part of the processor object) uses a multiplier of 0.01, giving the y-axis a range of 0–10,000. If you rarely have a high number of interrupts/second, you can change the multiplier to 0.1 to more accurately view the information collected. Finally, you can configure more options by clicking on Options, Chart. From here, you can modify display settings and set the update interval (which is set to 1.000 seconds by default). Note that decreasing the interval increases the load on your system and can decrease overall performance.

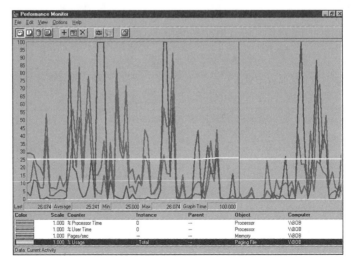

Figure 9.3   An example of Chart view in Performance Monitor.

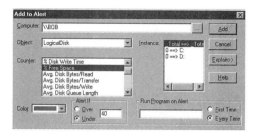

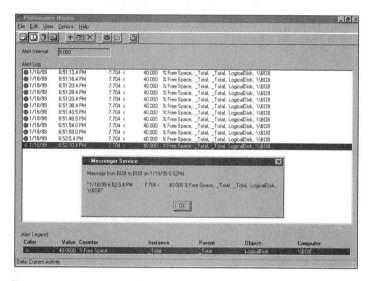

Figure 9.4   Performance Monitor is configured to warn the administrator whenever disk space is low.

Alert View

Performance Monitor can be set up in Alert view to warn a user or systems administrator whenever a specific threshold is exceeded. The threshold may be in the form of a maximum or minimum value for a counter or may be based on a percentage. In the case shown in Figure 9.4, Performance Monitor is configured to warn the systems administrator when disk space falls below 10% free (a very common occurrence on my laptop!). Here's how you set a threshold value:

On the CD-ROM

Demonstration 9.1, "Performance Monitor—Chart View," walks through the basic steps required to add counters to a Performance Monitor chart.

1. Click on View, Alert option.

2. Click on Add to set up a new alert.

3. Choose the % Free Space counter of the LogicalDisk object and specify the total instance.

4. To set a threshold value, select Under and 10 as values in the Alert If section. (If you have more than 10% disk space available on your system, choose a higher percentage, such as 75%.)

5. Because we haven't created a specific batch file in this example, we are leaving the Run Program on Alert section blank. We could have created a batch file that clears out typical temporary files, however. Click on Done to add this alert.

With these settings in place, if the combined free space on all your drives is less than 10% of your total disk space, alerts start to appear in the Performance Monitor window (see Figure 9.4). By default, an alert generates an entry in the Performance Monitor Alert view only. You can configure other Alert methods by clicking on Options, Alert. In this dialog box, you can choose to send a network message (making a dialog box appear on the user's screen) and/or add Alert information to the Windows NT Event Log (to view events using the Event Viewer).

Log View

You can choose to save performance-logging information to a disk file for later analysis or for keeping historical records. You can then use Performance Monitor or a third-party reporting program to report on this information. You use the following steps to save logging information with Performance Monitor:

1. Open Performance Monitor and select View, Log.

2. Click on the Add button and choose the following items: Processor, Physical Disk, and Server. Click Done to accept these choices.

3. Now, to activate the logging, we need to click on Options, Log to specify a file to which to save information. For the filename, choose any valid name (for example, PerfMon.log). Verify that the update interval is set to a reasonable time, and then click on the Start Log button.

4. The screen shows that logging has been started and shows the current size of the log file (in bytes). While data is being collected, you can choose to add a comment into the log by clicking the Place a Commented Bookmark into the Output Log button. This feature may be useful if you're performing specific operations on your system.

5. To stop the recording, click Options, Log, Stop Log.

On the CD-ROM

Demonstration 9.2, "Performance Monitor—Other Views," shows the basics of using Performance Monitor's Alert, Report, and Log views.

▶ For More
Information
5

Now that you've saved the information you're interested in, you can use Report and Chart views to see the results. From either view, choose Options, Data From and specify the log file from which you want to obtain data. Then just add counters and objects as you would if this information were live. Alternatively, you can prepare the data you are viewing to be examined outside Performance Monitor by clicking on the File, Export option and choosing either TSV (tab-separated values) or the CSV (comma-separated values) as the file type. These text file formats allow the data to be easily imported into reporting programs, such as Microsoft Excel.

Report View

So far, we've seen that Performance Monitor's Chart view displays data in a visual format that is ideal for viewing trends over time. If you only want to see data values at specific intervals, however, Report view is for you. Here's how you use it:

1. Click on View, Report.

2. Modify the sampling rate by clicking on the Options, Report command.

3. Click on Add and add counters as you did in Chart view.

Figure 9.5 shows an example of the information provided by the Report view.

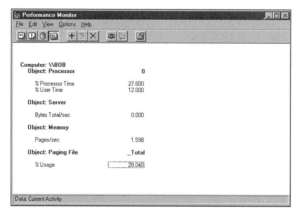

Figure 9.5 With Performance Monitor's Report view, you can see exact values
of the most recent measurements.

The Windows NT Task Manager

▷ For More
Information
6

For a quick snapshot of your system's current performance, you can use the Windows NT Task Manager. You access Task Manager by pressing Ctrl+Shift+Esc. Alternatively, you can right-click on the taskbar and choose Task Manager, or press Ctrl+Alt+Delete and click on Task Manager. The Task Manager interface has three tabs:

- *Applications*—Displays programs running on your system
- *Processes*—Displays current tasks executing on your system
- *Performance*—Displays a snapshot of vital CPU and memory statistics

Task Manager Settings

The Windows NT Task Manager can be configured to your own preferences. Some useful settings are in the Options menu:

- *Hide When Minimized*—When checked, this option makes Task Manager a tray icon when you minimize it.
- *Always on Top*—When checked, Task Manager overlaps any other Windows that are open. This option is useful when you want to measure performance while doing certain tasks in the background.

I often disable Always on Top and enable Hide When Minimized. Experiment with this utility—it will easily become your best friend when you're trying to figure out just what NT is up to!

On the View menu, you can choose to change the update frequency of Task Manager. Of course, the more frequently you update the display, the greater the performance load you exert on your system (notice that the `taskmgr.exe` task uses CPU time, as well). The following sections describe the tabs available within Task Manager.

The Applications Tab

The Applications tab shows which programs are currently running on the system. These programs are referred to as applications or tasks. This list includes only programs that run as tasks and excludes items such as Services and other background tasks. Figure 9.6 shows several tasks running on the machine. Each name is a specific instance of a program. From this screen, you can choose to end a specific task (shut down the program) or to switch to the highlighted task. You can also click on the New Task button, which simply allows you to run an executable program.

On the CD-ROM

Demonstration 9.3, "Task Manager," shows some of the valuable information that can be obtained by using the Task Manager.

Figure 9.6   The Applications tab in Task Manager.

A menu on this tab allows you to tile all applications horizontally or vertically. This feature is a useful way of seeing what your applications are up to at any given time. If the Status column shows [Not Responding], it's likely that the program either is waiting for you to input some information or has crashed.

The Processes Tab

The Processes tab, shown in Figure 9.7, displays the processes currently running on your system. Are you surprised to see so many? Even on a Windows NT System that is not running any visible programs, many background operations keep the operating system cranking—for example, threads that execute as part of an application, system services, and other background tasks. One item you are sure to recognize is the `taskmgr.exe` itself. In Figure 9.7, you'll see the following column headings:

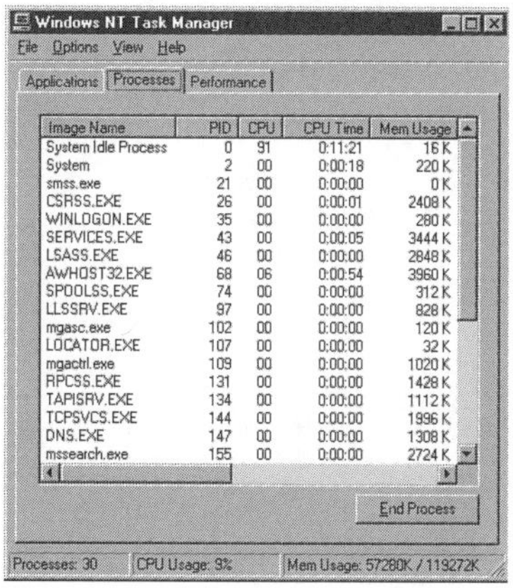

Figure 9.7   The Processes tab in Task Manager.

- *Image Name*—This entry names the task that is running. In some cases, the task has a friendly name (such as System or System Idle Process). Others have `*.exe` filenames that tell you what application is running.

- *PID*—This number is the process ID. Windows NT assigns a unique process ID to all tasks that run on the system. Note that these numbers may change when you run the same program several times.

- *CPU*—This number is the percentage of the current CPU time allocated to the specific process. If the operating system is not running a specific task, it is running the System Idle Process.

- *CPU Time*—This column tells you the amount of CPU time that the process has used. Windows NT automatically gives each process a certain amount of time to run its operations and then checks the next program in line. The format is in `HH:MM:SS` (Hours:Minutes:Seconds). This is a great way to find out which applications are slowing down your system the most.

- *Mem Usage*—This column shows how much memory is currently in use by the process. It is important to note that all this memory may not be RAM alone—some of it may be paged to disk as virtual memory. When the application needs it, these pages of memory can be loaded into RAM for quicker execution.

You can click on a column heading to sort by that value. For example, to sort programs by their memory usage, click on the Mem Usage column heading. To reverse the sort order, click on that heading again. You can also choose many additional parameters to view in this display; click on View, Select Columns to open the Select Columns dialog box. In it you can add and remove option statistics from the display. Figure 9.8 shows the available options.

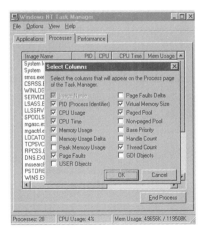

Figure 9.8 Selecting columns to view in the Processes tab of Task Manager.

The following example checks how much memory the system uses when running Internet Explorer 4.0 (you may be surprised by the results):

1. Make sure all programs are closed except for Task Manager.

2. Go to the Processes tab and click on the Mem Usage column to sort by this value. Make a mental note of the amount of total memory committed.

3. Launch Internet Explorer and wait until it is open.

4. Switch to the Performance tab and notice how much more memory is used when the Internet Explorer program is active. Also, click on the Processes tab and then click on the Mem Usage column to sort by this value to show exactly how much memory is currently in use.

You may not have realized it, but in performing this task, you have carried out the first two steps of performance monitoring: establishing a baseline (the amount of free memory before opening Internet Explorer) and making a single system change (opening Internet Explorer).

The Performance Tab

The Performance tab of Task Manager provides a readily available view of the current status of your system. It displays a quick snapshot of your CPU usage and memory statistics. Important information in the Performance tab includes the following values:

- *Totals*—The number of individual tasks running on the system.

- *Physical Memory*—The amount of RAM present in the system and its allocation.

- *Commit Charge*—The portion of memory currently being used by the system.

- *Kernel Memory*—The amount of memory being used by the operating system.

Figure 9.9   The Performance tab of the Task Manager interface.

Each of these counters can provide valuable information when you're determining the exact load on your system. If things are running slowly, be sure to check these counters.

The Windows NT Network Monitor

▶ For More Information 7

Windows NT Server includes a tool called Network Monitor. This useful application serves as a basic packet-level analyzer (sometimes referred to as a *sniffer*). Networking professionals often use dedicated devices to find information contained in packets traveling over the network. Network Monitor works in a similar way—it captures and examines all packets that are transferred over the network segment and saves them to a buffer. To install Network Monitor, simply add the Network Monitoring Tools and Agent option in the Services tab. You then need to restart the computer.

Network Monitor information can be especially useful for troubleshooting specific LAN connectivity problems. For example, suppose network clients have trouble receiving Dynamic Host Configuration Protocol (DHCP) information (for more information on DHCP, see Chapter 6, "TCP/IP Management"). You can use Network Monitor to determine whether or not the client is sending out the appropriate broadcast request and whether or not the server is sending out a valid response. Figure 9.10 shows the main interface of Network Monitor.

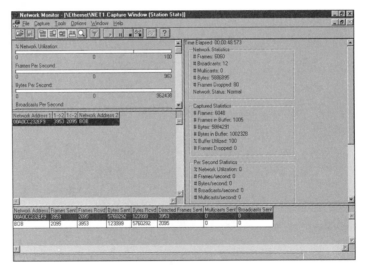

Figure 9.10   A typical Network Monitor capture.

Network Monitor Limitations

The version of Network Monitor that is included with Windows NT Server 4.0 is limited in that it can only monitor packets transmitted to and from the local machine. A full version of Network Monitor is included with Microsoft's Systems Management Server (SMS), which is also part of the BackOffice collection.

Collecting this type of data can affect the server's performance. One way to limit the impact is by restricting the buffer size that is used. To do so, click on Capture, Buffer Settings and specify the size of the buffer in megabytes. For most applications, a 2MB–3MB buffer is sufficient. If the server is unable to keep up with the flow of data packets, packets may be dropped. To increase performance, you can use the Dedicated Capture mode. This setting does not update display statistics while packets are being detected, thereby reducing the load on the machine.

You can use the filters available in the program to make the potentially huge collection of data more manageable.

Monitor Example: Isolating *ping* Problems

Suppose a network administrator suspects that a user is running an application that is generating excessive ping traffic, but is unsure of the data's origin.

The ping utility transmits and receives all data using Internet Control Messaging Protocol (ICMP) packets. The administrator begins a network capture and waits until the buffer (configured to be 2.0MB) is entirely full. He or she then enables a filter that restricts the captured frames to only ICMP data (the ping command sends ICMP packets only). The exact process is as follows:

1. Click on Capture, Buffer Settings and set the buffer size to 2.0MB.

2. Click on Capture, Start.

3. Wait until the buffer is full and then click on Capture, Stop and View.

4. Click on the Edit Display Filter button. Highlight the item that shows Protocol == Any and click on Expression in the Edit frame.

5. In the Protocols tab, click on Disable All. Then highlight ICMP and click on the Enable button. Click OK to accept these settings.

6. Click OK again to accept the new filter settings. The list of information should be restricted to ICMP requests.

Figure 9.11 shows a filtered capture with only ICMP data. By examining these packets, the administrator knows that the ping commands are originating from IP address 10.1.1.1.

With Network Monitor, you can also save the information that you captured in a file on your hard drive. This information can then be recalled later for analysis, if required.

On the CD–ROM

Demonstration 9.4, "Network Monitor," shows you how to capture and analyze packets sent over your network.

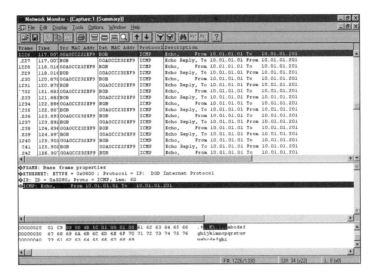

Figure 9.11 In this display, the captured data output is restricted to ICMP filters.

The Windows 95/98 System Monitor

You don't have to be running Windows NT to do performance monitoring. Windows 95 and Windows 98 were designed to be consumer/end-user operating systems, but they can still provide valuable performance information. Although the tools are somewhat different (and much more limited), the Windows 95/98 System Monitor can find basic information on the status of your system. To run System Monitor, click on Start, Programs, Accessories, System Tools, System Monitor. If the program is not installed, you can add it by using the Add/Remove Control Panel item. The interface for these tools is as user-friendly as their Windows NT counterparts, and a Help file is available to assist in determining the usefulness of information. Table 9.3 lists some useful items to monitor.

 For More Information 8

Figure 9.12 shows the Windows 98 System Monitor displaying basic statistics. This information can tell you, for example, whether your system is overloaded or whether a dial-up adapter is performing poorly because of line noise or a low connection speed.

On the CD-ROM

Demonstration 9.5, "System Monitor," shows the basics of measuring performance using the Windows 95/98 System Monitor tool.

Table 9.3   **Useful Windows 95/98 System Monitor Items**

Counter	Item	Purpose
Kernel	Processor Usage	Indicates CPU workload
Memory Manager	Allocated Memory— indicates memory in use	Indicates data paged to disk
Memory Manager	Swap-File Size	Indicates data paged to disk
Dial-Up Adapter	Bytes Received/Sec	Indicates modem speed
Dial-Up Adapter	CRC Errors	Detects corrupted data packets, possibly indicative of phone-line noise
File System	Bytes Read/Sec Bytes Written/Sec	Indicates the number of bytes read/written per second

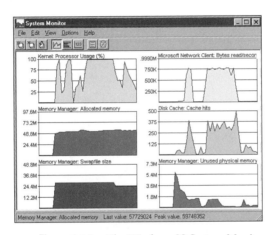

Figure 9.12   The Windows 98 System Monitor.

Case Study: Troubleshooting Server Performance

The IT staff at XYZ Corp. has decided that the current server's hardware configuration is inadequate to support the increase in workload it has experienced over the past several weeks. Specifically, the addition of several new users and the increased burden of working as a Web server have caused users to complain about slow access times, network browsing, and file copying. In attempting to identify the problems, a network administrator has decided to monitor current performance and compare it to a baseline created earlier. Figure 9.13 shows these charts.

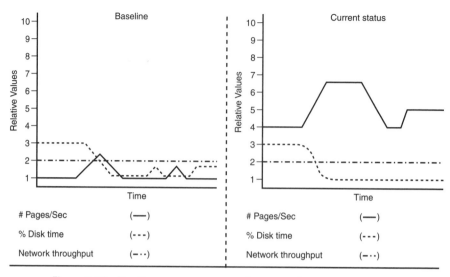

Figure 9.13 Baseline versus current performance of XYZ Corp.'s server.

Given this information, can you guess which of the following upgrades would help most?

- An increase in RAM

- A faster disk controller

- More available hard drive space

- A faster network adapter

The best answer in this case is to increase RAM. Notice that the Pages/Sec value is consistently much higher now than it was in the original baseline. Other parameters, such as CPU utilization, network throughput, and disk access are slightly elevated but still fairly consistent. A faster disk controller would not improve performance, as disk throughput is not an issue. Similarly, hard drive space is still at acceptable levels and would not normally affect performance. Finally, network throughput has remained fairly consistent, so the network adapter is not the bottleneck. Although upgrading these components would not have hurt performance, they probably would not have solved the reported problems.

The Bottom Line

Monitoring the performance of a system is a great way to see how your assets are performing. In many cases, something as simple as an inexpensive RAM upgrade can greatly increase the life span of a server and postpone a potentially expensive and time-consuming replacement. When handled properly, performance information is crucial to your daily network operations. Carefully tracking the performance of items you routinely rely on helps in planning for the future, in maximizing the usage of your current systems, and in lowering TCO.

Now that you've done some basic performance monitoring, you've probably found some areas that could be improved. The next step is to use this information to remove bottlenecks and perform troubleshooting. In Chapter 10, "Performance Optimization," we look at ways to optimize performance in your environment.

For More Information

1. Chapter 9, "The Art of Performance Monitoring," Microsoft Windows NT Workstation 4.0 Resource Kit

2. "Extensible Counters in Performance Monitor," Q179456, Microsoft Knowledge Base

3. "How to Monitor Disk Performance with Performance Monitor," Q102020, Microsoft Knowledge Base

4. "Troubleshooting Performance Monitor Counter Problems," Q152513, Microsoft Knowledge Base

5. "How to Create a Performance Monitor Log for NT Troubleshooting," Q150934, Microsoft Knowledge Base

6. Chapter 11, "Performance Monitoring Tools," Microsoft Windows NT Workstation 4.0 Resource Kit

7. Chapter 10, "Monitoring Your Network," Concepts and Planning Manual, Windows NT Server Manuals

8. Chapter 26, "Performance Tuning," Windows 98 Resource Kit

Further Reading

- "Network Traffic Analysis and Optimization (Windows NT 3.5x and 4.0 and Windows 95)," Microsoft TechNet

- "Optimizing Windows NT for Performance," Q146005, Microsoft Knowledge Base

- "Performance Analysis and Optimization of Microsoft Windows NT Server," Microsoft TechNet

- "INF: Optimizing Microsoft SQL Server Performance," Q110352, Microsoft Knowledge Base

- Chapter 8, "Monitoring Performance," Concepts and Planning Manual, Windows NT Server Manuals

10

Performance Optimization

I N CHAPTER 9, "PERFORMANCE MONITORING," we looked at the various ways to monitor Windows NT hardware, software, and network performance. After you've measured performance, you'll naturally want to know about what you can do with this information. If you haven't yet read Chapter 9, I recommend that you do so now. This chapter builds on those ideas by examining various ways to increase the performance of system components. Unfortunately, no blanket solutions exist for performance issues. Many of the solutions are environment dependent, and others may not be possible due to business concerns. As shown in Figure 10.1, performance optimization is a constant cycle of measuring/testing, finding a bottleneck, and making changes.

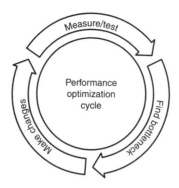

Figure 10.1 The performance optimization cycle.

The Goal: Moving the Bottleneck

The goal of optimizing performance is to move a performance bottleneck from one area to another. Why isn't the goal to remove the bottleneck entirely? Well, a *bottleneck* can be defined simply as the slowest step in a given process. Suppose the process is competing in a triathlon (that's a 100-mile bike ride, 26-mile run, and 5-mile swim). If you are good at cycling and swimming, but running is your weakness, you may work to improve your running. If you succeed, then one of the other two skills will be the slowest step. Overall, however, you will be faster than when you started. In the case of computers, bottlenecks vary based on the overall usage of the machine. For example, a hard disk controller may be the bottleneck if you're copying data between two physical drives on the same computer. The same operation on the same physical drive puts a much greater load on the hard drive itself. It's important to think of bottlenecks as relative values and not absolute numbers.

The Windows NT Server and Workstation operating systems are installed with standard settings that are determined to be the best for the average user. Unfortunately, few people fit this description exactly. Based on your specific usage of operating system features, you may benefit from tailoring some of the settings for your own network. Where does this cycle end? Before you change your job description to performance optimization specialist, you should recognize that the goal of the process is to reach acceptable or improved performance based on the time and resources you have available.

Hardware Basics

In order to understand how upgrades and changes might have an impact on performance, you need to understand the interactions of various hardware components. In this section, we look at the basics of caching data, managing and optimizing hard disks, and keeping current with new technologies. (For the sake of consistency, all relevant references are to Intel-based computers, the predominant platform for Windows NT and Windows 95/98 computers.)

Caching Data and Access Times

The goal of caching data is to store frequently used information in a faster type of memory. This idea is used in many subsystems within a modern computer. The *access time* of an operation can be loosely defined as the time that elapses before a request for information is complete. Different devices have widely ranging access times. For example, accessing data on a hard disk requires access times on the order of milliseconds (thousandths of a second). Access times for RAM, however, are on the order of 10,000 times faster (nanoseconds, or billionths of a second), so it is always a good idea to store frequently accessed data in memory. Similarly, frequently used RAM data should be stored in the much faster CPU Level 2 (L2) cache. This approach prevents the even faster processor from waiting for the relatively lethargic RAM.

You should also have an idea of the comparative access times for hardware such as CPUs, RAM, and other types of memory. In modern PCs, the CPU is the fastest component. The CPU often waits for data stored in slower system memory. Hard disks are relatively slower, followed by other types of storage such as tape and CD-ROM drives.

Physical Versus Logical Drives

The term *physical drive* refers to a hardware device. Most operating systems allow the creation of multiple logical drives within this device. The terminology varies between environments, but these partitions, or *volumes,* increase manageability and help in setting up more advanced disk configurations with multiple operating systems. A many-to-many correspondence exists between logical drives, as is shown in Figure 10.2. Multiple physical devices can be chained together to form a single logical device, as is the case for stripe sets and volume sets created in RAID configurations.

The Windows NT Disk Administrator provides a useful depiction of the layout of your physical and logical drives. Figure 10.3 shows the setup on one of my machines. Disk Administrator can be used to partition and format a hard disk and to assign drive letters to each partition.

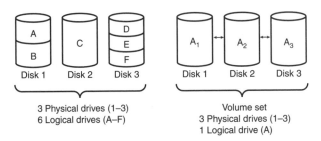

Figure 10.2 Physical and logical drives.

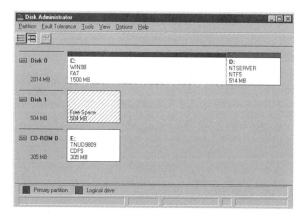

Figure 10.3   Using Disk Administrator to view logical and physical device information.

Improving Disk Throughput

▶ For More
Information
1

You can increase the performance of the disk subsystem in many ways. The first, of course, is to upgrade to faster hardware, including the controller and hard disk devices. For example, compared to IDE devices, SCSI hard disk devices perform much faster for disk-intensive applications. SCSI controllers also off-load much of the input/output work from the CPU and other devices to the SCSI controller. Implementing disk striping can also increase performance by enabling multiple disk controllers to access data at the same time.

Keeping Up with Technology

▶ For More
Information
2

Keeping up with changes in hardware specifications and the associated performance implications can be a major challenge. Even as this book goes to press, many changes are under way. It's important to try to separate the marketing hype from the real performance increases. For example, you might think that using a 400MHz CPU will make your system twice as fast as a 200MHz one. Pricing and marketing hype seem to confirm this, and you'll probably pay twice as much for the faster CPU. CPUs were often performance bottlenecks in 486-based or slower machines, but with today's faster machines, that's no longer the case. Unless you're running extremely processor-intensive applications (such as a database server or CAD application), your money might be better invested elsewhere.

A good way to verify claims about performance increases is by using benchmarking tools—software programs that measure the time it takes the machine to perform overall tests. The problem, of course, is that benchmarks can be very misleading and not report true real-world applications usage. Ziff-Davis Benchmark Operations has made its WinStone and WinBench programs freely available. WinStone uses a set of popular applications, such as Microsoft Word and WordPerfect, to measure the time it takes to complete simple tasks.

Optimizing Memory Settings

To optimize performance, I mentioned that it's important for hard disk data to be stored in RAM. Windows 95/98 and Windows NT attempt to place as much information in physical RAM as possible. When the system is low on available RAM, information can be stored in a special file on the hard disk that can quickly swap information to and from RAM. Though the default settings are fine for general use, several options are available for tuning memory access.

The Windows NT Paging File

Windows NT gives each application and process a separate set of memory addresses upon execution. When applications are executing, they address a portion of memory on the system. However, Windows NT may choose to store a portion of this information on the hard disk by using a paging file to take the place of physical RAM. This data is stored in the root directory of a logical partition in a hidden file called `pagefile.sys`. Windows NT uses special calculations for determining which information should be swapped to disk and which data should remain in memory. Regardless of the amount of physical RAM on your system, Windows NT requires this file to function.

The initial paging file settings are calculated by measuring the amount of available RAM in the machine and adding 12MB, which is a good basic rule of thumb. If you have more than one physical drive in your system, try spreading the paging file across multiple physical disks. The performance increase is due to the usage of multiple hard drives working concurrently to access information from the system. However, placing multiple paging files on different logical partitions of the same device is not recommended, as excessive movement of the drive heads may cause a performance penalty. Similarly, placing the paging file on fault-tolerant RAID volumes decreases performance because of increased processing overhead for reading and writing data.

The amount of memory you specify for the paging file is very important because you can incur performance penalties if Windows NT must frequently resize this file. When Windows NT encounters a kernel-level error (referred to as a STOP error), the default action is to write the contents of all memory to the hard disk. For this process to work, there must be a paging file equal to the size of RAM installed in the machine on the boot device. If you typically run many memory-intensive applications on your system, you should make the setting higher. The monitoring information presented in Chapter 9 provides a good guideline.

On the CD-ROM

Demonstration 10.1, "Paging File," shows how to modify the size and location(s) of the Windows NT paging file.

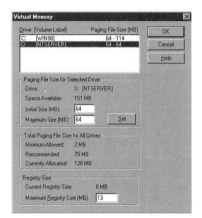

Figure 10.4   Defining Windows NT paging file settings.

To change the paging file settings, complete the following steps:

1. Click on Control Panel, System.

2. Click on Performance, Virtual Memory, Change. The screen that opens is similar to the one shown in Figure 10.4.

3. Highlight the partition for which you want to change settings (options vary based on the hard disk configuration of the machine).

4. Specify the initial and maximum sizes of the paging file and click on Set to accept these changes. To remove the paging file from a partition entirely, enter 0 for the minimum and maximum values.

5. (Optional) Repeat steps 3 and 4 to add paging files to other partitions or devices.

6. Click on OK to confirm and accept the changes. You need to restart the computer before these settings take effect.

The Windows 95/98 Swap File Settings

Windows 95/98 uses a single virtual memory file for virtual memory. The file is called the *swap file,* and by default, this information is stored in a hidden file called Win386.swp, which is located in the root directory of the installation drive. If you have another physical hard disk, you should change the location of this file by following these steps:

1. Click on Control Panel, System.

2. Select the Performance tab and then click on Virtual Memory.

Figure 10.5   The Windows 98 virtual memory settings.

3. Select Let Me Specify My Own Virtual Memory Settings. Change the Hard Disk value to a partition located on a separate physical disk (if available). Figure 10.5 shows this screen.

   You need to make sure that the drive containing the swap file will always be available. Therefore, you should not use removable media and should make sure that enough free space is present on the selected device.

4. (Optional) If you have a fairly good estimate of the amount of virtual memory you will be using on this system at any given time, you may choose to set the minimum and maximum swap file settings to the same value. This setting prevents overhead caused by shrinking and expanding of the paging file but also causes application errors if more memory is needed. The wording in this dialog box is somewhat misleading because the operating system continues to manage the size of the swap file after restarting unless you specify the same number for the minimum and maximum size.

5. Click OK to accept the changes. You need to reboot the computer before these changes take effect.

Optimize the Server Service

The Server service is available on Windows NT Server computers and is responsible for determining how memory is allocated on the local machine. The options are shown in Figure 10.6.

On the CD-ROM

Demonstration 10.2, "Server Service," demonstrates the various optimizations that can be chosen based on the specific role of your server.

Figure 10.6 The properties of the Server service.

Based on the role of your server, you can choose one of the following settings:

- *Minimize Memory Used*—Best for machines that support few users, such as work-stations or small servers. This setting leaves the most memory for local applications.

- *Balance*—Should be used for medium-size environments where memory is balanced between caching and application performance.

- *Maximize Throughput for File Sharing*—Should be used on servers that support many users and that are primarily used for basic file- and print-sharing functions.

- *Maximize Throughput for Network Applications*—This option is for servers that primarily run client/server applications that perform their own memory management. Microsoft's Exchange Server and SQL Server applications fit this category.

Shutting Down Unnecessary Services

By default, Windows NT installs several services that run on the system. Other services are registered with the system when you install certain software. For example, tape backup software might install an agent service that executes scheduled tape backups. Each service requires memory and some CPU time. So be sure to stop any service you're not currently using. For example, the Windows NT Option Pack includes WWW and FTP services.

Modifying Services

If you don't use certain services or options, set them to start manually. On the other hand, if you're not sure what a service does, leave it alone! Stopping services haphazardly can cause all kinds of problems on your system.

Windows NT Services have three possible states:

- *Started*—The service is currently running on the machine.

- *Paused*—This option is not available for all services, and its function is based on the properties of the service itself. For example, a paused WWW service does not disconnect current users but does prevent new connections from being made.

- *Stopped*—The service stops executing and is unloaded from memory.

The Log On As setting allows you to specify the user permissions of a service. Most services use the local system account, which has permissions to run applications on the local computer, but cannot access network resources. For this case, you need to create a separate account for the application and specify the account name and password in this dialog box.

Services also have startup settings:

- *Automatic*—Specifies that the service loads and remains in memory on Windows NT startup.

- *Manual*—Specifies that the service does not run on startup and must be manually started by the user.

- *Disabled*—Does not allow a user or another application to start this service under any circumstance until an administrator resets this option to manual or automatic.

To modify the startup options of a service, complete the following steps:

1. Click on Control Panel, Services. Highlight the name of the service for which you want to change the startup option and click on Startup. Figure 10.7 shows the Service control properties for the FTP publishing service.

2. Change the Startup value to Manual and click OK to accept the changes.

Figure 10.7   Changing Service settings.

Deciding What to Change

The Windows NT operating system requires certain services for normal functions. If you are unsure of the purpose of a specific service, try not to modify it.

Often, shutting down only a few services can make a large amount of memory available for the operating system to perform other tasks. For a description of the functions of each of these services, consult application-specific documentation.

Optimizing Network Performance

▶ For More Information 3 If you have more than a few computers on your network, managing network bandwidth may be an important step in optimizing performance. You can use several easy techniques to optimize network settings.

Controlling Broadcasts

▶ For More Information 4 The Windows Internet Naming Service (WINS) allows machines to register and query a single database instead of making broadcasts when trying to access network resources. This technique conserves bandwidth by sending direct messages between computers instead of networkwide requests. WINS requires relatively little configuration and maintenance when compared to manual address allocation methods and helps network performance dramatically in large environments.

Managing Protocol Bindings

Many computer manufacturers ship computers with all available protocol configurations enabled as a way to minimize support calls and achieve maximum compatibility. If your environment is using only specific protocols, you can uninstall those that aren't in use. Windows NT and Windows 95/98 operating systems allow the binding of specific protocols with specific adapters. For example, your dial-up networking connection may require only TCP/IP, but your network access may require both TCP/IP and IPX/SPX. When attempting to make connections to remote resources, protocols are tried in an order of preference. If you use more than one protocol, be sure to specify the most commonly used one earlier in the binding order.

On a Windows NT machine, you can change bindings by following these steps:

1. Click on Control Panel, Network.

2. Click on the Bindings tab. You can sort the information by services, protocols, or adapters.

3. Highlight a specific protocol or service and use Move Up (to place the protocol higher in the bindings list) or Move Down, as shown in Figure 10.8. You can also selectively enable or disable protocol bindings for certain components.

4. Click OK to confirm the changes; if prompted, restart the computer to make them take effect.

Potential Effects of Protocol Changes

Changing network protocol settings incorrectly may prevent the machine from connecting to certain resources. Be sure to determine which protocols your clients require before making any changes.

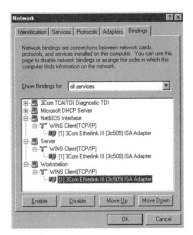

Figure 10.8 Windows NT protocol binding options.

The process is similar on Windows 95/98 computers:

1. Click on Control Panel, Network.

2. If you will never use one or more of the listed protocols, you can remove it entirely. Otherwise, double-click on the name of a network or dial-up adapter.

3. In the Bindings tab, check or uncheck the protocols as needed. Click OK to accept the changes and then restart the computer.

Segmenting Your Network

Isolating network traffic by segmentation can greatly increase the available bandwidth of a network. Ethernet, by far the most popular type of LAN, uses carrier sense media access/collision detection (CSMA/CD) for sending data on the network. With this method, a computer first checks the medium (the network cable) to sense whether another machine is sending a packet on the wire. If one is not, the computer sends the information; otherwise, it waits. If two packets are placed on the medium at the same time, however, a collision occurs, and both packets need to be resent. In this case, the sending machines wait for a random period of time and then attempt to re-send the packet. The term *collision domain* is often used to describe the number of machines that compete for the same medium.

Another characteristic of Ethernet topology is that all network adapters on the network monitor each packet to check whether it is destined for them. To illustrate this point, let's assume that 100 machines are on a subnet (a fairly large collision domain). To reduce the amount of contention, a network administrator may choose to place some machines on a specific subnet and others on a separate one. For example, if the subnet serves 25 sales and marketing users and 50 engineers, you could separate the servers for these two groups and place a router between the two subnets. Figure 10.9 shows this scenario.

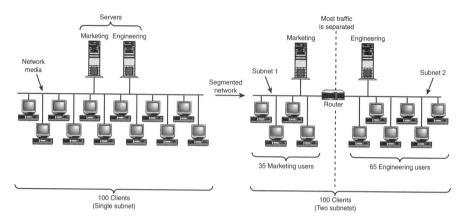

Figure 10.9   Segmenting a 100-user network.

Of course, as long as your router allows it, machines from either subnet may access the others' resources. Windows NT Server is capable of working as a router supporting multiple protocols.

It is beyond the scope of this book to describe more in-depth network design issues. However, many new technologies, such as switching, have become a very popular way to increase performance on large subnets without the hassle of having to reconfigure client computers. Switching is much faster than routing and only requires the network device to look at the first few bytes in a packet to determine its destination. Switches are also protocol independent and can be used to transmit any kind of network traffic. Additionally, you may want to locate all your servers on a single, faster subnet and implement switching to send data to slower clients. Specific best practices should be based on the needs of your environment.

Hardware Tuning

After you've made software and operating system tweaks, it's time to look at how your hardware may be causing performance bottlenecks. In this section, we look at upgrading hardware and keeping drivers current.

▷ For More
Information
4

Easily Managing IP Addresses

If you're planning to readdress your network clients, you can save a lot of time and trouble by using Dynamic Host Configuration Protocol (DHCP). DHCP allows you to assign all IP address information (including address, subnet mask, gateway, DNS servers, and so on) from a single central location.

Replacing and Upgrading Hardware

One of the best ways to optimize performance is to purchase additional or faster hardware. Here's a list of hardware upgrades and their potential impact on overall system performance:

- *Memory*—Standard RAM prices have dropped dramatically over the past several years. In most cases, a RAM upgrade can be a quick, inexpensive, and efficient way to improve performance. By measuring the amount of memory used by applications, you can find a good general guideline for how much RAM to use. Additional RAM has the benefit of decreasing disk activity due to virtual memory.

- *Network adapters*—The network adapter in modern systems is rarely a performance bottleneck. The network itself, however, does limit performance. If you want to improve performance for a single server, you may place an additional network card on the server. Figure 10.10 shows a multihomed server (a machine with more than one network interface). This server has two network adapters—on different subnets—for optimizing performance. Also, if you frequently perform network-intensive operations (such as large file copies) on a relatively low-traffic network, you should consider 100MB network cards to improve data throughput.

- *CPUs*—Modern processors are rarely a rate-limiting step on business desktop machines. For example, the performance difference between a 300MHz processor and a 400MHz processor (based on the same internal architecture) may be negligible if the end-user is primarily running business applications such as Microsoft Word or Excel. On highly active servers, increases in processor clock speed may have a nearly linear effect.

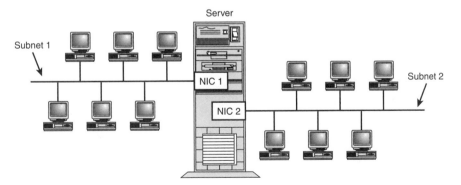

Figure 10.10   A multihomed server.

Most modern server and workstation hardware platforms can support additional processors. To take advantage of symmetric multiprocessing (SMP), you need to be using Windows NT. The Windows 95/98 operating system does not recognize the presence of more than one CPU.

SMP is useful on machines that perform an excessive amount of number-crunching operations, for example, database application servers or engineering workstations. In these scenarios, a CPU upgrade can greatly increase the useful life span of a desktop computer.

▷ For More
Information
5

■ *Video cards*—Certain graphics-intensive applications such as computer-aided design (CAD) packages can benefit from high-end graphics cards. Utilizing standards such as OpenGL and Microsoft's DirectX, much of the processing overhead associated with creating and manipulating visual objects can be off-loaded to the optimized video card. Modern video cards also include plenty of on-board memory for freeing up resources for other tasks. And let's not forget that recent advances in three-dimensional video cards have brought some amazing computer games.

Updating Device Drivers

All modern operating systems use device drivers to interact with hardware. Windows 95/98 and Windows NT have made device driver development easier by including basic hardware functionality within *unidrivers* included with the operating system. Hardware manufacturers then must write only *minidrivers* that handle functionality specific to their devices. For example, all modern modems use the same basic functionality. However, they do have different features, and these options can be included in a separate file. The unidriver contains the common functionality, and the minidriver addresses the model-specific features.

▷ For More
Information
6, 7

Although in their current versions the driver models are still different from one another, they will be unified in future releases of Windows. To ensure that your operating system is taking full advantage of the performance features of your hardware, you need to keep your drivers current. Manufacturers often implement new features and bug fixes in updates that are made freely available over the Internet. Windows 98 includes the Windows Update feature, which you can use to automatically download product updates, new functionality, and updated drivers. The Windows Device Manager also includes the capability to check the Internet for updated drivers not available on CD or disks. These changes are planned for future versions of Windows NT. Until then, you can use several Web sites that make it easy to find drivers and updates.

Windows NT Licensing

The most commonly sold versions of Windows NT Workstation and Server allow the use of up to two CPUs. If you use more than two CPUs on a Windows NT Workstation or Server, you need to have the appropriate version of the operating system license.

More Performance Optimization Tips

In addition to the performance optimization techniques already described, you can take several other steps to maximize your technology investments.

Reassigning Resources

Marketing hype for new machines, especially in the area of servers, would make you believe that a high-speed CPU and fast disk subsystem are required for any server operations. In the real world, the only difference between a server and a workstation is the tasks that these machines perform. For example, an outdated Pentium workstation may be very useful as a backup domain controller (for fault-tolerance purposes) or as a backup server for WINS or DHCP operations. Also, if you're in doubt about whether a given hardware configuration will give you acceptable performance, you should probably take the time to try it. Reassigning resources not only saves money on purchasing and configuring a new computer but also assists in reducing the management of many new machines. It might make much more sense to swap hardware between machines based on usage patterns than to reinstall servers. Keep in mind, however, that maintaining and supporting older systems may create an increased financial burden as a trade-off.

Scheduling Resource-Intensive Tasks

For More Information 8

Just as you wouldn't schedule a tape backup process during a busy time of day, you might want to run certain applications at night or at other off-hours. Scripting and scheduling of tasks can be used to perform large, time-intensive processes at times when system usage is low.

Conducting Disk Defragmentation

A fact of life of using disk storage is that data often gets fragmented. That is, information that was once stored all together on a disk becomes spread out. Defragmenting a hard disk makes sure that all related data is stored in contiguous sectors. This configuration minimizes the time the hard disk must spend searching for data. For example, suppose you often use a single large Microsoft Access database. Over time, the file will increase in size, and segments of it will be spread out over the disk. These factors increase the loading time and the work the drive must perform. After defragmentation, the data will be together in one area of the drive. Defragmentation is a process that must be performed periodically. Table 10.1 lists the defragmenting capabilities of Microsoft operating systems.

Table 10.1 **Windows Defragmenting Capabilities**

Operating System	File Systems Supported	Can Defragment	Notes
Windows 95	FAT	FAT	FAT32 support available only in hardware-vendor releases.
Windows 9x	FAT, FAT32	Both	Defrag can be scheduled; application access is monitored.
Windows NT 4.0	FAT, NTFS	FAT only	Defrag tool not included with O/S.
Windows 2000 (expected)	FAT, FAT32, NTFS, NTFS v5	All (expected)	Application access is monitored.

Although Microsoft doesn't include a tool for doing so, you can use third-party products to defragment NTFS partitions. The defragmenting utility included with Windows 98 offers the added benefit monitoring application usage and placing frequently used programs near each other on the disk.

Using Special Applications

▷ For More Information 9

Several specialized applications require different performance optimization techniques. These programs generally handle their own memory usage and are not configured directly within the operating system. For example, Microsoft's Exchange Server and SQL Server products can benefit dramatically from changing application settings. Although I can't adequately describe them here, several resources are available for optimizing these tools. The default settings for SQL Server installations assume that you are supporting small applications and relatively few users. Depending on your environment, you may want to change these defaults. To make a determination, the SQL Server Resource Kit contains a tool called LoadSim that tests database response times. LoadSim is also a great way to check whether any changes have affected performance.

The performance characteristics of other applications, such as Internet Information Server, are based largely on the content of their Web pages. Poorly created Active Server Pages, for example, may perform slowly; in this case, changing a few lines of code can often dramatically improve performance.

It's important to test applications for performance, as well. A poorly coded program running on the best hardware available will not give good results.

Case Study: Increasing Memory Performance

The case study in Chapter 9 involved examining performance data collected from a specific server. The systems administrator determined that the machine was running low on memory. Let's apply some of the ideas from this chapter to look at multiple ways of solving the problem.

Solution 1: Adding More Memory

The most obvious solution would be to purchase more RAM and install it in the same machine. This solution would alleviate some of the problems associated with the excessive pages per second rate. However, we're not sure whether the server is overloaded in general. Perhaps adding the RAM will show that other bottlenecks are severely affecting the machine. Another potential obstacle to this solution is that the hardware architecture of the server may limit the amount of RAM it can accommodate.

Solution 2: Optimizing the Configuration

Without needing to change hardware, the systems administrator can examine the configuration of the server. Perhaps the initial paging file settings are too low and the server is constantly expanding the paging file, causing additional overhead. Also, the disk subsystem may be slowing access to the hard disk. A RAID solution may help, depending on the usage of the data. Finally, device drivers or applications may be outdated or have bugs that cause memory leaks. The administrator should check for updates, patches, and/or known issues.

Solution 3: Reassigning Resources

Perhaps the server is truly being used beyond its capacity. Though it still functions, overall performance is low. In this case, it might be easiest to use another machine (perhaps a spare or older computer) to off-load some functions. For example, if the server is a domain controller and is running WINS, DHCP, and a Microsoft SQL Server, you might move the database to another machine.

Although there are several possible solutions, the best one will be based on information regarding the usage of the machine and the constraints of the environment. If your budget allows for buying a new machine and scrapping the old one, doing so may be the quickest and easiest way to improve the situation. If, however, funding is tight, you may have to make the best of what you have!

The Bottom Line

One of the best ways to maximize the performance of your environment and make the most of your investments may be to make a few minor tweaks and modifications. Computers are complex tools that require understanding of their various components. Often, the simplest changes or a relatively inexpensive hardware upgrade can increase the life span of a computer by many months. And the best way to lower your TCO is to maximize your usage of existing hardware, software, and networking equipment. If you need convincing, think about the performance benefits of increasing your technology refresh cycle by 3 to 6 months. Over time, these savings will be significant.

For More Information

1. Chapter 8 of this book: "Data Protection"

2. Ziff-Davis Benchmark Operations (ZDBOp) home page (www.zdnet.com/zdbop/)

3. "Network Traffic Analysis and Optimization (Windows NT 3.5x and 4.0 and Windows 95)," NT Server Tips and Techniques, Microsoft TechNet

4. Chapter 6 of this book: "TCP/IP Management"

5. Microsoft DirectX home page (www.microsoft.com/directx)

6. WinDrivers.com Web site (www.windrivers.com)

7. Winfiles.com 32-bit hardware drivers Web site (www.winfiles.com/drivers)

8. Chapter 19 of this book: "Scripting"

9. "Microsoft SQL Server Performance Tuning and Optimization for Developers, Part 1: Overview of Performance Issues," Microsoft TechNet

Further Reading

For more information on optimizing performance in general, see

- Suhy, Scott B. "Optimization and Tuning of Windows NT," Microsoft TechNet
- "Optimizing Windows NT for Performance," Q146005, Microsoft Knowledge Base
- Chapter 17, "Performance Tuning," Windows 95 Resource Kit
- Chapter 26, "Performance Tuning," Windows 98 Resource Kit

Advanced Network Administration

11 Remote Management

12 Remote Access Service

13 Virtual Private Networking

14 Automated Software Installations

15 Web-Based Technologies

16 Web Applications

17 Implementing a Secure FTP Site

18 Enforcing System Policies

19 Scripting

11

Remote Management

MOST ADMINISTRATORS AGREE THAT TIME spent going to a user's desk to configure a printer or to check on a cryptic error message could be better spent. Even if the
problems are unavoidable, wouldn't it be much more efficient to handle them from a
centralized location? If that argument doesn't convince you, think about the number
of times that you've had to return to the IT office to grab a CD-ROM or license
information that you forgot.

Users of other network operating systems, such as UNIX, often complain that
Windows NT does not support multiple concurrent logins on a single machine. One
reason you'd want to use multiple logins would be to allow for remotely controlling a
server or workstation. Additionally, multiple users cannot run applications off a single
server computer. However, Windows NT does allow for the management of almost all
resources on another computer via several tools and utilities. In this chapter, we look
at these methods.

Server Management

You can manage a Windows NT computer in many different ways without logging on
locally. The advantages of remote access include your being able to perform remote
administration and modify configuration settings from a central location. This section
looks at some of the tools and techniques for monitoring and configuring servers from

the convenience of your own workstation. In all cases, you need permissions to access the destination computer over the network and must have appropriate permissions to perform the operations you want to carry out.

Using Server Manager

The Server Manager application included with Windows NT allows you to view remote information Windows NT Workstation and Server computers on your network. You can access Server Manager by clicking on Start, Programs, Administrative Tools, Server Manager. You can use this tool to manage resources located in workgroups, the current domain, and other domains. Again, you need appropriate permissions and trust relationships before you can perform any tasks.

Notifying Remote Users

If you need to restart a machine or to notify users of problems regarding a particular server, you can use Server Manager to send a message as follows:

1. In Server Manager, highlight the computer from which you want to send a message.

2. All users who are currently connected to that computer receive a dialog box containing the text you entered. Note that you are sending a message to users connected to that machine over the network, not only to the user logged on to that machine itself.

▷ For More
Information
1

   The Messenger service must be started in order for machines to send and receive messages. If this requirement is met, users receive a dialog box containing the message and an OK button. You can also send messages from the command line by using the NET SEND command.

Managing Remote Services

If you're having a specific problem on a remote machine, you might want to make sure the requested service is working properly by following these steps:

1. In Server Manager, highlight the name of the computer for which you want to view service information. This machine must be running Windows NT Workstation or Server.

2. Click on Computer, Services.

3. From this interface (see Figure 11.1), you can start, stop, and pause services on the remote machine.

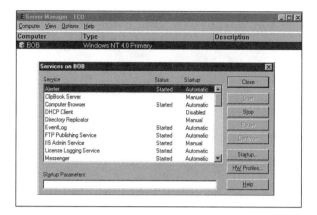

Figure 11.1   Viewing services on a remote computer.

Managing Remote Shares

In order to more efficiently share resources, the Windows NT operating system allows for the creation of network shares. A share is a pointer to a local system resource that is available to users of other machines. Windows NT directories and printers may be shared. You cannot create shares on remote computers using the Windows NT file system directly. That is, Windows Explorer can create shares only on local resources. You can, however, create shares on other Windows NT computers from within Server Manager:

1. In Server Manager, highlight the name of the computer for which you want to view/modify network share information.

2. Click on Computer, Shared Directories.

3. From this screen (shown in Figure 11.2), you can stop sharing specific directories and create new shares on the remote system.

Other NT Server Tools

In addition to Server Manager, several other Windows NT tools enable you to administer remote servers and workstations. (See Table 11.1.)

Creating Useful Shares

It's a good idea to create an Admin share on a server and to place in it copies of your most-used programs. For example, you might want to include installation directories for Microsoft Office 97 and WIndows NT Workstation so you don't need to carry these CD-ROMs around.

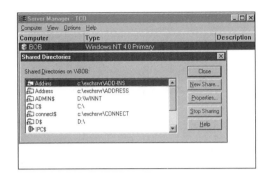

Figure 11.2 Administering remote shares with Server Manager.

Table 11.1 **Windows NT Administrative Tools That Support Remote Management**

Tool	Purpose	Notes	For More Information...
DHCP Manager, DNS Manager, WINS Manager	View and modify DNS, WINS, and DHCP information	Can view/ modify configuration information from multiple NT Servers	Chapter 5, "Network Management"
Event Viewer	View Security, Application, and System logs	Can view all event information from remote machines	Chapter 5, "Network Management"
License Manager	Manage license history	Can view/modify license information on all machines in a domain	Chapter 5, "Network Management"
Network Monitor	Monitor network traffic and packets	Can view network traffic originating from a remote machine	Chapter 9, "Performance Monitoring"
NT Backup	Back up and restore files	Can be used to back up remote files using shared network drives	Chapter 8, "Data Protection"

Tool	Purpose	Notes	For More Information...
NT Diagnostics	Viewing Windows NT configuration information	Can view remote machine information (limited)	Chapter 9, "Performance Monitoring"
Performance Monitor	Monitor local machine performance statistics	Can view remote performance information in real time	Chapter 9, "Performance Monitoring"
RAS or RRAS Administrator	Monitor remote access service properties	Can view/modify remote machine configurations	Chapter 12, "Remote Access Service"
Server Manager	Manage users, connections, and shares	Can view/modify remote configurations	This chapter
System Policy Editor	View/modify system policies	Can view/modify remote machine Registry	Chapter 18, "Enforcing System Policies"
User Manager for Domains	View/modify domain user accounts	Can view/modify remote domain accounts	Chapter 5, "Network Management"

Unfortunately, Windows NT's remote monitoring tools are not as organized as they could be. For example, in Windows NT Performance Monitor, you can click on Edit, Add To. In the Computer text box, you can enter the path to a remote machine on your network. Other tools, such as Windows NT Diagnostics allow you to use the File menu and click on Select Computer to connect to remote computers.

Windows 95/98 and NT Server Tools

It's often inconvenient to be located physically near a server. Other than the fact that server rooms are often so cold that you'll need a jacket and a pair of gloves, security reasons may restrict physical server access. It's much more convenient to use familiar tools such as User Manager from your workstation. On the Windows NT Server CD-ROM, Microsoft includes Windows 95/98 and Windows NT Workstation utilities that allow you to do just that. These tools are very useful because Windows NT Workstation machines and Windows 95/98 machines lack these utilities out of the box. (See Table 11.2.)

Table 11.2 **Client–Based Network Administration Tools**

Windows 95	Windows NT
User Manager for Domains	User Manager for Domains
Server Manager	Server Manager
Event Viewer	Event Viewer
	RAS Administrator
	WINS Administrator
	Policy Editor
	DHCP Administrator
	Remote Boot Service Manager

To set up the Client-Based Network Administration Tools on a server, complete the following steps:

1. Click on Start, Programs, Administrative Tools, Network Client Administrator to open the Network Client Administrator dialog box, shown in Figure 11.3.

2. Choose Copy Client-Based Network Administration Tools and click Continue.

3. In the Path box, enter the path to `\clients\srvtools` on the NT Server CD-ROM.

4. The Share Files option allows you to share the files from the CD-ROM. If disk space is low and the CD-ROM will always be available, choose this option. For most cases, however, you'll want to copy the files to a local directory and then create a share (see Figure 11.4).

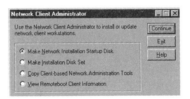

Figure 11.3 Installing the Client-Based Network Administration Tools on an NT server.

On the CD-ROM

Demonstration 11.1, "Client Administration Tools," shows how to remotely view and configure your Windows NT Server using Windows 95/98 and Windows NT Workstation client administration tools.

Figure 11.4   Creating a Client-Based Network Administration Tools share.

Be sure to set appropriate permissions on the newly created share to prevent unauthorized access. To run the tools, simply connect over the network to the shared directory in which the Admin tools are located. You can run the executable program files from the share by themselves. Windows 95/98 users can run the programs from the share by double-clicking on them. Figure 11.5 shows Server Manager being run on a Windows 98 computer. On Windows NT, you can run the Setup program to copy the files locally:

1. Create a mapped network drive to the ServerTools share on the machine you want to administer.

2. Run the Setup program in the WinNT folder of the ServerTools share. The DOS-based batch file copies the required files to your WINNT\system32 directory.

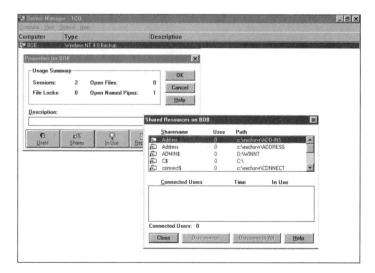

Figure 11.5   Running Server Manager from a Windows 98 computer.

Workstation and User Management

Although being able to manage your servers from remote locations is a very useful feature, most computers on your network are clients. In this section, we look at several tools for viewing information about remote workstations.

Windows NT Diagnostics

You can use the Windows NT Diagnostics program to view a variety of information about the local machine and about remote Windows NT computers. Figure 11.6 shows some of the information that's available. To use Windows NT Diagnostics, both computers must be running Windows NT 4.0. To view remote information, follow these steps:

1. Click Start, Programs, Administrative Tools, Windows NT Diagnostics.

2. Click File, Select Computer and then browse to or enter the name of a remote Windows NT computer.

Network Monitor Agent

▷ For More
Information
2

Windows NT Server includes Network Monitor Agent, which can serve as a basic packet sniffer. This utility captures raw data as it is transferred over the network and displays the information in a readable format. For example, if you're having problems with the DHCP service, make sure broadcasts are being sent and received properly. Network Monitor Agent can be installed as a service on Windows NT Server and Workstation computers. When it is started, it allows other machines to use Network Monitor to view packet-transfer information.

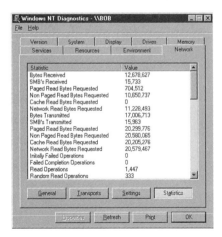

Figure 11.6   Viewing network statistics with Windows NT Diagnostics.

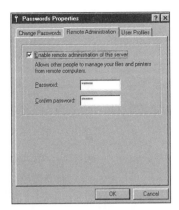

Figure 11.7   Setting a Remote Administration password in Windows 98.

Windows 95/98 Remote Administration

Windows 95/98 includes a service that allows a systems administrator to access the Registry of a remote client machine. This very powerful feature allows you to modify the system without logging on locally. If you've already set up your clients to allow remote modification of the Registry, you're all set. If not, you need to enable Remote Administration by doing the following:

1. Click on Control Panel, Passwords.

2. Select Enable Remote Administration of This Server in the Remote Administration tab.

3. Specify users who may remotely administer this machine. If you're using user-level security, you can click on Add and select Domain Accounts. If you're using share-level security, you need to set up a password (as shown in Figure 11.7). Remember that anyone who knows this password can modify this machine's settings from a remote location.

Now that the Remote Administration service is enabled, you can do the following:

- Use NetWatcher to monitor network users accessing the machine

- Use System Monitor to view remote performance information

- Use the Remote Registry feature to connect to this computer using RegEdit from a remote machine

▷ For More
Information
3

You can most easily access these features by using the Network Neighborhood icon to find a computer on the network. Then right-click on the name of the machine and select Properties. In the Administration Tools tab, you have the option to run the tools.

▷ For More
Information
4

Windows NT supports the capability to display network-based messages using the Messenger service. This service works well for server-based alerts and messages to all users connected to a computer. However, it does not allow two-way communications. On Windows 95/98 computers, you can use the WinPopUp utility to send and receive messages to remote machines. Although not quite as feature packed as

Microsoft's NetMeeting (described in Chapter 15, "Web-Based Technologies"), WinPopUp is useful for making system announcements and sending quick messages to active users. The program must remain running to send and receive messages. To start it on Windows 95/98, you can click on Start, Run and type WinPopUp.

Web-Based Management

One of the most significant impacts of the popularity of the Internet is the ubiquity of the Web browser. All modern operating systems enable users to access information via the standardized interface of the browser. Although the technology is not yet mature enough to provide all the functionality of complex client/server applications, browsers do provide an attractive alternative to installing programs on client computers to perform tasks on another machine. Web-based management techniques not only allow you to manage resources remotely but also are largely platform independent. All current operating systems offer some form of support for Web browsers. The Web-based programs and utilities discussed in this section are accessible from UNIX, Macintosh, and, of course, Windows-based operating systems. Many programs are now offering a method of access via the World Wide Web. In Chapter 16, "Web Applications," we take a look at Web-based communications.

Internet Service Manager Administration

What better way can you think of for administering a Web server than via a Web browser? Microsoft's Web-based Internet Service Manager allows you to do exactly that.

The Web-based Internet Information Server (IIS) Administrator (shown in Figure 11.8) is installed by default when you install the Windows NT 4.0 Option Pack. To access Internet Service Manager on the local machine, click Start, Programs, Windows NT 4.0 Option Pack, Microsoft Internet Information Server, Internet Service Manager (HTML). Alternatively, you can open a browser and connect to http://machinename/iisadmin. The default permissions set for this virtual root allow only the local machine to access this page (a good example of IP address restrictions). You need to allow other systems to access this page if you want to enable remote IIS administration. To use the Web-based administrator to modify security settings, follow these steps:

1. Run the Internet Service Manager Web-based application by clicking on Start, Programs, Windows NT 4.0 Option Pack, Microsoft Internet Information Server, Internet Service Manager (HTML).

2. Expand the IISAdmin virtual root in the interface and click on Properties.

3. Choose the Security option in the left navigation bar and then click Edit in the IP Address and Domain Name Restrictions section. Notice that the access

On the CD-ROM

Demonstration 11.2, "Web-Based Internet Service Manager," shows the configuration options available for administering IIS using a standard Web browser.

is currently denied to everyone except the IP address `127.0.0.1` (see Figure 11.9). In TCP/IP this address is a special, reserved address for the local machine.

4. Click on Add and enter another IP address from which you want to administer the service. Alternatively, you can choose to grant access to all except specific users or include an entire subnet or domain in the granted list.

5. Click OK to accept the configuration. Then click on the Save icon to commit the changes. You should now be able to administer this server by accessing `http://machinename/iisadmin`.

Figure 11.8   Administering Internet Service Manager via a Web browser.

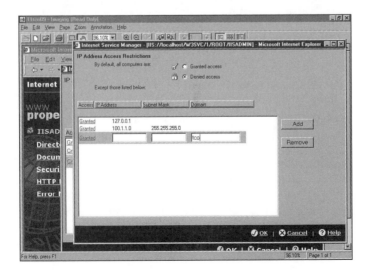

Figure 11.9   Changing IP address restrictions with the Web-based Internet Service Manager.

Web-Based Administrator 2.0 for NT Server

Microsoft has made available the Web-Based Administrator 2.0 (WBA) for Windows NT Server 4.0 as a separate download. This Web-based application runs on Internet Information Server 4.0 and allows you to remotely manage your NT Server from any current Web browser. Figure 11.10 shows the main page of the WBA. It is important to assess the security implications of making Web-based server administration possible. For example, if the server accepts connections from the Internet, you should take appropriate steps to hide this site from potential unauthorized users. You can do so by changing the TCP/IP port used for communications and restricting access by specific IP addresses. Both techniques are described in Chapter 17, "Implementing a Secure FTP Site."

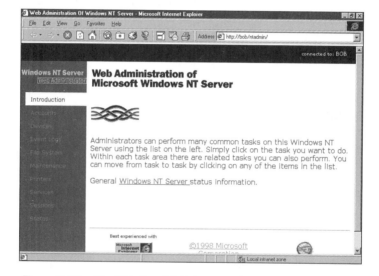

Figure 11.10   The Web-Based Administrator for Windows NT Server.

Limitations of Web-Based Administration

The World Wide Web Publishing Service must be started on the system before you can use the Web-based Internet Service Manager. If you use the Web-based Internet Service Manager to stop this service, you will not be able to restart it because Web administration will not be possible.

Browser Authentication Capabilities

Although any browser that supports standard HTML will work, Microsoft's Internet Explorer 3.0 or later is currently the only one that supports using secure Windows NT Authentication. Netscape's Navigator and other browsers work via basic authentication, but these methods send clear-text passwords over the network. If you're working in a relatively secure environment, this situation may not be much of an issue. However, be sure you understand the ramifications if you're using basic authentication on the Internet or an insecure network.

To install the WBA 2.0 package, simply double-click on the installation file. The program asks for a location to install its files. The setup program automatically copies all the WBA files to your local directory and makes the appropriate changes to the IIS 4.0 configuration.

You can access NT Admin Tools from a Web browser by going to `http://machinename/ntadmin`. The NT Admin Tools application includes the same basic security as Internet Service Manager (described earlier in the chapter), so you need to make sure that you allow IP addresses of remote users to access the service. If you already have permissions on this server and you are using Microsoft's Internet Explorer, the default screen greets you. Otherwise, you need to enter a username and password for a user who has access to administer this server.

The basic WBA interface is self-explanatory and intuitive for those that are familiar with browsing active Web sites. For example, to view the Windows NT Event Log, click on Event Logs from the main page. Here the familiar Event Viewer has a slightly different interface (shown in Figure 11.11). You use the other administrative tools much the same way you use the Event Log. One very useful way of quickly getting basic information about a server is to click on the Windows NT Server link in the main page of the application. This step opens the screen shown in Figure 11.2 (although I hope your server's memory utilization is better than mine).

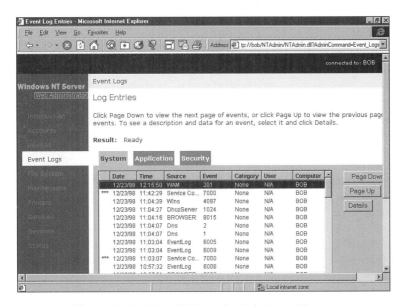

Figure 11.11 Using WBA to check the Event Viewer.

On the CD-ROM

Demonstration 11.2, "Web-Based Administrator," walks through the types of information and configuration settings you can access using a Web browser and Web-Based Administrator 2.0 for NT Server.

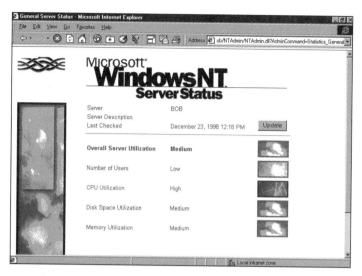

Figure 11.12 Using WBA to monitor the status of a server.

Windows Management Instrumentation

▶ For More
Information
5

To better manage remote hardware and software devices, standards are necessary for collecting information. The Desktop Management Task Force (DMTF) has developed a specification called the Common Information Model (CIM). This standard specifies a method for stored hardware- and software-related information that compatible programs can access. I'll add to the abbreviation soup and say that Microsoft developed the Windows Management Interface (WMI) to work with the Windows Driver Model (WDM) and CIM. WMI allows for centralized reporting and monitoring of hardware devices and software applications stored in CIM-compatible formats. For example, if a hard drive begins to report bad sectors, a network administrator may be notified so that the data can be backed up and the drive replaced.

▶ For More
Information
6, 7

Web-based enterprise management (WBEM) allows you to use a Web browser to view information collected from WMI components. Many hardware and software vendors currently support this standard. Microsoft's implementation of WBEM features is included with Windows 98 and will be included in future versions of Windows. It is also a downloadable upgrade for Windows 95/98 computers and is included with the latest Windows NT Service Pack. This software is an open specification through which independent software and hardware vendors can write components for managing their applications and devices. More information is available on the Internet.

More Remote Management Techniques

Keeping users informed and providing timely information to staff are constant challenges for individuals working in IT. Several tools can ease this problem.

Remote Control Applications

So far we've looked at ways to modify remote workstations and servers by connecting to them over the network and altering their configurations. This method is great for running all features that are supported via specific functions in the operating system. If you need to configure applications to not allow remote access or want to run a program on a remote machine, alternatives are available. For a more direct method of remote management, you may consider a remote control application. Remote control applications support the use of a remote keyboard and monitor for working with another computer (called the host). All processing and execution of programs continues to occur on the host, but a user may interact with programs from a remote location. Though this functionality is not included with basic versions of Windows, several third-party packages perform remote control. Remote control is useful for the following functions:

- Administering multiple workstations from the same machine
- Training remote users and/or demonstrating products
- Remote troubleshooting
- Logging on to a machine at work to check email
- Running programs that are not installed locally (such as compiling programs and databases, and server administration) on a remote machine

However, a drawback is that remote control sessions take up a lot of bandwidth for performing operations. Also, graphics-intensive applications run poorly over this type of link because all screen-related information must be passed over the network. One way to maximize performance is to run in lower screen resolutions and color depths. Figure 11.13 illustrates the difference between remote access and remote control. In a remote access scenario, when a user attempts to execute a remote file, all processing occurs on the user's machine. Remote control causes the file to execute on the host. Security for these applications is often password based. In most cases, users are required to authenticate on the remote machine as if they were logging on to it locally. Therefore, all default system security remain in effect. It is also a good idea to include data encryption for secure environments.

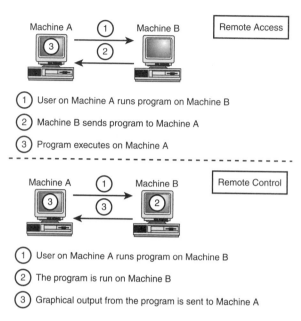

Figure 11.13 Remote access versus remote control.

▷ For More
Information
8
Microsoft's Systems Management Server (SMS) product includes a remote control utility. Also, several third-party vendors have written similar software. Figure 11.14 shows a remote session using Symantec Software's pcANYWHERE 8.0 remote control software.

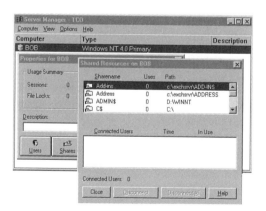

Figure 11.14 Remotely controlling a computer using pcANYWHERE.

Windows NT Resource Kit Utilities

In addition to the tools included with Windows NT by default, the Windows NT Resource Kit includes several utilities that can perform tasks on remote machines. (See Table 11.3.) Many of these utilities require the corresponding service to be running on the server before a connection can be made. In most cases, the Resource Kit includes both server and client utilities.

Table 11.3 **Remote Management Utilities Available in the Windows NT Resource Kit**

Application	Purpose	Notes
NetWatch	Views and modifies local and remote shares	
Remote Command Client (rcmd) and Server Service (rcmdsvc)	Runs command-line programs on remote machines	Requires Remote Command Service to be running on remote machine
Remote Execute (rexec)	Executes a program on a remote machine	Can be used with UNIX machines; must log on as root user
Remote Registry Service	Allows modification of the Registry and OS settings from remote computers	Only valid with Windows NT Workstation computers; must be logged on as a Domain Administrator
Remote Shell (rsh)	Creates a remote command-line logon on another machine	Can be used with UNIX machines
Service Monitor Configuration	Polls the status of NT services	Can send email in response to service events (see Figure 11.15)
Shutdown Manager	Can shut down remote workstations	See Figure 11.16
SNMP Monitor	View Simple Network Monitor Protocol (SNMP) network statistics	

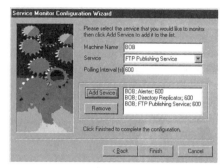

Figure 11.15   Service Monitor Configuration Wizard.

Figure 11.16   Using Shutdown Manager to shut down a remote workstation.

▶ For More
Information
9

   Performing a remote shutdown can cause issues if programs that require user interaction are currently running on the computer. In this case, the machine may not shut
down properly. Before using Shutdown Manager, be sure to experiment on systems in
your own environment. Complete documentation for each of these utilities is included with the Windows NT Resource Kit.

Thin Clients and Windows NT Terminal Server

Though we've looked at many useful ways of managing information on remote workstations and servers, none of these methods gives you the feeling of really "being
there" when logging on to another machine. Windows NT Server, Terminal Server
Edition (WTS) has been designed to make Windows NT Server a full-fledged multiuser operating system. WTS is available as a separate product and requires the purchase
of additional client licenses based on the number of machines that will be used. Client
computers can log on to a WTS computer and open a separate session. This system is
similar in theory to the remote control applications (explained earlier in this chapter).

That is, it redirects all input and output to a remote terminal. However, WTS allows multiple connections to occur concurrently and independently of each other. WTS allows computers that would otherwise be incapable of running resource-intensive applications to do so.

However, the "thinner" the client is, the "fatter" the server must be. That is, the server becomes responsible for providing processing power, RAM, and storage space. Network bandwidth is also consumed for each client connection. No set amounts of resources are required to support a specific number of users. Before deploying a thin-client solution, you need to perform adequate load testing to determine how many concurrent connections can realistically be supported. Then, based on the measurements and the needs of your users, you must decide whether a thin-client solution will be a cost-effective way to provide the functionality required.

Network administrators who have worked with mainframes are familiar with the concept of a dumb terminal. All application processing occurs centrally at the more powerful server, and clients simply serve as an interface between the user and mainframe. However, each user receives a separate process on the server. A *thin client* is a machine that can perform some local processing but has no local storage. Thin clients can be implemented in specific-task computers (such as those that run only Java applications) or scaled-down versions of PCs. Figure 11.17 shows multiple thin clients accessing a single WTS server. Each application runs in its own memory space on the server, but all user input and output is redirected to the remote client.

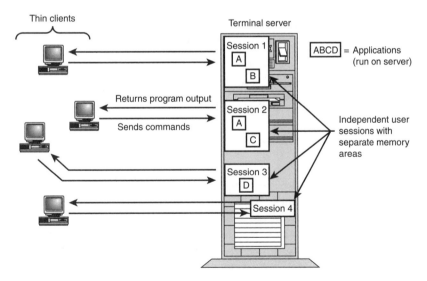

Figure 11.17 A basic terminal server scenario.

Much marketing hype surrounds thin clients and their impact on TCO. Basically, a thin client is a computer with reduced local computing power and no hard disk. Often, these machines are referred to as network computers, or NCs. Though there are many legitimate claims—such as decreased initial hardware investments, increased supportability, and centralized administration—thin clients also have many drawbacks. First, the greater reliance on the network can introduce single points of failure. For example, if the server is unavailable or if a network outage occurs for any reason, none of the clients are able to do any work. In contrast to situations where users can use their desktop computers to run applications locally, thin clients are not even able to start up. Additionally, with the dramatic decrease in costs of full-fledged desktop computers, having a hard drive and the capability to perform local processing is hardly a big expense. Finally, the part of the equation that's often left out in marketing hype is that the thinner your clients, the fatter your server must be. In many cases, server storage and processing resources can be much more expensive than client resources.

▶ For More
Information
10, 11, 12
The thin client debate will doubtless continue, but the bottom line will always be that thin clients are appropriate in certain situations. For now, they are appropriate for single-task situations and as replacements for traditional dumb terminals. Many changes will occur in the future. For example, future versions of Windows will probably treat local storage as intelligent caching devices instead of places for applications storage. Additionally, advances in network and hardware technologies will make balancing client and server processing much more flexible. These innovations will blur the line between thin clients and standard PCs.

Case Study: Remote Troubleshooting

A novice user calls into the help desk reporting a problem with his Microsoft Word settings. The user states only that he "cannot access his data." After trying some basic troubleshooting, the help desk technician is unable to understand the problem. She suspects that there is a file corruption on the server, that a database is unavailable, or that the client has a misconfigured application.

Solution

First, to adequately assess the problem, the help desk technician decides to use a remote control package installed on the user's machine. She watches as the user tries to access his application and makes note of the error message. The application seems to start correctly, but the user is getting an error message stating that "the database server is unavailable or access is denied."

To verify that the database server is running, she connects to an NT Server using Web-Based Administration. She checks the server status page to make sure that the server is up. She then notices the SQL Server database (the one the user usually connects to) is stopped. She attempts to restart the service and is unsuccessful. She then checks the Event Viewer and notices that one of the database devices is full. She fixes the problem by adding more disk space to the device, informs the user of the problem, has him try again, and watches as the attempt is successful. Using these techniques, the technician solved the problem without leaving her desk and before the client hung up the phone!

The Bottom Line

It's always a customer service plus when you can listen to a user complain about a problem, make a change from your own desk, and say, "Well, try it now." If you can fix a problem remotely, you save the time you would have spent in assigning the task to a specific person, coordinating a convenient time for that person and the user to access that machine, and making follow-up calls.

In the future, we'll see the idea of a single point of administration as vital to the management of networks of any size. Future hardware, software, and network devices will offer the ability to configure and manage settings independent of location.

Web-based and remote administration is certainly useful for situations in which you want to solve a problem quickly. In addition, by being able to perform most functions from a remote console, you can increase security, convenience, and efficiency.

For More Information

1. "Messenger Service of Windows NT," Q168893, Microsoft Knowledge Base
2. Chapter 9 of this book: "Performance Monitoring"
3. "How to Install Remote Administration Services," Q141460, Microsoft Knowledge Base
4. "Installing and Configuring WinPopUp," from Chapter 14, "Introduction to Network Configurations," Windows 98 Resource Kit
5. "Windows Management Instrumentation (Windows NT 5.0 and Windows 98)," Windows NT Server Technical Notes, Microsoft TechNet
6. Web-Based Enterprise Management home page (wbem.freerange.com/)
7. Microsoft WBEM home page (www.microsoft.com/management/wbem/default.htm)
8. Symantec Corporation home page (www.symantec.com)
9. Windows NT 4.0 Server Resource Kit, Microsoft Press
10. "Microsoft Windows NT Server 4.0, Terminal Server Edition Product Facts: Bringing Microsoft Windows to Desktops That Can't Run Windows Today," Microsoft Windows NT Server, Terminal Server Edition; Microsoft TechNet

11. "Microsoft Windows NT Server, Terminal Server Edition, version 4.0: An Architectural Overview," Microsoft Windows NT Server, Terminal Server Edition Technical Notes; Microsoft TechNet

12. "The 'Network Computer'—The Hype and the Hope," Total Cost of Ownership, Technical Notes; Microsoft TechNet

Further Reading

For more information regarding remote management in general, see

■ "Windows NT 4.0 Remote Troubleshooting and Diagnostics," Windows NT Server Technical Notes, Microsoft TechNet

■ Chapter 16, "Remote Administration," Windows 95 Resource Kit

■ Chapter 23, "System and Remote Administration Tools," Windows 98 Resource Kit

■ Microsoft's Management Web site (www.microsoft.com/management)

12

Remote Access Service

ONE OF THE BIGGEST CHALLENGES IT ORGANIZATIONS face today is allowing access to corporate resources from remote locations. The rapid rise in popularity and accessibility of the Internet has brought with it not only demands on information but also on its accessibility. To support truly location-independent computing, IT departments must allow remote users to access the same resources they have available in the office.

Windows NT includes the Remote Access Service (RAS), which allows computers to dial in to the network by using standard connectivity options such as analog modems and ISDN adapters. RAS supports the Point-to-Point Protocol (PPP) standard and can therefore support any client that is PPP enabled. Most current operating systems, including Macintosh, UNIX, and all Windows clients, support this functionality. For this reason, Windows NT RAS is an excellent option for companies that want to provide remote access connectivity for their users. It is a cost-effective, scalable solution and can lower TCO by making remote users more productive.

Security is discussed in greater detail later in this chapter. However, before implementing RAS on your network, you should assess the security implications of allowing remote users to dial in through this connection. For example, dial-in connections accepted on a local machine can circumvent firewall restrictions and other security implementations. A good general policy forbids clients from installing and running RAS on their local computers without first obtaining permission from IT. In most cases, RAS should be set up on a central server through which IT can control all authentication and security permissions. This configuration ensures that there is one more point of entry to the network and that IT can control this point.

Before using RAS, it's a good idea to update your server and clients. For Windows 95/98 users, Microsoft has released the Dial-Up Networking 1.3 Upgrade. This package updates the TCP/IP stack and several portions of the NDIS layer. For Windows 95 users, the Microsoft package includes support for ISDN adapters and makes available the PPP multilink feature (described later in this chapter) and the Point-to-Point Tunneling Protocol (PPTP, described in Chapter 13, "Virtual Private Networking"). Configuration enhancements include easier connection setup and more options via the Dial-Up Networking Phonebook Entries interface. For Windows NT Workstation and Server 4.0, you need to be sure to apply the latest Service Pack. Both updates are available free from Microsoft at www.microsoft.com/communications.

Windows NT RAS Basics

▶ For More
Information
1, 2, 3

Windows NT allows users to log on to the operating system from remote locations using a standard telecommunications device. The client software must support the PPP standard specified by the Internet Engineering Task Force (IETF). Windows NT Workstation allows only a single user to connect from a remote location at any given time. It is also limited in the types of RAS tools it offers. Windows NT Server, on the other hand, supports a maximum of 256 concurrent connections and offers several useful utilities for managing remote users. The information in this chapter focuses on Windows NT Server (on the server side) and Windows NT Workstation/Windows 95/98 on the client side.

Server Configuration

To set up a Windows NT–based remote access server, you need a machine that at least meets the minimum hardware requirements for Windows NT Server 4.0. In addition, you need at least one compatible wide area network (WAN) device (such as a modem or an ISDN adapter). Optionally, this server may have access to the Internet, your LAN, or other network resources such as printers or mainframes. (See Figure 12.1.)

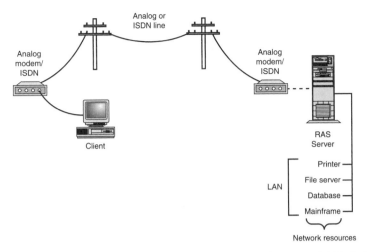

Figure 12.1 A typical RAS configuration: The client accesses the remote LAN via the RAS server through which it can access network resources.

Setting Up Your Modems

The first step in setting up RAS on the server is to enable all the available dial-in devices you may have. Dial-in devices supported by Windows NT include X.25 adapters, standard analog modems, and ISDN adapters. Collectively, these devices are referred to as *WAN adapters*. In many cases, Windows NT detects your WAN device during installation. If Windows NT does not detect your device, you need to access the Modems applet in the Control Panel. If Windows NT supports your device, simply click on Add and choose your device from the list. If drivers are not included, follow the instructions that came with your device.

Installing RAS

The tutorial in this section assumes that you are using TCP/IP for connecting remote users. You may just as easily use another protocol, such as IPX/SPX or NetBEUI. If TCP/IP is not yet installed on your computer, add and configure that protocol first. For help on this, see Chapter 6, "TCP/IP Management."

Supporting New Technologies

The purpose of RAS is to allow users to directly dial in to a corporate network. Newer Internet-based technologies, such as Asymmetric Digital Subscriber Line (ADSL) and cable modems must be handled differently. For more information on this topic, see Chapter 13.

On the CD-ROM

Demonstration 12.1, "RAS Setup," explains the installation and configuration of RAS on a Windows NT Server.

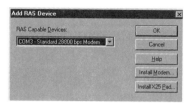

Figure 12.2   Adding a port to RAS.

Next, you need to install RAS on your NT server:

1. Click on Control Panel, Network, Services.

2. If Remote Access Service is not already listed, click on Add and then select it from the list.

3. After the service is installed, you are prompted to assign ports to RAS (see Figure 12.2). You can add any or all of the WAN devices available on your system. Choose those devices that will be used for RAS.

4. Click on Configure to assign the ports as available for dial-in, dial-out, or both. Dial-in ports allow remote users to call in and connect to the device. Windows NT places these devices in auto answer mode. Dial-out ports may be used to create your own RAS connections to other machines or for use by another telecommunications program. Although I don't recommend doing so, you can specify Both if people will be dialing in only occasionally or if a busy signal caused by an outgoing call is not a big deal. Keep in mind that you won't be able to dial out without first disconnecting any users connected to that port.

5. Accept this configuration by clicking on OK. If you have added either RAS or TCP/IP, Windows NT prompts you to restart.

Configuring the Protocols

In the properties for Remote Access Service, you have the option of enabling any or all of the protocols you have on your system. Figure 12.3 shows the available options. Each protocol allows you to specify which resources the user can access. The options are as follows:

- *Entire Network*—This setting allows the protocol to be routed across the network, and end users have access to any machines or applications on other computers.

- *This Computer Only*—This setting means that users can access only the local server (to transfer files from home directories, for example). This option does not allow contacting remote resources via the protocol.

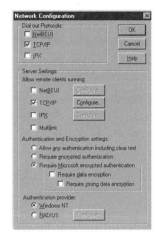

Figure 12.3 Selecting protocols from the Network Configuration dialog box.

► For More
Information
4
In most cases, you'll choose TCP/IP by default, but if you have other applications
that require NetBEUI or IPX/SPX, be sure to enable them as well. The configuration
options for TCP/IP allow you to use the Dynamic Host Configuration Protocol
(DHCP; explained in Chapter 6) if it is enabled on the network. Alternatively, you can
specify a manually defined pool of IP addresses for remote clients. Choosing the latter
may be useful if you want to determine whether a user is connecting locally or
remotely by his or her IP address. Figure 12.4 shows the dialog box you use when you
click on Configure.

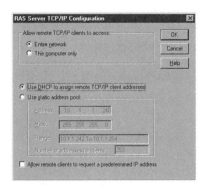

Figure 12.4 Configuring TCP/IP properties for RAS.

Using Remote Access Administrator

After RAS is installed and the computer is restarted, the Remote Access Administrator icon is available in the Administrative Tools program group. The Remote Access Administrator can be used to start, stop, and pause RAS and can manage dial-in users and ports. From this console, you can see who's connected to your RAS machine and view basic statistics on the connections. You can also disconnect users and perform other maintenance functions.

Granting Dial-in Permissions

Although you've installed RAS, you're not quite finished. You need to grant permissions for your users to dial in from a remote location. You can grant the permissions in one of two ways. First, you can use the Remote Access Administrator:

1. Open the Remote Access Administrator.

2. In the Users menu, select Permissions. This dialog box (shown in Figure 12.5) allows you to change specific user permissions. Simply highlight the users who require remote connectivity and check Grant Dialin Permission to User.

Alternatively, you can use the User Manager to grant dial-in permissions:

1. Open User Manager and double-click on any user account.

2. Click on the Dialin button. The options are similar to those available via the Remote Access Administrator applet. Figure 12.6 shows the dialog box for granting permission to users.

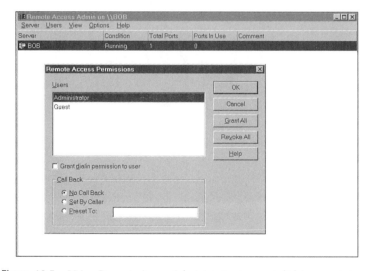

Figure 12.5   Using Remote Access Administrator to grant dial-in permissions.

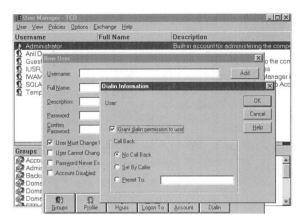

Figure 12.6   Granting dial-in permissions to users from the User Manager application.

Authentication Methods

Because a company does not normally own its dial-up networking infrastructure (for example, phone lines and ISDN links), it is very important to protect all data traveling on these links. For example, even if an intruder manages to intercept data during transmission, he or she must not be able to see sensitive information such as passwords. To ensure that remote logins are at least as secure as logins over the LAN, various options are available for sending passwords in encoded form. Clicking on Configure in the Remote Access Service properties brings you to these options. Authentication mechanisms include the following:

■ *Password Authentication Protocol* (PAP) uses clear text passwords and is the least sophisticated authentication protocol. It should be used only if the remote workstation and server cannot negotiate a more secure form of validation and the threat of intercepted passwords is acceptable.

■ *Challenge-Handshake Authentication Protocol* (CHAP) uses a challenge-response method with a one-way encryption of the user's login information. The response never actually sends the password over the line, so it is theoretically impossible to use, even if intercepted.

You can choose from among the authentication options listed in Table 12.1.

On the CD-ROM

Demonstration 12.2, "RAS Security," covers several ways you can increase the security of your RAS implementation.

Table 12.1 **RAS Authentication Mechanisms**

Option	Security Level	Recommendation
Allow Any Authentication Including Clear Text	Lowest	Use this option as a last resort if you are supporting non-Windows clients that cannot authenticate with any type of encryption method requirement.
Require Encrypted Authentication	Medium	Allows any encryption type except PAP (clear text passwords). Start with this option if you will be supporting non-Windows clients.
Require Microsoft Encrypted Authentication	Highest	Use when clients are Windows based.

Data Encryption

Windows NT RAS also allows you to force all data sent over a connection to be encrypted. Keep in mind that clients must also support this functionality and that it adds some processing overhead that slows down data transfer rates. Data encryption is supported for Windows 95/98 and Windows NT clients. In general, it is not necessary to encrypt all data because an intruder is not likely to tap in to the public phone network to intercept data. However, if highly sensitive information will be transferred, you might want to consider encryption.

Call-Back Verification

In certain situations, you will want RAS to dial directly to users. Using the Call-Back Verification option allowed by Windows NT has several benefits. First, this option can provide an additional level of security. If you know that users are allowed to dial in only from their home phone numbers and not from elsewhere, you can enforce this policy by using the Preset To option. You may also choose to use the Set by Caller option, which allows the remote user to specify the phone number at which he or she is available. This setting might be useful if you want long-distance charges to be incurred on the server side. In either case, the order of events is as follows:

1. The remote caller dials the RAS Server and authenticates normally.

2. If Set by Caller is selected, the remote user enters the phone number to which the RAS server should call back. (The number might directly call the user's computer.) If the Preset To option is used, the specified number is used for the callback.

3. The RAS server disconnects the user and immediately dials the provided phone number, using the same RAS port that was used to accept the original call.

4. The user authenticates again on the remote server, and the connection is made.

Deciding which security options should be enabled largely depends on the details of your environment. If, for example, most users dial in to the network from their home offices, then call-back security is a great idea. However, if users also call from hotel rooms and while on the road, call-back security may not work.

In addition to the basic security mechanisms, third-party alternatives are available. By default, Windows NT does not support functionality such as CallerID or Automatic Number Identification (both of which send the caller's phone number automatically with the call). This information can be used to automatically reject or route calls to the appropriate place. You may also want to have several phone lines attached to a single phone number. This configuration is called a hunt group and is used to automatically find the first non-busy phone line and route the call to it. If you're interested in implementing these options, you need to contact your local telephone service provider.

Your RAS server is now open for business! You've just configured the basics of the Remote Access Service, and the server is ready to accept connections. All that's left is to configure your clients.

Client Configuration

Windows NT RAS supports any PPP client for dial-in. All modern operating systems support remote access connectivity via this standard. PPP was designed to allow relatively slow analog connections and is able to encapsulate (that is, contain within its own packets) any type of protocol data. It is now most commonly used to carry TCP/IP for Internet access. PPP allows various authentication mechanisms and supports dynamic IP address allocation.

▶ For More
Information
5, 6
Dial-Up Networking (DUN) is now Microsoft's official term for client-side connections. Anyone who has ever set up a connection to an Internet service provider (ISP) is familiar with the procedure for setting up a DUN connection. In Windows 95/98 and Windows NT 4.0, you can click on My Computer, Dial-Up Networking, and select Make New Connection. Depending on the specific revision of your operating system, you are either greeted by a wizard or shown a new connection creation screen (as seen in Figure 12.7). In either case, the only configuration options that are required include specification of the protocols to be used and the phone number of the RAS server.

Figure 12.7   The Windows 98 Dial-Up Networking Connection Wizard.

Other New Features in Windows NT RAS

Keeping users connected to resources has always been a fundamental concern for IT, but configuration was often difficult and required training for users. Microsoft has focused its attention on making remote connectivity easier to configure and more powerful for end users and system administrators alike. This section describes several improvements in the Windows NT Remote Access Service.

Operating System Enhancements

There are several improvements that add functionality or allow easier access to remote resources. In this section, we look at features that make using resources accessed through RAS similar to being on a network. In most cases, the changes are automatic, but I point out where additional configuration is necessary:

■ *Logon dialing*—When RAS is installed on a Windows NT Workstation or Server computer, the Logon Information dialog box gives the user the option of being authenticated on a remote server. Figure 12.8 shows the Logon Using Dial-Up Networking option.

Figure 12.8   The Logon Using Dial-Up Networking option.

■ *Dial-up networking setup Wizards*—In an effort to simplify the creation of DUN connections, Wizards have been included for performing common functions such as adding new connections and changing dialing locations.

■ *Dialing location settings*—Users can now use separate dialing profiles for specifying the sequence to dial a calling card number of a long-distance carrier. The easiest way to access this feature is by clicking on Control Panel, Modems, Dialing Properties.

■ *Restartable file copy*—Enabled automatically for all RAS connections, it allows aborted transfers to be resumed from the point of disconnection.

■ *Idle disconnect*—A client and/or server configuration option that automatically disconnects users after a specified period of inactivity.

■ *Internet Connection Services for RAS*—A separate product available from Microsoft that is intended for large-scale RAS deployments. Allows the storage of a central phone book for RAS clients on a Windows NT Server. Whenever dial-up phone numbers or other parameters are changed, administrators need only change the centralized database.

■ *Microsoft Connection Manager for RAS*—This update is part of the Windows NT Option Pack and allows systems administrators to create custom dialing routines for users. This feature is especially useful when many clients need to be config- ured or a commercial ISP role is being assumed.

PPP Multilink

▶ For More
Information
7

PPP Multilink is based on an extension to the PPP specification and is an open stan- dard. Multilink allows the combination of multiple WAN connections into a single logical bundle. For example, if you have two 28.8Kbps analog modems and two analog phone lines, you can combine the bandwidth of both connections to form a single 57.6Kbps pipe. What's the catch? All connections must be made to the same RAS server. This might be an issue if you have multiple RAS servers and are having your phone company automatically configure a hunt group that finds the first non-busy line. However, PPP Multilink can often provide a cost-effective way to increase band- width over relatively slow connections. In Figure 12.9, for example, the client is using three 28.8Kbps analog modem connections and three separate phone lines to connect to the same RAS server. Using Multilink, this user effectively obtains 86.4Kbps total bandwidth for the connection. More information on setting up Multilink is available from Microsoft.

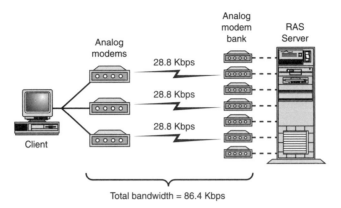

Figure 12.9   A PPP Multilink scenario.

The Routing and Remote Access Service Update

The Routing and Remote Access Server (RRAS) Update for Windows NT Server adds many useful features to Windows NT networking and remote access capabilities. Figure 12.10 shows the main interface of the RRAS Administrator program.

With the features of this update you can do the following:

- Connect to a router (or a Windows NT Server serving as a router) over the network.

- View all routers and RAS servers within the domain from a single location.

- View TCP/IP information and statistics for remote devices.

- View information based on the Simple Network Monitoring Protocol (SNMP), Open Shortest Path First (OSPF), and Routing Information Protocol Version 2 (RIP–2).

- Add a demand-dial interface that can dynamically make WAN connections as needed. This functionality can use a given set of credentials to automatically connect to and authenticate on a remote router or Windows NT Server computer.

- Enable packet filtering for network security.

- Support the Remote Authentication Dial-In User Service (RADIUS) standard for dial-in user authentication. RADIUS allows the use of several third-party security devices for securing logons.

- Implement 128-bit strong encryption for increased security.

▶ For More
Information
8

Installing RRAS uninstalls your existing RAS service and replaces it with the newer version. You then need to reassign your ports to RAS. For specifics about using the RRAS update, see the online Help file that is installed as part of the update.

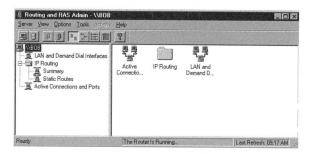

Figure 12.10 The RRAS Administrator main window.

Personal Fax Server for Windows NT Workstation

For More
Information
9, 10

Okay, so it's not strictly part of RAS, but Personal Fax Server is so useful that I had to include information on it here. Windows NT 4.0 did not originally ship with fax software. However, Microsoft has made the Personal Fax Server for Windows NT available for free via its Web site. Installing this program allows you to use any available dial-out port to send faxes. This port acts like any other printer and can be shared over the network. However, true to its name, the Personal Fax Server does not support advanced faxing functionality for multiple concurrent users. You can download Personal Fax Server for Windows NT from Microsoft's Web site.

Case Study: Making Applications Available Remotely

XYZ Corporation has 30 sales/marketing users who travel several days every month and require access to LAN resources. The solution you implement must support up to seven concurrent connections. Users must have access to their local intranet and Microsoft SQL Server to enter and query sales information. Additionally, these users currently use a TCP/IP-based network application to obtain sales-related data and also need to access information that is stored in their home directories (stored locally on the RAS server).

Solution

First, lease seven analog phone lines and instruct the telephone company to form a hunt group, which allows users to find a free line without dialing another phone number. Next, purchase and install a third-party hardware-based modem bank with seven ports.

Then, set up the Remote Access Service on the server:

1. Configure the modem bank per the hardware vendor's instructions.

2. Enable each port for dial-in through the Remote Access Service properties.

3. Grant dial-in permissions to the appropriate users and disallow callbacks (because a user may connect from one of many locations).

4. Configure the TCP/IP protocol to select from a static pool of IP addresses and enable the option to access the entire network for TCP/IP.

5. Because all users are running Windows clients, the Require Microsoft Authenticated Encryption option is enabled.

6. Additionally, the NetBEUI protocol is enabled for efficient transfers to and from users' home directories. The protocol is configured to allow access to This Computer Only, meaning that remote users can access resources only on the RAS server that is using NetBEUI.

7. When RAS configuration is complete, RAS Administrator and User Manager are used to grant dial-in permissions to users.

Then create a dial-up networking client connection on the remote users' laptops. All users will be dialing a single phone number because the company has set up a hunt group to find the first non-busy line. It may be necessary to provide documentation for laptops that cannot be accessed by IT for setup.

You can optionally set up various dialing profiles for different dial-in scenarios. In this case, there is one setup each for Hotel, Branch Office, and In-Town. Each specifies a different area code (999 is used for the Hotel setting) and specifies any additional dialing options.

This solution easily satisfies the requirements set forth and enables remote users to obtain network access from many locations. To improve security, you can also implement several more features. For example, if some employees regularly dial in from specific locations, you can use call-back security. To secure network access for remote connections, the RAS server could be set up behind a firewall and only specific types of packets could be allowed to pass. As is always the case, specific security implementations are based on the details of the environment.

The Bottom Line

A corporation's information is useless if it is not accessible when needed. Remote dial-in options offer many benefits. Traveling users often need to access files and network data they use in the office. In addition, the greater reliance on laptop computers and server-based storage means that many users need to access information from remote locations. If that information is simply a phone call away, users will be better empowered to do their jobs. Furthermore, remote access availability can ensure that employees will be available via email whether they are at their desks or on the road. Because you probably already have at least one Windows NT Server in your environment, the overall cost of implementation should be low. Remote dial-in options help to reduce TCO by providing employees with the information they need when they need it through a solution that is easy to implement and maintain.

Now that you're familiar with setting up remote access in Windows NT, check out the cost savings by using the Internet as your communications infrastructure. Details are covered in Chapter 13, "Virtual Private Networking."

For More Information

1. Chapter 5, "Understanding Remote Access Service," Microsoft Windows NT Server Manuals, Networking Supplement Manual

2. RFC 1171, "The Point-to Point Protocol for the Transmission of Multi-Protocol Datagrams Over Point-to-Point Links," Internet Engineering Task Force (www.ietf.org)

3. "The Point-to-Point Protocol (PPP): An Overview," Windows NT Server Technical Notes

4. Chapter 6, "Installing And Configuring Remote Access Service," Microsoft Windows NT Server Manuals, Networking Supplement Manual

5. "How to Configure Windows 95 to Dial into a RAS/RRAS Server," Q178729, Microsoft Knowledge Base

6. Part 6, "Communications," Windows 95 Resource Kit

7. "Dial-Up Networking Multilink Channel Aggregation," Windows NT Workstation Reviewers Guide

8. "Routing and Remote Access Service for Windows NT Server 4.0 and 5.0: New Opportunities Today and Looking Ahead," Microsoft Windows NT Server Technical Notes

9. Microsoft Personal Fax for Windows Web site (www.microsoft.com/windows/downloads/contents/Updates/NTPersonalFax/)

10. "Microsoft Fax and Modem Services: Usage and Troubleshooting Guide," Microsoft BackOffice Technical Notes

Further Reading

For more information on the Remote Access Service in general, see

- "Windows NT 4.0 FAQs: Dial-Up Networking and RAS Questions," Microsoft TechNet

- "Windows NT Remote Access Services—Common Questions and Answers," Microsoft Knowledge Base

- "Troubleshooting Problems with Windows NT Remote Access Services," Microsoft TechNet

- Chapter 13 of this book: "Virtual Private Networking"

- Microsoft Windows NT Server Communications home page (www.microsoft.com/communications)

13

Virtual Private Networking

IN CHAPTER 12, "REMOTE ACCESS SERVICE," you learned how to set up Windows NT remote access using modems for dialing in to a network. In this chapter, we take that idea one step further by allowing users to connect to your NT Server over the Internet. The basic idea is that you don't have to build a network connection from New York to Los Angeles because one already exists: the Internet. By utilizing cost-effective Internet access, you can reduce remote connection costs and ease administration. Despite the benefits it can promise, many companies have been reluctant to allow widespread remote access to their corporate LANs. Security is, perhaps, the greatest of their concerns. Following closely is the cost and administrative burden of creating modem pools, assigning login permissions, and configuring client machines. Fear of trying to keep pace with rapidly changing WAN technologies creates potential problems for the future. In traditional remote access scenarios, proprietary hardware-based solutions are often used in this capacity; however, they do not address all of the mentioned issues and can sometimes present additional problems of their own.

In this chapter, we look at how to set up a Windows NT–based virtual private network (VPN). It's quick and easy to do, plus you already have the software required! If you currently support or plan to support remote users, a VPN is a great way to lower your TCO.

Virtual Private Networking Basics

Virtual private networking is the use of an insecure public network for securely transferring sensitive information. The general idea is that users can connect to the Internet—via a LAN or through their ISP—and then make a secure, encrypted connection to their remote server. Figure 13.1 shows a basic VPN: All remote clients connect to the Internet and then form a secure tunnel to their remote network.

▶ For More
Information
1

The most obvious benefit of VPNs is a reduction in long-distance phone charges. However, this is only a small part of the equation. Before getting into the details of how to set up a VPN, we first look at problems with standard remote access solutions and how a VPN can address them.

Problems with Traditional Remote Access Practices

We talked earlier about the benefits of allowing remote access to your network. The proposed solution in Chapter 12 is great for supporting users who occasionally dial in to check email. However, it has several limitations and problems when remote access demands increase:

- *Hardware costs and support*—Not only are modem banks expensive, but they often lock you into a solution from a specific vendor. Upgrading a modem bank can be a significant expense, which increases hardware costs and support and administration headaches.

- *Data transport costs*—For supporting traveling users, toll-free numbers and long-distance charges can be incredible. The costs of leasing and maintaining higher-bandwidth site-to-site connections, although they're decreasing, are still significant.

- *Low bandwidth*—Traditional methods require you to access a phone line at low bandwidth even if you already have T1-speed Internet access from a local LAN.

- *Inefficient bandwidth usage*—When users are connected to a remote connectivity device, they are effectively using bandwidth, whether or not they are actually transferring any real data. Figure 13.2 shows how multiple ports are effectively used on a server where little data transfer is occurring.

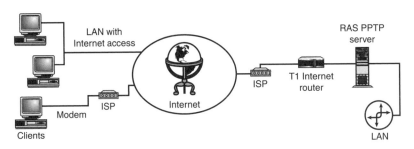

Figure 13.1   A basic VPN.

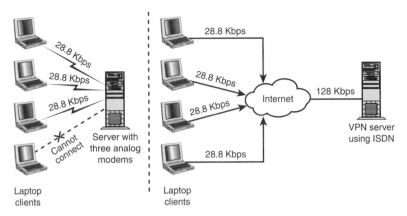

Figure 13.2 VPNs improve effective bandwidth usage efficiency.

The VPN Solution

VPNs address some of the issues associated with traditional remote access practices. The benefits of VPNs are considerable:

■ *Keep up with technology*—The technology applied by users is independent of that used on the server side; each user may choose the best available method. For example, a single T1 line (approximately 1.54Mbps) on the server side can support many remote clients using analog lines, ISDN, ADSL, cable modems, or a network router. The clients' ISPs—not the company's server—must support the technology they're using. ISPs are often better able to serve end users with technical support and quicker response times than are companies that view this function as secondary.

■ *No more busy signals*—In contrast to the traditional remote access situation, with a VPN if 10 users remain idle while reading email messages, they won't be wasting any bandwidth. Clients use resources only when they actually *transfer* data. Avoiding the "one port, one connection" effect allows many more concurrent connections within a fixed bandwidth.

■ *Convenience*—Internet access is often more readily available than analog phone lines in many corporate offices. Even those that use analog connections have some sort of Internet connectivity. Regardless of the type of connection, this data transport mechanism can be used to securely access remote resources without the need for modems or free telephone lines.

■ *Easy to implement and manage*—Although you have many options, a Windows NT Server–based VPN can be implemented in about an hour and does not require the purchase of any additional software.

Now that we've looked at some compelling reasons to consider a VPN, let's look at how Microsoft addresses this demand using Windows NT's Remote Access Service (RAS).

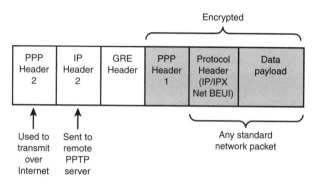

Figure 13.3 The layout of a typical PPTP packet.

Windows NT RAS and the Point-to-Point Tunneling Protocol

▶ For More
Information
2

The Windows NT 4.0 RAS includes the capability to form a secure, encrypted connection over the Internet for remote access users. The Point-to-Point Tunneling Protocol (PPTP) is based on an Internet standard (RFC 1171) and is an extension to the Point-to-Point Protocol (PPP) specification (described in Chapter 12). PPTP allows for the encapsulation of any type of network packet in an encrypted data packet that can be sent over the Internet. This protocol is included with current versions of Microsoft's operating systems (Windows 95/98 and Windows NT 4.0). Because PPTP is protocol independent, it can carry TCP/IP, IPX/SPX, or NetBEUI traffic. The diagram in Figure 13.3 shows the layout of a PPTP packet. The basic Windows NT RAS limitation of 1 concurrent connection on Windows NT Workstation and up to 256 concurrent connections on Windows NT Server also applies to PPTP-based connections.

Server Configuration and Client Setup

▶ For More
Information
1, 3, 4

Windows NT 4.0 supports PPTP connectivity out of the box. However, you need to make sure you've installed the latest Service Pack as well as any security fixes before proceeding with a live server. More information on security is provided later in the chapter. The hardware requirements for setting up a VPN are basically the same as those for RAS, although you do not need analog modems. You need a Windows NT Server (if you are supporting more than one connection at a time) and a connection to the Internet. The Internet connection may use any of a variety of technologies, including a modem, ISDN, T1, Frame Relay, and so on.

On the CD-ROM

Demonstration 13.1, "VPN Setup," covers the basic steps in setting up a Windows NT–based VPN.

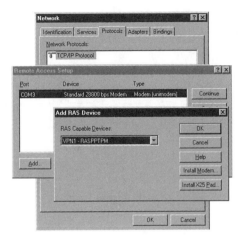

Figure 13.4 Adding VPN ports to RAS.

The first step in setting up a VPN, as in setting up RAS, is to enable the appropriate services on the server. Additionally, you need to install PPTP:

1. If you haven't yet installed the Remote Access Service, click on Control Panel, Network, Services, Add. Select Remote Access Service from the available choices and confirm the selection by clicking OK.

2. While you're in the area, install PPTP by clicking on the Protocols tab and then clicking on Add. You are asked how many VPNs you want to set up. Make this number equal to the maximum number of concurrent connections you plan to support.

3. The VPN ports (named VPN# - RASPPTPM) are logical devices that work exactly like modems. You can configure them for dial-out, dial-in, or both. Simply click on Add, as shown in Figure 13.4, and select the VPN devices you want to make available for dial-in. Then, click on Configure and enable the dial-in option.

4. Accept the new configuration and restart the computer if prompted to do so.

Server Security

Because your server will have access to the Internet, you need to consider enabling certain security measures. In this section, we look at configuring packet filtering and authentication and encryption.

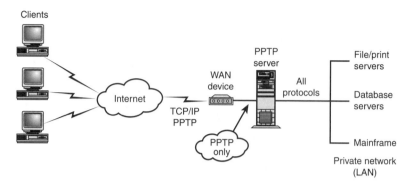

Figure 13.5   Packet filtering on a multihomed server.

Packet Filtering

Packet filtering examines all the data destined for a particular server or network and discards any data that does not meet certain criteria. Packet filtering allows the administrator to specify certain criteria for any information to be received and processed by the server. All other information is ignored. An example would be to allow all PPTP packets to a server, but to ignore any TCP/IP, IPX/SPX, or NetBEUI packets. This still allows for connectivity via PPTP but prevents the possibility of TCP/IP-based attacks.

Packet filtering is set up on a per adapter basis, so it is important that the filters are set up on the appropriate adapters in the case of a multihomed system. Figure 13.5 shows a multihomed server (a machine with more than one network adapter) with different packet-filtering options on each adapter. This server's network adapter allows all protocol traffic, whereas the ISDN Internet connection accepts only PPTP traffic.

To set up packet filtering for Windows NT, complete the following steps:

1. Click on Control Panel, Network, Protocols. Highlight TCP/IP Protocol and click on Properties.

2. If you have multiple adapters in this machine, select the adapter you want to configure in the Adapter drop-down box.

3. In the IP Address tab, click on Advanced. Place a check mark in the Enable PPTP Filtering box (as shown in Figure 13.6).

On the CD-ROM

Demonstration 13.2, "PPTP Security," walks you through enabling the PPTP filtering options.

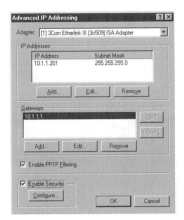

Figure 13.6 Enabling packet filtering in the Advanced IP Addressing dialog box.

Packet filtering effectively disables any non-PPTP traffic from being accessed on this interface. That is, before any users can access the resources of this server, they must first authenticate and form a secure connection. If you require other types of data transfer using an Internet connection (such as email, Web browsing, and FTP), you need to be less restrictive in which traffic is allowed to pass. To set up more detailed packet-filtering options, follow these steps:

1. Click on Control Panel, Network, Protocols. Highlight TCP/IP Protocol and click on Properties.

2. If you have multiple adapters in this machine, select the adapter you want to configure in the Adapter drop-down box.

3. In the IP Address tab, click on Advanced. Be sure that there is no check mark in the Enable PPTP Filtering box. Check the Enable Security box and then click on Configure.

4. The resulting dialog box, shown in Figure 13.7, allows you to permit or deny data on specific TCP, UDP, and IP ports. Before making changes, verify that the proper adapter is highlighted in the Adapter drop-down box.

▶ For More
Information
5, 6

It is beyond the scope of this chapter to examine this information in detail, but more information is available.

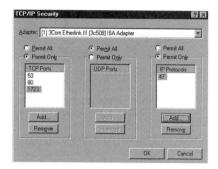

Figure 13.7 Setting packet-filtering options.

Your server is now configured to accept only PPTP connections via the WAN adapter and only specific TCP/IP communications. This is a reasonably secure config-uration and will prevent the vast majority of Internet-based intrusion methods.

Authentication and Encryption

In tunneling over a public network (such as the Internet), protection is required for data encryption and authentication. For securely transmitting data, PPTP uses a default of 40-bit encryption. This encryption is always enabled for data transfers and requires no additional configuration. A 128-bit strong encryption patch is available from Microsoft, but federal export restrictions limit its use to North American users.

Several methods are available for authentication. Windows NT Challenge Handshake Authentication Protocol (CHAP) is recommended because it does not actually send the password over the network. Instead, it sends a string determined by a one-way function that is made up of the client machine name and the current user account. Although CHAP is the most secure method of authentication, its drawback is that it is limited in use to clients that support this protocol—namely Windows 95/98 and Windows NT. For all other types of clients, Password Authentication Protocol (PAP) is available. This method sends a clear text password over the connection, but it is the most compatible standard available.

PPTP and Firewalls

To allow PPTP packets into a network, all routers along the virtual circuit must allow the passage of control information on TCP Port 1723 and allow data transfer via Protocol 47 (Generic Routing Encapsulation) to be passed. This is not a concern for most implementations because most ISPs for-ward these packets by default. However, if your company has a firewall, you need to verify that it allows this information to pass.

▶ For More
Information
7

PPTP Filtering Considerations

Incorrectly enabling PPTP filtering or TCP/IP security can make the server unavailable to the rest of the network via TCP/IP. This restriction forces any remote clients to connect via PPTP. This approach is fine if you want the server to be accessible only via your VPN but can cause problems if other network users must also access the server.

After the service is installed and configured, you need to grant dial-in permissions to users that require them. As in the case of the standard RAS, this can be done in the User Manager application or in the Remote Access Administrator. For more information, see Chapter 12.

Client Setup

Currently, PPTP is available on Windows 95/98 and Windows NT Workstation 4.0 operating systems. For Windows 95, you need to download and install the Dial-Up Networking 1.3 Upgrade to add this functionality. To set up Windows 95/98 and Windows NT clients, the general procedure is similar:

1. If it's not already installed, install Dial-Up Networking.

2. Install PPTP and configure at least one virtual port. For Windows NT, this procedure is identical to the NT Server setup procedure described in the "Server Configuration and Client Setup" section. For Windows 95/98, you need to add the PPTP protocol.

3. After PPTP is installed, you need to configure at least one dial-up adapter to use this protocol. For Windows NT machines, you can do so by specifying the number of virtual ports that will be supported. These ports will be made available to RAS for dial-in or dial-out similar to any other communications port. Windows 95/98 users need to configure an additional dial-up networking adapter to use PPTP (as shown in Figure 13.8) before continuing.

4. After restarting your computer, set up a new dial-up networking connection. However, instead of entering a phone number for the destination server, enter the name or IP address of the remote server. For the device that will be used to dial this connection, choose one of the virtual ports created in the previous step.

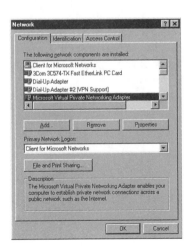

Figure 13.8 Windows 95/98 Dial-Up Networking configuration with a VPN adapter.

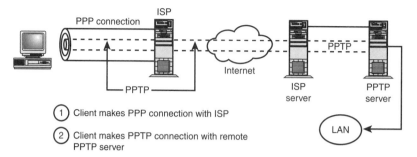

Figure 13.9 The procedure for making PPTP client connections.

To establish a VPN connection with a server, a client must do the following:

1. The client obtains an Internet connection. On the road, this connection is usually via a dial-up ISP account using PPP, although it may be via a LAN.

2. The client then dials a second dial-up networking connection that specifies a VPN device and an IP address instead of a phone number.

3. The client is prompted to authenticate on the remote server.

Figure 13.9 shows the procedure for making these connections. As long as authentication is successful, the user can work with any network resources for which he or she has permissions. Users also have access to the Internet via their ISP connection.

Internet Reliability and Service Levels

Because we take it for granted, we often forget that the Internet is a public network. As such, it is subject to the same limitations as other public utilities, such as roads. It is very difficult to predict the amount of traffic that you will encounter on your way to an important meeting across town. On the Internet, transmission times and reliability may vary. Although the redundant nature of the Internet provides for a fairly reasonable level of reliability, network outages are possible. Additionally, performance may vary based on traffic at any particular time of day. If you're using a VPN to handle the transfer of time-sensitive or mission-critical data, you may want to get a guaranteed service-level agreement from your ISP. This is especially important for time-dependent applications such as voice or video.

You can generally expect the performance hit incurred by encryption on the client side of the transmissions to be negligible. Because most WAN connection methods are relatively slow, a 5% to 10% decrease in speed is not a major cause for concern. On the server side, however, it is important to perform load testing to check whether a significant amount of processing overhead is incurred. For more information on measuring performance parameters, see Chapter 9, "Performance Monitoring."

The Routing and Remote Access Server Update

▶ For More
Information
8, 9
Described in Chapter 12, the Routing and Remote Access Server (RRAS) Update adds server-to-server PPTP connection capabilities. This allows a company to connect an entire LAN with branch offices using the Internet for transport. It also enables the creation of a dial-on-demand PPTP interface that allows Windows NT Server to create a RAS or PPTP connection as needed by client computers of network users. The update is designed for users that support advanced RAS functions such as temporary VPN connections and advanced routing configurations.

Microsoft has released a special package designed to make deploying remote access features easier for ISPs and medium- to large-sized companies. Internet Connection Services for RAS provides the following additions and benefits:

- Improved wizards for installing dial-up adapters and configuring connections

- Centralized phone books for administering dial-up numbers and other information in a single location

- Custom graphics and icons for indicating connections to company or ISP servers

- Broader support for Internet authentication mechanisms and protocols

▶ For More
Information
10, 11
If these options seem helpful for managing your environment, be sure to consider using the Internet Connection Services.

Alternatives to a Windows NT VPN

Although the Windows NT VPN solutions may be appropriate for several situations, many alternatives are available. In this section, we look at VPN solutions that support Windows NT–based environments, but do not necessarily rely on the operating system.

VPN Protocols

The VPN marketplace is based on several incompatible standards. Until these problems are ironed out, it is important to understand some of the differences. There are currently three major protocol standards that may be used to set up a virtual private network:

- *PPTP*—Microsoft's software-based protocol. PPTP is freely available and is included with Windows NT and Windows 95/98 operating systems. PPTP must be used over an IP-based network (such as the Internet) and can form only a single tunnel per connection.

On the CD-ROM

Demonstration 13.3, "RRAS Administrator," introduces the RRAS Administrator interface and provides an overview of possible uses for this service.

- *L2TP*—A combination of Cisco Systems's Layer 2 Forwarding (L2F) protocol and PPTP. This protocol will become the new standard for client/server VPN connectivity. A benefit of L2TP is that it supports multiple data transfer types, including frame relay, ATM, and IP-based networks. It also supports the establishment of multiple tunnels within a single connection. Microsoft will support this specification in future updates of Windows NT.

- *IPSecure (IPSec)*—An Internet Engineering Task Force standard, IPSec is still not finalized. IPSec will be initially designed for use in server-to-server connections over the Internet and will be incorporated in a future revision of the Internet Protocol, IPv6. Its primary weakness currently lies in its lack of flexible authentication mechanism support. In addition, it only supports the transmission of IP-based traffic. Microsoft will most likely support IPSec in future updates of Windows NT.

Using Encryption

The purpose of sending information via a virtual private network is to prevent the usability of information in the event that it is intercepted. PPTP does this by using data encryption for all transmissions at the packet level. But suppose you only want to send small pieces of information—such as weekly sales information email—by using an encrypted method. There are several software packages for performing file- and message-based encryption. These include

- *Public key encryption*—Pretty good privacy (PGP) is an example of public key encryption. Don't let the name fool you—PGP is one of the strongest encryption methods available. You can find more information and download the software from `www.pgp.com`.

- *Third-party authentication*—Another method used to ensure that only the intended recipient can view a message is through the use of a third party that can verify the identities of the sender and the receiver. Verisign, Inc. (`www.verisign.com`) is one such service. The sender and recipient must register for identification, based on some type of subscription cost for the service.

- *Secure Sockets Layer (SSL)*—Designed for transferring secure data over the Internet, SSL is a secure method for transferring socket-based data such as that carried by the Hypertext Transfer Protocol (HTTP). For example, if passwords or credit card information must be sent via a Web site, this information can be encrypted. Alternatively, highly secure sites can specify that all data transfers between clients and the server be protected.

Hardware-Based VPNs

Although it is beyond the scope of this book to describe other specific products and services, dedicated hardware routers can be used to set up a VPN. The benefit of using hardware-based solutions is that they are often fast and can support many users. Another major benefit is that hardware-based solutions can be implemented transparently to the users. If hardware devices are responsible for encrypting and decrypting data, client computers require no reconfiguration. Figure 13.10 shows a hardware-based VPN in which the routers handle all data encryption. The drawback is that hardware-based solutions are often expensive and may require committing to proprietary standards. Additionally, they require some networking knowledge to implement and maintain. More information is available from the VPN hardware manufacturers mentioned in the "Further Reading" section at the end of this chapter.

VPN Outsourcing

▶ For More
Information
12
Another alternative for organizations is to outsource their VPN to an ISP. In this situation, the ISP is responsible for automatically encrypting all data that is sent between the ISP's local points of presence (POPs) and the connection to the server. In Figure 13.11, the ISP is responsible for encrypting all data between point A (the ISP dial-in) and point B (the server's Internet connection). Again, the benefit is that client reconfiguration is not required and that a third-party specialist handles support and management of the service. Costs for outsourced VPNs vary based on the provider, service-level guarantees, and amount of bandwidth required.

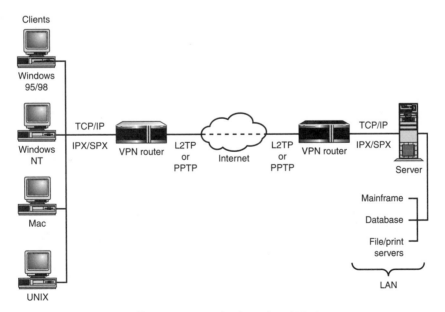

Figure 13.10 A hardware-based VPN.

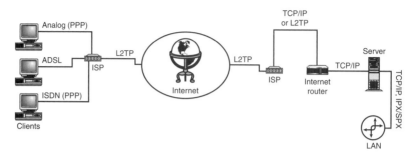

Figure 13.11   An outsourced VPN.

Case Study: Improving Remote Access

XYZ Corp. is looking for a way to reduce costs for remote access to its LAN and to support a greater number of remote access technologies. Currently, support for up to 20 concurrent users is required. Specific problems with the current modem-bank situation include high costs for users who are traveling out of the country and lack of support for 56Kbps modems, ADSL, and cable modems. A large proportion of IT's support time is taken away for training and troubleshooting remote access problems. Finally, there are several problems with the incoming phone lines on the server, including busy signals and maintenance costs from the telephone company.

Solution

The network administrator determines that a VPN can address most of these issues and decides to implement it using Windows NT because of the low cost and ease of setup and administration. First, she sets up a PPTP server inside the company's firewall. She determines that the firewall will allow PPTP packets to be passed onto the network. As an added precaution, she enables packet filtering for the Internet connection. Finally, she enables IP forwarding to allow remote users to access the rest of the network after they authenticate on this server.

XYZ Corp. enters into an agreement with an international ISP that has POPs in each of the major cities in which users will be connecting. Each client is each given an individual username and password and is instructed to use a local POP whenever possible. The ISP also supports cable modems and ADSL in select areas and handles all configuration and troubleshooting for the users of XYZ Corp. Client machines are configured with PPTP, and additional dial-up networking connections are created. Clients are instructed to connect to the Internet using the ISP's accounts and then to use a second dial-up networking connection to access the remote PPTP server.

Cost Savings Analysis

A major motivation in this case study was to reduce the costs of providing remote access. Tables 13.1 and 13.2 compare implementation and ongoing costs of the traditional solution and the solution using Windows NT PPTP.

Table 13.1 **Setup (One Time) Costs**

Item	Traditional RAS	PPTP
Phone line group setup (20 lines @ $20/each)	$400	N/A
Modem bank (20 ports @ $100/each)	$2,000	N/A
Total (one-time cost)	$2,400	$0

Table 13.2 **Monthly (Recurrent) Costs**

Item	Traditional RAS	PPTP
Phone line maintenance (20 lines @ $15/month/line)	$300	N/A
ISP charges for Internet access (50 total users)	N/A	$1,000 ($20 per user, unlimited use)
Long-distance charges	$1,404	N/A (assumed local dialing)
Total (per month)	$1,704	$1,000

▶ For More Information 13

Cost Calculation Details

The following calculations do not include these items because they are similar in both cases: Internet connectivity (line and adapter cost); server hardware, software, and licenses; installation and setup; and modem costs for clients. The data in Tables 13.1 and 13.2 is based on the assumption that, on average, each user spends 12 hours per month connected to the network, the average number of connected users at any given time is 15, and the cost for long-distance charges averages $.13 per minute.

The Bottom Line

Traditional remote access methods are fine for supporting few users and where long-distance and data transport charges are minimal. However, for supporting more users, a virtual private network can clearly be the method of choice. In the case study, we can see that the problems associated with maintaining a large number of analog lines and proprietary modem banks have been eliminated. Instead, the server has a single, easily upgradable Internet connection, and the ISP is responsible for handling all client access requirements.

By controlling the various costs and problems associated with providing remote access solutions, IT staffers can focus on other tasks such as making information more accessible for network users. Additionally, the cost-effective outsourcing of remote user support to ISPs can be of tremendous value. In most implementations, financial benefits can be realized immediately. The less tangible end-user satisfaction may also increase because of better support and more readily available connection options. Finally, IT will thank you for reducing the costs and burdens of using modem banks. What more could you hope for in reducing TCO?

For More Information

1. "How to Set Up a Private Network Over the Internet Using PPTP," Q161410, Microsoft Knowledge Base

2. "Understanding PPTP (Windows 95 and Windows NT 4.0)," Microsoft Windows NT Server Technical Notes, Microsoft TechNet

3. "Installing, Configuring, and Using PPTP with Microsoft Clients and Servers (Windows 95 and Windows NT 4.0)," Microsoft Windows NT Server 4.0 Resource Kit Supplement 2

4. "Microsoft Windows NT Server 4.0 PPTP White Paper," Microsoft Windows NT Server Technical Notes, Microsoft TechNet

5. Chapter 6 of this book: "TCP/IP Management"

6. Appendix B, "Port Reference for Microsoft TCP/IP," NT Server 4.0 Resource Kit

7. "Troubleshooting PPTP Connectivity Issues in Windows NT 4.0," Q162847, Microsoft Knowledge Base

8. "Microsoft Routing and Remote Access Service Update for Windows NT Server 4.0—Frequently Asked Questions," Microsoft TechNet

9. "How to Create a Demand Dial PPTP Interface," Q177335, Microsoft Knowledge Base

10. "Internet Connection Services for Microsoft RAS Features At-A-Glance," Microsoft Windows NT Server Product Facts

11. "Internet Connection Services for Microsoft RAS," Microsoft Windows NT Server Manuals

12. "Using PPTP Over a Non-PPTP Enabled Internet Provider," Q154062, Microsoft Knowledge Base

13. "Evaluating Microsoft Point to Point Tunneling Cost Factors," Microsoft Windows NT Server Technical Notes—Planning, Microsoft TechNet

Further Reading

For more information on virtual private networking in general, see

- "Virtual Private Networking: An Overview," Microsoft TechNet
- Third-party vendor Web sites:
    - 3Com Corp.: www.3com.com
    - Ascend Communications, Inc.: www.ascend.com
    - Aventail Corp.: www.aventail.com
    - Cisco Systems, Inc.: www.cisco.com
    - Shiva Corp.: www.shiva.com
- Chapter 11, "Point-to-Point Tunneling Protocol (PPTP)," Microsoft Windows NT Server Manuals, Networking Supplement Manual
- Chapter 7, "Internet Connections," Windows NT Server Technical Notes

14

Automated Software Installations

L ARGE AND SMALL COMPANIES ALIKE require their IT organizations to roll out new operating systems and applications. This process is often regarded as the most important function of IT. Unfortunately, it can also be the most boring, repetitive, and troublesome. Automating the process offers many benefits:

- *Saves time and costs*—By taking the time to plan a specific installation only once, you can save subsequent time on manual installations. Additionally, many installations can be performed in parallel.

- *Ensures consistency and reduces errors*—Help desk staffers can attest to the fact that supporting systems with identical configurations can be much easier than supporting many disparate systems. Automated installations ensure that all machines have the same basic setup.

- *Improves recoverability and troubleshooting*—If you run across problems (hardware or software) that keep the user from working, you can easily back up any user data and then re-run the automated installation routine. By resetting the system to a default configuration, you can save time and work on other responsibilities.

In this chapter, we look at ways to automate Windows 95/98 and Windows NT operating system installations. We also see that installing groups of applications can be done quickly and easily via freely available tools. All these tools and techniques help reduce the TCO of managing and supporting systems across your business.

When to Automate

Although there are no concrete rules regarding when automation would be beneficial, some useful guidelines are to automate when:

- Groups of clients have similar basic configurations. For example, if all administrative users require Microsoft Office applications and some need a company database, create a basic configuration including Microsoft Office. Then, create a setup routine that adds the additional company-specific application.

- You often restore systems to a standard configuration. Training labs and test environments fit nicely into this category.

- You want to customize the installation defaults for a specific program. For example, suppose you want all Word users to use the company's default template for all documents and store files on a specific network share.

- You are performing a rollout of a new application or operating system to multiple users. Automation can help many users make the transition in a short period of time.

Automating a Windows NT Workstation Installation

If you're rolling out a large number of Windows NT Workstation computers, you may have wished for a robot that could click through the numerous prompts that you are required to answer. Fortunately, Windows NT includes a small but useful program called Setup Manager that can help. This application allows you to easily create a file that contains all the information required by Windows NT Setup *before* you start the process.

Creating a Network Installation Boot Disk

If the system to which you want to copy files does not have an operating system installed, you need to have some method for accessing data. The easiest way would be to use a CD-ROM if you can create one. Alternatively, you could create a DOS-based boot disk that loads a minimal set of network drivers and allows you to connect to a share on a server. An easy way to create such a disk is to use the Network Client Administrator program that is included with Windows NT Server. Just select the Make Network Installation Startup Disk option. You need to ensure that Windows NT supports the network interface card drivers required by your client machine. For more information, see the program's Help file.

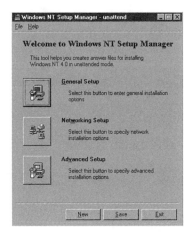

Figure 14.1 The main Setup Manager window.

Creating an Answer File with Setup Manager

You can use the Setup Manager utility to create an answer file that contains the information usually requested by a user during the Windows NT operating system installation. This file contains the responses you would normally be required to enter during installation. Setup Manager also includes support for modifying the Registry with application- or operating system–specific settings. As you'll soon see, the simplicity of using the utility may hide its value.

The Setup Manager utility is located on the Windows NT Workstation and Server media in the `\Support\deptools` directory. Choose the appropriate directory for the platform you are using. Simply double-click on the `Setupmgr.exe` file to run the program. For ease of use, you can copy that file to a local directory. Figure 14.1 shows the main screen of Setup Manager.

Finding Setup Manager

Original equipment manufacturers (OEMs) may move/omit some files on the Windows NT CD-ROM. The path specified is for the retail CD-ROM. If the file is not available in the location specified, just do a search for `Setupmgr.exe`.

On the CD-ROM

Demonstration 14.1, "Setup Manager," walks you through the basics of creating a setup information file with Setup Manager and shows you the layout of the resulting file.

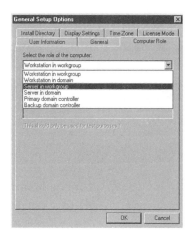

Figure 14.2 General Options in Setup Manager.

You use the Setup Manager's graphical user interface (GUI) to specify responses to setup prompts. These responses can then be saved using the File, Save command at any time. Any filename works (I'm using `unattend.txt` in this tutorial). Here's how you create an answer file:

1. Click on the General tab to view the general setup options (see Figure 14.2). The various tabs allow you to enter basic information, including the install directory, display settings, and user information.

2. The Network tab allows you to select the various adapters, protocols, and services you want to support. If you have a standard configuration, it's a good idea to specify the adapter (as shown in Figure 14.3). If your client hardware configurations vary, it's best to allow setup to manually find the first adapter. However, note that if the adapter is not one for which Windows NT has a driver, the installation prompts you for the drivers.

3. The Advanced section was created mainly for OEMs that want to specify their setup screens with banners, customer hardware abstraction layers (HALs), and vendor-specific drivers. Although you may not need to modify any of these options now, look through them to see which may be useful.

4. Click on File, Save to save all your settings to a text file. The name of this file is arbitrary, but the following examples refer to it as `unattend.txt`.

Choosing Information to Specify

During installation the user is required to enter any information not already specified in Setup Manager. In these steps, I note some important settings, but it's likely that modifications will be required to support specific hardware and software configurations.

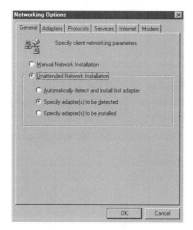

Figure 14.3   Specifying a network adapter in the network settings.

That's it! You've pre-answered many, if not all, of the questions asked by Windows NT Setup. Note that if you need to modify these settings in the future, Setup Manager allows you to reopen the text file by clicking on File, Open. The `unattend.txt` file that we created is shown in Listing 14.1.

Listing 14.1   **The *unattend.txt* File Generated by Setup Manager**

```
[Unattended]
OemPreinstall = yes
NoWaitAfterTextMode = 0
NoWaitAfterGUIMode = 0
FileSystem = LeaveAlone
ExtendOEMPartition = 0
ConfirmHardware = yes
NtUpgrade = no
Win31Upgrade = no
TargetPath = manual
OverwriteOemFilesOnUpgrade = no

[OEM_Ads]
Banner = "This is an example of an automated installation!"

[UserData]
FullName = "Anil Desai"
OrgName = "Sprint Paranet, Inc."
ComputerName = FROGGY
```

▶ For More
Information
1 Unfortunately, Setup Manager does not include its own documentation. However, Microsoft provides detailed information on the available options.

Using the *unattend.txt* File

Now that you've created the unattend.txt file, it's time to use it in an actual installation. To use this answer file, change to the installation share (on the network or on a CD-ROM) and type the following at a command line:

```
Winnt /b /s:\\server\ntws\i386 /u:c:\download\unattend.txt
```

In this syntax:

/b	Indicates a floppyless installation (all startup files are copied to a local drive).
/s	Tells the path to the source files (in this case, a universal naming convention [UNC] name is used because the data is coming from a remote server; you could just as easily specify a local path, such as c:\download). This location must also contain the unattend.txt file.
/u	Specifies that the installation should be unattended and gives the path to the unattend.txt file.
/e	Can be used to execute a batch file at the end of the GUI phase of setup (not used in this example).

▶ For More
Information
2, 3 Documentation for the options available for creating an unattended installation file is available from Microsoft.

Modifying the **unattend.txt** File

It is possible to edit the unattend.txt text file manually, but it is also very easy to enter an invalid response when doing so. Unless you know exactly what you're doing, it's recommended that you stick with the Setup Manager tool.

Running Windows NT Setup

WINNT32 is a 32-bit application you can use if you are installing from within another Windows NT Installation. The WINNT program is the 16-bit Windows NT installer and should be used in all other cases (i.e., installing from Windows 3.x or 95/98, or MS-DOS). To get a useful list of all the available command-line switches, use WINNT /? or WINNT32 /?.

Handling Machine-Specific Settings

One apparent limitation of the Setup Manager program is that it does not allow you to set system-specific information. For example, even though you are installing the same operating system on multiple machines, each computer has a different machine name, unique network address, and so on. Although you could create multiple answer files—one for each machine—this effort would hardly save any time. Fortunately, you can handle this information by using a uniqueness database file (UDF), which can be referenced by Windows NT Setup. Within this text file, you can specify the machine name and any other unique settings for the destination computer. This information is stored in a text file with a `.udb` extension. It includes a table of arbitrary machine ID's along with configuration information specific to each. Listing 14.2 shows the entire contents of a sample `.udb` file.

This file defines two arbitrary machine IDs: `Workstation1` and `Workstation2`. The parameters provided in the `.udb` file override any equivalent parameters in the `unnatend.txt` file and can be used to add, delete, and modify any answer file settings. In the file in Listing 14.2, if the `unattend.txt` file specifies that the `FullName` variable should be `Joe Admin` and the `.udb` file specifies the value `Jane Doe`, the effective user setting will be `Jane Doe`. To apply a `.udb` file to an installation, use the `/UDF` switch with Windows NT Setup. An example using the preceding file would be

```
Winnt /u:c:\download\unattend.txt /s:\\server\ntws\i386
➥/UDF:Workstation2,c:\download\unique.udb
```

For More
Information
1, 4 Although it is not included with the programs themselves, documentation for working with UDFs is available.

Listing 14.2 **The Contents of *unique.udb***

```
[UniqueIDs]
Workstation1 = Config, NetworkSettings
Workstation2 = Config, NetworkSettings

[Workstation1:Config]
FullName = "John Doe"
ComputerName = "Machine1"

[Workstation1:NetworkSettings]
JoinDomain = "Domain1"

[Workstation2:Config]
FullName="Jane Doe"
ComputerName = "Machine2"
```

Making Registry Changes

▶ For More
Information
5
The `Regini` program is a command-line utility included with the Windows NT 4.0 Resource Kit. It can be used to make specific modifications and add security settings to the Windows NT Registry. This is useful when you need to modify the installation of specific operating system features that are not available via the Setup Manager installation utility. A possible use for this feature would be to make a change to the default desktop settings for clients after setup is complete. Typing `Regini` at the command line shows the basic options for the utility. More complete documentation is available.

It's important to note that automating a setup routine that does not prompt for user input and performs without any hitches requires some degree of trial and error on the part of the administrator. Different hardware configurations can make handling heterogeneous clients quite a challenge.

Installing Applications with SysDiff

Thus far, we've discussed a way to install the Windows NT operating system. Now comes the pleasure of getting to install all the applications your users have come to rely on. What's the best way to do this?

Imagine that you could take a picture of your system as it appeared before and after installing applications. You could use this information to generate and record only the differences between the initial state and the final state of the system. Okay, let's take this one step further: Let's superimpose this difference snapshot on top of a plain, unmodified installation on multiple machines.

Yes, it can be done. The best news is that it requires only a free 65K utility and a little command-line work. The SysDiff program, included on the Windows NT CD-ROM, captures all the files installed or changed on the system, records all Registry additions and changes, and makes note of all other settings for applications and the operating system. SysDiff has no graphical interface, so you need to run the program from the command line. Let's go through the process.

Step 1: Create an Initial Snapshot

Complete the following steps to create a "before" snapshot of your system:

1. Start with an already completed Windows NT installation. This machine should be in as similar a state as possible to all the other clients that will be receiving applications. Remember that SysDiff records all the *changes* made to the current state of the operating system, so make sure you change any machine-specific settings to the defaults before moving to step 2.

On the CD-ROM

Demonstration 14.2, "SysDiff," shows the steps necessary to define the `sysdiff.inf` file and then take a system snapshot.

2. The `SysDiff.inf` file contains information about which directories you want SysDiff to scan. Edit this plain text file to include or exclude specific drives, directories, and Registry entries. Save the changes to the same file and be sure that it is located in the same directory as the `SysDiff.exe` file. The default file, shown in Listing 14.3, is well documented (lines beginning with a semicolon character are comments) and should be self-explanatory.

3. Take a preliminary snapshot of the system by typing

   `SysDiff /snap before.bin`

   SysDiff records all configuration information to the file you specified and presents the dialog box shown in Figure 14.4 when complete.

Listing 14.3 **The default *SysDiff.inf* file**

```
[Version]
Signature = "$Windows NT$"


[ExcludeDrives]
;
; The first character on each line is the drive letter
; of a drive to exclude.
;
;c
;d
;e


;
; General notes for file/dir exclusion sections:
;
; *: refers to all drives.
; ?: refers to the drive with the system on it.
; :: is substituted with %systemroot%
;
; Lines that are not in valid format (such as those that
; don't start with x:\) are ignored.
;


[ExcludeDirectoryTrees]
;
; Each line is a fully qualified path of a tree to
; be excluded. The directory and all of its subtrees
; are excluded.
;
*:\recycled
*:\recycler
```

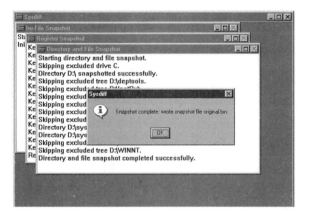

Figure 14.4   SysDiff has completed a snapshot.

The filename you assign is arbitrary. I chose the name `before` because the snapshot is taken before installing any applications and `.bin` because the file includes binary data. Depending on your environment, you might want to make this more specific. Something like `CleanNTInstall.bin` or `EngineeringWorkstation.bin` may be more appropriate. Be sure to use something that's easy for you to recognize.

Step 2: Generate a Difference File

Now it's time to have some fun. Let's make some changes to the operating system configuration. Because the purpose of this tutorial is just to show you what *can* be done, the choices are up to you—you can add, move, and delete files and change desktop and other user settings.

Excluding the Snapshot Directory

If you are storing the snapshot on the local drive, be sure to exclude this directory by modifying the `SysDiff.inf` file. Otherwise, SysDiff may try to save its own file as part of the configuration and cause an error. You can avoid this problem by saving files to a network share.

SysDiff and System Settings

If you change the network settings of a system, this information is automatically forced on all the clients on which you run the SysDiff /`apply` command (described later in this chapter). For example, if you change the IP address, all subsequent machines also change to the *same* IP address. Therefore, be sure you handle these cases before taking the initial snapshot of your system.

In my example, I've done the following:

- Added the Windows NT Logo bitmap to the default background and made the active screen saver 3D Flying Objects

- Installed all of the optional Windows NT Games (who could live without Minesweeper?)

  Changed my default Internet Explorer home page to `www.microsoft.com` and set the Windows Explorer window configurations to hide text labels and show the Address box on the same line as the toolbar

- Included the Windows NT Task Manager in my Startup group

- Installed Microsoft's TechNet and added a desktop shortcut (never leave home without it!)

- Uninstalled Microsoft's Outlook Express email client

- Created a User Data Source Name in the ODBC Administrator

After you've released as much creativity as your mouse allows, it's time to take another snapshot of the system. This time, however, you only want to record any changes between the initial state of the system and how it is set up now. To do this, type the following:

```
SysDiff /diff before.bin Difference.bin
```

The utility starts to compare all the Registry settings and files on the local hard drives with the information stored in the before SysDiff snapshot. Figure 14.5 shows the utility saving these changes. All files and information are stored in the `Difference.bin` file.

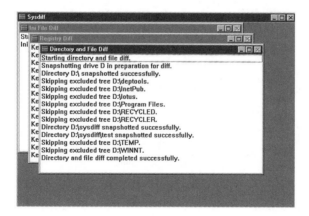

Figure 14.5 The SysDiff `/diff` command at work.

Step 3: Apply the Snapshot

Now that we've generated a file with the information we need, all that's left to do is apply it on another system. Copy the `SysDiff.exe` application locally on the destination machine and type:

```
SysDiff /m /apply \\server\share\Difference.bin
```

The /m specifies that the programs will be installed for the default user instead of for the user account that was logged on when the snapshot was created. In this example, I've chosen to pull the file over the network using a UNC pathname. This approach is extremely useful and convenient for rolling out different software updates to multiple machines, because you can store all files on a central distribution server. After applying the file, be sure to restart the machine, because some files and Registry settings are accessed only during the startup process.

SysDiff also has several other useful features. For example, you can use SysDiff to create a logfile that includes information generated by SysDiff while it gathers difference information. You can use the `/log:filename.txt` switch (in conjunction with `/difference`) to provide a human-readable file containing information on differences.

▷ For More
Information
6, 7
In order to create files that will automatically be applied at the end of Windows NT setup, you can dump the values of a snapshot to a text file via the `/dump` switch. In addition to its many benefits, there are limitations to SysDiff, specifically in its inability to install applications that add services to the system. The steps in this section give you an idea of what can be done using the SysDiff utility. You already have enough information to perform basic application installations, but troubleshooting tips are also available.

Combining SysDiff with Setup Manager

To further automate the setup process, you can choose to have the SysDiff snapshot file automatically run at the end of an unattended installation script. To do so, you need to create an `.inf` file by using the following command:

```
SysDiff.exe /inf c:\download\after.bin \\server\nt\i386
```

Leave SysDiff Alone!

SysDiff can be very picky about when and how you let it run on the system. If you switch tasks or even move the mouse at certain points during its execution, you may end up with a crashed program or a corrupt file. In short, stand back and keep your hands away from the machine while SysDiff is running.

SysDiff and File Locations

For this process to work, the names of the Windows NT directories must be the same for all machines. This includes the name of the directory to which Windows NT is installed and the names of any application directories that exist prior to running the command.

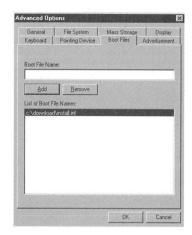

Figure 14.6   Specifying a boot file's value in Setup Manager.

or More
nformation

In this example, the destination file is called `after.inf` and is stored in the `\\server\nt\i386` directory. You have an image directory called `$OEM$`, containing all the files needed to install the applications. If Windows NT sees this directory within the installation share, it will automatically execute the necessary files. In Setup Manager, you need to add the path to this file in the Advanced, Boot Files option (see Figure 14.6).

To execute this setup, simply use the same command line as shown in the Setup Manager section earlier in the chapter:

```
Winnt /u:c:\path\unattend.txt /s:\\server\ntws\i386
```

More Automation Options

In addition to using the Setup Manager and SysDiff utilities, there are several other ways to deploy operating systems and applications to multiple users.

Creating Batch Files for Simple Tasks

Have you ever wished you could run a single command on every machine on your network without physically accessing them? Through the use of command-line utilities, you can send a batch file to your users in email to do exactly this. Tell them to simply double-click on a file, and the changes should be made without any user intervention.

For example, suppose XYZ Corp. wants to automatically copy the contents of a local spreadsheet to certain users on the network. The IT department is not sure which users need the file, and it is completely voluntary for users to download it. A simple solution is to create a batch file that connects a user to a network share, downloads a copy of the selected file, and creates a shortcut to the user's desktop. Listing 14.4 shows an example of such a batch file.

Listing 14.4 **The *spreadsheet-download.bat* file**

```
net use x: \\server1\common\spreadsheets
Copy x:\Spreadsheet.xls c:\download
Net use x: /delete
```

▶ For More
Information
9, 10

You can take this one step further by having Windows NT audit the installation share and record who has copied the spreadsheet. More examples and techniques of writing batch files and scripts are provided in Chapter 19, "Scripting."

Automating a Windows 95/98 Installation

▶ For More
Information
11

There are different—but just as useful—tools available for rolling out Windows 95/98 installations. The Windows 98 Resource Kit includes a utility called Batch 98 that OEMs and system administrators can use to pre-answer the important setup questions. (See Figure 14.7.) For information on this utility, see the Windows 98 Resource Kit documentation. The Windows 98 Batch program is similar in function to the Windows NT Setup Manager but also includes a useful command called Gather Now, which uses the system settings of the current Windows 98 installation as defaults.

Other Automated Installation Methods

There are several other options for automating system installations and rolling out software. In fact, many programs are dedicated to these important tasks. If you want to do more advanced application rollouts or wide-scale software distribution, the information in this section familiarizes you with various options.

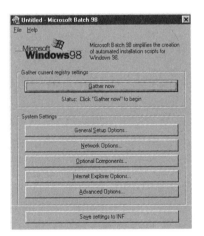

Figure 14.7   The Batch 98 application.

Application Package Installers

Programs such as Microsoft's Systems Management Server (SMS) can distribute application packages across the network to client machines. *Packages* are scripts that answer all the basic installation questions a program may ask. Distribution can be performed on demand or automatically at user login. Several companies have created applications that combine some of the most needed benefits for large environments. SMS is a good option for larger environments, but it involves the installation of software that is loaded when clients are started. Purchasing licenses for the package can also be a significant expense. Overall, SMS is a good solution if you plan to implement its other functions such as remote troubleshooting and automatic inventory of hardware and software.

Difference Detectors

For More
Information
12

Software packages have been designed to allow administrators to track the settings changes a specific application makes. These programs work much like the SysDiff application that we looked at earlier. However, they offer a more elegant user interface, more options for multiple snapshots, and better distribution capabilities. For more information on these products, see the Web sites of the various vendors.

Disk Duplicators

If you support complicated configurations with various partition types and multiple operating systems on a single machine, it might be worthwhile to consider making an exact duplicate of a working configuration. Disk duplicators do just what you might guess—they examine all information on a hard disk and copy every bit from one source to one or several destination drives. This information includes partition tables and heterogeneous partition types. Dedicated hardware devices perform this task quite quickly, but a potential drawback is that you must remove the hard drives from new or existing systems before performing the data transfer. Use a hardware method if you will be rolling out many desktops at a specific time.

For More
Information
13

Software-based disk duplicators (often called *imagers* or *bit-level copiers*) give the same result but use a different method. Basically, an image of an existing hard drive is taken and stored in a single, large file. This file is then used to partition, format, and write the information to one or many destination machines. Most systems provide a boot disk from which a system with a blank hard drive can be started. The disk loads minimal network drivers (usually based on Microsoft's MS-DOS) and attaches to the necessary server.

Disk Duplicator Considerations

All hardware-based and some software-based disk duplicators require the source and destination hard drives to be the same size and to have identical physical geometry (that is, number of heads, tracks, cylinders, and so on). When investigating a solution, be sure to keep your exact needs in mind.

Office 97 Network Installations

▶ For More Information 14

Suppose you have plenty of network bandwidth available, but your clients are running low on hard drive space. Also, like any efficient network administrator, you hate going to every computer each time you need to add a patch or install a new version of a program. An easy way to centralize applications administration is by allowing multiple users to access the same installation from a network share. How do you set this up? Well, to begin with, you need a copy of Microsoft Office 97.

There are several potential drawbacks to running applications off a server. First, the application must support storing individual user settings on a local system. Second, you are introducing a single point of failure for several users. That is, if this application server is not available (because of a server or network failure), many users may be unable to access required applications. Be sure to measure these potential problems when determining whether or not to run applications locally or from a server.

Automatic Application Upgrades

What could be better than an operating system or an application that can upgrade itself? New programs and the Windows 98 operating system itself offer such an option. Perhaps you're worried about having multiple users running various versions of an operating system. And you should be concerned: How can you maintain all users on the same version of an application when applications update themselves? Furthermore, how can you be sure that an upgrade does not introduce more problems than fixes? Both are very real concerns and affect the usability of these tools. However, it is always good to have the option to download updates without reloading an entire application or visiting workstations.

Windows NT Security and Disk Duplicators

Remember that modern operating systems install drivers and other operating system software based on the exact hardware configuration of machines. To ensure success with disk duplication methods, be sure that all systems have an identical configuration.

Also, there is an issue with duplicating systems running Windows NT. The problem lies in the fact that Windows NT expects unique security identifiers (SIDs) for each user and each machine on a network. These unique values are created upon installation of a Windows NT computer. If disks are duplicated, all machines will have the same values for these identifiers. Several vendors have solved this problem by using SID changing software. For more information, see the specific documentation that accompanies these utilities.

Licensing Issues for Network Application Installations

Be sure to check with your reseller and/or Microsoft about licensing options when you are running network-based applications. Some programs might require you to purchase licenses for each user, whereas others allow a certain number of "concurrent users." Remember that just because you have the software media doesn't mean you have the legal right to use a program. The Office 97 Resource Kit includes information on the Network Installation Wizard utility that can customize the setup options for these applications.

Case Study: Automating Installations Based on User Requirements

XYZ Corp. is planning an operating system and application rollout for three major groups of users. All client machines will run Windows NT Workstation but have different software requirements:

Job Function	Applications Required
Engineers	Microsoft Office 97, AutoCAD, and Microsoft Visual Studio
Administrators	Microsoft Office 97 only
Accountants	Microsoft Office 97 and mainframe access via a terminal emulator

Solution

To save time and ensure consistency in installations, the systems administrator creates an answer file and generic uniqueness database files for installing Windows NT Workstation using Setup Manager. She then uses SysDiff to generate an initial snapshot of this configuration. Because all users require Microsoft Office 97, it is installed on the system. Then, she chooses to make the corporate logo the default background, disables the screen saver, and makes the company's intranet the default browsing Web page. She also generates a difference file called `Basic.bin`. Although she could start over with a clean Windows NT installation at this point, it is better to make another snapshot of the system (remember that SysDiff only records changes to the current system). Next she adds AutoCAD and Microsoft Visual Studio and generates a second difference file called `Engineers.bin`. Because she has not made any other changes to the system, she chooses to take another snapshot on the same system. Finally, she adds and configures the mainframe terminal emulator and creates a difference file from this configuration (`Accounting.bin`). To deploy these applications, she applies the following difference files to these machines:

Intended Users	SysDiff File(s) Applied
Engineers	`Basic.bin` plus `Engineers.bin`
Administrators	`Basic.bin` only
Accountants	`Basic.bin` plus `Accounting.bin`

Finally, to further automate the process, she chooses to automatically apply these difference files at the end of the automated Windows NT Setup process.

The Bottom Line

There's a solution available for everyone who has ever asked, "Isn't there an easier way?" when faced with the task of manually rolling out multiple copies of programs or operating systems throughout their environment. The small amount of time it takes to properly automate these processes can pay for itself in just a few system installations. Most tools are freely available and are easy to use. As computing environments get larger and IT must support more users, automated system installations will become increasingly important. Using a combination of batch files, setup scripts, and other tools, you'll be able to automate one of the most mundane—yet essential—responsibilities of IT.

Let's not forget the bottom line—the TCO! By saving time and resources and ensuring consistency, you can be sure that automated installations will reduce the burden of installing new applications for your clients. You don't have to purchase expensive software to achieve these ends (although you do have that option if you can justify the cost). Instead, you can use simple utilities and a little ingenuity to optimize the operations of your environment. And, if that doesn't convince you, imagine never sitting in front of a machine clicking on OK 100 times!

For More Information

For more information on the topics mentioned in this chapter, see

1. Appendix A, "Answer Files and UDFs," Windows NT Workstation 4.0 Resource Kit

2. "Unattended Setup Parameters for Unattend.txt File," Q155197, Microsoft Knowledge Base

3. "Troubleshooting Cmdlines.txt during an Unattended Setup," Q177462, Microsoft Knowledge Base

4. "Using UDF Files with Windows NT 4.0 Unattended Setup," Q156876, Microsoft Knowledge Base

5. "How to use Regini.exe to modify HKEY_CURRENT_USER," Q142265, Microsoft Knowledge Base

6. "General SysDiff Troubleshooting Tips," Q165533, Microsoft Knowledge Base

7. "How to Troubleshoot the SysDiff Tool in Windows NT," Q157576, Microsoft Knowledge Base

8. "Using Sysdiff.exe with Unattended Setup and Windows NT 4.0," Q156795, Microsoft Knowledge Base

9. Chapter 7 of this book: "Security"

10. Chapter 19 of this book: "Scripting"

11. "'Deploying Windows 98 Using Batch98 and Infinst.exe' White Paper," Q169539, Microsoft Knowledge Base

12. Seagate Software's WinInstall product information: `www.seagatesoftware.com`

13. Symantec Software's Ghost product information: `www.ghost.com`

14. Chapter 6, "Customizing Client Installations," Microsoft Office 97 Resource Kit

Further Reading

For more information on performing automated installation in general, see

- Chapter 2, "Customizing Setup," Windows NT 4.0 Resource Kit

- "Automating Microsoft Windows NT Setup Deployment Guide," `www.microsoft.com/ntworkstation/info/Deployment-guide.htm`, Microsoft TechNet

- "Windows NT 4.0 FAQs: Deployment and Unattended Setup Questions," Microsoft TechNet

- "Microsoft Windows NT Workstation Deployment Guide—Automating Windows NT Setup," Microsoft TechNet

- *Windows NT Automated Deployment and Customization*, Macmillan Technical Publishing, Indianapolis, IN, 1998 (Richard Puckett)

15

Web-Based Technologies

Oₙₑ OF THE MOST POPULAR APPLICATIONS for network PCs is sending electronic messages. Email is an excellent way to communicate; instead of taking up someone's time when they are in the middle of something else, you can be sure that most people at least check their email at regular intervals. Apart from being unobtrusive, email is also very functional. It makes it easy to send carbon copies, forward messages, and communicate with large groups of people. Anyone who remembers interoffice memos and hard-copy messages on his or her desk every morning knows that the use of email is indeed a step forward. Even if they now receive more messages, information is much easier to deal with through electronic distribution lists and user-friendly software.

A major challenge IT organizations face is supporting heterogeneous clients while maintaining communications between all sets of users. For example, Macintosh clients may use specific email software that is very different from its Windows-based counter-parts. Even among Windows-based PCs, there may be fragmentation. Some desktops may be using cc:Mail or Lotus Notes, whereas others access Microsoft Exchange servers. If you add the requirements of calendaring and scheduling functionality, large organizations often find that a major migration to a single platform is the best way to go. There is, however, an attractive alternative that uses a common medium. Web-based communications have the potential of replacing tedious paper-based and fax-based procedures with much more efficient ones.

It's important to keep in mind the business considerations of implementing an intranet- or Internet-based solution. For example, development efforts are rarely worthwhile if they require many months of effort and yield solutions that would be applicable to only a few users. The end product is not the only design goal, either—the solution must be quick, easy, and simple to set up. It's also important to never consider the task "done." Instead, these applications must be maintained and updated as business needs change. If implemented properly, Web-based technologies can greatly reduce a company's total cost of ownership by increasing efficiency of information transfer, improving standardization, decreasing development time, and providing a better end-user experience. In this chapter, we look at the technologies that can be used as building blocks for a Web site. In Chapter 16, "Web Applications," we see some useful implementations of these ideas.

Web-Based Solutions

In the past several years, there has been much hype about the importance and true potential of the Web. At first, commercial Internet sites served as little more than kiosks, inviting Web users to call the company for more information. This technology quickly evolved to include the addition of much more useful information. New developments in Web standards made truly interactive applications a reality. Today, Web-based applications are often considered as replacements for traditional client/server programs. Figure 15.1 shows how a Web application can be used in a multitier application. The multiple tiers include the client interface, the Web server, and the data repository. In this section, we look at some of the benefits of Web-based solutions, as well as their drawbacks.

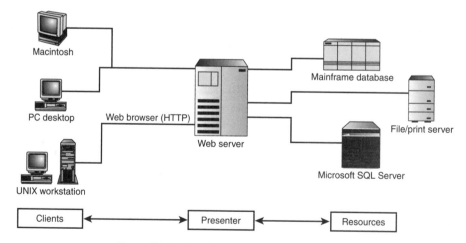

Figure 15.1   A Web-based multitier application.

Problems with Traditional Applications

Although they may not be perceived as such, many of the inefficiencies of business have to do with paperwork traffic and the difficulty of streamlining workflow. Common complaints are with processes for entering time-sheet information, expense reports, requesting services, benefits administration, and so on. The list of items that people view with the question, Isn't there a better way? is endless.

Of course, this information is useless if no one can access it. In fact, the value of the information is reduced if it is so difficult to use that people choose not to go through the trouble. For example, suppose your sales and marketing staff is supposed to check on inventory levels before placing an order, but the method for accessing this information is a cumbersome and often inaccurate client/server-based application. Furthermore, IT has problems with maintaining and updating program code, coordinating development efforts, rolling out new applications to clients, and training users. It is easy to see why users and IT alike would view this "tool" as more of a hindrance than help.

A traditional application is written in some programming language and then compiled separately for each supported client type. For example, if I write a program using the C++ language, I need to compile separate versions for Windows NT, UNIX, OS/2, and Macintosh clients. The actual code involves adapting to changes and limitations of separate operating system platforms. The program is then deployed to the various clients via some installation method. Although this definition is somewhat vague, it does cover a wide variety of programs. Figure 15.2 shows the cumbersome process of developing and maintaining code.

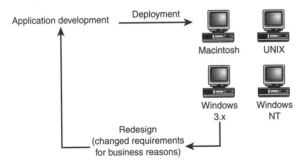

Figure 15.2 An overview of the traditional application development cycle.

There are several problems with developing applications in this manner:

■ *Long/inefficient development cycles*—When new applications are needed, programmers often start from scratch, developing their own components and database constructs—essentially, reinventing the wheel.

■ *Lack of consistency*—Each new application brings with it a different interface to learn. Programmers use their own documentation conventions, abbreviations, and keyboard shortcuts. All this leads to frustration for new users and increased training time.

■ *Monolithic code*—Often, when some part of an application has to be changed, the entire program must be recompiled for each client type and redeployed to all affected users. This makes the client applications less reactive to changes in business needs and adds significant time between development and widespread adoption.

■ *Inconvenient security implementations*—Older applications include their own security databases, and it is not uncommon for users to have to log in to many different programs at the start of each day. Maintaining these lists of users and passwords is very difficult when several programs are supported. Often, the problem is that users may require several separate applications—each with its own security information—to complete their business functions.

Advantages of the Web

What makes a good application? Clearly, metrics such as performance and ease of use can be used to measure the capability of a program. Software developers attest to the fact that a powerful yet usable user interface is also very important. Finally, applications must be easy to maintain and continue to evolve in response to changing business needs. It may not be the only solution, but Web-based information access can solve many of the problems associated with obtaining and managing information.

Among the major benefits of accessing data via a Web-based system are the following:

▶ For More
Information
1

■ *Usability*—The existence of an application can hardly be justified if its use is cumbersome and its results are inaccurate. Web-based client/server applications allow users to utilize a familiar program—the browser—while taking advantage of unique features of the application itself. Intranet pages take a very visual approach, and users are not forced to memorize a large number of custom keystrokes for accomplishing simple tasks. Figure 15.3 shows Microsoft's Expedia Web site, through which users can book airline tickets, make hotel reservations, and read about potential travel destinations.

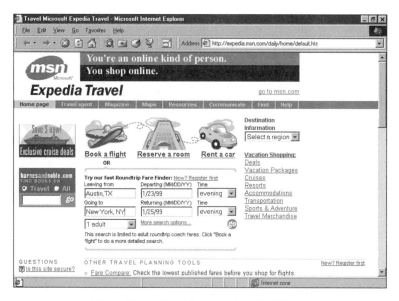

Figure 15.3 The Microsoft Expedia Web site.

- *Consistency*—Users can expect a consistent user interface presented through a Web browser for all applications. This will serve to decrease end-user–training time and allows developers to work within a well-developed framework. Of course, to make this happen, developers must cooperate and agree on standards.

- *Increased responsiveness*—Companies can quickly and easily deploy information continually, instead of through traditional "point releases" accompanied by a scheduled deployment. As with any development effort, programmers must coordinate with others and test their code before releasing the solution to users. With effective content management, Web-based interfaces can respond and evolve much more quickly than traditional compiled programs.

- *Multitier performance*—The true information processing of Web-based applications can be performed by server-side code. If information is required from several different sources, a middle transaction-processing layer can be added for coalescing the data and presenting it to the Web server. The database queries and information access techniques can be modified independently of the client front end. Various configurations of load sharing between servers and clients can be tested. This not only allows developers to easily experiment with performance parameters in a production environment but also provides much quicker turnaround times on performance tuning of the code.

- *Flexibility*—Web-based code is highly portable because static information such as SQL queries, pathnames, and resource names are not hard-coded. That is, they can be easily changed on the back-end database without rewriting the client software. Furthermore, these benefits are available instantly for all client types because there is no need to recompile and redeploy an application when these changes are made. Because the client front end is independent of the back-end database processes, performance can be easily optimized based on real-world usage data.

- *Modular components*—When new functionality is required for an application, there is no need to redesign, recompile, and redistribute the application. Instead, new or modified Web pages can be added to the existing intranet site with minimal impact to the existing functionality. It is similarly easy for other applications to borrow code to reduce development time and cost.

- *Efficiency*—For the purpose of inter-employee communications, Web-based publishing has become, in many cases, just as simple as sending email messages to a large group. Furthermore, it helps ensure that information is stored only in one place and is always available for reference. A prime use of this technology would be when specific groups provide status information on their projects for the peers who can easily find their progress if needed.

- *Accessibility*—Remote users and network users alike are able to access Web-based information. Web-based applications are often designed to conserve bandwidth and reduce the amount of data transferred between the client and the server. Users who use applications on many different types of client platforms will get a similar end-user experience.

Intranet-Unfriendly Situations

Even the most dedicated Web developers admit that Web applications, in their current state, cannot address all application issues. There are currently several limitations to Web-based application front ends. Many of these are due to the need for security. For example, Java programs run from within a Web browser (described later in this chapter) can operate only in their own restricted virtual machine. That is, certain functions, such as reading or writing from a user's hard disk, are not possible. Programs that require large amounts of local processing are also not appropriate for use as intranet apps. For example, a tool that reads data stored on a user's hard drive and generates a report based on this data would perform best as a traditionally compiled program. Similarly, design tools and larger programs that use many customized screens are easier to work with as executable code. Finally, the current performance of Web servers may not be adequate to handle large numbers of users. This problem will be addressed with faster hardware and software that can scale much more easily. For now, however, measuring load capacity for Web applications should be an integral part of any testing process. Overall, the main benefits of traditional, compiled applications include optimized client-side performance and greater flexibility in interface design. However, in the future, look for more and more applications to support Web-based functionality.

Focusing on Content

When the Web made its entry as a vital part of a business's presence, developing HTML pages was reserved for those who called themselves Webmasters. Nowadays, even the worst Web page creation tools are better than old word processors. The goal of developing an intranet or Internet site is to choose a solution that will be easy to maintain. The overall goal is to focus on content and not on the technology required. Programs like FrontPage 98 (described later in this chapter) have automated tedious and complex tasks, such as maintaining navigation bars in large sites and giving a consistent appearance to all pages (see Figure 15.4).

Figure 15.4   Choosing a theme in FrontPage 98.

Web-Based Publishing Tools

Due to the rise in popularity of Web-based solutions, several tools and technologies have been made available for filling in gaps between client/server applications and otherwise static HTML pages. In this section, we take an overview of Web-publishing technologies.

HTML Editors

▶ For More
Information
2, 3, 4

Static Web pages are developed to be unchanging documents. They are written in Hypertext Markup Language (HTML), which includes basic formatting commands in a text file. This information is sent to a client upon request via Hypertext Transfer Protocol (HTTP). Client Web browsers interpret these files into a graphical display, including formatting and pictures. Although HTML files can easily be created in any text editor, many HTML development tools are currently available. Several of these applications are intended for novice end users and have intuitive user interfaces that work like basic word processors. Good examples in this category are Microsoft's FrontPage 98, HotDog Professional from Sausage Software, Inc., and Allaire's HomeSite.

Dynamic Web Page Editors

▶ For More
Information
5, 6

Although static HTML pages are sufficient for posting information that does not often change, many business applications require much more power and flexibility. One solution to this demand is the use of dynamic Web page technology. Several techniques are currently available to aid in the creation of attractive and useful Web pages (described in detail later). Popular programs for creating and editing dynamic Web pages include Microsoft's Visual InterDev and Net Objects Fusion.

Web Browsers

▶ For More
Information
7, 8

On the client side, the overwhelming majority of client computers use either Netscape Navigator or Microsoft's Internet Explorer 3.x or higher (see Figure 15.5). Both browsers are now available for free from their respective companies. Both support Java, HTML 3.2, and Web page-caching technology. Both browsers are available as standalone products or as part of a suite of applications, including email and newsgroup clients. For many users, however, the choice of whether to use Microsoft or Netscape products is based on the user interface.

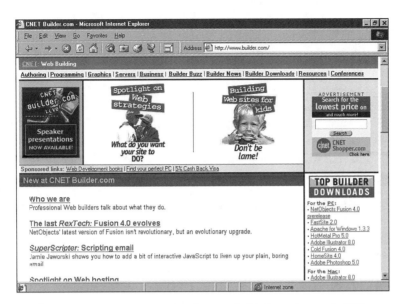

Figure 15.5 Using Internet Explorer to find information on the Web.

Scripting

Scripting languages create programs that execute on a Web server or on a client machine. They allow for performing calculations and providing unique dynamic content to end users. These pieces of code can be embedded in HTML and are executed upon request on either the client or the server. There are currently several popular types of scripts, including

- *Common Gateway Interface (CGI)*—Although it is an older standard, CGI scripts can be written in a variety of programming languages. Most commonly, scripts are based on the Perl language, but authors can also use C, C++, Visual Basic, and other languages. Almost all Web server types support these applications, but they do not allow for easily coding many multimedia and advanced programming functions.

- *JScript/JavaScript*—Java was originally designed by Sun Microsystems to be a multiplatform, client-independent language. High-level code is written, and the instructions are compiled by the client at the time of use. Java has evolved since its introduction and is now supported by all current major Web browsers in an implementation developed by Netscape called JavaScript. JavaScript code is compiled by developers before deployment. The code is then downloaded and interpreted by client Web browsers. The Java Virtual Machine is a runtime compiler that executes the compiled instructions in a limited environment. Java is best used for simple programs and animations on otherwise static Web pages or for data-dependent Web objects. For example, a working clock or an animated logo

For More Information 9

may be implemented via Java. Somewhat more complex applications such as a database front end can also be designed. Microsoft has dubbed its implementation JScript. Developers should be aware that Java support from various companies' products may differ. For example, Microsoft's implementation of the language includes some functionality not specific in the original specification of the language. Currently, major criticisms of this language have to do with the limited capabilities of the code, poor performance, and questions regarding it as an open standard.

▷ For More
Information
10, 11

■ *Visual Basic, Scripting Edition (VBScript)*—Microsoft's VBScript is based on the popular Visual Basic programming language. Visual Basic is an easy language for nonprogrammers to learn but is still powerful enough to handle complex code. VBScript allows for the use of a subset of functions that are limited for the purpose of security. For example, VBScript applications do not allow file I/O operations on a client computer and cannot call external functions from within the code. Although these restrictions limit VBScript's power, it can be used to quickly develop multimedia and database-access applications. Another current drawback is that VBScript is currently supported only on Microsoft's Internet Explorer Web browser and using the Windows Scripting Host application. VBScript is well-suited for Web development because it is an event-driven language. That is, code is written to respond to user events such as the clicking of a button or the dragging of an icon. For example, a simple script might animate an icon when a user double-clicks or hovers the mouse over it (see Figure 15.6). A wealth of information for new and experienced programmers is available on the Web.

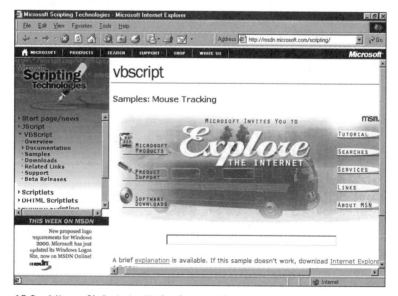

Figure 15.6 Microsoft's Scripting Technologies Web site provides real-world code examples.

ActiveX

For More
Information
12

Microsoft created ActiveX to facilitate the sharing of program code between applications and platforms. ActiveX controls can be used to easily create objects containing events and logic. Currently a major drawback of ActiveX components is that only Microsoft's Internet Explorer browser supports them by default. Netscape Navigator and Communicator packages may use third-party ActiveX plug-ins to add this functionality, however. ActiveX components may be developed based on Microsoft's popular Visual Basic or Visual C++ programming languages. For example, using Visual Basic's wide array of controls, attractive and functional front-end interfaces can be created with minimal effort. Developers more familiar with these languages can also use other popular third-party programs such as Delphi and Visual J++. ActiveX controls allow complex functions to run in precompiled code that is executed at the client side. This can improve performance and give Web developers more functionality than is available in standard Web browsers.

Data Access Using ODBC, OLEDB, and ADO

A fundamental aspect of working with many Web-based applications is obtaining access to data. The goal is to make obtaining information from many different database sources easier for programmers. To make this happen, you first need to wade through some alphabet soup!

Open database connectivity (ODBC) was created to be a universal interface between SQL-compatible databases and application code. An application that executes a Structured Query Language (SQL) query written for Microsoft's SQL Server should work unmodified against an Oracle database (as long as both the driver and the database support the requested functions).

Object linking and embedding for databases (OLEDB) is a newer and more powerful standard based on the Component Object Model (COM; described later in this chapter). OLE itself has been largely replaced by the ActiveX standard for sharing code and functionality between applications. However, many applications still use OLEDB for their database access functions. OLEDB allows developers of data management software to create logically organized connections to data that other programmers can use for accessing their program code. In addition to supporting ODBC-compliant data sources, OLEDB can access data from mainframes and other custom repositories. Data service providers use standards to make information available from within their repositories. A typical data service provider may intertwine information from a human resources database and combine it with sales performance information. Data consumers (usually applications) can then take advantage of this information easily without regard to the source of the data, its storage format, or its location.

For More
Information
13

Finally, ActiveX Data Objects (ADO) provides a single unified interface for working with any type of data source. From within an application, the programmer must only use simple commands to open a data connection and request information. Figure 15.7 shows the relationships among ODBC, OLEDB, and ADO. Variations and additions to the ADO specification include ActiveX Data Objects Multi-Dimensional (ADO-MD) for complex data analysis and Remote Data Services (RDS) for working with distributed information systems.

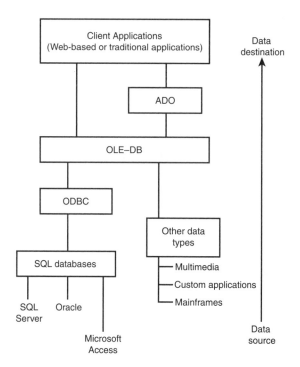

Figure 15.7 The relationships among data access technologies.

Dynamic HTML

Dynamic HTML (DHTML) is a World Wide Web Consortium (W3C)-approved specification that includes new functionality not previously available in HTML. In addition to supporting the HTML 3.2 specification for static pages, DHTML documents can contain absolute positioning information (in three dimensions). It also supports cascading style sheets (CSS)—a technology that allows Web developers to create a single template file for defining color and appearance information. If a change in the look of an entire site is desired, the developer must make the change only in a single CSS document. Uses of DHTML scripting would be to create menu bars, command buttons, and program code for applications that work through the Web browser interface. Microsoft's Visual Basic 6.0 development environment supports the creation of DHTML code. In fact, you can create a basic Web-based calculator in less than 10 lines of code!

▶ For More
Information
11, 14

There are currently some issues involved with differing support for DHTML in the most common browser types (from Netscape and Microsoft). For this reason, it is recommended that any developed pages be thoroughly tested on both platforms. More information is available from these companies' Web sites. DHTML also supports JavaScript and the Document Object Model (DOM) for hierarchical Web page organization.

Active Server Pages

Active Server Pages (ASP) are a set of standard HTML documents that contain special code. Tags specify to the server that some code interpretation must be done before the page is sent to the client. The code itself may be written in either JScript or VBScript. The major benefit of this method is that all clients receive only pure HTML documents, thus ensuring compatibility across multiple different platforms. For example, a simple ASP document might have a section that automatically looks up a value in a database (by executing a SQL query on a database) and displays this value to the user every time the page is requested. A simple example is the following ASP code inserted within the body of an HTML file:

```
<%
For I = 1 to 10
Response.Write I & "<hr>"
Next
%>
```

This VBScript fragment embedded in a Web page results in the screen shown in Figure 15.8 when viewed from a Web browser. The code creates a simple loop and increments the variable *I* 10 times. Each time, the `Response.Write` action sends the value of the variable followed by a horizontal line character. If the client views the source file, he or she sees only the following string:

```
1<hr>2<hr>3<hr>4<hr>5<hr>6<hr>7<hr>8<hr>9<hr>10<hr>.
```

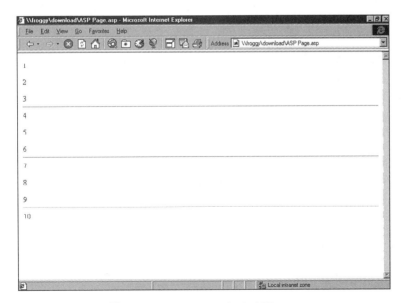

Figure 15.8 Viewing a basic ASP page.

ASP works on any server that has the active server extensions installed. The extensions are responsible for executing all the server-side instructions in the document before it is sent to the client. By default, Microsoft's Internet Information Server installs this code. For other platforms, such as UNIX-based or Netscape Web servers, the extensions are available from Microsoft.

► For More
Information
15, 16
The actual process begins with the reading of the ASP page by the Web server. The Web server interprets the special ASP tags, and the page is converted to plain HTML content. This information is then sent to the client, who receives only a basic HTML document. This method is useful in many ways because it hides the application logic from the client. The drawback to ASP is that it can incur a significant performance penalty if many concurrent requests are being made.

The Component Object Model

► For More
Information
17
With the overwhelming popularity of object-oriented design in programming languages, new methods have been developed for programmers to share code across applications. COM is a specification that allows programming "objects" to expose their functionality to other programs. For example, if a COM spell checker is in use in one application, another program can use these instructions. COM is one of the most widely supported standards in the industry and is compatible with thousands of existing applications. The Distributed Component Object Model (DCOM) is designed to be used on networks and the Internet. It allows for applications to share program code on remote machines and distribute processing requirements. Both technologies will be increasingly useful as large corporations start to adopt universal directory services.

Building a Windows NT Web Platform

Windows NT servers offer several tools that can be used to quickly and easily implement a functional Web site solution. Some of these products include

► For More
Information
18
- *Internet Information Server (IIS) 4.0*—Available free as part of the Windows NT 4.0 Option Pack (see Appendix A, "Windows Updates"), IIS 4.0 is a powerful and full-featured Web server that supports many of the newest server-side scripting technologies. A version of IIS, called Personal Web Server, can be run on Windows NT Workstation and Windows 95/98 computers.

► For More
Information
5
- *Microsoft Visual InterDev 6.0*—Included separately and as part of Visual Studio 6.0, Visual InterDev is a powerful tool designed to allow Web developers to create and manage complex Web sites. It allows for the simple creation of Active Server Pages (described earlier in this chapter), including database connections and dynamic navigation bars. It also includes several tools for the management of large Web sites.

► For More
Information
2
- *Microsoft FrontPage 98*—Targeted toward end users and novice Web developers, FrontPage 98 offers several of the same features as Visual InterDev. It allows users to focus on content by automatically managing Web styles and navigation bars. Figure 15.9 shows FrontPage 98's theme browser.

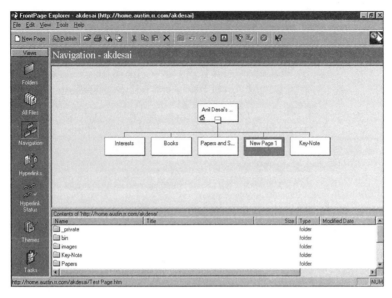

Figure 15.9 Viewing site navigation information in FrontPage 98.

- *Databases tools*—The creation of Web-based applications often requires some repository for storing data. In many cases, simpler tools such as Microsoft Access 97 will be sufficient. For larger solutions, where supporting many concurrent users is a possibility, relational database management systems such as Microsoft SQL Server and Oracle platforms will be more appropriate.

▶ For More Information 19

- *Web browsers*—In order to view the applications created on an intranet or Internet site, clients require Web browsers. There is still much controversy over the two leading Web browsers: Microsoft Internet Explorer and Netscape Navigator. Both products are available free and support standard HTML. They differ, however, in advanced features. As of this writing, Internet Explorer supports more new technologies than does its competitors. However, the overall decision of which browser to use is usually based on user preference.

If you're new to developing Web-based content, it might be difficult to see why so many pieces are required to complete the puzzle. Figure 15.10 shows the purpose of Web servers, development tools, and databases. We see how all of these tools fit together in Chapter 16, "Web Applications."

On the CD-ROM

Demonstration 15.1, "FrontPage 98," walks you through some of the most powerful and useful features of the program. Included are steps to create and maintain navigation bars and to apply themes for consistent Web site design.

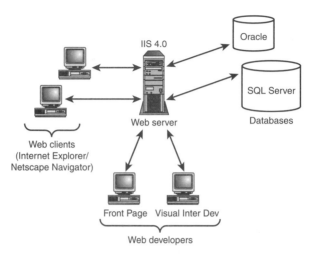

Figure 15.10   A Windows NT Web platform.

Web-Based Security

As is the case with most business applications, security is a major concern. In the past, proprietary applications used their own security databases. It wasn't uncommon for a user to start the day by spending several minutes entering passwords for each system he or she intended to use. More modern database applications allow for pass-through security (that is, using the same security identifiers as the network operating system). Depending on the type of security desired, Web-based connections can be encrypted and users can be forced to authenticate securely over the Web before accessing sensitive information. For example, on Microsoft's Internet Information Server, the following sequence of events occurs when a user attempts to access a Web page:

- The file and network permissions on the data are checked: If anonymous access is allowed, the user is given the data. If it is not, the user will be required to provide authentication information.

- If the client is a 32-bit Windows-based machine and the user has already authenticated, IIS tries to use this information. That is, information about a user logged in to a Windows NT computer is automatically sent securely to the Web server. If this user does not have permissions to access the data, more information will be required.

▷ For More
Information
20

- The user is prompted with a dialog box that asks for a username and password that is valid for accessing this information.

Other Web-Enabling Technologies

For More
Information
21, 22

Several extremely popular and free Web-based email services are available. These Web sites use technology that, much like Outlook Web Access, offer an HTML interface for sending and receiving email. Examples include the Hotmail service (www.hotmail.com) and Yahoo email (mail.yahoo.com). The sites are supported by advertisement-based revenue. Users have the benefit of using a single email account. Corporations may reach the same end by combining Web-based messaging and a virtual private network.

Voice Over IP

Voice over IP is based on the idea of carrying voice-based telephone traffic over less expensive IP connections. Entire buildings may be able to use the bandwidth provided by a single Internet connection to transfer voice data all over the world. Similar in idea to virtual private networks (covered in Chapter 13, "Virtual Private Networking"), this technology can help reduce data transport costs and provide location-independent access to communications. Additionally, it can help ease the administration of tele-communications and networking functionality by integrating both. Of course, several challenges—such as reliability and guaranteed service levels—stand in the way of broad-scale voice over IP integration. However, it is clear that this technology will become the voice-based communications networks of the future.

Videoconferencing

The traditional way of getting people together is to schedule meetings. However, these meetings usually require people to be in the same place at the same time—a task that is both costly and difficult for distributed corporations and busy individuals. It also requires the availability of resources such as meeting rooms, whiteboards, and laptop projectors. A much better way of handling meetings is via computer applications that send video and audio among multiple users. Major challenges to this technology include working within low-bandwidth situations and adequate hardware to compress the audio and video adequately. Developments such as dedicated compression chips and the availability of ever-increasing bandwidth will make videoconferencing a very real alternative in the future. Additionally, the H.323 protocol standard aims to provide compatibility between different platforms and applications. Currently, popular software clients include White Pines Software's CU-SeeMe (www.wpine.com) and Intel's Business Video Conferencing solutions (www.intel.com/proshare/conferencing/index.htm).

IP Multicasting

One problem with traditional audio- and video-on-demand applications is that a single session must be set up for each user who will be viewing the information. For example, if 100 users request a Web page, that same page is sent over the network 100 times. This type of transmission is referred to as *unicast* because each packet sent is intended for only one recipient. Multicast technologies, however, send information that can be received by many different clients. Real-world examples include television and radio—all possible channels are always being sent over the air, and the recipient only needs to choose which signals to tune in to. Figure 15.11 shows the difference in network bandwidth used in unicast versus multicast situations. In both examples, 10 clients are requesting a video clip that requires a sustained bandwidth of 40KBps. Using unicast communications, the total data transfer rate is 400KBps. Multicast communications, on the other hand, use only 1/10 of this data throughput. Many Internet applications such as RealPlayer (www.real.com) and Web sites such as Live Concerts (www.liveconcerts.com) use this technology to stream content to users.

Push Technology

▷ For More
Information
7, 8, 23
The idea of push technology is to automatically send Web pages and other content to a client at regular intervals. For example, a client may choose to have her browser automatically updated with stock prices several times during the day. Another client may want to be notified of changes to specific corporate information. Several commercial software applications support push technology. Perhaps the most popular is the PointCast client software (see Figure 15.12). PointCast provides newsfeeds that are updated many times during the day without direct cost to the user. Commercial content is available free and is supported by an advertisement-based model. Although the client software is free for personal use, businesses need to license the PointCast I-Server to generate their own newsfeeds. Current browsers from Microsoft and Netscape also support push content. Microsoft's Internet Explorer 4.0 supports Active Channels, a subscription-based service. When a user subscribes to a channel, she may automatically have the browser download the updates and can optionally be notified of updates. Netscape's Netcaster works in a similar way.

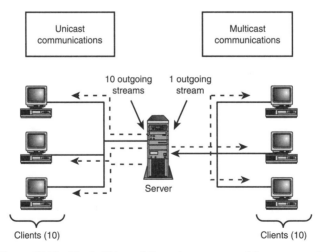

Figure 15.11   Bandwidth used for unicast versus multicast communications.

Figure 15.12   Viewing news using the PointCast Network client software.

Content Management

In an actively used Web-based environment, it is critically important to make sure that all Web developers are working on current code. There must also be a process in place for modifying existing content. (Visual InterDev and Visual SourceSafe are products released by Microsoft that fill this need.)

For More
Information
24
When multiple developers are working on the same pieces of code, it is often difficult to keep track of various revisions. Visual SourceSafe is designed to ease some of these problems. When developers want to edit code, they simply "check out" that piece of the program. They are then free to modify it. While one developer is using the code, others may only open the files for viewing. When finished making the modifications, the developer can return the updated code. It is now available in a central location for all team members to view. Visual SourceSafe also provides for version tracking and gives others the ability to add comments to code. The program is compatible with all current Microsoft development products.

Microsoft Transaction Server

For More
Information
25
Microsoft Transaction Server (MTS) has been developed to ease the development of some of the most complicated portions of Web application development. Namely, connection pooling, transaction processing, and state management are items that are handled by this software. *Transaction processing* ensures that all data changes and modifications required for a specific operation are carried out before the change is committed. For example, I would not want to update a customer's shipping address without

making necessary changes to her billing address (which might be stored in another database). MTS ensures that either both transactions occur or that they are both rolled back. *Connection polling* occurs when multiple users request access to the same data. Traditionally, several independent database connections—each using system resources—were required. MTS allows on-demand use of a fixed set of connections. Finally, *state management* refers to the maintenance of user identification as a client moves between Web pages. This functionality can be implemented in Web-based applications, but MTS can be used to maintain the state of users as they request data-dependent content. The major advantage of MTS is that it saves time and performance tuning in code development by allowing the author to compose pages that seem to be written for a single user. MTS handles all the operations required to make the page available to many users at once.

Microsoft Message Queue Server

▶ For More
Information
26

Microsoft Message Queue Server (MSMQ) is designed for easily replicating data between applications in remote sites over slow or nonpersistent connections. It allows for a storage mechanism for applications to queue information. This data is then sent periodically to other sites or to a central repository at a predetermined interval. MSMQ is very useful for large, distributed networks or for organizations that have many small remote offices and do not otherwise require expensive, full-time WAN connections.

Case Study: Making Information Access Easier

Currently, many users at XYZ Corp. log in to three different database front-end applications every morning. One stores customer billing information, another contains current inventory levels, and the third includes an order history for customers. Clients may be running on a variety of platforms including UNIX, Windows NT, and Macintosh. The information available is very useful to employees, but certain functions—such as finding customer billing information and order history at the same time—are very difficult. Also, there is no easy way for users to report on data from these three different sources. A systems administrator is asked to develop a solution for combining results from these data sources while maintaining ease of use.

Solution

The systems administrator has basic programming skills and some database experience. He decides to create a simple solution for all the platform types, using their Web browsers as a common interface. First, he creates ODBC connections for each data source. Then, he uses Microsoft's Visual InterDev to graphically add certain data fields from the various sources on an ASP Web page. By using these tools, he is able to focus on the actual processing and manipulation of information within the program logic.

Next, he implements password-based security to support any client type. The passwords are stored in a Microsoft Access database, and the application automatically queries users for this information the first time a user accesses the Web-based application. Finally, the systems administrator copies the ASP pages to a Windows NT Server running IIS 4.0. After thoroughly testing the code and functionality, he tests the applications with several volunteers who are eager to use the system.

When he feels that the code meets the functional environments, he allows more volunteers to use it and provide feedback. To train them on the new Web-based application, he creates a brief multimedia tutorial and makes it available via the application's help page.

The major benefits of the solution are that is was relatively easy to create and deploy. For example, the application was written in high-level Visual Basic code and did not have to be rewritten to support various platforms. As business needs change, the systems administrator can easily modify existing code and update the Web pages with minimal impact to users.

The Bottom Line

In this chapter, we've taken a brief look at many Web-based technologies that you can use to provide easier access to your information. Data access technologies, Web-publishing tools, and integrated Web server platforms work together to provide a unified platform for publishing data. This platform can provide an excellent vehicle for focusing on content instead of technology. Many companies fall into the mindset of collecting and storing all possible information but fall short of making it easily available. After all, few things are more important to a company than its information. Making accessibility a priority is the best way to realize potential benefits. This attitude can work toward reducing your total cost of ownership and maximizing your IT-related investments.

Now that you have an idea of the basics of current Web-based development, move on to Chapter 16 to put them to use!

For More Information

1. The Microsoft Expedia Web site: www.expedia.msn.com
2. Microsoft FrontPage home page www.microsoft.com/frontpage
3. Sausage Software's Hot Dog Web site: www.sausage.com/hotdog5/
4. Allaire's HomeSite home page: www.allaire.com/products/homesite/
5. Microsoft Visual InterDev home page: www.microsoft.com/vinterdev
6. NetObjects, Inc. home page: www.netobjects.com
7. Netscape home page: www.netscape.com
8. Microsoft Internet Explorer home page: www.microsoft.com/ie

9. Sun Microsystems Java home page: `www.sun.com/java`

10. Chapter 19 of this book: "Scripting"

11. Microsoft Scripting Technologies home page: `msdn.microsoft.com/scripting`

12. ChiliSoft home page: `www.chilisoft.com`

13. Microsoft Universal Data Access home page: `www.microsoft.com/data/`

14. SiteBuilder Network DHTML Workshop:
    `www.microsoft.com/workshop/author/default.asp`

15. Appendix B, "ASP Standards," Microsoft Internet Information Server
    Resource Kit

16. "Microsoft Active Server Pages Overview," Microsoft TechNet

17. Microsoft COM Technologies Web site: `www.microsoft.com/com/`

18. Microsoft Web Server home page: `www.microsoft.com/iis`

19. CNet browser reviews: `www.cnet.com`

20. Chapter 8, "Security," Microsoft Internet Information Server Resource Kit

21. Chapter 13 of this book: "Virtual Private Networking"

22. Hotmail Web site: `www.hotmail.com`

23. PointCast Network Web site: `www.pointcast.com`

24. Microsoft Visual Studio Web site: `www.microsoft.com/vstudio`

25. "INFO: Example: Simple DCOM VB Client Talking to an MTS Component,"
    Q191766, Microsoft Knowledge Base

26. "INFO: MSMQ and MTS Design Programming Considerations," Q176307,
    Microsoft Knowledge Base

Further Reading

For more information on Web-based technologies in general, see

- Microsoft's SiteBuilder Network: `www.microsoft.com/sitebuilder`
- CNet's Builder Web site: `www.builder.com`
- Microsoft Developer Network Online: `msdn.microsoft.com`

16

Web Applications

THE PURPOSE OF INFORMATION TECHNOLOGY is to manage data and make it easily available. Most useful data is stored in some organized format. On networks we use databases and file servers to share information. The technology used may be Microsoft Office applications, Microsoft SQL Server, Oracle, Sybase, Informix, or a number of other database platforms. But that's only part of the solution. This information would be worthless if those who need it couldn't easily access it.

In this chapter, we look at several ways to improve accessibility by making information available via a Web interface—either through your corporate intranet or on the public Internet. We also see just how easy it is to create a basic Web-based application (minimal programming required)! Finally, I point you in the right direction for finding information on creating more complex and sophisticated Web-based applications. The goal of this chapter is not to make you a programmer or a master of Web development. I hope only to help you get your feet wet in an extremely useful and exciting technology. If you're a complete stranger to HTML, you may find a few of the references to be a little over your head. Don't worry, though—you'll still get useful ideas of what can be done and links to resources you can use to learn how to do them. Be sure to check out the references in "For More Information" to get up to speed on anything you don't understand. Also, I recommend that you read through

Chapter 15, "Web-Based Technologies," before tackling the material in this chapter to gain an understanding of basic Web development standards and techniques. After you've done that, get ready to learn how to apply what you've learned!

Outlook Web Access

▷ For More
Information
1, 2, 3

Outlook Web Access (OWA) is a Web-based interface for Microsoft Exchange Server. With it, any Web-enabled client can access his or her email without installing any client software. OWA is based on Microsoft's Active Server Pages (ASP) technology. The information in this chapter focuses on Exchange Server 5.5, although earlier versions do still have some of this functionality. OWA can be installed as part of the Exchange Server installation process. All it requires is IIS 4.0 (available as part of the NT Option Pack) and network access to Exchange Server. Although it is possible for OWA and Exchange Server to run on different machines, this chapter assumes that both are on the same machine for the sake of simplicity. Figure 16.1 shows the relationship between a Web client, a Web server, and Exchange Server.

Installing and Configuring OWA

When you are installing Exchange Server 5.5, you have the opportunity to also install the OWA component. If you choose this option, the setup program automatically copies all necessary files and code to the Web server you specify.

The default OWA setup should be sufficient for most users. The Web pages are based on Microsoft's ASP technology (introduced in Chapter 15). ASPs use server-side scripting to dynamically generate standard HTML pages based on application logic. The actual data may be based on information stored anywhere on the network. In the case of OWA, the source of the information is Exchange Server.

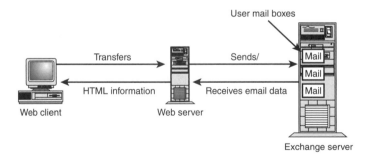

Figure 16.1   Outlook Web Access integrates the Web with Exchange Server.

On the CD-ROM

Demonstration 16.1, "Outlook Web Access," walks you through logging into the OWA system, using a Web browser. Included are common operations such as viewing messages, sending messages, and working with a calendar.

For More
Information
5 To configure OWA, you need to access the Internet Service Manager. From this
tool, you can modify directory and file permissions for the appropriate directories and
even modify the various files that make up the OWA application. The default permissions for this Web site are appropriate for most environments, but restricting access by
IP address can provide more granular security to select users or groups of users.

Client Setup

The main benefit of using OWA is that there is no client setup at all. That is, no code
needs to be installed on client machines. By default, a user can access OWA by point-
ing his or her Web browser to `http://servername/exchange`. From this main page
(shown in Figure 16.2), users can log in to Exchange Server from the Web. They can
then view and send email and access their calendar and schedule information.

The only browser requirement for using OWA is the ability to run Java scripts.
Netscape Navigator 4.0 or later and Microsoft Internet Explorer 4.0 or later browsers
support these technologies. In Figure 16.3, an administrator is viewing a message that
requests an email account to be created. From this screen, the administrator can view,
reply to, and forward email messages through the Web browser.

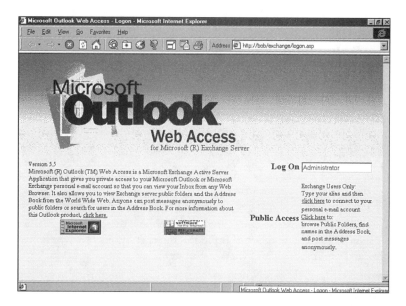

Figure 16.2   Logging in to Exchange Server using a Web browser and OWA.

For More
Information
4 **Outlook Web Access Licensing**

To use OWA, you must obtain sufficient licenses for each client with an actual mailbox on your
Exchange Server. For more information on licensing, see the program documentation.

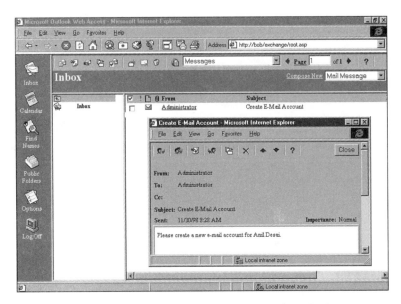

Figure 16.3 Viewing Exchange Server email via OWA.

Outlook Web Access Applications

Microsoft Exchange Server and OWA support functionality that goes far beyond the basics of sending and receiving email:

▶ For More
Information
6

- *Calendaring and scheduling*—OWA users have most of the same functionality as Windows-based Outlook 97/98 users, including the ability to access their calendars and view their contacts lists. Users who are familiar with the Outlook 97/98 interface should already be quite familiar with these features.

▶ For More
Information
7

- *Public folders and newsgroups*—An excellent way to communicate on the Internet or on an intranet is to set up public Web discussion folders. These public folders store messages that all users can view and respond to. Unlike email, all responses are available in a "thread" view so users can follow them and keep conversations separate. For public discussions using the Internet, access to newsgroups can be provided through the same Web-based interface.

▶ For More
Information
8

- *Creating specialized forms*—OWA enables users to create forms for collecting and sharing information. Creating areas for users to enter data can standardize many processes that would otherwise require email or paper-based methods. This data can then be automatically processed. Procedures such as changing health care enrollments or requesting a new computer installation can be done via the email client. These forms can create an easy method for all types of clients—including Internet users—to work with this data.

Web Database Publishing

One of the most powerful applications of Web-based technology is to make database information available via Web browsers. For decades, organizations have stored their most important information in database tables. The common practice was to make this information easily available to end users by writing proprietary applications. Today's data-enabled Web pages are a revolutionary change over the static HTML pages that were commonplace just a few years ago.

In this section, we create a sample Microsoft Access database and publish it as a Web site. Via the Web-based front end, users can view, add, and modify database information. The software you need includes the following:

■ Microsoft Internet Information Server (Windows NT Server) or Personal Web Server 4.0 (Windows 95/98, Windows NT Workstation) with ASP extensions installed

■ Microsoft Access 95/97

▶ For More Information
9

■ Microsoft Visual InterDev 6.0 (part of Visual Studio 6.0)

To perform the following procedures, you need to be familiar with the basics of Microsoft Access. The program's online Help file is an excellent place to start. It is also helpful if you have a grasp of the basics of HTML.

Step 1: Creating a Database

Before we can publish information on an intranet, we are going to create a sample database that we want to make viewable via a Web browser. In this example, I've used Microsoft Access to create a basic company phone list database. Here's how you create the database:

1. Open Microsoft Access and create a new blank database. Save the file as `PhoneList.mdb` and make note of its location.

2. Create a new table including the columns shown in Table 16.1. Save the table with the name `Employees`.

Choosing a Database

In this example, I've used Microsoft Access because it is user friendly and is familiar to most readers. If you want to use another database design tool, feel free to do so. Note, however, that you need to have an ODBC driver (described in the section "Step 2: Creating an ODBC Connection") that provides the same functionality for whatever platform you choose in order to complete this example.

Table 16.1 **Columns in the PhoneList Database**

Field Name	Data Type
EmployeeID	Number (primary key)
FirstName	Text
LastName	Text
PhoneExtension	Number

3. Add some sample data to the table. If you set up the table as shown in Table 16.1, you need to make sure that the EmployeeID fields are unique for each record. Figure 16.4 shows the layout of the database, along with some sample data.

4. Save the changes and exit Microsoft Access.

Step 2: Creating an ODBC Connection

In order to access this database via the Visual InterDev application, it is necessary to create an Open Database Connectivity (ODBC) connection. ODBC drivers are used to mask program code from the differences between multiple database platforms and allow for a single programming interface to view data from heterogeneous sources. For example, if you're using Oracle, SQL Server, and Microsoft Access databases on your network, you will only need to write one piece of code that calls on an ODBC driver that specifies from where you want to get your data. The ODBC driver translates this request into the actual syntax required for obtaining that information. If, at a later date, you decide to switch database servers, you need only update the data connection to reflect this change. Figure 16.5 shows the role of an ODBC driver in making database connections.

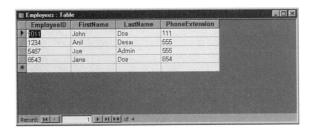

Figure 16.4 The PhoneList database includes contact information for various employees.

On the CD-ROM

Demonstration 16.2, "ODBC Connections," shows you how to create and configure a new ODBC connection.

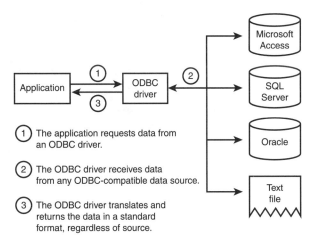

Figure 16.5 The role of ODBC drivers.

To set up an ODBC connection for the PhoneList database, follow these steps:

1. Double-click on either ODBC or 32-bit ODBC Drivers in the Control Panel.

2. On the System DSN tab (also called Machine DSN), click on Add. System DSNs allow all users on a specific machine to access the created ODBC connection. User DSNs, on the other hand, are created for use only by a single user account and are not available if an application is run under different logins. File DSNs must be accessed manually via the file system and are generally more cumbersome to use than the other types.

3. From the available options, choose Microsoft Access driver and click Finish. For the name of the connection, type PhoneList. Next, use the Select button to find the database we just created (see Figure 16.6). Because we haven't set any security or additional options on the database, these are the only settings that must be configured.

ODBC Driver Versions

Several versions of Microsoft's ODBC drivers are available for Windows 95/98 and Windows NT operating systems. The above steps were run using Windows 98. The version you have installed may differ slightly from this one, but in all cases the basic functionality should be the same.

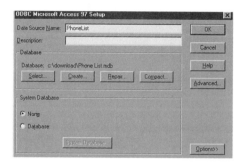

Figure 16.6 Creating a new ODBC connection for the PhoneList database.

4. Click OK to accept the new connection and OK again to exit the ODBC Control Panel.

▷ For More
Information
10

We now have an ODBC connection that we can use to read and write information from this database. In the future, if we move the database to another platform or simply move the file to a different location, only the ODBC connection must change. The application will continue to run, unmodified. Note that ODBC connections are machine specific, so if I want to run my Web-based application on another computer (such as a dedicated Web server), I would need to add another ODBC connection on that machine.

Step 3: Creating an ASP Page

Microsoft's Visual InterDev 6.0 application makes the creation of ASP pages simple. ASP pages can use database connections to dynamically generate HTML Web pages that are then sent to the client. To create an ASP page using Visual InterDev 6.0, complete the following steps:

1. Click on File, New Project. Click on New Web Project and enter a name and folder in which you want to store files (see Figure 16.7). To accept these settings, click Open.

2. The Web Project Wizard walks you through the next few steps. In Step 1, choose the name of a Web server to use (as shown in Figure 16.8). If a Web server is available over the network, you can specify the name of that machine. Otherwise, you can use a Web server on the local machine. Choose Master Mode as the mode in which you want to work. Click Next to continue.

On the CD-ROM

Demonstration 16.3, "Visual InterDev," shows you the basics of creating a Web-based application using this development tool.

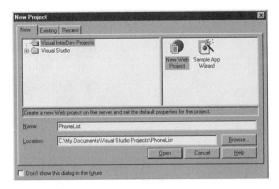

Figure 16.7 Creating a new project in Visual InterDev.

3. In Step 2, specify that you want to create a new Web application and give it the name PhoneList.

4. Steps 3 and 4 allow you to choose navigation buttons and a theme for the Web site. For the sake of this example, leave the default setting of None and click Finish. Visual InterDev automatically copies all necessary files to the Web server and begins building the default project.

Now that we've created a Web project that specifies which server to use and where to store files, we're ready to create the first Web page! To create the database-enabled page, we first create a database connection in the existing project:

1. In the Project Explorer window, right-click on the name of the project and select Add Data Connection. This opens the ODBC Control Panel window and allows you to select the PhoneList ODBC connection we created earlier.

2. You now have an opportunity to name the database connection. In this example, we are keeping the default name, Connection1. To accept all the default settings, click OK.

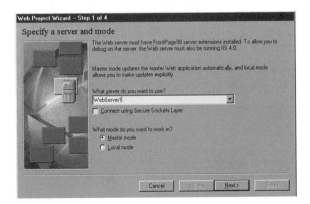

Figure 16.8 Specifying a Web server to use for a Visual InterDev Web project.

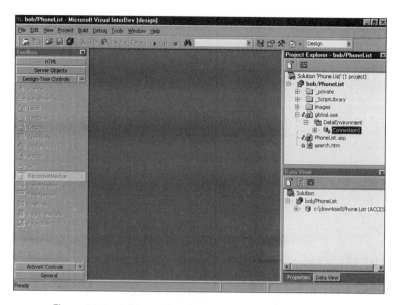

Figure 16.9   Adding a data connection using Visual InterDev.

3. A Data View window should appear on the right side of the screen (see Figure 16.9). If it's not visible, click on View, Other Windows, Data View. To make the Employees table accessible, click and drag it from the Data View to the Connection1 icon (located in Project Explorer, under `global.asa`).

Now that we have a data connection, we can use it in the creation of a new ASP page:

1. In the Project Explorer window, right-click on the name of the Project and select Add, Active Server Page (as shown in Figure 16.10).

2. Specify the name `PhoneList.asp` for the name of the file and click OK to create it. Switch to Design view for the page and type `Employee Phone List:` as the first line.

3. To add database information to the page, drag and drop the Employee table (from the Project Explorer, located under `global.asa`, Data Environment, Connection1) onto the page. This creates a recordset object that tells the server the location of the data you want to obtain.

4. Next, we need to add a control that actually displays specific data values. To do this, hold down the Ctrl key and select each column in the data collection. Drag and drop them onto the Web page under the recordset object. Visual InterDev automatically creates a data-bound control that includes the field names and placeholders for database values (see Figure 16.11).

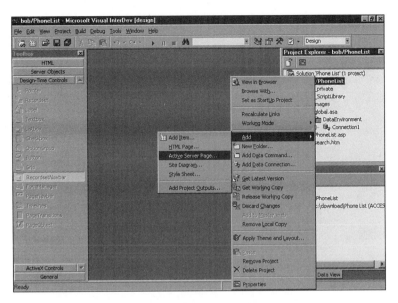

Figure 16.10   Adding a new ASP page to the Visual InterDev project.

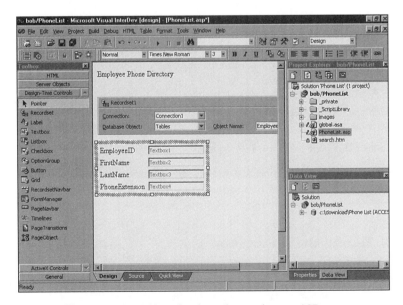

Figure 16.11   Adding data-bound controls to an ASP page.

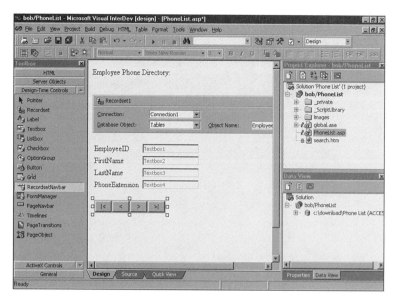

Figure 16.12   The final PhoneList ASP page.

5. Finally, we need to add a way to navigate through the records of the database. Visual InterDev includes the `RecordNavBar` control to do just that. From the Design-Time Controls section of the toolbox, click and drag this item to an area below the data area. If the toolbox is not visible, click on View, Toolbox. Next we need to tell the control to which recordset we're referring. Right-click on the control and select Properties. For the recordset value, choose RecordSet1 from the drop-down list. Click OK to accept the setting. When you're done, your screen should look similar to the one in Figure 16.12.

6. To save this page, click on File, Save All.

▶ For More
Information
11

   If you want to view the code that was actually generated by these actions, you can switch to Source view. It is beyond the scope of this book to examine the code in detail, but complete documentation is available from Microsoft.

Step 4: Testing the Application

To test this Web page, open your Web browser and point to `WebServerName/phonelist/phonelist.asp`. The information you see is drawn directly from the database at the time that you request the page. If you want to test it, modify the database from within Microsoft Access and then refresh the page in your Web browser. You should see the changes. That's it! You've created your first database-enabled Web application.

Application Improvements

▶ For More
Information
12
To add security to your Web pages, you have several options. First, you can use NTFS permissions. Second, you could create a lookup table in your database; this database could contain information that maps user login names to any column in the given table and verifies that the user is authorized before sending information. In this way, users could be able to access only their own records in the database.

▶ For More
Information
9, 13
The purpose of these examples was to show you just how easily you can publish Web-based information on an intranet. To learn how these pages work, take a look at the code that was magically generated by the wizard. Details on the many possibilities of applications using Visual InterDev, ASP, and databases could fill (and has filled) entire books! There's also a wealth of information on the Web for new Web coders.

Streaming Media Content

▶ For More
Information
14, 15
A wide variety of tools and technologies have recently become available for enhancing the usefulness of the Internet and corporate intranets. Mainly, the static Web pages that were the norm a few years ago have been replaced with more dynamic content. There are many examples of live audio and video sites on the public Internet.

One push in this direction is the availability of technology to deliver live and recorded audio and video content via TCP/IP. Traditional audio and video on the Web requires users to wait to download an entire media clip that they want to access and then play it. "Streaming" technologies, on the other hand, allow data to be sent sequentially to the client as it is being viewed. For example, a user may have to wait 30 minutes to download a 5-minute audio/video file. However, this same user could utilize a streamed content file and start viewing the content almost immediately (see Figure 16.13).

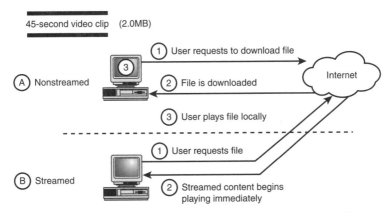

Figure 16.13 Downloading streamed versus nonstreamed media files.

Streaming Standards and Players

▶ For More
Information
16, 17
Compression/decompression algorithms (codecs) minimize the amount of data generated by audio and video content. Most methods incur some loss in the quality of the
data. Some video standards make better use of data space by recording only the differences between frames in a video sequence. Currently, there are several competing standards in the streaming audio marketplace. Real Networks, Inc., for example, has
RealAudio and RealVideo specifications. Microsoft has introduced NetShow.
Macromedia has developed Shockwave plug-ins. Finally, in the arena of audio compression, MPEG Layer 3 (MP3) audio files have become very popular. In an effort to
consolidate the various Web browser plug-ins and player-file downloads that would be
required of the average user, Microsoft has released the Windows Media Player. This
single interface can use a variety of codecs that may be downloaded on demand from
various content providers' Web sites.

NetShow Services for Windows NT Server

▶ For More
Information
18, 19
Microsoft has made available a free streaming service that runs on Windows NT
Server. NetShow Server Tools works by allowing Internet Information Server to send
files to a client sequentially instead of requiring them to be downloaded. For non-
Internet multimedia streaming, Microsoft has released the NetShow Theater Server.
This tool can provide audio and video data streams for high-bandwidth situations.
Among its many features is the capability to automatically adjust content based on
client bandwidth.

Despite the advances in streaming content, there are still several concerns. First,
many of the protocols used may not be able to traverse a company's firewalls (depending on the configuration). Also, managing compression schemes and keeping content
updated can present a challenge for system administrators. Finally, the actual creation
of video footage can be expensive. Streaming techniques will continue to evolve, as
will other technologies, such as high-speed Internet access for businesses. Despite the
challenges, it's clear that streaming multimedia data will provide a much better user
experience in the near future.

More Web-Based Applications

By now you've had a good overview of the tools and technologies available for creating and maintaining Web-based content. In this section, I briefly touch on some other
usage ideas.

Daily Company News

It's difficult for employees to feel appreciated in large companies. One very inexpensive and easy solution is to post daily news about non–business-critical information.
Posting a happy birthday message or documenting one employee's achievements can
go a long way toward improving job satisfaction. Perhaps this can be managed by an
assistant who types short messages into a Microsoft Word document and saves them as

HTML files. The files can then be included in the intranet home page so all users can view the information.

Automated Forms

I briefly mentioned that Microsoft's Outlook messaging products (including OWA) support the creation of custom forms for collecting different types of information. Instead of only being able to send email with requests for information, you can use Web-based forms. This way, you can enforce the consistency of the message and easily track information in a database. For example, a company help desk could easily set up an automated problem-reporting page for handling noncritical errors. Not only does this save time for the IT staff, but it also allows the user to continue his or her job without waiting on hold for routine assistance.

Web-Based Training

Computer-based training methods have long been seen as a potential alternative to traditional classroom-based training. Among other benefits, computer-based training offers the following:

- *Location-independent training*—There's no longer a need to fly employees across the country to learn how to use a simple application. A computer monitor and multimedia demonstrations can take the place of live instructors and paper-based materials. Additionally, with products like Microsoft's NetMeeting, groups of users can be trained through multi-person videoconferences. These virtual meetings can include viewing multimedia demonstrations and remotely interacting with other PCs.

- *Lower material costs*—In many cases, producing multimedia content can be much cheaper and more efficient than printing and distributing paper-based documentation.

- *Flexible hours*—A computer-based training package is always available and can be tailored around employees' schedules. Even the busiest traveling employee can view information on a CD-ROM on a laptop computer.

For the multimedia demonstrations and tutorials included on the accompanying CD-ROM, I used the Lotus ScreenCam application. Most demonstrations were created quite quickly and easily.

Case Studies

In this chapter, I've provided an overview of just some of the applications of Web-based technologies. This is just scratching the surface of possibilities, however. In the real world, few Webmasters would be satisfied with the simplistic phone list application we created. The following hypothetical case studies provide some ideas for utilizing these tools in your own environment.

Case Study 1: Web-Based Messaging

XYZ Corp. has a very large network environment, including remote clients, Macintosh users, Windows users, and UNIX users. The company has been using a variety of messaging systems, but now wants all users to be able to share scheduling information without a costly and time-consuming email system migration. Additionally, XYZ wants to make a Web-based training class available for new users to learn how to use this solution.

Solution

OWA can be used for all remote and local network users. Additionally, the Microsoft Outlook 98 client can be supported for users who choose to install it. Also, some applications require the use of simple SMTP services. All of these features are configured on Microsoft Exchange Server 5.5.

To simplify the administration of mail accounts, the email administrators decide to make a form available via Microsoft Outlook. This form can be used to request changes to service, email troubleshooting, and technical support. Finally, the Engineering group is given access to a public folder that can be used for sharing information and project status reports.

To handle training on the new system, XYZ Corp. will create a streamed audio/video file that walks a user through logging in to the OWA application and performing basic functions such as sending and receiving email and working with the calendar. This file is authored using Microsoft's NetShow Tools and is compressed and placed on the server. NetShow Services is placed on a separate Windows NT Server, and links to this application are created. After measuring available network bandwidth, the files are optimized for the use of 30Kbps of bandwidth. Finally, a link on the corporate intranet is created, and users are made aware of the training.

Case Study 2: An Employee Survey

XYZ Corp. must receive information about how employees feel about their current insurance service as quickly as possible. The many employees, data entry, and paper forms increase the chance for error, so an automated process is required. Responding to the survey is optional for all company employees, and each employee should respond only once.

Solution

The Webmaster creates a simple database containing fields for the requested information. An ASP page is created that performs the following functions:

- Presents the user with a form through which he or she can enter information.
- Validates each entry to make sure that the values entered are acceptable.
- Automatically captures the user's network login name and stores it in the database. If the name already exists, the employee is asked whether she wants to change her answers.

Optionally, the Webmaster can make results of the survey available to upper management by another protected Web page that queries the same database and generates statistics.

Case Study 3: The Help Desk

XYZ Corp. has a basic help desk database system that tracks problems and resolutions for help desk issues. Currently, only help desk staffers have access to this system. They enter, view, and modify data using Microsoft's Access 97 database. The help desk would like to allow users to view the status of their requests and view common questions and answers for problems similar to those they have encountered. Few users have Microsoft Access installed, and the environment includes heterogeneous client types, such as Macintosh, Windows, and UNIX machines. Microsoft Internet Information Server can manage issues regarding multiple users accessing the same database. In the future, if business needs demand it, the database platform can be upgraded to a relational database management system such as Oracle or Microsoft's SQL Server simply by changing ODBC connection properties.

Solution

To support the various client types, a Web-based application is an excellent solution. All users have access to the company's intranet and are able to view any Web-based information. The XYZ Corp. Webmaster creates a front end for viewing specified information in the help desk database. This front end is also configured to send email to help desk staffers who require notification of critical and important problems. The application allows users to find the status of their trouble tickets, enter new trouble tickets, and cancel their own requests. Users may also enter additional information about a previously submitted ticket. To take it one step further, the Webmaster plans to implement a Web-based application that generates statistics on help desk tickets. IT managers will be able to view these pages to obtain up-to-the-minute help desk statistics.

The Bottom Line

Publishing database information on the Web provides a client-independent and efficient way of getting important information to users. It can also be used to collect data without the traditional inefficiencies of paper forms and manual data entry. Using these techniques, you can easily lower the often-unmeasured costs of doing business the old way. Web technologies can also be quite cost-effective. Usually, companies can avoid purchasing database software or client access licenses for users who only need to view information by making it available via Web browsers. All these factors help reduce your overall TCO. Better yet, you might see a less quantifiable benefit from employees who thank you for automating otherwise annoying processes!

For More Information

1. "Microsoft Exchange Server 5.5 Reviewer's Guide," Microsoft TechNet

2. "Microsoft Exchange FAQs from Support Online," Microsoft TechNet

3. "Microsoft Active Server Pages Overview," Microsoft TechNet

4. Microsoft Exchange Server home page: `www.microsoft.com/exchange`

5. Chapter 17 of this book: "Implementing a Secure FTP Site"

6. Chapter 31, "Workgroup Features in Microsoft Outlook," Microsoft Office 97 Resource Kit

7. Chapter 6, "Public Folders," Exchange Server 5.5 Resource Guide, Microsoft TechNet

8. "Building Microsoft Exchange and Outlook Solutions," Microsoft TechNet

9. Microsoft's Visual InterDev home page: `www.microsoft.com/vinterdev`

10. Chapter 27, "Sharing Information with Microsoft Office Applications," Microsoft Office 97 Resource Kit

11. Microsoft Developer Network home page: `msdn.microsoft.com/developer/`

12. Chapter 5 of this book: "Network Management"

13. Microsoft SiteBuilder Network home page: `www.microsoft.com/sitebuilder/`

14. ABC News's Windows Media home page: `www.abcnews.com/sections/us/dailynews/windowsmedia.html`

15. VideoSeeker Web site: `www.videoseeker.com/`

16. Microsoft Windows Media Player home page: `www.microsoft.com/windows/windowsmedia/default.asp`

17. Real Networks RealAudio home page: `www.realaudio.com/`

18. Microsoft Windows NT Media Services Web site: `www.microsoft.com/ntserver/nts/mediaserv/default.asp`

19. Microsoft NetShow Theater Server home page: `www.microsoft.com/theater/`

Further Reading

For more information on creating and managing Web-based applications in general, see

- 15 Seconds ASP development Web site: `www.15seconds.com`

- Support and troubleshooting for Microsoft Visual InterDev home page: `http://support.microsoft.com/support/vinterdev/`

- Microsoft's Site Builder Network Web site: `www.sitebuilder.com`

- "Troubleshooting Guide for Outlook Web Access," Microsoft TechNet

- "Microsoft Active Messaging: Combining Microsoft Exchange with the Web," Microsoft TechNet

Implementing a Secure FTP Site

AN ESSENTIAL FUNCTION OF ALL NETWORKS is sharing files, and in a Windows NT–based environment, many file-sharing methods are available. For example, users can map network drives that actually reside on a server to their home directory or use the Network Neighborhood to browse resources. Although the World Wide Web is a great technology for sharing information, File Transfer Protocol (FTP) is a much simpler and more efficient way to transfer program and data files between computers. Accessing intranets and other Web-based content may be transparent to the user but is actually based on information pulled from various servers and databases throughout an environment. Client/server applications make data seem to be stored locally, though such applications often pull information from remote sources.

In heterogeneous environments, file sharing between operating system platforms is an important challenge for IT. There are incompatibilities and limitations on functions that may not be supported between operating systems. For example, UNIX and Macintosh clients cannot automatically map network drives as easily as can Windows-based clients. Depending on how the network is set up, some clients may also be unable to browse the network via a graphical user interface (GUI).

This chapter looks at FTP and how it can be used to share data across your environment and the intranet. One important step is to assess the security implications of making this old workhorse protocol work in your environment. Be forewarned: FTP does not include any modern built-in security mechanisms such as data encryption or secure authentication. However, with proper configuration you can make it a viable protocol in your environment. You can greatly reduce your TCO by properly installing and configuring this simple, yet powerful, Windows NT Service.

What Is FTP?

Since the early days of the Internet, FTP has been a TCP/IP standard used to transfer files across machines. FTP servers allow users to connect to them using this protocol. FTP clients are included as part of most major operating systems, including Windows 95/98 and Windows NT, all flavors of UNIX, OS/2, and Macintosh computers. Though they may differ slightly in their implementations, most command-line FTP applications function in the same way. For GUI-based operating systems, a wealth of tools are available for making an FTP session look and feel as comfortable as Windows Explorer! This is one of the reasons that FTP remains in such widespread use on the Internet. It is also one of the reasons that FTP may work well for your own environment.

There are many resources on setting up Web sites with Internet Information Server (IIS). In fact, Chapter 16, "Web Applications," describes a specific application. Figure 17.1 provides an overview of how users, using a variety of connection methods, can access an FTP server. Nevertheless, administrators often overlook the FTP service.

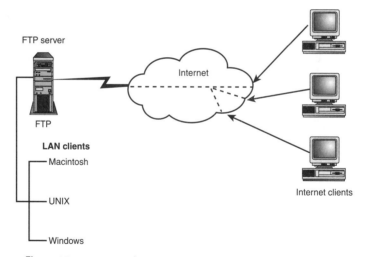

Figure 17.1 Various client types connecting to a single FTP server.

Configuring the FTP Service

The FTP service is available as part of Microsoft's IIS and can be installed as part of the Windows NT Option Pack (see Appendix A, "Windows Updates," for more information). All versions of IIS support the FTP service. However, this chapter focuses on the configuration options available for IIS 4.0 on Windows NT Server. Much of the information contained herein is similar for earlier versions of the FTP service and for the Windows NT Workstation FTP service.

Using Microsoft Management Console

For More Information 1

Microsoft Management Console (MMC) is designed to serve as a single point of administration for various Windows NT services. After the FTP service is installed, the Internet Service Manager can be used to start, stop, and configure the service. This application is well hidden in Programs, Windows NT 4.0 Option Pack, Internet Information Server. Figure 17.2 shows the MMC interface.

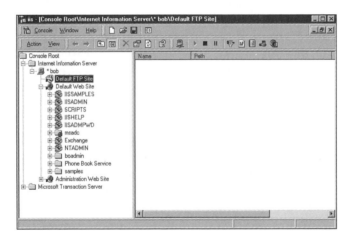

Figure 17.2   The MMC interface.

On the CD-ROM

Demonstration 17.1, "FTP Setup," walks you through the various configuration options available in the properties of the FTP service.

Automatically Starting the FTP Service

To have the FTP service start on every reboot of the machine, be sure the Control Panel Services Startup value is set to Automatic for FTP Publishing Service.

Figure 17.3   Basic FTP site options available in the Internet Service Manager.

The left side of the MMC displays the various options available for configuration. Clicking the plus (+) sign next to FTP Service opens up this branch. You can then see the various FTP sites that are available via the service. By viewing the properties of a site, you can see the available configuration options (see Figure 17.3).

Specifying the Home Directory

When you installed the Windows NT Option Pack, you were asked to specify the default WWW and FTP directories. The initial default setting is the `\inetpub\ftproot` directory (located on the Windows NT system partition). You can change this directory by clicking on the properties for the FTP Service, selecting the Home Directory tab, and changing the Local Path setting to a different directory. All users who access the FTP site will begin in this area of the file system. Now that you've set up the defaults, let's move on to managing directories.

Managing Sites and Directories

The FTP service allows you to share data that is located anywhere on your network, so you're not limited to making files available only through your default FTP root directory. Virtual Directories allow you to create pathnames visible via the FTP server that link to files located elsewhere on your server or even on a remote machine. For example, if you want all users to have access to files located in your `c:\download` directory, do the following:

▶ For More
Information
2

Web-Based Administration

Newer versions of Microsoft's program interfaces can be accessed via the Web through the HTML tools, although the native applications are still usually more user friendly. For more information, see Chapter 11, "Remote Management."

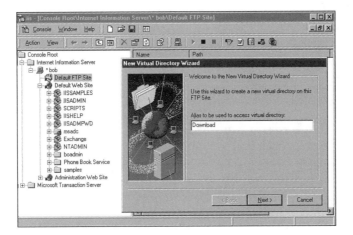

Figure 17.4   The New Virtual Directory Wizard.

1. Highlight Default FTP Site and choose File, New, Virtual Directory. This step starts the New Virtual Directory Wizard (shown in Figure 17.4).

2. On the first screen, enter an alias by which users can access this directory. In my example, I call it `Downloads`.

3. The next screen allows you to specify the physical path to the resources you want to make available. The path may be a local path (such as `c:\downloads`) or a relative Universal Naming Convention (UNC) path (such as `\\server1\ downloads`). Note that if you're supporting MS-DOS–based computers, the UNC names must not exceed eight characters.

▷ For More
Information
3, 4

4. If you choose a local directory, you need to make sure that the `IUSR_machinename` account has the appropriate Windows NT File System (NTFS) access permissions. If you choose a file that resides on a remote computer, you need to specify a user account that has access to these files. All FTP users assume the identity of this user and are given the same user permissions as this account.

5. Choose whether you want to allow read and/or write access to this directory. These settings override the NTFS permissions you set in step 4. Finally, click on Finish to accept your choices.

When a remote client logs on to the FTP server, he or she is able to access this directory by typing `cd download`. Note, however, that the directory does not appear in the list of available paths, so the user has to know that it exists before proceeding. A new FTP site can be created if you want to make all shared files in a different location available via your FTP server. The new site and the default site may have completely different properties. Using these configuration options, you can instruct the FTP service to share any files you want.

Managing Security

The FTP service is designed to allow remote users to send and receive files from remote clients. As mentioned earlier, it is especially useful when transferring files between multiple client types. It is also useful for transferring files over the Internet. However, in this case, security can be a very important consideration. This section describes how to set up the FTP service to give only the permissions required by your remote users.

Authentication

A basic security limitation of FTP is that this type of communication sends unencrypted passwords over the network. Intruders on the network can use a protocol analyzer (also known as a *sniffer*) to intercept data and learn passwords. Though this security lapse may not be much of a concern over a LAN, it is very important to consider for public Internet sites. Therefore, the FTP service should be set up to accept anonymous connections only. This way, users are never actually required to send passwords over the network.

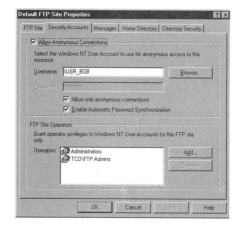

Figure 17.5 Authentication options for an FTP site.

On the CD-ROM

Demonstration 17.2, "FTP Security Settings," shows some of the ways you can secure your implementation of the FTP servers.

File System Security Issues

▶ For More Information 5

The File Allocation Table (FAT and FAT32) file systems were not created to be secure methods for file storage on networked machines. A limitation of FAT is that it cannot prevent users from accessing files from outside the operating system. For this reason, I recommend that you use NTFS on all shared network drives and data. NTFS allows for granular access control based on domain users and allows for auditing of access attempts.

The authentication levels you choose largely depend on the needs of your environment. If you are fairly sure that sending clear text passwords over the network will not cause huge security problems, uncheck the Allow Only Anonymous Connections option in the Security Accounts tab. This setting allows users to type in a valid Windows NT username and password to enter the site. They then have all of the permissions assigned to this Windows NT account. Figure 17.5 shows the configuration options for setting authentication types.

To set security permissions on files for anonymous users, you can use the standard NTFS permissions. When anonymous or unauthenticated users attempt to access a resource via the FTP service, they impersonate a specific Windows NT user (named IUSR_machinename by default). They assume any file-system permissions given to this account. For most applications of an FTP server, remote users should have read-only access to files and directories.

Another very powerful method of security is to place a restriction on the IP addresses from which the FTP Service can be accessed. For more information on TCP/IP, see Chapter 6, "TCP/IP Management." For example, to restrict access to IP addresses on subnet 192.168.1.x, you would do the following:

1. Open the properties for the FTP site and click on the Directory Security tab.

2. Choose the Denied Access option for the TCP/IP Address Restrictions to prevent access from all machines except those you explicitly allow.

3. Now, to add IP addresses that will have access to this site, click on the Add button. Figure 17.6 shows the Grant Access On dialog box.

4. Specify the Group of Computers option. The network ID should be set to 192.168.1.0, and the subnet mask should be set to 255.255.255.0.

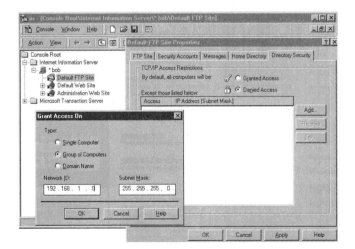

Figure 17.6 Granting access to specific IP addresses.

▶ For More
Information
6, 7
Note that in addition to IP address requirements, you can also restrict FTP access
to users who have authenticated on a Windows NT domain. This setting eliminates
the need to know all possible source IP addresses but retains a good level of security in
most cases.

Creating Special-Purpose Directories

In most situations, the sole purpose of an FTP site is to allow remote users to download applications, documents, and other files. For these directories, it is appropriate to
allow the IUSR_machinename account to have read and list permissions to files and
directories. This allows them to download files but not to delete, modify, or upload
them.

An Incoming (also called Upload) directory is usually designated as a place where
users can upload files for review by either the systems administrator or another designated user. To prevent misuse of the system, the files cannot be downloaded until a
system administrator moves them to an appropriate download directory. To set this,
give the IUSR_machinename account add directory permissions. Note that this setting
does not allow any users (including the uploader) to see files in these directories.
Figure 17.7 shows typical NTFS permissions for this situation on a server named Bob.
Finally, for organizations you may give the anonymous user account the ability to create new directories. This setting allows the user to create directories for specific sets of
files to be uploaded.

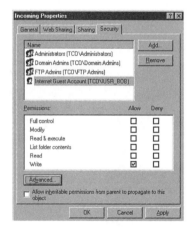

Figure 17.7   Permissions for an upload-only FTP directory.

On the CD-ROM

Demonstration 17.3, "FTP NTFS Settings," displays some basic file system security settings for limiting
access to resources made available by the FTP service.

Giving Users the Right Message

The IIS 4.0 FTP service allows you to specify messages to be received by users as they connect to the FTP server. Though a warning message may not directly add security, a statement regarding the purpose of the site can deter the casual snooper. To set up the messages, complete the following steps:

1. Open the properties for the FTP site.

2. Click on the Messages tab.

3. The Welcome text box allows you to enter information about your FTP site. This information is displayed to users after they successfully log in. Type in the text `This site is intended for authorized users only` (or something equal-ly scary). You may also want to add a disclaimer stating the purpose of the site and that the site administrators cannot be held responsible for its content.

4. The Exit text box allows you to enter a message that is seen immediately prior to closing the user's connection.

5. The Maximum Connections box displays a message if the user is denied access because there are currently too many connections.

6. Click on OK to accept the changes. Users will then see these messages when they log in to the service.

Configuring the FTP Log

It is useful to know who is accessing your FTP site, when, and from where. You can set the FTP service to record this information by logging connections and file trans-fers. You have the option of storing this information in any ODBC-compliant database (see Chapter 15, "Web-Based Technologies," for more information). Or, you can save to a standard text file. To view the options available, click on the FTP site properties, check the Enable Logging box, and then click on Properties. In the Extended Properties tab, you can specify which information to retain. Figure 17.8 shows the types of information that the FTP service can log.

By default, the log files are stored as simple text and are located in the `winnt\`
`system32\logfiles` directory. It's unlikely that parsing through these files manually will give you the information you need. To create reports, you need to import these files into a spreadsheet program or use a reporting tool such as Seagate Software's Crystal Reports.

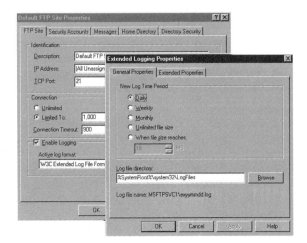

Figure 17.8 Configuring logging options for the FTP service.

Network and Protocol Security

A firewall is an essential part of protecting any server that has access to or from the Internet. If you're implementing a public Web server for general use, then the solution may be to simply place the server outside the firewall. If, however, you want to restrict access to authorized users, you need to permit the transfer of data on specific ports based on the functionality required. The basics of firewalls are discussed in Chapter 7, "Security," and more information on FTP-specific configuration is available from your firewall vendor.

Ensuring that users are permitted access and protecting data during transfer are both important concerns. One popular method of securing data transmitted over the Internet is the Secure Sockets Layer (SSL). SSL is supported by IIS and can be used for transferring data using HTTP and/or FTP. SSL provides a mechanism for clients to securely perform "handshaking" with a server. Server "certificates" use a third-party security provider to prove the identity of users. Servers and clients then agree to use some form of encrypted communications (usually the highest level supported by both parties) to transfer data. SSL is relatively easy to configure and is a widely supported standard. Consider implementing it for your servers that require security on the Internet.

Accessing the FTP Site

Various client types use slightly different methods to access an FTP server. For example, Macintosh and UNIX operating systems both provide FTP utilities, but they differ in usage. In general, there are two main ways to access FTP sites—via a command line or via a GUI.

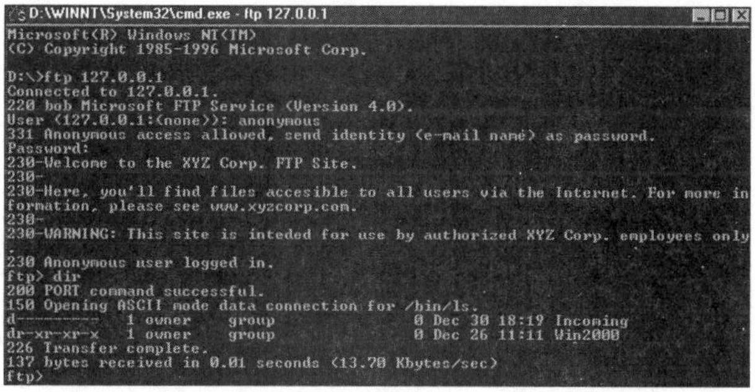

Figure 17.9 Accessing an anonymous FTP server from the command line.

The Command Line

So far, you've set up your new FTP Site just the way you want it. Now it's time to connect your clients. Windows 95/98 and Windows NT computers automatically have the necessary tools for connecting to an FTP site via the command line. To open an FTP session, go to a command prompt and type `ftp`, followed by the server name or IP address. For example, type `ftp ftp.microsoft.com`. If you are able to connect, you will be prompted for login information. Figure 17.9 shows a command-line FTP session.

A typical login consists of a username of anonymous and the user's email address for a password. FTP commands are similar to those in DOS. For example, you can type `cd` to change directories. For transferring files, you can upload files using `put` and download files using `get`. If you plan to transfer binary files (such as programs or multimedia content), you need to first set the binary transfer mode by typing `bin`. For a list of available commands, type `help` at any prompt.

The command-line versions of the FTP Program in both Windows 95/98 and Windows NT 4.0 allow for the automation of various FTP functions. For example, consider a company that wants all users to automatically transmit a time sheet spreadsheet from their local machine to a central server. To avoid complications due to user intervention, you can make this a one-step process by doing the following:

1. Create a text file called `SendTimeSheet.bat` (the name is arbitrary).

2. Type the following lines into the text file and then save it:
   ```
   anonymous
   username@xyzcorp.com
   cd TimeSheets
   put c:\myfiles\timesheet.xls
   quit
   ```

On the CD-ROM

Demonstration 17.4, "FTP Clients," shows you how to use the command-line FTP program to log in to and download files from an FTP site.

3. Create a desktop shortcut and specify the following for the command line:

```
ftp -s:c:\download\SendTimeSheet.bat
```

▷ For More
Information
4

4. Now, whenever users want to send the file, they can just click on this icon and the file is transferred automatically. In addition, you can schedule this command to run automatically by using the Windows NT AT command or the Windows 95/98 Task Scheduler (both discussed in Chapter 19, "Scripting").

You have now implemented an automated method for sending information to a server. With a little imagination, you can extend this process to perform more extensive file housekeeping.

Other Methods of FTP Access

Most current Web browsers (including Netscape Navigator and Internet Explorer 2.0 and higher) can be used to access an FTP site. If users are familiar with browsing and downloading files from the Web, obtaining files this way will be familiar. To access the site via a browser, the user can simply type `ftp://servername`. If anonymous access is allowed, users are automatically logged in using the email address that is set up in their browser. Otherwise, they are prompted for a username and password. Figure 17.10 shows the screen a Web-based user sees when accessing an FTP site.

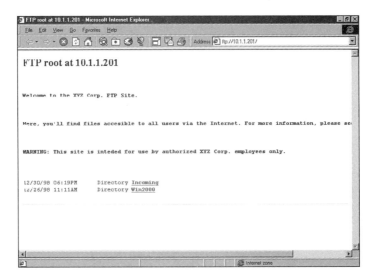

Figure 17.10 Browsing an FTP site.

For More
Information
8, 9 The command-line interface is suitable for systems administrators, but it may be too complicated for Windows-based users. The Web browser interface solves this problem, but it allows only for downloading data. To get the best of both worlds, several FTP client applications use a GUI available from third-party vendors. These programs provide a powerful and user-friendly interface for sending files. Some are so good, in fact, that users have a hard time distinguishing them from Windows Explorer. These programs can be downloaded from several shareware collection Web sites.

Case Study: Using FTP for Cross-Platform, Secure File Sharing

XYZ Corp. wants to set up a temporary file storage area in which clients can place large files for analysis. Additionally, network users utilizing a variety of operating systems (all of which support FTP) need to share files. The accounting department requires Excel spreadsheets of financial information to be stored in a central location. However, only the supervisor should have access to these files.

Solution

A basic IIS 4.0 FTP site is set up. This site specifies that only anonymous access is allowed. A download directory is created with read permissions for all users. The Upload directory specifies only add permissions. Only administrators and the Accounting Supervisors group are given change permissions so that they may view/modify files in these directories. For security, the IT staff restricts access of accounting department data to valid IP addresses for these internal users.

One Step Further: Creating a Web Interface

For More
Information
10 Current versions of the most popular Web browsers (Internet Explorer 4.0 or later, or Netscape Navigator 4.0 or later) support uploading files by using HTTP functionality. Web-based connections have the added advantage of supporting the SSL functionality for encrypting sensitive information before it is sent over the Internet. If you're looking for an easy way for Web users to send files over the Internet, third-party products are available for adding this functionality on the server side.

The Bottom Line

Sharing files via the FTP service is a quick and easy way to connect a heterogeneous mix of computers on your network or over the global Internet. Instead of using various client connectivity packages for handling interoperability issues, system administrators can save time and money by using FTP on Windows NT servers. The Windows NT Option Pack is freely available from Microsoft. It's easy to configure and provides extended functionality. All these features can significantly affect your TCO in the core functioning of IT—providing access to files and information. What more reason do you need to set up the FTP service?

For More Information

1. "Microsoft Management Console," Microsoft Windows NT Server Technical Notes: Windows NT 4.0 Option Pack Deployment Guide
2. Chapter 11 of this book: "Remote Management"
3. "How NTFS Permissions Work," NT Server Manuals: Concepts and Planning
4. Chapter 5 of this book: "Network Management"
5. Chapter 3, "Server Security on the Internet: FTP Security," Windows NT Server 4.0 Resource Kit
6. "IIS Authentication Models" in Chapter 8, "Security," Microsoft Internet Information Server Resource Kit
7. "IIS: Authentication & Security Features," Q142868, Microsoft Knowledge Base
8. The Ultimate Collection of Windows Shareware (www.tucows.com)
9. CNet's Shareware (www.shareware.com)
10. 15 Seconds Web Site (www.15seconds.com)

Further Reading

For more information on setting up and managing FTP servers in general, see

- Chapter 1, "Internet Information Server Architecture: FTP Service," Windows NT Server 4.0 Resource Kit

- "Using FTP," Windows NT Server 4.0 Resource Kit

18

Enforcing System Policies

I N Chapter 4, "Policies and Procedures," we discussed the importance of having a general acceptable network usage policy and making this policy known to all users. Voluntary acceptance of these policies can make life much easier for the IT support staff, but universal compliance with usage policies isn't likely in practice. For example, users may feel that they should be able to install new applications on their desktops at will. Also, novice users may accidentally make settings changes that affect their programs. IT policies that try to prevent these problems may be ignored or circumvented. The associated increase in support issues and the difficulty of maintaining heterogeneous configurations can negatively affect TCO.

Modern desktop operating systems were created to be powerful and to allow a broad range of flexibility in usage. Though this functionality is great for those who need it, many business users do not require all the features available. For example, data entry clerks may only require access to two applications to perform their job. A systems or network administrator can take several measures to restrict the options available to end users of the operating system. In this chapter, we consider ways to control the desktop environment and to enforce security and usage policies. The proper use of the System Policy Editor and user profiles can make life easier for IT departments and users alike.

The Importance of Enforcing Policies

One of the major costs that IT departments and support services incur is based on problems caused by user errors. This category includes inadvertent or deliberate changes to system settings that adversely affect the system's operation. Every systems administrator has received calls from users who claim, "It was working yesterday" or "I haven't made any changes to the system." These words are often a preamble to the truth: "Well, actually I did install an application and change my Control Panel settings. Plus, there's a utility that I've had problems with since I installed it." For many administrators, solving problems caused by users is often an area that requires a lot of time. Maintaining identical configurations on multiple systems is all but impossible. Wouldn't it be great if all help desk calls were for *real* troubleshooting issues?

In certain situations where IT staff is thinly spread over a large number of users, it may be appropriate to emphasize that the sole responsibility of IT is to provide a working operating environment. To this end, if problems crop up that are not easy to fix, an IT staffer may choose to reload the entire system. If an automated application installation process (described in Chapter 14, "Automated Software Installations") is in place, this policy can save many hours of needless troubleshooting. Most of the information in this chapter assumes that you are running in a Windows NT domain-based environment and require access to a domain controller to perform the features mentioned.

Managing User Profiles

One of the best parts of working with a GUI-based operating system is that you have the ability to configure your computing environment the way you like it. Windows 95 provides an enhanced interface that allows users to create desktop shortcuts, customize display settings, and rearrange the Windows desktop. Windows NT has always supported multiple users' settings and configurations, as well. In this section, we look at how *user profiles*—desktop settings and related information—can be managed for efficiency and conformity. We start with an overview of the Windows Registry.

The Windows Registry

Windows 3.1 and earlier Microsoft operating systems and applications stored their information in initialization (.INI) files. .INI files are simple text documents that contain lines for assigning values to parameters, system settings, and variables. Managing these files was very difficult because it required a complete understanding of how a program functioned. Also, a simple typo or omission of a line could cause an entire application to fail. Moreover, the files themselves were often found in various areas of the hard drive, including the operating system directory and/or the application's own directory.

Table 18.1 **Windows 95/98/NT Registry Filenames and Locations**

Contents	Filename(s)	Default Location
Windows 95/98 system settings	system.dat	Windows root
Windows 95/98 user settings	user.dat	Windows root
Windows NT system settings	Various	Winnt\
	*.log files	System32\Config
Windows NT user settings	NTUser.dat	Winnt\
		Profiles\UserName

Windows 95/98 and Windows NT computers store operating system and application-specific information in a single location called the *Registry*. These files contain information on hardware devices and drivers, application settings, and user settings. The Registry itself consists of files that serve as a central repository of this data. Microsoft's latest generation of development tools (including Visual Basic) makes it very easy for programmers to store their own settings in the Registry without dealing with text files. Table 18.1 shows the default Registry filenames and where they're located. The operating system automatically makes modifications to the Registry whenever user or system changes such as changing service startup options or installing new programs are made.

For More
Information
1, 2, 3 Incorrectly modifying the Registry can prevent system startup and can force you to reinstall your operating system. Most modifications to the Registry and system settings can be performed through the Windows user interface. If you must make Registry modifications, be sure to back up the appropriate files. To easily back up the Windows NT Registry, use the Emergency Rescue Disk utility. In Windows 95/98, you can manually copy the system.dat and user.dat files to another directory. Windows 98 also includes a handy utility called ScanReg for backing up and troubleshooting the Registry automatically.

For editing the Registry, Windows 95/98 and NT users can use the Registry Editor, or RegEdit, program. This tool provides an Explorer-style interface; the user can run it by clicking on Start, Run and then typing RegEdit. Windows NT supports RegEdit and also includes the RegEdt32 program (shown in Figure 18.1) that allows for the setting of security on Registry keys. This utility, however, cannot view or modify remote Windows 95/98 Registry settings.

Viewing Registry Files

As a safety precaution, the Registry files have the Hidden attribute enabled. To see these files from within the file system, you need to make sure that you're viewing hidden files. In DOS, you can use the dir /a command, and in Windows Explorer, you can click on View, Options.

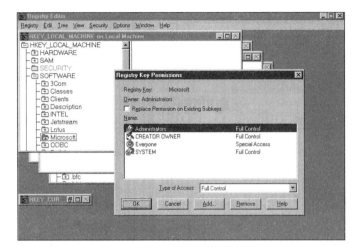

Figure 18.1 The Windows NT RegEdt32 application.

▶ For More
Information
4, 5
Though there is no single authoritative source for all possible Registry keys and settings, documentation is available from multiple sources. If you're looking for Registry settings specific to a certain application, you'll need to contact the program's vendor.

Windows NT 4.0 User Profiles

Windows NT 4.0 was created for use in networked, multiuser environments. It is designed to automatically create a new local user profile the first time a user logs in to a machine. By default, the Windows NT user profiles are stored in the `\winnt\profiles` folder. Figure 18.2 shows the folders stored within this path. The following subdirectories are contained therein:

- `All Users`—This directory stores desktop shortcuts and programs that are available to all local users in this machine.

- `Default User`—This folder stores the icons and shortcuts that are given to any user when he or she logs in to the system for the first time.

- *User-specific folders*—Any application or desktop shortcuts that the user creates are stored in the user-specific folders on the local machine. The exact names of these directories reflect the account names of users who have logged in to the system.

On the CD-ROM

Demonstration 18.1, "Profile Directories," shows where profile directories are located in the file system and the types of information they contain.

Figure 18.2 The subfolders of the Profiles directory.

Having access to a program icon does not necessarily mean that the user will be able to use a program. To perform certain functions, the user must have appropriate NTFS permissions, user rights, and any required application settings. All of these must be made independently of user profiles.

Profile Storage

Windows NT profiles store desktop shortcuts and basic user-specific application settings. Information retained for each user profile is stored in one of two locations. For user-specific desktop, application, and operating system settings, Registry information is stored in a single file called NTUser.dat. When a user logs in, this information is copied into the current Registry. In the Registry Editor, the information appears as the HKEY_CURRENT_USER key. Desktop items, network shortcuts, Start menu settings, and so on are all stored in the file system under the winnt\profiles directory.

Types of Profiles

User profiles store preferences and basic information for users. These settings include desktop color preferences, shortcuts and icons, and application settings. Though they all store the same information, there are three main types of profiles:

Accessing Program Groups

You can quickly access these folders by right-clicking the Start button. Choose Explore or Open to show the current user's program groups. On Windows NT, you can also choose Explore All Users or Open All Users to open the All Users directory.

- *Local user profiles*—Local profiles are stored on each workstation. This profile is the default type of profile that is created when a user logs in to a Windows NT machine.

- *Roaming user profiles*—In networked Windows NT environments, it is possible to store all user profile information centrally on a server. This way, a user logging in to the network has the same desktop settings on one machine as he or she would have on another computer. Roaming profiles are especially useful when users move between computers for various tasks or when people work in shifts.

- *Mandatory profiles*—A systems administrator may specify profiles as mandatory. These, like roaming profiles, are stored on a server. However, the end user is unable to save any changes to the profile when he or she logs out.

Creating User Profiles

You can manually create a user profile by logging in to a system as any user. For example, if several members of the administrative staff require the same desktop shortcuts and Start menu programs, you can log on under one of these user accounts and make the necessary changes. This step includes the creation of desktop shortcuts, screen saver and desktop settings, and any other elements that are stored as part of the profile. When you log off, the settings are stored on the local machine. Now that the profile is created, you can click on Control Panel, System, Profiles and then click on Copy To to assign the profile to other users.

Assigning Roaming User Profiles

There are several situations in which a user may need to log on to different physical machines but still need to access the same resources. For example, in offices with multiple clerical staffers, users may switch between machines frequently. Roaming user profiles that store information centrally on a server can be created. First, create a share on a server and give all necessary users read access to this directory. Within the share, create a folder for each user who requires a roaming profile.

To assign a roaming user profile to a user's account:

1. Run User Manager for Domains.

2. Double-click on an account name or create a new account.

3. Click on the Profile button to open the User Environment Profile dialog box, shown in Figure 18.3. For the User Profile Path, enter the UNC name for the server (for example, \\server1\profiles\JoeUser).

4. Click OK to accept these settings. If the directory does not yet exist, Windows prompts you to create one.

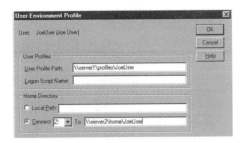

Figure 18.3   Assigning a roaming user profile in User Manager.

Mandatory User Profiles

For More
Information
6, 7 A systems administrator can designate a permanent profile for a user. Mandatory profiles have the same functionality as roaming profiles with one exception: Any changes
a user makes are not saved. Mandatory profiles are particularly useful when several
people use the same profile (such as in a training lab environment). To convert a roaming profile to a mandatory one, do the following:

1. In User Manager for Domains, add a `.man` extension to the end of the profile
   directory. From the earlier example, I would make the setting `\\server1\`
   `profiles\JoeUser.man`.

2. Next, use Windows Explorer to rename the actual profile file. Use Windows
   Explorer to navigate to the directory in which the profile is stored. Then
   rename the `NTUser.dat` file to `NTUser.man`.

Managing User Profiles

A user profile can be copied from a user's machine or a server and assigned to another
user. Effectively, you are copying all settings and information stored in the profile to
another user or another machine. This procedure is useful if you want to give multiple
users the same default settings or you want to change the default settings on remote
machines. To copy an existing user profile:

1. Click on the System icon in the Control Panel.

2. On the User Profiles tab, highlight the profile you want to copy and click on
   Copy To. The dialog box shown in Figure 18.4 opens.

3. Choose the location to which you want to copy the profile. This location may
   be a local directory path or a remote network path (such as `\\server1\`
   `profiles\User1`).

4. In the Permitted to Use section, click on Change to specify the user or group
   that should have access to this profile.

5. Click OK to save the settings. Changes take place the next time affected users
   log in.

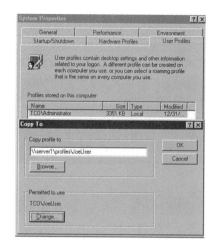

Figure 18.4   Using Windows NT to copy a user profile.

▷ For More
Information
8, 9

Local copies of the roaming user profile are created when a user logs in. This locally cached copy is checked against the server-based copy each time the user logs in. If any differences exist between the server and local copies of the profile, the newest version is used. Also, if the server is unavailable for any reason, the user can still log in if a locally cached profile is available.

Transferring profile information may cause performance problems on typically slow remote access links. To force a Windows NT client to use the locally cached profile by default:

1. Click on Control Panel, System and select the User Profiles tab.

2. Highlight the profile you want to change and click Change Type.

3. Check the Use Cached Profile for Slow Connections box (see Figure 18.5).

Maintaining Profile Permissions

It is important to use the Copy To function instead of the file system to copy profiles because this places appropriate user permissions on these directories.

Replicating Profiles to All Domain Controllers

If you want all domain users to use the same default profile, you can copy the profile to the NETLOGON share of the PDC in a directory called Default User. This profile overwrites the local default user profile for any users who are logging in to the domain for the first time and ensures that all BDCs are also able to provide the same profile.

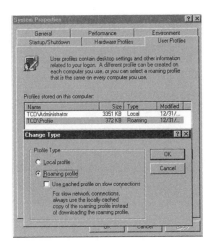

Figure 18.5 Changing the roaming user profile settings.

For More
Information
10 New with Windows NT 4.0 Service Pack 4 is the ability to manage the size of a profile. The `Proquota.exe` file can be used to set a maximum limit for a profile size. If the set limit is exceeded, the user cannot log off until files are deleted and/or moved. The benefit is that setting the quota can prevent users from storing very large downloads or other files on their desktop, thereby reducing the amount of data transfer during logins. More information on implementing profile quotas using system policies is available with the Service Pack 4 documentation.

Windows 95/98 Profiles

Profiles in Windows 95/98 are similar to Windows NT profiles. However, Windows 95/98 operating systems were designed primarily for home use. Therefore, the default setting for Windows 95/98 is to maintain a single profile. To change this profile:

1. Click on Control Panel, Passwords.

2. On the User Profiles tab, click on the Users Can Customize Their Preferences and Desktop Settings option (shown in Figure 18.6).

3. Optionally, you may choose to save individual desktops and/or Start menu programs with the user settings. If either of these options is left unchecked, all user profiles include common settings.

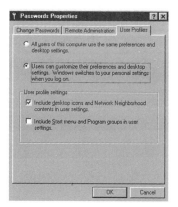

Figure 18.6   The Windows 95/98 passwords control panel.

▶ For More
Information
11

Windows 95/98 profiles must be created on computers running the same operating system because Windows NT Workstation and Server machines generate profiles differently. By default, the profile information is stored locally on the client machines in the Windows\Profiles directory. The profile name is user.dat (for a roaming user profile) or user.man (for a mandatory profile). You can also make these roaming profiles by storing them on a server. To do so, simply copy the user.dat or user.man file to a user's home directory on a machine running Windows NT Server. Windows 95/98 clients obtain profiles from the user's home directory and not from the Profile Path value specified for their user account.

System Policies

System policies are based on Windows 95/98/NT Registry settings and restrict the functions that users can perform on specific machines. Although you can use the Registry Editor tool to make these changes, finding the keys you want to modify, out of the thousands present, is often difficult. The System Policy Editor tool included with Windows NT makes this process easier and more manageable. In this section, we see how policies can be created based on templates and then assigned to user accounts.

System Policy Templates

The System Policy Editor tool provides a graphical interface for setting various Registry options. Policy templates are special text files that specify the available options. The diagram in Figure 18.7 shows how these pieces fit together: A policy template lists Registry settings, along with options for that setting, and provides a friendly prompt that describes its effects.

Profile Permissions

In order for mandatory profiles to work, the user must have at least read NTFS permissions to the profile directory. For roaming profiles, the user must have change access.

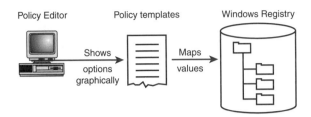

Figure 18.7 Policy templates, the Policy Editor, and the Registry.

The Registry models of Windows 95/98 and Windows NT vary, and performing the same function on these operating systems may require the modification of different Registry keys. By default, Windows NT includes the following templates:

- `Winnt.adm`—Options for Windows NT computers
- `Windows.adm`—Options for Windows 95/98 computers
- `Common.adm`—Options that are common to both Windows 95/98 and Windows NT

By default, the system policy files are installed in the `winnt\inf` directory. Listing 18.1 shows a portion of the `common.adm` file.

▶ For More Information
12

System policy templates can be created for any Registry settings you want to change. This may be helpful if you want to set options for specific company applications or to change Registry settings not specified in the default `*.adm` files.

Defining System Policies with the System Policy Editor

The System Policy Editor provides a graphical interface for creating and assigning policies. It uses the information stored in policy templates to provide the list of options that may be set for a specific value. Figure 18.8 shows the System Policy Editor interface.

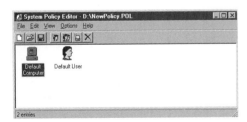

Figure 18.8 The Windows NT System Policy Editor.

Listing 18.1 **An Example of the Settings Available in the** *common.adm* **Policy Template File**

```
CLASS MACHINE


CATEGORY !!Network
    CATEGORY !!Update
        POLICY !!RemoteUpdate
        KEYNAME System\CurrentControlSet\Control\Update
        ACTIONLISTOFF
            VALUENAME "UpdateMode"      VALUE NUMERIC 0
        END ACTIONLISTOFF
            PART !!UpdateMode           DROPDOWNLIST REQUIRED
            VALUENAME "UpdateMode"
            ITEMLIST
                NAME !!UM_Automatic     VALUE NUMERIC 1
                NAME !!UM_Manual        VALUE NUMERIC 2
            END ITEMLIST
            END PART

            PART !!UM_Manual_Path       EDITTEXT
            VALUENAME "NetworkPath"
            END PART

            PART !!DisplayErrors        CHECKBOX
            VALUENAME "Verbose"
            END PART

            PART !!LoadBalance          CHECKBOX
            VALUENAME "LoadBalance"
            END PART
        END POLICY
    END CATEGORY    ; Update

END CATEGORY    ; Network
```

In this example, we set up a system policy that does the following:

- Runs the WordPad application on startup
- Specifies a directory that holds all desktop icons
- Enables a logon banner that warns users that the system is for authorized use only

Keeping a "Spare Key"

It is possible to lock yourself out of the system by placing policies that are too restrictive. Be careful when you make changes and be sure to always leave a user account available as a safety net to make changes.

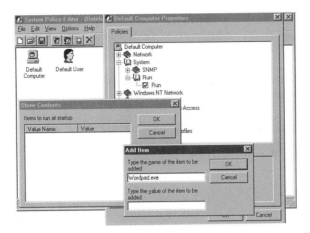

Figure 18.9 Setting default computer properties with the System Policy Editor.

To set up system policies:

1. Start the System Policy Editor from the Administrative Tools program group.

2. Click on File, New Policy to create a new policy file. The basic default policy template files are already loaded.

3. Select Default Computer, Run and place a check mark next to the Run command. The values in this section are either Selected (checked), Not Selected (unchecked), or Unspecified (a grayed-out box). Next, click Show, Add and type Wordpad.exe for the name of the item to be added (as shown in Figure 18.9). Click OK to accept the changes.

4. Select Windows NT Shell, Custom Shared Folders and place a check mark next to Custom Shared Desktop Icons. This setting allows you to specify a path to use for shared icons. In this example, I'm using the path c:\desktop.

5. Select Windows NT System, Logon, Logon Banner and enable the selection. For this example, I'm keeping the default warning, but you will probably want to add something more relevant to your environment. A well-worded banner states that the machines are to be used by authorized users for business purposes only. Reminders about password policies and usage information can also be added.

6. Click on OK to accept these settings. The final step is to save the settings (File, Save). For this example, name the file NtConfig.pol and make note of where you saved it.

On the CD-ROM

Demonstration 18.2, "System Policies," shows the basic steps required to create and apply new user and machine profiles.

Applying System Policies

Thus far, we've created a system policy, but we have not yet assigned it to any machine or users. To assign the policy file to a machine or to a user:

1. Click on File, Open in System Policy Editor and select the `NTConfig.pol` file we created in the previous section.

2. Click on Add Computer and then select the computer to which you want to apply the machine settings.

3. Click on Add User and then select the user account to which you want to apply the user settings.

4. Save the updated policy file by clicking on File, Save.

Both the user account and computer inherit the default settings that you have already defined. You can, however, override or change any of these settings by double-clicking on the user or computer icon you want to affect. You can also use the System Policy Editor to directly modify the settings in a local or remote Registry. To do so, click on File, Open Registry (for the local Registry) or File, Connect (to access remote computers).

Finally, we need to make this new policy file available to all network users. Simply copy the `NTConfig.pol` file to the `NETLOGON` share on the PDC. This step ensures that the file is replicated to all other domain controllers if they are present. Make sure that users have at least read permissions to this directory. Any computers that are not specifically added to the policy file inherit the Default User and Default Computer settings. To change these settings, simply reopen the `NTConfig.pol` file in the System Policy Editor and add or remove users and machines.

Creating Policy Groups

To facilitate the administration of environments with many workstations, you can place users and computers in policy groups. To use the System Policy Editor to create a policy group, click on Edit, Add Group. Specific user profiles take precedence over group profiles if both exist. If users or computers belong to more than one group, you need to set a precedence order in which policies are to be applied. In this case, the highest precedence settings that are enabled are chosen. An enabled setting is one that is either checked or blank. The unspecified setting is represented by a grayed-out box and indicates that the setting should not be affected by this policy. To modify group priorities:

Enabling Remote Registry Modification

To directly modify policy settings on remote computers, the host machine must have the Remote Registry service installed.

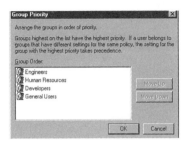

Figure 18.10   Setting system policy group priorities with the System Policy Editor.

1. Create the group by clicking Edit, Add Group and enter a name.
2. Make any settings that you want members of this group to use.
3. To specify the order of precedence, click on Options, Group Priority. From this screen (shown in Figure 18.10), you can move groups up and down in the list to assign their order of precedence.

Multidomain Policy Issues

By default, the NTConfig.pol file is downloaded from a domain controller of the domain in which the machine is a member. However, if a user of this computer chooses to log in to another domain, he or she receives the user policy from the domain controller of that domain instead. Additionally, you can specify a manual update path for users to obtain policy information from a predefined path by specifying it explicitly in User Manager (for example, \\server1\policies).

For more information on changing the update mode, see the To Change the System Policy File Path for Manual Update entry in System Policy Editor Help.

Policies on Windows 95/98

▶ For More
Information
13

Windows 95/98 policies must be created using the System Policy Editor on computers running the Windows 95/98 operating system. These policy files are not compatible with Windows NT computers (or vice versa). Windows 95/98 policy files are named Config.pol and must be stored in the user's home directory on a server (instead of the NETLOGON share). Also, to enable support for group policies, you need to add group policy support. To do so, click on Control Panel, Add/Remove Programs, Windows Setup, System Tools. If it's not already checked, install the Group Policies option. Windows 98 additionally includes special policy template files that you can use for customizing the settings of Internet Explorer, Outlook Express, and other applications. More information is available in Windows 95/98 documentation.

Security Notes

Even though a policy file can restrict a user from performing specific functions, it is enforced only when a user logs in to a domain. Therefore, system policies, by themselves, may not provide sufficient security. For example, preventing users from accessing the Control Panel does not directly prevent them from deleting system files or making Registry modifications manually. It's important that system policies be used in conjunction with well-managed file-system permissions and user rights.

More Policy Templates

▶ For More
Information
14

Microsoft Office 97 includes setup templates for customizing the setup and use of Office 97. You can use these template files to restrict certain functions, to create defaults for Office application users, and to configure Registry settings. However, these settings are specific to Microsoft Office 97 applications. If you're planning a rollout of Office applications and want to keep user default settings consistent, system policies are very useful. Other application vendors can include their own .adm files for enforcing policy options specific to their software.

The Windows NT Zero Administration Kit

▶ For More
Information
15

In an effort to address the problems associated with end users changing their system configuration and causing additional support problems, Microsoft introduced the Zero Administration Kit (ZAK) for Windows. Although the underlying technology in this model is not new, ZAK provides an integrated solution designed to restrict access on computers used for single tasks or for only a few business-critical applications. ZAK is perfect for training environments, Internet kiosks, or users whose jobs involve few applications (such as accounting data-entry clerks). ZAK is available as a free download from Microsoft and is can be used on Windows NT Workstation and Server computers.

ZAK Modes

ZAK is a preconfigured set of system policies, user profiles, and automated installation scripts. ZAK works in two basic modes:

- *App Station*—Designed for machines that run a few specific business-related applications. For example, users may require Microsoft Office 97 applications, such as Word and Excel, and access to the company's mainframe system. It is not necessary, however, for users to manage various features of their hardware and software configuration or install new programs. They should also be unable to change display, user, and network settings.

- *Task Station*—Some users may use a PC to run only a single application. For example, administrative personnel may be responsible only for data entry into a companywide mainframe using a terminal emulation program. In this case, they don't need to see the Windows user interface—all these users require is the program's main interface. Another example of a Task Station is an Internet-access kiosk. Because the sole purpose of this machine is to run a Web browser, the Start menu and taskbar are not necessary.

The Task Station mode is really a subset of the App Station mode. Therefore, if you plan to support both roles in your environment, it is only necessary to configure the App Station and then make a few changes to user permissions and logon scripts.

Implementing ZAK

▶ For More
Information
16
This section provides a basic overview of what's required of the systems administrator to set up an App Station or Task Station. The ZAK online course provides a clear, step-by-step method for implementing this process. Detailed installation instructions and step-by-step procedures are freely available from Microsoft. In the ZAK environment

- A single program interface handles all setup options.

- All applications are stored centrally on a server and are run over the network.

- Operating system installations are automated for easy rollout and minimal administrator interaction.

- System policies are included to limit the functions a user may perform.

- Access to the local machine is secured via NTFS permissions.

- Users can run only specific programs on their computers and may not be able to access the Start menu and other configuration settings.

The ZAK setup program copies various configuration files and applications to server locations. The process for implementing ZAK involves storing all ZAK-related files, including Windows NT Workstation, the latest Service Pack, and files used by ZAK for configuration, on a Distribution Server. Optionally, applications for end users, such as Microsoft Office 97, can also be stored on this machine. Here's the procedure for implementing ZAK:

1. The ZAK Setup program prompts the user for a network share or a CD-ROM with the programs to be copied and copies them to the server. Figure 18.11 shows the initial ZAK Setup screen.

2. Windows NT Workstation, along with the ZAK configuration files, are installed on client machines using the unattended installation mode.

3. A systems administrator assigns permissions to users, using groups and built-in policies.

4. Users access programs through a limited operating system interface by logging in to their client workstations and running programs from the server.

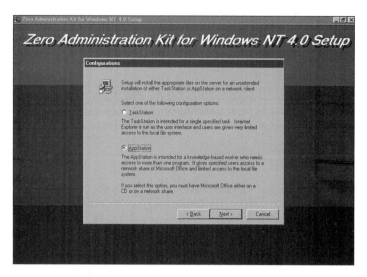

Figure 18.11   The Zero Administration Kit Setup program.

All restrictions on functionality are performed on a per user basis. Therefore, if you need to make changes to system configurations, you can simply log on to a machine as an Administrator and not have the same system policies enforced.

In summary, ZAK does not provide any new technology. It does, however, integrate several otherwise disorganized methods for simplifying the installation process and restricting users. In the real world, it is unlikely that ZAK, by itself, will solve all of your problems. Instead, it serves as an illustration of how things may be done better. ZAK unifies the ideas of automated installations and using policies and profiles to restrict user access.

Other Concerns

Apart from utilizing policies and profiles, there are many different concerns for IT staff. Despite all the technical solutions that are available, there are obstacles that must be overcome before policies can be effectively enforced. In this section, I briefly mention some of these obstacles and offer suggestions for overcoming them.

Useful ZAK Tools

In the \Tools directory of ZAK, there are several useful utilities. Though they don't come with much documentation, one—RUNAPP.exe—can be quite useful. This small utility runs any program you choose. But as soon as a user tries to close the program, Windows restarts it automatically. This utility is great for single-task environments—just add it to the Startup program group!

The People Factor

When implementing system policies, getting buy-in from users and management is critical but may be quite difficult. Appropriate business cases should be presented and approved before changing any functionality or user permissions. In many cases, people resent not being able to install new software on their computers or customize their environments to their liking. Also, the 80/20 rule estimates that most of the problems will come from only a few users. For many technical staffers, addressing these issues is the most complicated part of implementing policies. However, with adequate communication, it might be easy to solve common complaints without compromising security and/or functionality. The benefits of implementing appropriate system policies can be great—license management, decreased troubleshooting, and greater focus on business-critical job functions.

Finally, managing policies requires time and effort. As users' needs change and new applications are introduced, policy files will probably need to be modified. For these reasons, it's best to view system policies as a flexible set of guidelines that evolve with business needs.

Running Applications from the Server

One limitation of the use of policies and profiles is that they can only restrict access to programs and features available on the local installation of a client machine. That is, if I have a profile with a Microsoft Word shortcut, I can run the program only if it is installed on the local machine. If you're in an environment where such restrictions are a problem, you might want to install your applications so that they run from a central server. As shown in the section "The Windows NT Zero Administration Kit," not all programs support this functionality. Consider storing applications on the server if network bandwidth is available and universal application access is desired. Other options are available in Windows NT Terminal Server (mentioned in the next section) and will be integrated into Windows 2000.

Windows NT Terminal Server

Microsoft's Windows NT Server, Terminal Server Edition, has been created to assist IT departments in providing remote users with information and application access via thin clients. This product is discussed in more detail in Chapter 11, "Remote Management." Terminal Server enables you to set all policies, profiles, and user permissions on a single computer. This machine can then be accessed by simple, scaled-down clients that rely on Terminal Server for all information processing. The main benefit is that less powerful client computers can run resource-intensive programs that execute on a server. Although many hurdles remain before wide-scale terminal adoption, thin clients are worthy of consideration for many single-task situations.

Case Study: Managing Profiles and Policies Based on User Requirements

The IT department at XYZ Corp. supports 100 users running Windows 95/98 and Windows NT. Several staff members are spending most of their time troubleshooting problems caused by users tinkering with their system settings. The IT department is looking for a way to reduce these problems so that it can focus on other issues. By function, these users are

- Secretarial/administrative staff
- Human resources staff
- Engineers
- Software developers

Each of these groups has different requirements. For example, the administrative staff primarily uses Microsoft Office applications and accesses files from a single departmental server. Software developers and engineers, on the other hand, require almost unrestricted access to their own machines for testing and software installation. Human resources users require access to specific company databases and basic word processing applications only.

Solution

The systems administrator decides to implement roaming user profiles for all of the secretarial staff because they move between computers. ZAK options were considered for these users, but because the group is small, policies alone should be sufficient. Other users have assigned computers and rarely use other machines. For all users, system policies with different levels of permissions are established. First, the administrator decides to create a default profile group. She places all users in the default group and adds a logon banner and default program startup options. She then makes changes to this default profile for the several different types of users who will be supported and places appropriate group priorities.

Users in the human resources department are given a modified Start menu that contains only the icons necessary for running applications such as the employee database and Microsoft Word. Engineers and software developers do not require immediate access to the corporate intranet upon login, so their profiles do not specify any programs to run at startup. This setting overrides other group options, so no programs automatically execute upon login.

Before rolling out the solution to many users, the systems administrator tests the configuration with volunteers and adds/removes permissions as needed. Finally, she deploys the policy file on the domain controllers of the environment. Using these steps, the administrator has ensured that roving users will have a consistent experience regardless of which machine they decide to use. Additionally, users are permitted to perform only the functions required for their jobs. Both solutions help to cut down on support costs and ensure that machines are used for their intended purpose.

The Bottom Line

The purpose of computers in business is to assist users in completing a job. All too often, however, users may purposely or accidentally make changes to their systems that are against corporate policies. By limiting what users can do on their own machines, you can be fairly sure that they do not accidentally change any system settings that might have an adverse impact on their system. Enforcing user rights via policy profiles and templates can solve one of the most common IT support headaches and can ensure that users will always be able to use their local machines for business purposes.

For More Information

1. Chapter 8 of this book: "Data Protection"
2. "Description of the Windows Registry Checker Tool (Scanreg.exe)," Q183887, Microsoft Knowledge Base
3. "How to Back Up the Registry," Q132332, Microsoft Knowledge Base
4. Appendix A, "Windows NT Registry," Windows NT Server Manuals, Concepts and Planning Manual
5. Chapter 23, "Overview of the Windows NT Registry," Windows NT Workstation 4.0 Resource Kit
6. "How to Create a Base Profile for All Users," Q168475, Microsoft Knowledge Base
7. "How to Create Mandatory Profiles for Windows 95 Users," Q161809, Microsoft Knowledge Base
8. "User Profile Scenario Summaries," Q174491, Microsoft Knowledge Base
9. "How to Create and Copy Roaming User Profiles in NT 4.0," Q142682, Microsoft Knowledge Base
10. "How to Enable Profile Quotas in Windows NT 4.0," Q185561, Microsoft Knowledge Base
11. "User Profiles and System Policies in Windows 95," Windows 95 Technical Notes, Microsoft TechNet
12. "Creating a Custom System Policy Template" in Chapter 8, "System Policies," Microsoft Windows 98 Resource Kit, Part 2 "System Configuration"
13. Chapter 15, "User Profiles and System Policies," Windows 95 Resource Kit
14. "Microsoft Office 97 System Policies Whitepaper," Microsoft TechNet
15. Chapter 14 of this book: "Automated Software Installation"
16. Microsoft Management home page (www.microsoft.com/management)

Further Reading

For more information on working with profiles and enforcing system policies in general, see

- "Guide to Microsoft Windows NT 4.0 Profiles and Policies," Microsoft TechNet

- Chapter 7, "User Profiles," and Chapter 8, "System Policies," Windows 98 Resource Kit

- Chapter 3, "Managing User Work Environments," Windows NT Server Manuals, Microsoft TechNet

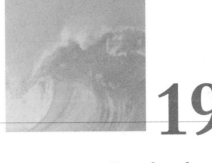

19

Scripting

Oの NE OF THE LIMITATIONS OF GUI-BASED operating systems is that they often sacrifice the functionality that is available in scripting. Of course, there's good reason for this: For the average desktop operating system user, writing batch files—simple sequences of operating system commands—borders on being a programmer. However, scripting enables network and systems administrators to do many things we cannot easily do otherwise. For example, obtaining and changing Registry entries from the command line requires the use of a cryptic utility.

Batch files are no longer limited to simple command-line operating system tools. Microsoft has recently made available the Windows Scripting Host (WSH), which allows any type of scripting language to be used to perform operating system tasks. By default, WSH supports JScript (Microsoft's version of JavaScript) and VBScript (a scaled-down, specific subset of the Visual Basic programming language). Those who have programmed in a language like Visual Basic will see the true usefulness of these scripts.

If you've done some programming, you'll feel right at home with the scripts in this chapter. If you haven't, then you may find it a little challenging to follow some of the more complex scripts. In this chapter, I show you how to write and execute scripts. A discussion of programming concepts and techniques (such as defining variables and using loops or other control structures) is beyond our scope. A good source for this type of information is the documentation that accompanies program development environments (such as Microsoft's Visual Studio or Oracle's PowerBuilder). By the end of this chapter, I hope to prove just how easy and useful generating scripts can be. I won't accept "I'm not a programmer" as a response, so let's get started!

Scripting Basics

Before we get started with the details of implementing scripts, let's look at what scripts are, how they can be written, and how they are executed.

The Usefulness of Scripting

Scripts fill in the gap between the basic functionality provided by DOS batch files and the full-featured functionality of applications created in languages such as Visual Basic. Figure 19.1 shows the relationship between the various types of coding.

How exactly does scripting empower systems administrators? In a distributed network environment, the amount of control you have over desktop computers may be limited. The graphical user interface (GUI), with its ease of use and protection of the user from the behind-the-scenes workings of the operating system forms a perfect interface for the most common functions accessed by end users. For example, you can set up Dynamic Host Configuration Protocol (DHCP, described in Chapter 6, "TCP/IP Management") options by clicking on Start, Settings, Control Panel, Network, Protocols, TCP/IP, Properties and then selecting the option to use DHCP. This is not a very daunting task for administrators, but when end users perform the same task, there is some room for error. Also, imagine performing the task on a hundred computers—each click would significantly multiply your work.

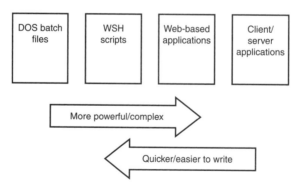

Figure 19.1   Properties of scripts, batch files, and applications.

The Windows Scripting Host

Scripts are not confined to performing operating system functions and modifying the Registry, however. You can access code and modules from other applications. On the sample files that are installed by default with the WSH is the Chart example. This short script opens an Excel window, creates a basic graph, and then rotates this graph through multiple frames. We look at the specifics of these types of scripts later in the chapter. For now, just know that such functions are easily possible with a few lines of code.

Finally, scripting is important in that it allows the use of newer programming concepts such as nonlinear program flow and event-driven code. You can easily define and call subroutines and share code between different script modules. This helps in realizing the true usefulness of scripts in general.

WSH Supported Languages

One of the main benefits of WSH is that it is written to be language independent. It is a basic shell for allowing interactions with a scripting language. By default, WSH is installed with support for the VBScript and JScript languages. Scripting engines for other languages, such as Perl, TCL, REXX, and Python, are either available or are in development from other companies. Although WSH provides a single scripting interface, separate programs are available for running scripts generated in most other languages directly. Scripting is an evolving technology, and changes in language details and WSH will occur periodically. Information is available from Microsoft (see Figure 19.2).

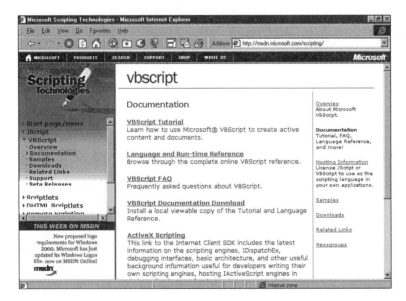

Figure 19.2 Microsoft's Scripting Technologies Web site.

Obtaining WSH

▶ For More
Information
1
WSH is preinstalled with the Windows 98 operating system and will be included as
part of all future versions of Windows. Windows NT 4.0 users need to install either
Service Pack 4 or the Windows NT Option Pack to install WSH. Windows 95 users
need to download WSH support files from Microsoft. If newer versions of WSH are
available, they also can be downloaded from Microsoft.

The Registry

Before embarking on the basics of designing scripts, let's take a quick look at how
Microsoft's current operating systems store configuration information. This discussion
will be useful if you decide, for example, to create a script that automatically changes
all users' network configuration. The Windows 95/98 and Windows NT Registry is a
centralized location for storing all application settings and program information. In
addition, the Registry stores all operating system settings, including a list of hardware
devices installed on your system. There are differences in the organization and content
of the Windows 95/98 and Windows NT Registries. In fact, one of the major reasons
that Microsoft has cited for not creating an automatic upgrade path from Windows
95/98 to Windows NT 4.0 is the difference in the Registry structures. One difference
is that the Windows NT Registry supports the management of security settings for
information stored there. Also, Windows NT was designed to easily support multiple
users, and this is seen in the Registry structure. Finally, Plug and Play (the standard for
automatic detection of compatible devices) is not supported on Windows NT 4.0, thus
making hardware-specific keys different. Table 19.1 lists the major sections and a brief
description of the data they store.

Table 19.1   **Major Registry Keys and the Information They Hold**

Registry Key	Type of Information
HKEY_LOCAL_MACHINE	System settings and information specific to the hardware settings of this computer
HKEY_CURRENT_USER	A subset of HKEY_USER that stores basic settings and information about the user currently logged in to the machine
HKEY_SOFTWARE	Software- and application-specific information
HKEY_CLASSES_ROOT	Information on registered dynamic link libraries (DLLs) and ActiveX controls

On the CD-ROM

Demonstration 19.1, "RegEdit," walks you through the basics of viewing Registry information on a
Windows NT 4.0 computer.

For More
Information
2

Before the days of the Registry (i.e., in MS-DOS and Windows 3.x), applications stored all their settings in individual `.ini` files. These files would either be stored in the program's directory or in the Windows root directory. For example, programs that would load at startup or make other operating system changes modified the `System.ini` or `Win.ini` files. These files are still preserved for backward compatibility in current versions of 32-bit Windows, but they are not the preferred way of storing information. Because each program was responsible for maintaining its own information, there was no central database to query to find out which programs were installed on a computer. A major advantage of the Registry is that system administrators can look in one central location for operating system and application settings. However, the Registry is far from perfect—it is poorly documented, and its lack of organization makes it cumbersome. Furthermore, there is no way to enforce where applications store their settings, and much of this is in the hands of developers. Microsoft includes the RegEdit tool, which can be used to view and modify Registry settings (shown in Figure 19.3) with all current operating systems.

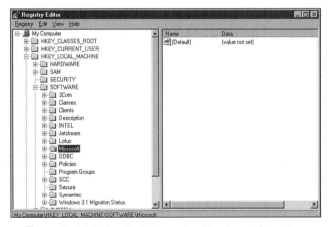

Figure 19.3   Using RegEdit to view Registry information.

Backing Up the Registry Before Making Changes

Anyone who often relies on Microsoft's Knowledge Base will have read warnings about modifying the Registry and information on the importance of backing it up. Making changes and/or deleting keys from the Registry can potentially cause serious problems to your operating system. Some may force you to reinstall the operating system. For this reason, it's worth taking the time to back up the Registry before making any changes.

▶ For More
Information
3, 4   So far we've seen that the Windows Registry holds a great deal of useful information. The obvious question is, Where can one get information on all the different Registry keys and application objects? Unfortunately, there is no single comprehensive source describing all of the possible settings. For specific applications, you need to receive information from the manufacturer. Regarding operating system settings, Microsoft's TechNet and Knowledge Base articles often provide information on specific settings that can be made only via the Registry. In general, most configuration changes can be made through the GUI. However, if you want to make an application-specific change to multiple computers, changing Registry settings with scripts can be much more efficient.

Limitations of Scripting

Using WSH and creating scripts have their limitations. For example, there is not much of a mechanism for interacting with the user. The inability to create a client interface is one of the major differences between scripting and traditional programming. Scripting is better suited to functions such as handling network administration tasks, creating login scripts, and automating simple functions.

Choosing a Scripting Language

WSH supports both the VBScript and JScript programming languages. Choosing between the two languages will usually be based on the preference of the programmer. In general, if you're familiar with C, C++, or Java programming language, JScript is a good bet. JScript is Microsoft's version of the JavaScript language and is compatible with most current Web browsers. Visual Basic scripting language (VBScript) was originally created as a subset of the Visual Basic language and provides an easy-to-learn and powerful basis for new programmers. Its feature set provides for the same functionality as JScript, but it is currently supported only in the Microsoft Internet Explorer browser for UNIX and Windows-based platforms. If you're using Netscape, this solution is clearly not one you can choose. However, if you'll be making operating system-level scripts, VBScript is probably the better choice due to ease-of-use, code accessibility and convenience. For comparison, Listings 19.1 and 19.2 show fragments of code taken from the Shortcut.vbs WSH sample scripts. They have the exact same functionality but use a different syntax. For now, just know that there are multiple ways to perform the same task. Don't worry if you don't understand the syntax of each code line because we look at these in detail later in the chapter.

Listing 19.1 **Creating a Welcome Message in VBcript**

```
Sub Welcome()
    Dim intDoIt
    intDoIt = MsgBox(L_Welcome_MsgBox_Message_Text,
                     vbOKCancel + vbInformation,
                     L_Welcome_MsgBox_Title_Text )
    If intDoIt = vbCancel Then
        WScript.Quit
    End If
End Sub
```

Listing 19.2 **Creating a Welcome Message in JScript**

```
function Welcome() {
    var WSHShell = WScript.CreateObject("WScript.Shell");
    var intDoIt;
    intDoIt = WSHShell.Popup(L_Welcome_MsgBox_Message_Text,
                             0,
                             L_Welcome_MsgBox_Title_Text,
                             vbOKCancel + vbInformation );
    if (intDoIt == vbCancel) {
        WScript.Quit();
    }
}
```

Both of these script fragments provide the equivalent function of creating a simple message box. The values of the variables are actually assigned elsewhere in the scripts. Figure 19.4 shows the results of this code as it is used in the ShowVar.vbs WSH sample script. In this case, the text of the message box is defined as the values of current system variables.

Figure 19.4 Sample results from the ShowVar.vbs script.

In this chapter, I focus on VBScript programming because this language is much easier for new programmers to learn. Again, the goal of this chapter is not to make you an expert programmer, but to give you a sampling of what you can do with WSH.

VBScript Language Basics

Now that you know what scripting is and does, let's look at some of the details of actually implementing code in Visual Basic examples. The standard disclaimer still applies—this section won't make you a professional VB programmer, but you'll learn the basic steps in writing a script.

VBScript is an object-oriented language and allows you to reference numerous aspects of the operating system. Table 19.2 shows the various objects that are available from within the WScript language object. Most objects are not directly available to program code and must be accessed through other objects. We look at examples later in this chapter.

In addition to using the WScript object and its subobjects, you can also reference objects available from other Windows programs. In a WSH sample script described later in this chapter, a simple script uses Microsoft Excel to create and modify a spreadsheet.

Table 19.2 **WScript Objects**

Object Name	Accessed Through	Purpose
WshShell	Wscript.WSHShell	Creating desktop shortcuts; running programs; reading and writing from the Registry
WshArguments	Wscript.Arguments	Accessing command-line arguments
WshShortcut	WshShell.CreateShortcut	Creating program shortcuts
WshURLShortcut	WshShell.CreateShortcut	Creating Internet shortcuts
WshSpecialFolders	WshShell.Folders	Modifying contents of special folders (AllUsers, Desktop, and so on)
WshEnvironment	WshShell.Environment	Setting, removing, and querying environment variables

Running WSH Scripts

WSH provides two interfaces—one is run from within the Windows environment, and the other is run from the command line. Both tools execute files with a .vbs or a .js extension and execute those commands.

Using Windows: WScript

After you install WSH, you can execute scripts from within Windows 95/98 and Windows NT by double-clicking on any file with a .vbs or .js extension. Alternatively, you can click on Start, Run and type Wscript scriptname.vbs. Running WScript with no arguments (shown in Figure 19.5) allows you to modify some basic properties used when executing scripts.

The properties you can set are as follows:

- *Stop Scripts After Specified Number of Seconds*—Automatically ends execution of a script after the specific time has elapsed. You might use this to prevent scripts from using system resources in the event of an error.

- *Display Logo When Scripts Executed in MS-DOS Prompt*—Shows the WSH logo (or a logo of your choice) when you run command-line scripts.

To set the options for all scripts that you run on this machine, simply run the WScript program by itself and make the necessary changes. The properties may also be set on a per script basis by right-clicking on a script file, selecting Properties, and then making settings changes in the Script tab.

During installation, WSH copies several sample scripts to your c:\windows\ samples\wsh directory. The code samples are well documented and are a good place to start learning about the VBScript and JScript syntax. Table 19.3 lists the sample script names and their functions.

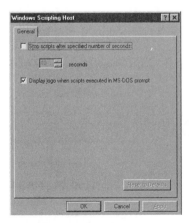

Figure 19.5 WScript script options.

Table 19.3 **WSH Sample Scripts**

Script	VBScript	JavaScript	Function
Chart	Yes	Yes	Creates and rotates a Microsoft Excel chart
Excel	Yes	Yes	Opens Microsoft Excel and creates a new spreadsheet with WSH information
Network	Yes	Yes	Displays network information and (optionally) maps network drives
Registry	Yes	Yes	Creates and deletes Registry keys (no permanent changes)
Shortcut	Yes	Yes	Creates a desktop shortcut for Notepad
ShowVar	Yes	No	Shows Windows Environment variables

Figure 19.6 shows the display you receive when running the `Chart.vbs` or `Chart.js` sample scripts.

Running scripts is as easy as double-clicking on them. For example, to run the `showvar.vbs` script included with the WSH installation, complete the following steps:

1. Use Windows Explorer to find the `showvar.vbs` file in the `Windows\Samples\Wsh` directory.

2. Double-click on the file to run it from within Windows.

3. Click on OK to execute the script. The dialog box shows the current settings of environment variables on your system (refer to Figure 19.4 for a sample).

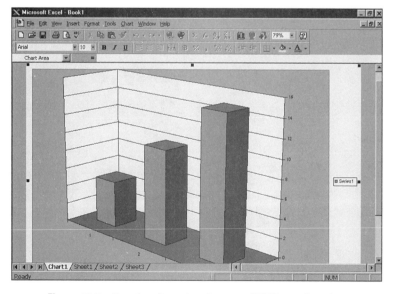

Figure 19.6   Results of running the `Chart` WSH sample script.

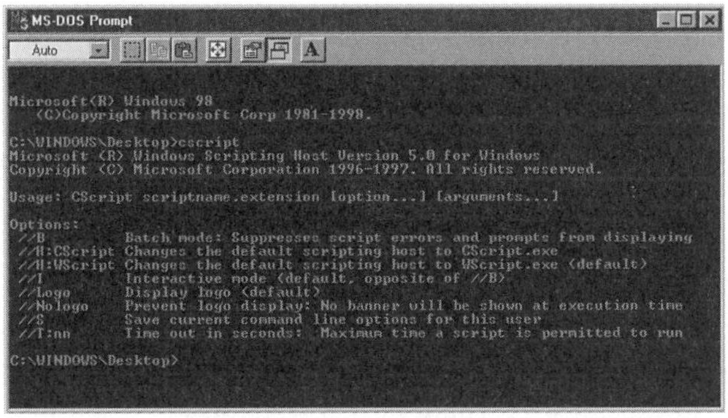

Figure 19.7   Command-line options available for the CScript utility.

If you need to specify command-line parameters for a script, you won't be able to simply double-click on the file (as this runs it without any arguments). Instead, you need to click on Start, Run and type wscript /argument1 /argument2 scriptname.vbs. Alternatively, you can create a shortcut that specifies this on the command line or create a .wsh text file that can automatically specify input parameters. We discuss the usage of command-line arguments later in the chapter.

Using the Command Line: *CScript*

You can use the CScript command to launch a WSH-compatible script from the command line. The main difference between using the CScript as opposed to WScript is that standard output is sent to the command line and input options are limited to the command-line interface. Figure 19.7 shows the possible parameters when using the CScript.exe command.

Note that options that are intended for WSH are preceded by a double slash (//). The single slash is reserved for parameters that are to be sent to the script itself. For example, the following command sets the timeout to 10 seconds and runs a script named test.vbs with the parameter TCOTest:

```
Cscript //t:10 test.vbs /TCOTest
```

To run the same showvar.vbs script from the command line, follow these steps:

1. Open a command prompt and change to the Windows\Samples\Wsh directory.
2. At the command line, type
   ```
   Cscript showvar.vbs
   ```
3. The results display from within Windows.

WSH Scripting Applications

This chapter is based on a fairly simple idea—creating programmatic constructs to perform and/or automate otherwise tedious tasks. It is beyond the scope of this book to provide extensive programming information. As always, see the "For More Information" section for pointers to more complete VBScript reference materials.

Example 1: The Basics

Programmers commonly use code to generate the output "Hello, World!" to test a programming language. In the following script, we do just that. To create the listing, type the following line in a text editor such as Notepad and save it to a file named Hello.vbs:

```
Wscript.Echo "Hello, User"
```

To execute the script, you need to have WSH installed. Simply double-click on the file you created from within Windows. Note that if you run this from the command line using the CScript program, the output is sent to a command line.

Let's take this script one step further and prompt the user for his or her name. The script in Listing 19.3 creates a somewhat personalized greeting.

The listing uses the Set statement to create the WSHNetwork object. This allows us to access network-related information from within the script. Next, we assign the value of the current username and machine name to the CurrentUser and CurrentComputer variables. Finally, the script displays this information as part of a message box, as shown in Figure 19.8.

Listing 19.3   **The "Hello, [*username*]" Script**

```
Set WSHNetwork = WScript.CreateObject("WScript.Network")
Dim CurrentUser
Dim CurrentComputer
CurrentComputer = wshnetwork.ComputerName
CurrentUser = wshnetwork.UserName
Wscript.echo "Hello, " & CurrentUser & "!  " &
     ➥ "Your machine name is: " & CurrentComputer
```

Creating Shortcuts for Editing Scripts

If you'll be editing scripts often, it might be convenient to create a shortcut to the Notepad program on your desktop. Also, you can copy this shortcut to the \windows\sendto directory to allow using the SendTo command when right-clicking on a script file.

VBScript and Case Sensitivity

The VBScript language is not case sensitive, but it does retain case. To make variables and other operations easier to read, it's a good idea to use mixed case.

Figure 19.8   The results of running the script in Listing 19.3.

Example 2: Creating Desktop Shortcuts

For our second trick, we'll create a simple Windows NT script that makes some common shortcuts on the user's desktop. In this example, I've chosen common programs included with Windows 98. For the shortcuts to work properly, you may need to modify them for your environment. The script in Listing 19.4 is similar to the Shortcut.vbs sample script but should be a little easier to follow.

Listing 19.4   **The *CreateShortcuts.vbs* Script**

```
'CreatShortcuts.vbs
'This script creates desktop icons for WordPad and Calculator
Dim Desktop, DesktopPath
Set Shell = WScript.CreateObject("WScript.Shell")
DesktopPath = Shell.SpecialFolders("Desktop")
'Create Notepad Shortcut, set properties, and save
Set Shortcut1 = Shell.CreateShortcut
    ➥(DesktopPath & "\Notepad.lnk")
Shortcut1.TargetPath = Shell.ExpandEnvironmentStrings
    ➥("%windir%\notepad.exe")
Shortcut1.WorkingDirectory = Shell.ExpandEnvironmentStrings
    ➥("%windir%")
Shortcut1.IconLocation = Shell.ExpandEnvironmentStrings
    ➥ ("%windir%\notepad.exe, 0")
Shortcut1.Save
'Create Wordpad Shortcut, set properties, and save
Set Shortcut2 = Shell.CreateShortcut
    ➥(DesktopPath & "\Wordpad.lnk")
Shortcut2.TargetPath = Shell.ExpandEnvironmentStrings
    ➥ ("c:\Program Files\Accessories\WordPad.exe")
Shortcut2.WorkingDirectory = Shell.ExpandEnvironmentStrings
    ➥("%windir%")
Shortcut2.IconLocation = Shell.ExpandEnvironmentStrings
    ➥ ("c:\Program Files\Accessories\WordPad.exe, 0")
Shortcut2.Save
WScript.Echo "Two shortcuts have been created on your desktop."
WScript.Quit
```

Special Characters in the Code

A single quote (') character in a line of code indicates that the remainder of the line is a comment. I include comments to explain what's going on, but it is not necessary to enter these lines when typing in scripts. An underscore (_) character indicates that a line is continued. You can type all the code on one line (up to 256 characters), or you can type them as they appear in the listings.

Note that the script in Listing 19.4 does not check for the existence of these short-cuts, so if they exist, they will be redefined. Also, if you run the script multiple times, you'll only have one set of shortcuts. It's unlikely that you'll have hours of pleasure with this script, so let's move onto something slightly more useful.

Example 3: Displaying Drive Mappings

Being able to create shortcuts on users' desktops may not demonstrate the full power of scripting, but it did provide an introduction to command syntax. Let's move on to generating more useful scripts. The code in Listing 19.5 prompts the user to select the drives he or she wishes to map and then creates drive mappings for them. It also auto-matically connects the user to specific printers. This script uses the same basic ideas as the network.vbs WSH sample file but should be easier to follow. (If this code is a little over your head, you might want to read up on the basics of VBScript.)

Listing 19.5   **The *MapNetworkDrives.vbs* Script**

```
'This script displays a listing of current
'drive mappings and allows
'the user to reset to default drive mappings
'as defined within the script
'Initiaize variables
Dim WSHNetwork, DriveMappings
Dim UserInformation, MappingInfo, RemapDrives
Dim CRLF
CRLF = Chr(13) & Chr(10) 'Used to start a new output line
Set WSHNetwork = WScript.CreateObject("WScript.Network")
Set DriveMappings = WSHNetwork.EnumNetworkDrives
'Store current network settings and drive mappings
UserInformation = "** User Information ** " & CRLF & _
   "Current Domain: " & WSHNetwork.UserDomain & CRLF & _
   "Current User: " & WSHNetwork.UserName & CRLF &    _
   "Computer Name: " & WSHNetwork.ComputerName
'Display Current Drive Mappings
If DriveMappings.Count = 0 Then
    MappingInfo = "You currently have no network drive mappings."
   Else 'Add drive mapping information to MappingInfo string
    MappingInfo = "*** Current Drive Mappings *** " & CRLF
    For i = 0 To DriveMappings.Count—1
       MappingInfo = MappingInfo & CRLF & DriveMappings(i)
    Next
   End If

' Output Current Information and query for remapping
MsgBox UserInformation & CRLF & CRLF & MappingInfo & CRLF & CRLF
'Ask to remap drive
```

```
RemapDrives = MsgBox ("Do you want to reset
  ➥drive mappings?",vbYesNo,"Remap Drives?")
If RemapDrives = vbNo then
  WScript.Quit 'Exit script if user chooses "Cancel"
  End If


  '*** Map Network drives
  On Error Resume Next 'Ignore errors and move to next step
  WshNetwork.MapNetworkDrive "H:","\\server1\"
    ➥& WshNetwork.UserName
  WshNetwork.MapNetworkDrive "P:","\\server1\public"
  WshNetwork.MapNetworkDrive "K:","\\server2\apps"
  WshNetwork.AddPrinterConnection
    ➥"LPT1","\\print-server\printer1"


  WScript.Echo "The command has been completed.
  ➥Click OK to exit the script."
  WScript.Quit
```

For More
Information
5 Figure 19.9 shows the output the user receives after running this script.

This script can easily be modified to run as part of the Windows NT login script or to provide custom mappings for departmental users.

Figure 19.9   User information displayed after running the `MapNetworkDrives` script.

More Scripting Tools

The scripting examples in this chapter pertain mostly to basic network management features. This is only the tip of the scripting iceberg, and the same language and tools can be used in other applications. If you're looking for other possibilities, be sure to check out the WSH sample files. Then, look for repetitive tasks in your environment that lend themselves to being done automatically. For example, if you routinely copy files between locations or you want to create shortcuts to important company files for users, consider doing so within script code. A more complex script might automatically open an Excel document, populate several cells with prompts for specific information, and automatically generate the spreadsheet. Using scripts in this way can greatly increase efficiency and cut down on tedious operations. Now that you have an idea of the potential of scripts, let's look at alternative ways to run them.

Web-Based Scripts and Active Server Pages

It seems that no matter where you look, applications are being presented on or are being ported to the Web. Scripts lend themselves well to running on a Web site, provided that your browser supports this functionality. It is very easy to incorporate VBScript elements into Web pages as long as the browser supports such elements. For more universal browser support, consider using JScript because it is supported by browsers from Netscape, Microsoft, and other vendors.

Listing 19.6 shows a basic Web page incorporating a VBScript component.

Listing 19.6 **Scripts Within Web Pages**

```
<HTML>
<HEAD><TITLE>A Simple First Page</TITLE>
<SCRIPT LANGUAGE="VBScript">
<!--
Sub Button1_OnClick
        MsgBox "Welcome, User."
End Sub
-->
</SCRIPT>
</HEAD>
<BODY>
<H3>A Simple First Page</H3><HR>
<FORM><INPUT NAME="Button1" TYPE="BUTTON" VALUE="Click Here">
    ➡</FORM>
</BODY>
</HTML>
```

For More
Information
6, 7
An extremely popular method of designing dynamically generated Web pages is to use Microsoft's ASP technology. Using this technology, Web developers can embed client- or server-side application logic within a Web page. Before this page is sent to the client, the Web server interprets it. For more information on scripting for the Web, see Chapter 15, "Web-Based Technology," and Chapter 16, "Web Applications."

The Remote Scripting Host

For More
Information
8
To better enable client/server interactivity via Web pages, Microsoft has created the Remote Scripting Host (RSH). One of the major problems with performing calculations or applying business rules via Web pages is that the pages must be reloaded when calculations are performed. Remote scripting allows Web pages to call scripts from the server without reloading text. A potential use is handling data validation as values are entered, instead of when the user completes the form. RSH also allows you to access Dynamic HTML functions if your client browser supports them. This functionality blurs the line between client/server applications and Web-based front ends by giving users and developers more control over data access. For help with using RSH, sample files are available from Microsoft.

Case Study: Automating Routine Tasks

XYZ Corp. has many remote branch offices and wants to implement an automated procedure that performs the following functions:

1. Extracts information from a local branch database and saves it in a separate text file
2. Automatically transfers this file, as an email attachment, to the corporate headquarters
3. Imports each of the smaller files into a single large database to be maintained on the corporate network
4. Notifies the sender when the operation is complete

Solution

All the requirements are excellent cases for using WSH. It is beyond the scope of this chapter to provide the exact code, but WScript objects can be used with either VBScript or JScript to perform all the functions XYZ Corp. requires. Although there is no built-in functionality for working with databases and data connections, external programs and applications can be called from within the script. Code from Microsoft Office applications (such as Outlook 98) can be used to automatically send the email notifications. Additionally, you can use a command-scheduling program to ensure that this process runs automatically on the system at predefined times. Getting this script to function as desired will take some work, but the time saved will be well worth the effort. Managing these tasks using scripts is a quick and simple way to automate a small task that does not require significant training or changes to business processes. It is, however, far from the perfect situation. In the long run, it might be worthwhile to develop a method of directly transferring data between users without using intermediate files.

The Bottom Line

Performing routine or complicated tasks via scripts can increase efficiency and maintain consistency between applications. This may also enable less-technical users to perform otherwise complex tasks. For example, an accountant may not feel comfortable examining information generated by Windows NT Backup. However, he or she would be able to double-click on a small script that can display and interpret log files. Automating common yet tedious tasks is a great way to lower TCO, even in large and complex environments. It's also another tool you can add to your box of useful techniques.

For More Information

1. Appendix A of this book: "Windows Updates"
2. "How to Modify the Windows Registry," Q136393, Microsoft Knowledge Base
3. Chapter 24, "Registry Editor and Registry Administration," Windows NT 4.0 Workstation Resource Kit
4. Chapter 33, "Windows 95 Registry," Windows 95 Resource Kit
5. Microsoft Visual Basic home page: `msdn.microsoft.com/vbasic/`
6. Chapter 15 of this book: "Web-Based Technologies"
7. Chapter 16 of this book: "Web Applications"
8. Microsoft Scripting Technologies home page: `www.microsoft.com/scripting`

Further Reading

For more information on Windows Scripting Host and scripting in general, see the following:

- Microsoft's Windows Scripting Web site: `msdn.microsoft.com/scripting/`
- Windows Scripting Host site: `wsh.glazier.co.nz/Frame.htm`
- Windows Scripting Host Programmer's Reference: `msdn.microsoft.com/developer/sdk/inetsdk/help/wsh/wobj.htm`
- The Development Exchange: `www.devx.com`

IV

The Future of TCO

20   Windows 2000 TCO Features

21   The Future of TCO Management

Windows 2000 TCO Features

ONE OF THE MAJOR DESIGN GOALS for Windows NT has been to increase the ease of use of network operating systems while still providing the same power, flexibility, and scalability of other operating systems. By addressing this problem from both the client and server sides, Microsoft continues to improve both the desktop and server operating systems. Windows 2000, the next version of Windows NT, represents the culmination of the calls from many IT organizations and incorporates the latest innovations in ease of use and functionality. These features will, in one way or another, act together to reduce the TCO for a networked environment.

At the time of this writing, Microsoft has not yet decided the fate of the desktop operating system. The company has, however, publicly announced that all future versions of Windows will be based on the Windows NT kernel and that Windows 98 was the last in the long line of DOS-based operating systems. Windows 2000 will be a major new upgrade. In this chapter, I provide an extremely high-level overview of this important upgrade with a focus on how it will affect TCO.

Windows 2000 Packaging

Windows NT 4.0 is available in several versions: Terminal Server, Cluster, Workstation, Enterprise Server, and Server Editions. Windows 2000 will be available in at least four different variations, each aimed at different segments of the business marketplace:

- *Windows 2000 Professional*—Windows 2000 Professional will replace the Windows NT Workstation product. This package is targeted toward corporate desktop users of all levels.

- *Windows 2000 Server*—Designed for smaller networks and hardware platforms, Windows 2000 Server will remain the default choice for users who use the product primarily for file and print services.

- *Windows 2000 Advanced Server*—Windows 2000 Advanced Server will include all the functionality of the Server product as well as support for clustering and hardware support for more processors and memory.

- *Windows 2000 Datacenter Server*—Aimed at the enterprise level, Windows 2000 Datacenter Server scales well for mission-critical, high-performance applications.

Table 20.1 lists the hardware configurations that are supported by the various versions of Windows 2000.

Table 20.1   **Windows 2000 Hardware Support**

Operating System	Processors	RAM	Purpose
Professional	1	2GB	For desktop, mobile, and work-station users
Server	Up to 2	2GB	Smaller file/print/Web servers
Advanced Server	Up to 4	64GB	Clustering and load-balancing support for larger applications
Datacenter Server	16	64GB	Very large enterprise-level application support

By making the name change to Microsoft 2000, Microsoft hopes to market operating systems based on the Windows NT kernel to all users, from consumers running home applications to multiprocessor servers managing terabytes of databases. Despite the names of the operating systems, hardware decisions will play an important part in the actual role of a server.

The Status of Windows 2000

At the time of this writing, Windows 2000 is still in the pre-release stage. Microsoft has not committed to a ship date for the product, and speculations on the release of the product range from its release by the time you read this to a second-quarter 2000 launch. In any case, the major features of the product have been determined, and functional changes are minimal. All of the screenshots and detailed information in this section are based on the latest available beta versions. You can expect to see variations in the interface between this and the final product.

Simplifying Administration

No matter how self-configuring a network operating system is, network and systems administrators must perform basic functions. Tasks such as adding new users and making accommodations for personnel changes are real daily tasks. Windows NT 4.0 offers many tools for handling these tasks. This variety is also a problem, however, because each tool (Server Manager, User Manager, and so on) has a different interface. Other tasks, such as starting and stopping services and configuring network settings, must be done from the Control Panel. Finally, some advanced configuration changes can only be made using the Registry Editor or command-line utilities. These shortcomings not only increase the learning time for new users but also make administration cumbersome for those who are familiar with the administration tools.

The Microsoft Management Console

Windows 2000 attempts to address administration headaches by utilizing several new technologies. A major advance in this area—Microsoft Management Console (MMC)—can already be seen in newer Microsoft applications such as SQL Server 7.0 and Internet Information Server 4.0 or later. MMC provides a single, consistent user interface for performing all common administrative tasks. The goal is to ease the learning curve and the need to access multiple tools. Windows 2000 administrative tools, called "snap-ins," work from within the main MMC interface (see Figure 20.1). Furthermore, MMC allows third-party developers to create their own snap-ins for configuring and managing their own applications. For example, a vendor of routers can create a snap-in that allows for the modification of route tables. Many vendors have already announced support for this approach. The use of snap-ins gives the dual benefit of providing a familiar and consistent end-user interface while making application interface easier for developers.

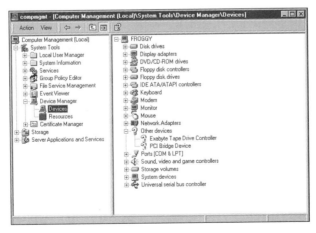

Figure 20.1   Viewing system information with MMC.

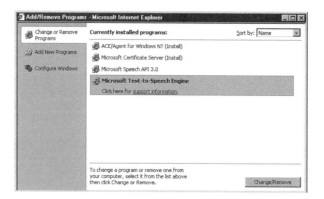

Figure 20.2   The Add/Remove Programs application.

Installing and Uninstalling Applications

With the introduction of Windows 95, Microsoft took a much-needed step forward in providing a consistent method for applications to install and uninstall themselves. However, many problems remained. Compliance with this standard was strictly voluntary, and applications often erased or overwrote files needed by other programs. Replacing a single shared component could often cause other programs to stop functioning properly. Also, programs that stored common files in their own directories wasted a large amount of disk space. All of this is restricted by the new Add/Remove Programs Control Panel application (shown in Figure 20.2). Standard packages that contain all Registry setting changes, executable files, and shared program libraries can be created. These easy-to-use files can be used for just-in-time application installations for users who need them. Only programs that adhere to these standards will be granted the Microsoft Windows 2000–compatible logo.

Client Management

A major aspect of managing a network is dealing with many different client systems. Windows 2000 includes several major features that can help centralize administration, provide for easy data recovery, and improve performance. IntelliMirror and group policy management functionality are central to reducing TCO in this area.

> **Upgrading to Windows 2000**
>
> Although pricing information was not available at the time of this writing, Microsoft has provided an upgrade path from many existing versions of Windows to Windows 2000. Details will be made available at www.microsoft.com/windows closer to the launch date.

IntelliMirror Technology

IntelliMirror is a function supported on all Windows 2000 Server products. It allows system administrators to centrally manage clients' data, settings, and applications on a single location. When a user logs in to a workstation, he or she will be able to automatically download any applications that may be needed from one or more servers available in the environment. In Windows 95/98 and Windows NT 4.0, user profiles and policies can allow users to store settings and shortcuts on a server. However, if I log in to a machine that does not have Office 97 installed, my Word 97 shortcut does not do much good. Using IntelliMirror settings, however, I can have the programs I use automatically downloaded and installed regardless of which computer I am using.

IntelliMirror can be configured to effectively make a PC's hard disk an intelligent caching device. That is, a replica of certain operating system files, applications, and program settings can be stored on a central server. When users move to different Windows 2000 Professional machines, they can simply log in to a new computer and automatically restore all data and settings stored on the server. The entire process can save hours of time and can preserve security settings, user preferences, and application installations. IntelliMirror technology combines many aspects of the Windows 2000 operating system, including the Active Directory, Group Policy Management, and enhanced application installation support (all features that are described elsewhere in this chapter) to ease administration and reduce TCO.

Group Policy Management

In Chapter 18, "Enforcing System Policies," you learned how system policies can restrict the functions that end users are allowed to perform. Although it is possible to place restrictions on almost any Registry-based function, the methods are far from easy to administer and use. Windows 2000 offers a simplified interface to group policy editing, using an MMC snap-in (see Figure 20.3). With this tool, users can easily be placed in policy groups for simplifying administration. When job functions change, administrators can simply reassign policy groups. Group policies allow for such varied functions as auditing, application installations, system usage permissions, password policies, and user rights. These improvements make it much easier for system administrators to limit end-user functionality based on the requirements of the user.

Storage Management

The information an organization possesses is one of its most important assets. Maintaining and protecting this resource is a fundamental function of Windows 2000. New functionality has been added to the areas of the file system, backup and restore tools, and storage device configuration and management.

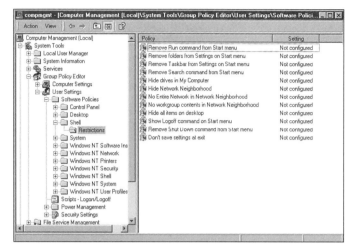

Figure 20.3   Using the Group Policy Editor MMC snap-in.

NTFS 5.0

The updated version of the Windows NT File System (NTFS)—NTFS 5.0—allows for new functionality. First, applications can be distributed across network partitions. In addition, NTFS adds the much-asked-for features of managing disk quotas and adding file system–level encryption. Encryption strength has not yet been determined, but Microsoft plans to add support for using a variety of methods. Quota management allows a systems administrator to limit the amount of disk space that a user may use. Finally, we can limit large home directories and force users to clean out old files. For security, encryption prevents the usability of any sensitive data; should it fall into the wrong hands. Encryption can be performed on a per file or per directory basis and can use several different methods. In addition, you can more easily find and organize files by the owner of the file. For example, you can search for all files created by a specific user on the server.

Hierarchical Storage Management

Hierarchical Storage Management (HSM) allows a server to store infrequently used data offline in some other form of storage. For example, old database files that have not been accessed in 60 days can be automatically offloaded to tape drives. Although this could have been performed in the past, it was tedious to set up and administer. Windows 2000 makes the automated backup procedure transparent to the user. Better yet, users can restore these files at will, without the intervention of a systems administrator. When they are viewing file and directory listings, end users will only know where a file is stored because of a different icon. If the files have been archived, they can be automatically restored for the user. The Removable Storage Manager MMC snap-in, shown in Figure 20.4, can configure devices for use by the operating system.

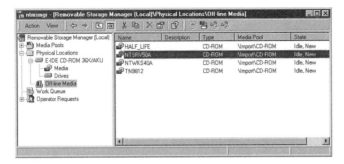

Figure 20.4   Using the Removable Storage Manager to view offline media types.

Backup Improvements

As we saw in Chapter 8, "Data Protection," Windows NT Backup can be used to handle basic backup operations. However, the tool is limited, mainly because it can only store information to tape media and because its user interface is cumbersome. Windows 2000 Backup supports the storage of information on various devices, including network shares, CD-RW drives, and a wide array of tape devices. Support is included for robotic media changers and dedicated network storage servers. It also offers a Windows Explorer–style interface that allows the easy selections of files to back up and restore. Also, with the new Backup program (see Figure 20.5), administrators can easily select files to back up or restore and schedule tape jobs to occur at a later time. For disaster recovery, administrators will be able to create a disk to automatically restore all necessary files without reinstalling the entire operating system from scratch.

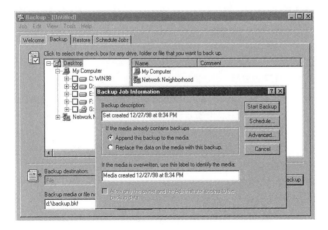

Figure 20.5   The Windows 2000 Backup program.

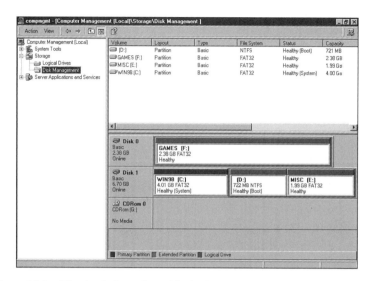

Figure 20.6   Viewing information with the Storage Management MMC snap-in.

Dynamic Volume Management

Windows 2000 gives administrators the ability to dynamically change and configure disk partitions to make the most effective use of space. It allows reformatting and repartitioning hard drives without restarting the system. Even complex configurations, such as stripe sets and disk mirroring, can be dynamically configured. This is a useful feature because it does not require any downtime, and it allows administrators to change disk configurations as needed. New hardware functionality includes support for the Intelligent Input/Output (I^2O) specification, Fiber Channel technology, and smart cards. These features can be easily accessed using the Storage Management MMC snap-in, as shown in Figure 20.6.

Active Directory Services

Perhaps one of the most requested and talked about features in Windows 2000 is the Active Directory service. Microsoft has decided to move away from flat domain-based schemes and allow for a hierarchical naming system that contains a wide variety of objects. In this section, we look at reasons the Active Directory is needed, how it is structured, and the steps required to set it up and manage it.

Domain Limitations

To truly appreciate what the Active Directory brings to the table, let's look at some problems and limitations with the Windows NT's domain model:

- *Lack of scalability*—Although the theoretical maximum number of users for a domain is quite high, managing domains with many users can cause great loads on servers. These loads translate into wait times for logging in and an overall decrease in performance.

- *Support for large environments*—Maintaining multiple domains is difficult and complicated. For distributing administration, the large number of trusts required between multiple domains is difficult to administer and manage.

- *Support for distributed resources*—Although logging in to different types of servers (such as Novell NetWare and UNIX computers) is possible, configuring and managing secure access to all the resources available in an environment is not easy. When servers and resources move or are renamed, applications may need to be redesigned and redeployed. Also, users might require training to find all the resources they are familiar with.

- *Centralized administration*—The many different parts of a network are managed quite differently. Disks, applications, users, and printers require separate management tools.

Benefits of the Active Directory

The Windows 2000 Active Directory will take a giant leap forward in solving these problems. The Active Directory works by creating a single, companywide database of information including users, disks, applications, security configuration, and other resources and settings. The directory is extensible and can be distributed throughout a network environment of virtually any size. This will be useful for applications developers, end users, and IT professionals, because they will all be able to use a single, enterprise-wide repository for storing useful information. Microsoft realizes that it is unrealistic to expect organizations of any size to quickly change their entire networks to take advantage of any new technology. Therefore, backward compatibility with Windows NT domains was a design goal for the Active Directory. However, to enjoy all the benefits of the Active Directory, you will need to have a fully Windows 2000 network.

The Active Directory supports distributed storage for performance and fault tolerance. Any number of servers can function as domain controllers. Each of these machines contains a complete replica of the entire directory. The Lightweight Directory Access Protocol (LDAP) has been chosen as the primary method to transfer directory-based data. LDAP can be used over TCP/IP. For authentication, the Kerberos methods (long supported on UNIX operating systems) are available.

The basic function of the directory is to store information regarding users, printers, applications, and file system objects. Each of these items is placed in containers. Application developers can tap information from the Active Directory to incorporate configuration information, user details, and application settings. Finding resources such as files and printers is much easier as well. A user can simply use the operating system shell to navigate through the directory and choose, for example, a printer in his or her department.

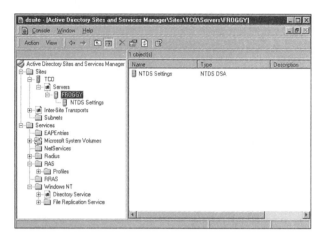

Figure 20.7   The Active Directory Sites and Services Manager.

Managing the Active Directory

To set up a directory, you will need at least one Windows 2000 server running as a domain controller. The Active Directory Sites and Services Manager (an MMC snap-in, shown in Figure 20.7) creates and manages the directory. Any number of domain controllers can be added to distribute the load of user accesses and decrease response times. Additional domain controllers also give the functionality of fault tolerance. It is very important for all domain controllers in an organization to remain synchronized with each other. Microsoft has chosen to use a version control system that ensures synchronization. However, synchronization depends on network connectivity. The replication options allow for temporary connections as long as the bandwidth is sufficient for communicating any directory changes to all domain controllers.

Network Support

Windows 2000 improves on the network functionality and support provided by previous Windows operating systems. It includes new versions of the IP stack, and IPSecure and IP version 6 support are planned. Familiar applications, including WINS, DNS, and DHCP, are still available. To address the many demands of the Internet and TCP/IP-based connectivity, a much better interface for IP security management throughout an entire networked environment is available. Look for multiprotocol dynamic routing to be a standard feature in Windows 2000. In this section, we take a brief look at some of the enhancements and their importance.

Domain Name System

In Chapter 6, "TCP/IP Management," we saw that Windows NT 4.0 includes several methods for managing TCP/IP name resolution. The easiest method to configure is

Microsoft's Windows Internet Naming Service (WINS). The Active Directory places a greater reliance on the Domain Name System (DNS) for handling name resolution. Windows 2000's implementation of DNS will be based on common standards and adds the functionality of being dynamic. The latter feature allows the automatic creation and maintenance of name-to-IP address listings for network resources. Microsoft's new DNS also works with DHCP and WINS for the best flexibility and automation in management, but pure Windows 2000-based networks will rely only on DNS. These features can be administered through the DNS Manager, which provides a graphical interface for making configuration changes and editing mappings.

Distributed File System

The Windows 2000 Server Distributed File System (DFS) has been created to offer flexible access to resources on different servers in a networked environment. Network administrators can present resources to end users, regardless of their actual type and location. For example, a Windows-based client can access information on a NetWare server using virtual roots. This works similarly to shortcuts that can be used to hide the true source of information. DFS has many benefits, including intelligent management of resources across multiple servers. To the end user, information access is transparent and does not require multiple system logins or connections to multiple servers. The end user sees only standard share names, although resources reside on machines distributed throughout the network environment. DFS uses DNS for handling naming of resources and integrates well with the Active Directory. Finally, DFS roots can be used for fault tolerance, whereby, if one resource path is unavailable, the user can be automatically redirected to another. As shown in Figure 20.8, DFS Manager makes the creation and management of DFS roots a simple task for administrators.

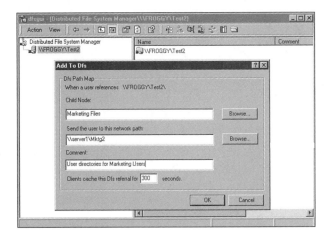

Figure 20.8 Creating a new DFS share by using DFS Manager.

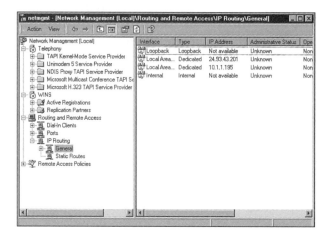

Figure 20.9   Viewing IP routing information using the Routing and Remote Access Administrator.

Remote Access Improvements

Remote access is currently an area of focus for many IT organizations. Windows 2000 continues to build on the architecture of the Remote Access Service by providing improved dialup and Virtual Private Network (VPN) services. Specifically, it adds all the numerous incremental releases for Windows NT 4.0, including the Internet Connection Services for RAS, which allows phonebooks to be centrally managed. Included are the new, integrated user interfaces shown in Figure 20.9. More importantly, it includes support for the Layer 2 Tunneling Protocol (L2TP) and IPSecure (IPSec) for virtual private networking (described in Chapter 13, "Virtual Private Networking"). Built-in support for managing access to multiple networks and remote resources are also included. The goal continues to provide location-independent network access in a method that is transparent to end users.

Additional Enhancements

In addition to the major improvements already described, Windows 2000 will include numerous other advances to make network operations easier, more reliable, and less costly. We don't have the space to discuss the details here, but this section gives an overview of new enhancements.

Greater Uptime

Systems administrators everywhere will breathe a sigh of relief when they find that Microsoft has dramatically reduced the number of situations that require a system restart. For example, network settings such as protocol bindings and protocol configurations can be changed on-the-fly. Additionally, the vast majority of software installations and modifications can be made on-the-fly, as can disk, network, and user configurations. This saves a great deal of time in configuring a system and allows all users to focus on doing work instead of waiting for their machines to restart.

Simplified Installation

Automating the installation process will be much easier with Windows 2000. If you choose to perform a manual installation, you'll be able to answer most setup questions during the beginning of installation and then let the machine continue with the remainder of the process. This allows administrators to easily automate installation processes and perform several installations at once. Figure 20.10 shows the options presented when beginning a Windows 2000 installation.

Synchronization Manager

A major challenge for mobile users is keeping multiple copies of files synchronized with each other. For example, if I change a file on my laptop, I want the changes to be written to my server files when I reconnect to the server. The Briefcase functions in Windows 95/98 and Windows NT 4.0 performed the basics of this functionality. In Windows 2000, the Synchronization Manager builds on these features by allowing users to copy files stored on servers to their local hard disks. By using the Offline Folders feature, users can easily take files normally stored on the network with them on their portable computers. Additionally, jobs can be scheduled to occur at login/logoff events, during idle times, or on a set schedule. Figure 20.11 shows the Synchronization Manager—a tool for managing all of these settings.

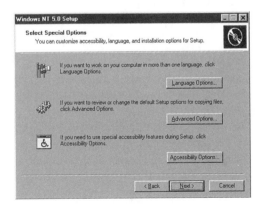

Figure 20.10   The Windows Setup interface.

Figure 20.11 Using the Synchronization Manager.

Unified Driver Models

At long last, all future versions of Windows will be truly Plug and Play compatible. All versions of Windows 2000 will use a driver model specification compatible with the one introduced with Windows 98. This serves the dual purpose of easing device driver compatibility for hardware vendors and making compatibility between the operating systems much simpler. No longer will users have to wait for vendors to offer specific support for Windows versions of their operating systems.

Multiuser Support

Windows 2000 will feature built-in multiuser support that allows clients to run their own independent sessions on a server. This functionality is very similar to that supported in Windows NT Server 4.0, Terminal Server Edition. Figure 20.12 shows the Terminal Server Administration tool. Although the software is built in, companies must purchase special licenses to use these multiuser capabilities. Details and pricing have not yet been determined.

Multilanguage Support

Few people could have predicted how quickly some of today's largest businesses would grow. In some cases, business growth involves the transition from a single coffee shop to a franchise system. For larger corporations, offering products and services globally is the next logical step. Microsoft kept this in mind when developing Windows 2000. Windows 2000 greatly eases the use of foreign languages for developers and users alike. In fact, Microsoft will release a single version of Windows 2000 that supports the Unicode character set. This will allow international users' distributed companies to use Windows 2000 installations by installing the necessary language packs.

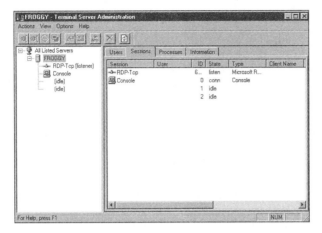

Figure 20.12   Viewing remote connections with the Terminal Server Administrator.

Improved Internet Support

Windows 2000 will provide greater integration with the Internet and Internet-based applications. Carrying forward user desktop and interface changes incorporated in Internet Explorer 4.0 and Windows 98, future versions of Windows will include the capability to contain active content on the desktop. The Internet Explorer Web browser will be a standard part of the operating system. Support for advanced Internet applications such as IP telephony using the H.323 protocol will also be included.

Preparing for Windows 2000

Despite its many improvements, new features, and simplified administration, you will need to plan before deploying Windows 2000 in your environment. First and foremost, with any large operating system release, Microsoft is faced with the same challenges that any software developer undertaking such stringent development requirements would face. Windows 2000 must not only provide reliable operations for mission-critical operations but also support many thousands of older applications designed for Windows 95/98 and Windows NT platforms. Concerns such as security, reliability, and scalability are of paramount importance for many companies that rely on their network operating systems to run their core operations. Microsoft has worked closely with early adopters of pre-release versions of Windows 2000 products. Beta programs have also been made available to further test the operating system in real-world environments by individuals and companies using the product in varied test labs. Before Windows 2000 is released, thousands of users will have used it in simulated and real-world environments, and feedback gained from these processes will be incorporated in the released product.

Despite all of these preparations and preliminary testing, there will be unexpected problems with Windows 2000. Some may be manifested in the operating system itself (such as security holes in the protocol stacks), and others will be environment specific (such as a Windows NT 4.0 application that does not run on Windows 2000). To ensure the smoothest transition, be sure to allocate time and resources to testing Windows 2000 in your environment before deploying it.

The Bottom Line

Windows 2000 promises many improvements and new functionality to reduce the burden of network administration. If you haven't yet heard about all the features to be included in this product line, you're probably amazed at the giant forward leaps Microsoft expects to make. When implemented properly, these tools and techniques will save time and money in ways that can be easily measured. Microsoft has kept TCO goals at the forefront of its development efforts for Windows 2000 products. As always, purchasing and moving to a new operating system platform will generate costs and migration pains for any organization; in this case, however, the return on investment is likely to be realized quickly. Although the new features are very important, it's up to you—the systems administrator—to make the most of them. Consider the benefits of Windows 2000 in your environment and how its new functionality can reduce your own TCO.

Further Reading

In the months preceding the release of Windows 2000, much information will become available about the features and usage of the new operating system. Microsoft has already made the feature sets and detailed information on the new product (including documentation) available on the Internet. For more information regarding Windows 2000 in general, see

- Microsoft Windows NT Server Web site: www.microsoft.com/ntserver
- What's New in Windows NT Server Web site:
  www.microsoft.com/ntserver/windowsnt5/exec/overview/WhatsNew.asp
- Windows 2000 beta site: ntbeta.microsoft.com

Preparing for a Major Upgrade

Fully taking advantage of new Windows 2000 features may require many changes to your existing environment. To prepare your network for supporting these new technologies, you may need to make changes to your domain architecture, client configurations, and TCP/IP settings. More information on planning for a Windows 2000 migration is available from Microsoft at www.microsoft.com/windows.

21

The Future of TCO Management

I N PART I, "AN INTRODUCTION TO TCO," we looked at some of the current issues, ideas, and practices related to calculating and reducing total cost of ownership (TCO). Throughout Parts II, "Network Administration," and III, "Advanced Network Administration and Implementation," I included information with a single goal—to provide methods that may make your Windows NT–based environment more efficient and reduce your operating costs.

Although it is still a relatively new concept, TCO will be seen as increasingly important by decision makers in the future. Companies will closely examine costs of maintaining hardware, software, and networks in addition to the initial cost of purchasing such items. To gain a competitive advantage, businesses of all sizes will realize that return on investment is much more important than a single one-time purchase. Although perception and awareness of TCO issues is important, the real trick is accurately measuring these values. The final step is to apply this information to reduce costs and increase value. As we saw in Chapter 1, "Measuring Total Cost of Ownership," the process is never complete because you need to continually reevaluate your practices.

Although these tasks will be challenging for environments of all sizes, IT decision makers will get more help from the industry in the future. In this chapter, we look at some developments we're likely to see in the near future. These are predictions, at best, but plausible ones based on the current directions of the industry.

Technology Advances

Advances in hardware, software, and networking technologies will help IT to better serve its users. In Chapter 20, "Windows 2000 TCO Features," we looked at new functionality and standards Microsoft will be supporting in its future operating systems. Here, we examine some general trends and expectations for hardware, software, and networks of the future.

A Greater Focus on TCO

In reading reviews of hardware, software, and networking products, you are most likely to see information on the initial purchase price of a product. Most products are reviewed based on important criteria such as usability, performance, and reliability. In the future, business software will be rated on some "cost of ownership" metric. Although there will be much disagreement about results and evaluations, some basic information will be accepted. The same has happened with automobiles. In the early part of this century, a consumer could buy any car he or she wanted as long as it was black and manufactured by Ford Motor Company. Nowadays, the marketplace is much more diverse. Automobile reviewers have responded by performing real-life tests of the usage of these vehicles and making available such information as total cost of maintenance and repairs. Similarly, IT product vendors will aim to satisfy the same criteria to obtain favorable reviews.

Better Software Integration

Having to learn new tools and techniques to master separate programs is a major burden on IT personnel. Even within Windows NT, for example, there are many different tools and utilities—each with different user interfaces—used for basic administration. In Windows 2000, all administration will be performed through Microsoft Management Console (MMC). MMC uses openly available standards that other vendors can use for their own applications. This provides the dual benefit of standardizing the user interface and making software development much easier.

▶ For More
Information
1, 2

In the future, look for tools and applications that support common and intuitive user interfaces. Software applications will better integrate into a user's current environment, and compatibility will be enforced through such features as Web-based management interfaces and other commonly accepted standards. For example, Microsoft Office 2000 supports HTML as a standard file type containing all Office-related formatting. This helps ensure that the broadest possible audience can be reached by using Office applications. When evaluating these products, IT professionals will focus on feature sets instead of compatibility issues. Overall, this will help reduce TCO by allowing IT to focus on solving business-related technical problems instead of interoperability issues.

Development of Cost-Related Benchmarks

▶ For More Information 3

In order to provide an easy way to reference TCO information, industry-accepted benchmarks will be necessary. Currently in the relational database management system (RDBMS) marketplace, the Transactional Processing Performance Council (TPC-C) has developed benchmarks to measure database performance. Cost of performing transactions is included as an important metric. The TPC-C benchmark is often used to compare price to performance. It is calculated by measuring the cost of specific hardware and software required to process a given number of transactions per unit time. This is an important consideration because many vendors claim that their software is faster than the competition, but do not specify that it runs on a much more expensive hardware platform. For example, comparing Oracle servers running on UNIX with Microsoft SQL Server running on Windows NT requires the use of different hardware platforms. By including cost in the equation, decision makers can get a more accurate comparison of technology versus cost.

However, this benchmark, like many others, falls short of evaluating factors such as administration and maintenance costs—both of which are very difficult to measure. To encompass the many factors that contribute to TCO, studies need to look at real-world operations. We looked at some examples of these in Chapter 2, "Total Cost of Ownership Studies and Tools." A major drawback to this approach is that the data obtained is specific to the environment(s) studied. However, increasing information will be available for making decisions based on costs. This information should help organizations compare their performance requirements to budget-related issues and make decisions that are more cost-effective.

Network Management for the Masses

▶ For More Information 4, 5, 6, 7, 8

Many companies are moving toward integrated business solutions that promise to unify and organize the various components of medium- to large-sized companies. Asset and network management involves the organized accounting and planning of all of a company's assets. This all-encompassing term includes people, information, hardware, and software. Today's network management packages are geared toward large companies. The main reason is the high price—smaller organizations simply cannot justify the expenditures required to purchase and implement large-scale solutions. Products from Tivoli, Hewlett-Packard, and Intel are aimed at such tasks as hardware and software inventory, software distribution, and remote troubleshooting. These features help companies provide support and track and manage their assets. Figure 21.1 shows a live online demonstration of Novell's ManageWise (www.novell.com/managewise).

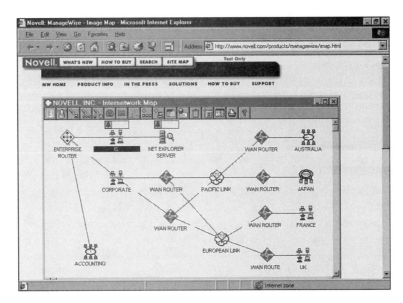

Figure 21.1   Using Novell's ManageWise to view router information.

In the future, look for network management packages to be tailored toward smaller businesses and organizations. One step in this direction is Microsoft's Active Directory (to be introduced in Windows 2000). The Active Directory will allow network administrators to organize their users, hardware, and applications in a central area. As the gap between network operating systems and network management packages is reduced, look for limited implementations of standard software-based management suites.

Future Technology Innovations

Although technology is notoriously difficult to predict, I'll take a stab at it. Table 21.1 shows some developments you're likely to see regarding the specific technical topics covered in this book.

Making Your Own Predictions

Don't take my word for it—make your own predictions! By browsing various trade publications (such as *PCWeek* at www.pcweek.com and CNet's News.com at www.news.com) and vendor Web sites, you'll see information on upcoming products and technologies. Some will be successful, and others will have little impact. Either way, you can get a good idea of what to look out for in the technology industry.

Table 21.1 **Future Trends**

Chapter Number	Chapter Title	What to Watch For
4	Policies and Procedures	As computers become more commonplace than staplers, organizations will enforce technology usage policies and make users more responsible for their use.
5	Network Management	Centralized administration of all resources; common interfaee for troubleshooting tools.
6	TCP/IP Management	Greater security built in to TCP/IP; automated IP address management using DHCP; IP becomes primary LAN and WAN protocol; IPv6 offers more flexible addressing and IP security.
7	Security	Non–password-based authentication (biometrics) and more emphasis on educating users and holding them responsible; companies will become more responsive to security flaws in their products.
8	Data Protection	Faster and more convenient methods of storage; centralized enterprise-wide backup solutions with distributed administration; built-in disaster recovery; automatic file archiving with user-initiated restore procedures.
9	Performance Monitoring	Better high-level interfaces for interpreting performance information and making recommendations.
10	Performance Optimization	More self-tuning features in operating systems and applications.
11	Remote Management	Universal Web-based standard interfaces for devices; common acceptance of Windows Management Interface, MMC, and other technologies; multi-user capabilities built in to server and workstation operating systems.
12	Remote Access Service	Reserved for special point-to-point applications; greater security and capabilities in operating system.

continues

Table 21.1 **Continued**

Chapter Number	Chapter Title	What to Watch For
13	Virtual Private Networking	Primary solution for supporting remote users; standardized protocols and widespread support; increased performance; better authentication mechanisms.
14	Automated Software Installations	Common setup procedures for all applications; all options are chosen before installation begins; all applications have options of local and/or server-based execution; clients store copies of all programs on central server for easy recovery and location independence.
15	Web-Based Technologies	More efficient design tools for creating Web-based content and applications; further developments of scripting and Web-based standards.
16	Web Applications	Greater reliance on Web-based applications as a primary method for information access.
17	Implementing a Secure FTP Site	Web-based FTP client applications; continued usage of this simple protocol for transferring files between users.
18	Enforcing System Policies	Operating systems with improved integrated policy administration; enforcing policies integral to IT requirements.
19	Scripting	Scripting will become both more powerful and more accessible. The distinction between programming and working with desktop applications will be blurred.

IT Industry Advances

The field of information technology is changing faster than perhaps any other field in history. Performing electronic transactions using a Web-based interface was a fantasy a few years ago. Now technologies such as e-commerce are on the brink of changing business practices. As these technologies become more important for organizations, IT departments will devise new practices and methods for dealing with changes in business requirements.

Service-Level Agreements

In many organizations, IT departments claim to do the best they can, given their time and resources. However, it is ultimately the burden of IT to meet business needs in any way that it can. An end user who cannot log in to the network does not care that a systems administrator quit during the previous week—she just wants to be able to get her job done. To meet this goal, IT must commit to some level of service. Service-level agreements (SLAs) specify goals for IT staff regarding problem resolutions, troubleshooting, and other common tasks. An SLA might specify, for example, that all moves, adds, or changes to functioning equipment will be completed within 24 hours, whereas critical system glitches affecting many users will be addresses within 4 hours. SLAs are consistent with human nature—people may not mind waiting 4 to 6 weeks for something in the mail if they know to expect the delay. Tell them that they'll receive it "very soon," however, and you'll have angry customers to deal with in a few days.

As an example, some computer manufacturers promise "guaranteed 24x7 technical support." They fail to mention that you may have to wait 2 hours before speaking to a technician. You needn't look at independent reviews to see which customers are happiest. In an absolute worst-case scenario, 5% of purchasers will call in, but these customers may be the most important the business ever has. If the support call is properly handled, the customer, despite his or her initial problem with the product, may hang up the phone happier with the company than he or she would have been if nothing had gone wrong. This is the nature of customer service and perception. General business ideas like "underpromising and overdelivering" are great for IT. And the benefits can be tremendous. In empowering employees to find the way to meet certain goals on their own, job satisfaction will clearly increase. Additionally, when an IT manager requests a specific network upgrade, he or she can allude to the fact that "in order to maintain the agreed-upon level of performance, additional resources will be required." Vital to such policies is seeking, obtaining, and responding to end-user feedback.

IT departments will not be forced to manage all aspects of their network on their own, however. In the past several years, many businesses have experimented with outsourcing certain operations. The goal is often to focus attention on what a company does best and to allow tasks such as managing the IT help desk to be outsourced. The cost analysis can be very complex for relying on external organizations for support. In the end, however, it's important for businesses to realize that this is an available option and to accurately gauge the actual pros and cons of outsourcing.

E-Commerce

A larger number of businesses will begin implementing electronic commerce (e-commerce), and many of those that are already doing so will see a tremendous growth in revenues. E-commerce involves the use of automatic transactions being performed between a business and a consumer (such as a retail outlet) or a business and its vendors. The success of an e-commerce solution is largely technology dependent. For example, Web sites must be fast, up-to-date, and user friendly. They must also be affordable and flexible to develop. These enabling technologies will be critical as companies find an economical and efficient method to connect to potential customers and business partners. Figure 21.2 shows the Dell Computer Corp. Web site. Dell already enjoys millions of dollars of sales on its Web site everyday. Couple this scenario with a great overall reduction in the cost of taking orders, and it provides a very compelling business case.

E-commerce will again place IT at the forefront of business operations. To meet this demand, more resources will be devoted to developing and maintaining a company's Web-based storefront. The end result will be a paradigm shift in the way transactions are processed between businesses and their customers.

The Evolution of Application Technology

Client/server technology distributes the burden of storing, processing, and presenting information to users who need it. Building applications is no longer as monumental a task as it was in the past. The idea of monolithic chunks of code written from the ground up is outdated. New applications will be more easily written with the help of programming aides such as Microsoft's wizards. In Chapter 16, "Web Applications," we saw that a few mouse clicks can easily create a live Web database. We generated all the necessary code in a few minutes. You may have identified many applications of this technology in your own environment. For an administrator or manager, collecting information over an intranet is a huge improvement over older methods.

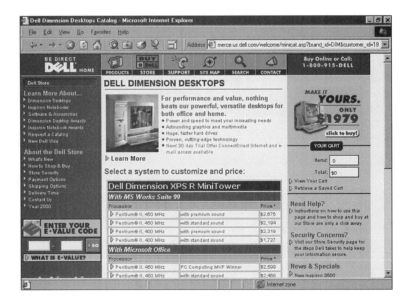

Figure 21.2   The Dell Web site allows visitors to purchase computers online.

Prepackaged software solutions will continue to keep their foothold in the marketplace. However, the new breed of systems administrators—armed with the power of scripting tools and rapid application development platforms—will increasingly conquer business-specific challenges on their own.

In the area of communications, cellular and wireless communications will help people remain in touch with their resources. The decreasing cost of these services (which were seen as luxuries a few short years ago) will make them commonplace for business users. Faster and more reliable residential Internet access will open up many possibilities for entertainment, news, retail, and other industries. We'll see new ways of dealing with government, technology, and businesses. Some changes will be good, others will be bad, but at least they'll all be technically possible. For many companies, adapting to these changes will be costly and time-consuming. However, the result will be a reduction in the cost of doing business and thus the TCO.

Business Advances

Meeting business needs should always be the focus of any IT implementation. More and more, companies will treat their IT departments less as a cost center and more as a strategic tool for increasing competitiveness in the marketplace.

Many companies today are rapidly expanding. Whether through takeovers, mergers, acquisitions, or an increase in market presence, successful businesses will increase in size. Changes in geographic distribution and number of users supported will place a large burden on IT organizations. At the other end of the spectrum, new technologies will allow smaller organizations to remain competitive in the marketplace by maintaining quality, efficiency, and service. In this section, we look at the changing role of IT and the effects of this shift.

IT Leading Business

Many people currently view IT as an organization that supports a business. After all, this department rarely generates revenues or sells a product to the public. Instead, IT is responsible for maintaining communications and information access. In the past, endusers rarely called their systems administrators unless they were experiencing a technical problem. In the future, IT will acquire an increasingly strategic position in a company. Even today, several new companies have been developed solely on the Internet and in software technologies. Without the contributions of IT, these businesses could hardly remain competitive. One example is Amazon.com (shown in Figure 21.3), the online-only book and music retailer from whom many of you may have purchased this book. Other businesses may not rely on IT to the same extent, but the fact remains that technology implementers must be able to see the big picture to help move a business toward its goals.

Figure 21.3 Finding books at Amazon.com *(www.amazon.com)*.

To meet the challenges of making information more available, IT departments will need to maintain a competent staff and increase their interactions with other departments. For example, no commercial Web site will be popular without the help of sales and marketing experts. Additionally, financial considerations will require the involvement of accounting departments and other key decision makers. The overall effect will be that IT departments will be seen as part of the team instead of just the support workers.

Meeting IT Staffing Demands

The high cost of finding, training, and retaining employees is often an area of concern for companies of any size. The issue is especially important in the information technology field, where finding and retaining qualified people is of paramount importance. The first and foremost requirement will be for more technology specialists who also understand business issues. Although there will always be a place for the "bit flipper," technical professionals who can see the big picture will assist in moving an organization forward. Dealing with these types of issues will also give many IT staffers the ability to solve problems in creative ways and to feel that they are part of a team.

We looked at some best practices for retaining employees in Chapter 3, "General Best Practices for Reducing TCO." Companies will see the value of truly involving technical staff in business decisions. The companies that succeed in this area will be able to meet business needs much more effectively than those that have a revolving door in their IT department. Ultimately, it will fall to the IT team to effectively implement, manage, and support the new technologies that businesses of the future will require.

Industry Research and Evaluations

In Chapter 2, we saw that many independent organizations currently perform industrywide research related to TCO issues. The demand for these types of studies will increase as companies try to compare themselves with their competitors.

For businesses that want to take a much more active approach to managing their own environments, help is available from third parties. For example, the GartnerGroup currently offers software products and services for evaluating TCO. GartnerGroup consultants can also be hired to assist with the evaluation of the environment and make recommendations for improvements. Many more IT consulting organizations will begin to offer such assistance, and making TCO studies a standardized service is not much further behind.

Reliance on Consulting and Outsourcing

Accounting departments have long understood the value of performing external financial audits for their organizations. In the same way, companies will call on consultants and outsourced staff to evaluate current practices and make recommendations. Involving a third party helps to avoid some of the corporate politics that often obscure an insider's view. For certain business functions, it just is not feasible to handle all management internally. For example, supporting 50 remote access users can create quite a burden on the support staff of a typical company. However, it may cost only $20 per month to allow an Internet service provider to handle all installation, support, maintenance, and troubleshooting. Outsourcing this area of support frees the IT organization to tend to what it's best at—working with the company's business goals.

The benefits of consulting and outsourcing certain functions depend on a company's environment and strategic directions. General considerations include evaluating what a company does effectively and what outsiders might do better. Consultants are available for handling IT functions from staffing the help desk to making strategic business recommendations. Measuring the relative costs and quality of service of both alternatives can be a difficult task. The information required for performing a TCO assessment can be applied in this area. In any case, IT managers should take comfort in knowing that external resources are available for performing these tasks.

Finding Employees and Employers Online

Especially in the IT industry, people are using the Internet to find and apply for jobs. If you're interested in working for a company, a good first step is to look for employment opportunities listed on the business's Web site. If that doesn't work, check out the Monster Board (www.monster.com)—it's the largest job database in the United States. If you want to provide more information to potential employers than is possible in a standard resume, put up a Web site and publish your credentials. Also, be sure to use email, newsgroups, and Web discussion forums for finding ideas of interest. With newer technologies, the gap between potential employer and potential employee is decreasing.

Social Changes

Computers and their use have become an everyday part of life for many of us. Even if we are not consciously working on a PC and downloading information from the Internet, our businesses depend on them. In this section, we take a look at some of the ways social changes will affect information technology.

Freedom of Information

It was once said that freedom of the press belongs to those who own presses. This statement used to be completely accurate—simply getting your ideas on paper was very difficult and costly. Distribution of that message was also very difficult. With the Internet, however, public forums are available for everyone with a personal computer to voice their opinions on products that they carry. In a world where unsolicited views are not hard to come by, people would be surprised at how much weight this electronic word of mouth can carry. Figure 21.4 shows messages posted to Internet newsgroups via the DejaNews Web site.

Participants in public discussion Web sites and newsgroups know that it doesn't take much for a discussion on any subject to escalate into an angry debate. It's easy to see why some critics question the usefulness of such resources. However, the ability to interact freely in appropriate forums will change the way people communicate.

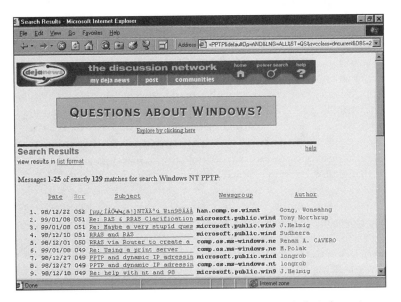

Figure 21.4 Using DejaNews (www.dejanews.com) to search for information.

Service Expectations

Some companies still believe that they can obtain the greatest profits by providing poor customer service. For example, if you purchase a box of matches and later find that they do not light, you probably won't bother to return the item (especially when the best you can find is an address, and the cost of postage is far more than the cost of the product). An unconcerned company would see your behavior as profitable: The sale was completed and never reversed. A more forward-thinking company would view this situation as a lost opportunity for more business and would find how to solve the problem in the future.

Customers may not always be external to a company. We already discussed how IT departments should view their internal customers as end users and strive to provide high levels of satisfaction. All types of businesses will be able to improve communications with their customers by using technologies such as the Internet. Businesses can use this technology to speed the distribution of product information, provide support, and obtain feedback from customers. Companies that do not provide such services are likely to lose customers.

The Future of Microsoft Windows

Is Windows 2000 *the* operating system of the future? No. Microsoft has clearly done an excellent job in meeting user needs with products such as Windows NT 4.0 and will continue to do so with the upcoming Windows 2000 operating system. Details of exciting new features in Windows 2000 were covered in Chapter 20. However, as we progress in networked environments, it will become increasingly unlikely for any one system to address all needs. Windows NT will remain a player at the forefront of the application services scene but will share the stage with other systems that offer different functionality. It is difficult to find an IT professional who doesn't feel very strongly that one platform is better than another. This may be true for certain applications, but the many thousands of businesses that rely on mixed environments are not wrong. In the future, we are likely to see greater reliance on commonly accepted standards for software, hardware, and networking devices. Perhaps there's no greater testament to the value of standards than TCP/IP—the aging technology upon which the framework of the Internet is based. Features presented for current and future products make it very likely that Microsoft and Windows will continue to be industry leaders for a long time. However, it is up to you—the IT professional—to determine how these products best fit in your own environment.

The Bottom Line

In the future, the function of many IT departments will shift from primary support tasks to business-driving activities. Increasingly, companies will include the words *information* and *technology* in their strategic plans. Advances in technology will help enable these changes. IT departments will begin to look much more closely at TCO information for making decisions on which best practices and hardware, software, and network products are appropriate for their environments. This information will be used to carefully look past initial sticker prices and factor in support and maintenance costs. Ultimately, this information will enable IT organizations to devise methods to meet new business goals based on available resources.

For More Information

1. Microsoft Office 2000 Preview Web site: www.microsoft.com/office/preview/
2. "Reducing the Cost of Ownership with Microsoft Office 2000," Microsoft TechNet
3. Transactional Processing Performance Council Web site: www.tpc.org
4. Microsoft Systems Management Server Web site: www.microsoft.com/smsmgmt/
5. Tivoli Systems, Inc. Web site: www.tivoli.com
6. Novel Managewise Web site: www.novell.com/products/managewise/
7. Hewlett-Packard OpenView Web site: www.openview.hp.com
8. Intel LANDesk Management Suite Web site: www.intel.com/network/products/landesk_mgmtsuite_v6.htm

V

Appendixes

A Windows Updates

B Resources for More Information

C What's on the CD

A

Windows Updates

To BETTER SUPPORT THE USERS of its products, Microsoft often releases patches, updates, and free options for its operating systems and applications. This book would be limited in its usefulness if it assumed that you had already installed all of the latest and greatest add-ons. In the technical chapters of this book, I have assumed that readers are using the following:

- Windows NT Server or Workstation with Service Pack 4. For chapters that reference it, Windows NT Option Pack (including IIS 4.0 and related components)
- Windows 95/98 with the latest Service Pack/Service Release

In most cases, changes with other operating system versions are minimal, so it may not be absolutely necessary to install these upgrades to follow the examples in this book.

Unfortunately for a book writer, trying to write for a specific version of an operating system is like taking a photograph of a moving target. That is, although you may be able to see the object of the picture, everything is blurry. To avoid that, I have chosen what I think is most representative of real-world Windows NT and Windows 95/98 installations. In many cases, your configuration may vary, and this will not cause any problems. In others, a certain option may be unavailable or may be found in another location. If you're like me, you probably chose IT as a profession because you enjoy the challenges and rewards of keeping up with new technologies. This appendix introduces the various major and minor upgrades available for Windows NT and Windows 95/98 operating systems. At the end, I provide a summary of the relevant fixes, patches, and updates that I've assumed throughout the book that you have.

Versions Used in This Book

Most of the information in this book is applicable to all current versions of Windows NT 4.0 (Workstation and Server) and Windows 95/98. By "current" versions, I'm referring to Windows NT 4.0 Server or Workstation with Service Pack 4 installed and Windows 95/98 with the latest Service Releases and patches. Current Web browsers include Netscape's Navigator 4.0 or Communicator 4.0 or higher, or Microsoft's Internet Explorer 4.0 or higher.

Windows NT Service Packs

Microsoft has been releasing operating system patches in collections called *Service Packs*. The setup utilities for these files simply back up some of your existing system files (optional) and replace them if older versions are found. In general, it is a good idea to make sure that you have the latest Service Pack installed on all of your Windows NT computers. It is also important to note that Service Packs must be reapplied any time you install software from the original Windows NT CD-ROM or from any other source.

The Routing and Remote Access Update for NT Server

The Routing and Remote Access Service (RRAS) update for Windows NT Server enhances the functionality of using Windows NT as a network router. The update supports dynamic routing for Windows NT and allows a virtual private network to be set up between two RAS servers. The RRAS update is covered in more detail in Chapter 13, "Virtual Private Networking."

Windows NT Option Packs

Microsoft made a conscious decision to release new features for operating systems in *Option Packs*. Option Packs include new programs and applets, increased functionality, and more features than the "stock" operating system. The first Windows NT 4.0 Option Pack is primarily aimed at people running Internet Web and/or FTP services and at those developing Web-based applications. Among the major additions and upgrades in this package are the following:

- *Internet Information Server 4.0*—Includes the 4.0 versions of the WWW and FTP services, including support for Active Server Pages, file uploading, and database connections.

- *Microsoft Transaction Server 2.0*—Allows developers to easily write programs that manage distributed transactions.

- *Microsoft Message Queue Server 1.0*—Can be used by Web developers to queue data to be sent to remote computers in batches. This is useful in situations involving slow and costly wide-area networking connections.

- *Internet Connection Services for Microsoft RAS*—Allows for easily managing dial-up connections.

The Option Pack also includes numerous other operating system extensions, many of which greatly aid Web developers, including

- *Certificate Server*—Used for creating authentication certificates.

- *Microsoft Index Server*—A search engine that can be used by visitors to your Web site.

- *FrontPage 98 server extensions*—Web server extensions used by Microsoft's FrontPage 98 and Visual InterDev 6.0 Web authoring tools.

- *Microsoft data access components*—New ODBC drivers and support for OLEDB, ADO, and RDO (explained in Chapter 15, "Web-Based Technologies").

- *Microsoft Management Console*—A new interface for administering the Internet Information Server components.

- *Microsoft Script Debugger*—A small tool that developers can use to debug Active Server Pages.

- *Microsoft Site Server Express 2.0*—A scaled-down version of the full product, Site Server Express allows administrators to view Web site usage information and verify sites for broken links.

- *Visual InterDev Rapid Application Deployment Components*—Tools for deploying, managing, and debugging Web-based applications written in Visual InterDev.

- *Windows Scripting Host*—For more information on this utility, see Chapter 19, "Scripting."

The Option Pack may be installed on Windows NT and Windows 95/98 computers. The specific components available vary based on the operating system you're using, and details are available in the Option Pack documentation. In general, it is a good idea to install only the components you require. Figure A.1 shows the Option Pack setup options. However, many of the components have dependencies on each other. If you are unsure what to install, choose the Typical option—it may take up a little more disk space but will prevent compatibility problems in the future. For details on components included with the Option Pack, see www.microsoft.com/ntserver.

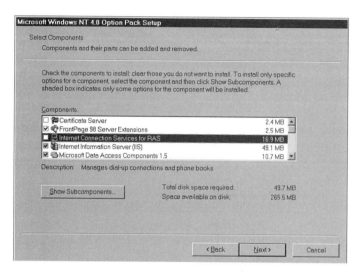

Figure A.1   Setup options for the Windows NT Option Pack.

Security-Related Hotfixes, Patches, and Bulletins

Every once in a while, a press release regarding a security hole, problem, or work-around surfaces in the media. Those who find the problem often claim that it's the end of the world or that Windows NT is no longer a useful operating system. Others claim that the problem is negligible or has already been addressed. Of course, the truth is somewhere between these two extremes. Nevertheless, security is very important, and it requires constant monitoring of responsible sources of information.
Microsoft's Security Advisor Program Web site (shown in Figure A.2) can be found at www.microsoft.com/security. You can also sign up for an email list to get information when new security patches are available.

Hotfixes are patches to fix a specific problem or add a specific feature to a portion of the operating system. These files are generally fairly small and are available for download. The fixes represent new code that should be implemented only by users who are experiencing a specific problem. In most cases, the fix will be released in the next Service Pack or operating system upgrade.

It's important to note that as any product matures and is tested in real-world environments, problems will be found. However, as more and more people use Windows NT, it will continue to become more secure and stable. The likelihood of finding a flaw in the operating system that will render it a serious security problem is low.

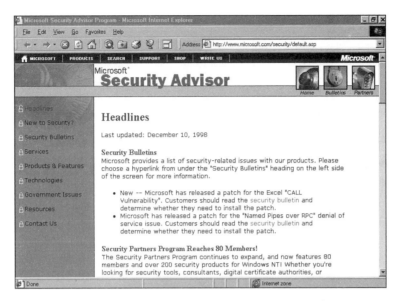

Figure A.2 The Microsoft Security Advisor Program Web site.

Windows 95/98 Updates

Many systems and network administrators do not realize that there are many different versions of Windows 95/98 available. At the time of this writing, there are at least four different versions of Windows 95. Most are original equipment manufacturer (OEM) releases available only on new systems purchased from vendors. These versions are named operating system release (OSR) 2.x. For example, versions of Windows 95 labeled OSR 2.1 and above support the FAT32 file system, whereas others do not. Microsoft has also released Service Release 1 (SR1) for Windows 95, which is freely available for download. It is important to determine whether you need this set of patches and enhancements before rolling them out to a large number of machines—the outcome may not be worth the trouble.

Downloading Updates

I've avoided direct links for downloading the updates mentioned here. Microsoft and other vendors frequently reorganize their Web sites and update filenames and content. The easiest way to find the patches and files you need is to use the Internet. To start searching for product updates, go to `www.microsoft.com/windows`. Choose your operating system from the main page and find the appropriate downloads. You can also find updates from `support.microsoft.com/support/downloads` or via FTP from `ftp.microsoft.com`.

The Bottom Line

You can't beat free software patches and upgrades for increasing the value of your existing systems. Upgrading software and keeping it current increases the life cycle of applications and operating systems. It may even delay an upgrade by filling the gap of some desired features. Keeping current on new technologies has always been a struggle for IT. Often all that's required is some additional driver support or enhanced functionality in applications. If they're available, find out whether they'll help you or your users and, if so, apply them. Downloading patches, drivers, and additional software can keep your machines consistent, up-to-date, and bug free, usually at a price you can't beat—free!

B

Resources for More Information

I N MANY AREAS OF THIS BOOK, I've referred to resources for more information. In this section, we look at exactly how you can use these references to find the information you need. In most cases, a wealth of information is freely available on the Web. Microsoft provides all levels of support and information for its products through various methods, including the World Wide Web, paid telephone-based support, and authorized technical training classes. Additionally, a wealth of third-party information is available from independent forums and publications.

Microsoft Resources

A major challenge for a company as large as Microsoft is supporting its products. The best software in the world is useless if people don't know how to use it effectively. To meet this need, Microsoft and other companies have made significant strides toward information and training dissemination in the past several years. The Internet has been the main carrier of this information, although traditional phone-based support is still available. Microsoft has proven its dedication to supporting its software products by providing extensive information to its end users. Many sources of information and support are freely available to end users.

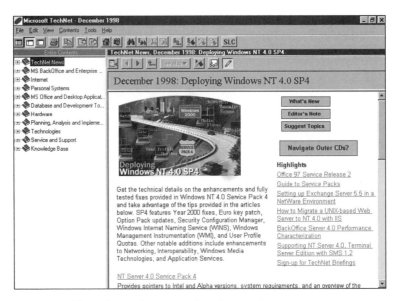

Figure B.1   The Microsoft TechNet welcome screen.

Microsoft TechNet

Microsoft's TechNet provides a wealth of information on implementing, supporting, managing, and troubleshooting Microsoft products. Microsoft TechNet is a subscription-based program. Subscribers receive TechNet issues monthly on CD-ROMs. These discs include the following:

- Microsoft Knowledge Base, including all support articles (updated each month)
- Technical articles regarding the use of Microsoft products
- Service Packs for Microsoft operating systems and BackOffice products
- Microsoft operating system and product resource kits with utilities
- Microsoft BackOffice evaluation products

The heart of Microsoft TechNet is the interface shown in Figure B.1. With this program, you can quickly and efficiently search through thousands of technical articles related to the keywords you supply.

Overall, TechNet is an invaluable resource for IT professionals who work with Microsoft products. If you need assistance with a specific error message or software bug, TechNet is the first place to look. Also, the monthly kits contain current updates and patches to keep your systems up-to-date.

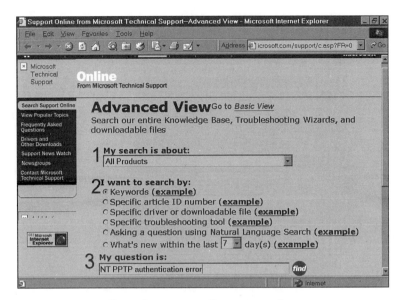

Figure B.2   Microsoft's Support Online.

Microsoft Knowledge Base

The Knowledge Base consists of product support bulletins, bug reports, and trouble-shooting information for working with Microsoft products. Microsoft uses the letter *Q* followed by six digits to uniquely identify each of the documents available. Through-out the technical chapters of the book, I've made references to many of these articles. Information in the Knowledge Base is available from Microsoft's TechNet and from Microsoft Support Online.

Microsoft Support Online

Microsoft has made its extensive Knowledge Base available online via the Internet. To access Support Online (see Figure B.2), point your browser to www.microsoft.com/support. The first time you visit the site, you must complete a free registration questionnaire. From then on, all information will be freely available to you.

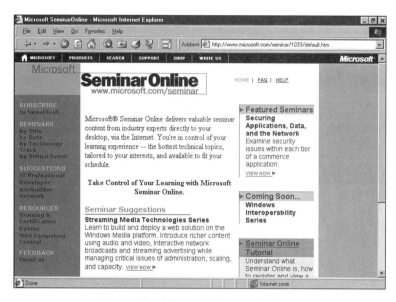

Figure B.3   Microsoft's Seminar Online.

Microsoft Seminar Online

Web-based product and technology information is available free from Microsoft via the Seminar Online Web site at `www.microsoft.com/seminar`. From here, you can click on a number of information titles. The format includes descriptive "slides" along with voice narration, as shown in Figure B.3. It's almost like being in a seminar or live presentation, and it's available on demand and works well even in low-bandwidth situations. In the future, you can expect live, multimedia demonstrations of software, technologies, and techniques (much like the ones on the CD-ROM accompanying this book).

Microsoft Phone-Based Technical Support

For technical and usage support on Microsoft products, users can call Microsoft's phone-based support. Pricing structures and levels of support vary based on the product, purchased support options, and special arrangements with companies. For more information on contacting Microsoft technical support, see `www.microsoft.com/support`.

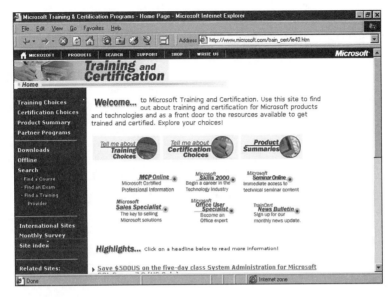

Figure B.4 The Microsoft Training and Certification home page.

Microsoft Authorized Technical Education Courses

If you want to learn the ins and outs of specific Microsoft products or technologies in an instructor-led classroom setting, Microsoft Authorized Technical Education courses may be for you. Classes range from half-day sessions to 2-week, in-depth training courses. For a complete list of classes and authorized training centers, see `www.microsoft.com/train_cert` (see Figure B.4). This site also provides a wealth of information for those who are seeking Microsoft certifications.

Internet Resources

We've already looked at some of the information available from Microsoft on the Internet. In addition to these sites, a wealth of other information is available on the Internet. In this section, I point you to some useful Web sites and other online resources.

World Wide Web Resources

In addition to the Microsoft resources covered earlier, several excellent Web sites are available for finding Windows NT and TCO-related information (see Table B.1).

Table B.1 **Windows NT and TCO-Related Web Sites**

Site Name	Web Address	Content/Purpose
Beverly Hills Software	`www.hs.com`	Reviews and download links Windows NT–related applications and utilities
CNet's News.Com	`www.news.com`	IT industry news and information updated daily
Forrester Research	`www.forrester.com`	IT market studies and predictions
GartnerGroup Interactive	`www.gartner.com`	TCO and IT industry market research and news (see Figure B.5)
Hardware Central	`www.hardwarecentral.com`	Hardware product reviews and technical discussions
Microsoft Certified Professional Magazine	`www.mcpmag.com`	Technical articles and information about Microsoft certification
NT Security.Net	`www.ntsecurity.net`	Up-to-date information about Windows NT security issues
The Ultimate Collection of Windows Shareware (TUCOWS)	`www.tucows.com`	A large repository of shareware programs, specializing in Internet applications
Winfiles.com	`www.winfiles.com`	A shareware repository of Windows- related programs available for free evaluation
Whatis.com	`www.whatis.com`	A good reference site that defines technical terms
Ziff-Davis Anchordesk	`www.anchordesk.com`	Daily information about IT products, events, and news

Usenet Newsgroups

Most of the information resources I've presented thus far have been mainly one-way communications. What if you want to ask a specific question or participate in interactive peer discussions on the Internet? Your best resource for doing so is Usenet, the Internet's public news network. Although Usenet newsgroups rarely receive the level of media attention accorded the World Wide Web, Internet users have long relied on these forums for discussing issues and obtaining information. Usenet uses a protocol called the Network News Transfer Protocol (NNTP) to share discussion group information worldwide. Almost all Internet service providers offer free access to news servers. Microsoft's public news server is available at `msnews.microsoft.com`.

Figure B.5 The GartnerGroup Interactive home page.

Popular newsgroup clients can be downloaded from the Internet. Figure B.6 shows Microsoft's Outlook Express being used to access a public Microsoft discussion group. In addition, several Web sites host their own Web-based forums. An excellent example is *Microsoft Certified Professional Magazine's* discussion area (`www.mcpmag.com`) through which Microsoft test takers can discuss questions and answers. Access to peer support on the Internet can be a great way to find exactly the information you need. Just be sure to consider the sources of information and get several opinions.

If you'll be working with news servers often, client software is the way to go. For casual news searches, however, it may be easier to use a Web-based interface. DejaNews (`www.dejanews.com`) provides exactly that—a Web-based engine for searching through millions of messages posted worldwide (see Figure B.7). If you're searching for obscure information, this is the place to go!

Searching for More

In addition to the information resources I've already mentioned, be sure to use popular Web search engines for finding information. Table B.2 lists a few of the most popular ones. Although you'll clearly need to do some mouse work to sift through thousands of results, search engines can help you find the information you need.

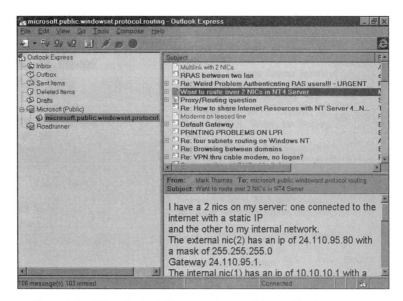

Figure B.6 Using Outlook Express to browse Microsoft's Usenet server.

Figure B.7 Using DejaNews to perform a newsgroup search.

Table B.2 **Web Search Engines**

Site	Address	Main Purpose
AltaVista	`www.altavista.com`	General Web page searches
Lycos	`www.lycos.com`	General Web page searches
MetaCrawler	`www.metacrawler.com`	Combines information from the major search engines
Yahoo!	`www.yahoo.com`	Provides hierarchical information trees

C

What's on the CD

GENERALLY, PEOPLE LEARN MOST EFFECTIVELY when they use visual tools. That's one reason you're unlikely to find this work as a "book on tape." The figures, screenshots, and procedures presented within Parts II, "Network Administration," and III, "Advanced Network Administration and Implementation," are best used when you're working with a computer and have the ability to test and experiment with the information you have. In addition to this information, I've included resources on the CD-ROM that you will find very useful in understanding concepts and procedures related to Windows NT network administration. Although you won't easily be able to learn how to reduce TCO in your car, the media clips included on the CD-ROM will be useful to supplement—not replace—the instructions in the book.

For example, if you want to get a better idea of how Outlook Web Access (OWA) works but don't have a spare server (or the time) for installing Windows NT Server, Exchange Server, and the Windows NT Option Pack, check out Demonstration 16.1. It walks you through the basics of using this Web-based application and should suggest some ways that you can use it in your own environment. Plus, if you decide to set it up, you will have seen the basics already. It's kind of like trying to get to a place you've been before instead of trying to get there by using directions alone. Note that both are important, and you'll probably want to read the information in the chapters and use the demonstrations as a supplement.

The accompanying disc also includes the Macmillan Technical Reference Knowledge Bases for Windows NT and Windows 98. This useful reference contains information excerpted from Macmillan Computer Publishing books. In this appendix, we look at the exact contents of the CD-ROM and how to best apply them.

Multimedia Demonstrations

If you have already taken a quick glance at the book, you have probably noticed that there are references to multimedia demonstrations within the chapters. These media clips were created with the Lotus ScreenCam utility. They present video captures of screen output along with audio narratives that describe some of the more technical features of Windows NT.

Using Lotus ScreenCam

The best way to access the media clips on the CD-ROM is to simply insert the disc into your CD-ROM drive. If you have the AutoPlay option enabled in Windows 95/98 or Windows NT, the software front end will load automatically. Using this interface, you'll be able to view short descriptions of each clip and easily launch those of interest. There's also help information available for first-time users. The Lotus ScreenCam media clips on the CD-ROM are self-running executable files. Rest assured, these programs do not require you to install a custom player and will not copy any permanent files onto your system. If you're so inclined, you may run them manually from the CD-ROM by double-clicking on their icons. You can control the playback of the media clip by using the Lotus ScreenCam command bar (shown in Figure C.1). The interface allows you to easily start and pause playback as well as fast-forward through portions of the clips.

Index of Multimedia Demonstrations

Table C.1 lists information about all the multimedia demonstrations included on the CD-ROM. You'll benefit most if you read them while you're covering information in the various chapters of the book. The titles and descriptions will help you find information on specific topics. Some of the longer clips have multiple segments that you can access by using the Segment button on the ScreenCam toolbar. If you're new to Lotus ScreenCam, be sure to start with the "Introduction" clip. Happy viewing!

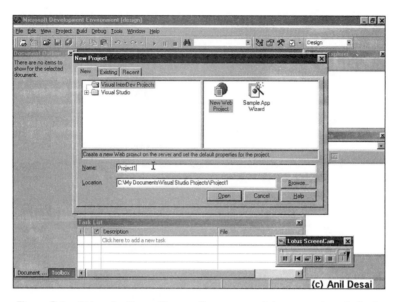

Figure C.1   Using the ScreenCam toolbar to control demonstration playback.

Table C.1 **Demonstrations on the CD-ROM**

Chapter Number	Clip Number	Title	Description
	0	Introduction	Introduction View an introduction to the CD-ROM from the author and basic instructions on viewing the other media clips
2	1	Server TCO Calculator	Use the Server TCO Calculator Excel spreadsheet for comparing TCO values for UNIX and Windows NT Server
5	1	Administrative Wizards	Allow nontechnical users to perform simple administration functions with Windows NT Administrative Wizards
5	2	Server Manager	Use the Server Manager to view computer configuration information such as shares, currently connected users, and files in use
5	3	Event Viewer	Use the Event Viewer to diagnose Windows NT operating system, service, and application events

continues

Table C.1 **Continued**

Chapter Number	Clip Number	Title	Description
5	4	Windows NT Diagnostics	Use Windows NT Diagnostics to view configuration information and statistics for local and remote computers
6	1	Viewing TCP/IP Configuration	Use the `ipconfig` and `winipcfg` commands to view and save TCP/IP configuration information
6	2	TCP/IP Diagnostic Tools	Use the `ping`, `tracert`, and `netstat` commands to diagnose and troubleshoot TCP/IP-based network devices
6	3	DHCP	Configure DHCP by defining a scope, activating it, and specifying various scope options
7	1	User Manager	Increase user account security settings with User Manager
7	2	Account Policies	Set password and account policies using User Manager
7	3	Auditing	Enable Windows NT Auditing in the User Manager
7	4	Packet Filtering	Increase TCP/IP Security by enabling and configuring packet filtering
8	1	Disk Administrator	Use Disk Administrator to view logical and physical disk configuration information
9	1	Performance Monitor—Chart View	Add counters to Performance Monitor Chart view
9	2	Performance Monitor—Other Views	Use the Report, Log, and Alert views of Performance Monitor to capture and analyze data in various ways
9	3	Task Manager	Use the Windows NT Task Manager to get a quick snapshot of system resource utilization
9	4	Network Monitor	Use the Windows NT Network Monitor to capture and analyze packets transferred on your network
9	5	System Monitor	Use System Monitor in Windows 95/98 to view, record, and analyze system performance statistics

Chapter Number	Clip Number	Title	Description
10	1	Paging File	View and modify Windows NT paging file settings
10	2	Server Service	Optimize the Windows NT Server Service for the specific role of each machine
11	1	Client Administration Tools	Use the Windows 95/98/NT client administration tools to remotely administer a Windows NT Server
11	2	Web-Based Internet Service	Use a Web browser to Service Manager administer Internet Information
11	3	Web-Based Administrator	Use a Web browser to administer your Windows NT servers
12	1	RAS Setup	Set up and configure the Remote Access Service to allow remote users to connect to your server using a modem
12	2	RAS Security	Use User Manager and other Windows NT settings to secure your Remote Access Service installation
13	1	VPN Setup	Use the Point-to-Point Tunneling Protocol to set up a Windows NT Server to allow virtual private networking
13	2	PPTP Security	Set up packet filtering to secure your Windows NT–based VPN server
13	3	RRAS Administrator	Use the Routing and Remote Access Service Administrator to easily configure advanced Windows NT routing functions
14	1	Setup Manager	Use the Windows NT Setup Manager to create a file that automatically responds to setup prompts
14	2	SysDiff	Use the SysDiff utility to create a snapshot of your current system configuration
15	1	FrontPage 98	See how Microsoft FrontPage 98 can ease the creation and maintenance of Web site themes, links, navigation bars, and content
16	1	Outlook Web Access	Use a Web browser with Outlook Web Access to view schedule and calendar information and email

continues

Table C.1 **Continued**

Chapter Number	Clip Number	Title	Description
16	2	ODBC Connections	Create an ODBC connection to a Microsoft Access database
16	3	Visual InterDev	Use Microsoft's Visual InterDev 6.0 to create database-driven Web-based applications
17	1	FTP Setup	Configure options for Internet Information Server's FTP service
17	2	FTP Security Settings	Configure security settings for the FTP service
17	3	FTP NTFS Settings	Configure Windows NT File Systems settings for the FTP service
17	4	FTP Clients	Use Windows NT's command-line FTP utility to access an FTP server
18	1	Profile Directories	View the location and types of information stored within a Windows NT profile
18	2	System Policy Editor	Use the System Policy Editor to create and modify Windows NT policy files
19	1	RegEdit	Use the RegEdit and Regedt32 utilities to view and modify Windows NT Registry information

Macmillan Knowledge Base

If you're looking for information on Windows NT 4.0 and Windows 98, just insert the CD-ROM into your drive. The CD-ROM includes the entire Macmillan Knowledge Base for these products. From the initial screen, you'll be able to choose the references you want. The interface allows you to quickly find information of interest, using a Web browser or a built-in viewer. Figure C.2 shows a sample of the types of information in the Knowledge Base. This resource is best used if you want more specific information on certain topics covered in the technical chapters of this book.

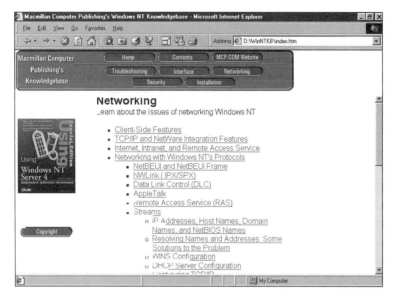

Figure C.2   Viewing the Macmillan Windows NT Knowledge Base in a Web browser.

Index

Symbols

80/20 rule, 341

A

access
  remote, 232-235
  time, 175
accessing
  command prompts, 79
  company information, 65
  computers, restricting, 339-340
  data, 279-280
  File Transfer Protocol (FTP) sites, 318-321
  program groups, 327
  Registry, Remote Administration, 201-202
account managers group, 77
accounts
  managing, 73-77, 117-121
  options, 83
Active Directory service, 372-374
Active Server Pages (ASP), 281-282, 298-302, 360-361
Active X controls, 279
ActiveX Data Objects (ADO), 279
adapters, network, 185, 217
adding
  Active Server Pages (ASP), 298-302
  batch files, 80
  Client-Based Network Administration Tools, 198
  connections
    Dial-Up Networking (DUN), 223
    Open Database Connectivity (ODBC), 296-298
  counters, default views, 155
  databases, 295-296
  forms, Outlook Web Access (OWA), 294
  modems, Remote Access Service (RAS), 217-223
  Point-to-Point Tunneling Protocol (PPTP), 235
  policy groups, 336-337
  profiles
    users, 328
    Windows 95/98, 332, 337
  security, Web pages, 303
  shortcuts, 356-358
  snapshots, 256-257
  special-purpose directories, File Transfer Protocol (FTP), 316
  static addresses, Dynamic Host Configuration Protocol (DHCP) Manager, 104
  system policies, 333-335
  templates, 75-76
  warning messages, File Transfer Protocol (FTP), 317
  Web platforms, Windows NT, 282-284
  Web-Based Administrator (WBA), 205
  Windows NT Zero Administration Kit (ZAK), 339-340
addresses
  Internet Protocol (IP)
    gathering information about, 96-97
    managing, 184
    resolving domain names, 92-96
  networks
    allocating, 102-106
    translation, 125
  static, creating, 104
administrative tools, wizards, 70
administrators
  groups, 77
  managing permissions, 118
  responsibilities, 12

ADO. *See ActiveX Data Objects*

advances in technology, 45, 59

agents
Dynamic Host Configuration Protocol (DHCP), 106
Network Monitor,
capturing data, 200

agreements, service-level, 57, 387

Alert view, Windows NT Performance Monitor, 158-160

All Users directory, 326-327

allocating network addresses, 102-106

Allow Any Authentication Including Clear Text option, 222

allowed traffic, 107

AltaVista, 411

Always on Top setting, Windows NT Task Manager, 162

analyzers, network, 116

answer files, creating, 251-256

App Station mode, Windows NT Zero Administration Kit (ZAK), 338

Application layer, 91

applications
administrative, wizards, 70
Client-Based Network Administration Tools, installing, 198
command-line
management, 78-81
Regini, 256
Transmission Control Protocol/Internet Protocol (TCP/IP), 96-102
database, 283
Difference detectors, 263
Disk Administrator, 77
Disk duplicators, 263
Event Viewer, 70-72
installing, 250-267, 368
Internet Connection Services for Microsoft RAS, 399
Internet Information Server (IIS), 282, 399
Internet Service Manager, 202
licensing, 43, 57, 83-85, 264
logs, 70
Lotus ScreenCam, 414
Microsoft Exchange Server, backing up data, 146
Microsoft FrontPage, 98, 282
Microsoft Message Queue Server (MSMQ), 288, 399
Microsoft Script Debugger, 399

Microsoft Site Server Express, 399
Microsoft SQL Server, backing up data, 146
Microsoft Transaction Server (MTS), 287-288, 399
Microsoft Visual InterDev, 282
NetWatch, 209
Network Client Administrator, 72
Network Monitor Agent, capturing data, 200
Office 97, network installations, 264
Outlook Web Access (OWA), 292-294
password-breaking, 116
Performance Monitor, 72
ping, isolating problems, 167
public key encryption, 242
Remote Access Administrator, 220
Remote Administration, accessing Registry, 201-202
Remote Command Client (rcmd), 209
remote control, managing servers and workstations, 207-208
Remote Execute (rexec), 209
remote management, Windows NT Resource Kit, 209-210
Remote Registry Service, 209
Remote Scripting Host (RSH), 361
Remote Shell (rsh), 209
Repair Disk utility (RDISK), backing up data, 144
running from servers, 341
Secure Sockets Layer (SSL), 242
Security Configuration Manager, 128
Server Manager, 70, 194-195, 199
Server Service (rcmdsvc), 209
Service Monitor Configuration, 209
Setup Manager
combining with SysDiff, 260-261
creating answer files, 251-256
Shutdown Manager, 209
SNMP Monitor, 209
standardizing, 58-59
Synchronization Manager, 377
System Policy Editor, 333-337
Systems Management Server (SMS), 263
testing, 302
third-party
authentication, 242
backing up data, 146
total cost of ownership (TCO), 19-32
uninstalling, 368
User Manager, 73-77
Visual InterDev Rapid Application Deployment Components, 399

Web-based, 270-297, 300, 303-308
Web-Based Administrator (WBA),
    managing Web servers, 204-206
WinBench, 176
Windows 2000, 366-380
Windows 95/98 System Monitor, 168-169
Windows NT Backup, 139-140
Windows NT Diagnostics, 73, 200
Windows NT Disk Administrator, backing
    up data, 141-142
Windows NT Network Monitor,
    166-167
Windows NT Performance Monitor,
    155-161
Windows NT Task Manager, 162-166
Windows NT Terminal Server (WTS),
    managing remote workstations and
    servers, 210
Windows NT Zero Administration Kit
    (ZAK), restricting access on computers,
    339-340
Windows Scripting Host (WSH),
    347-348, 353-359
WinPopUp utility, sending and receiving
    messages, 201
Applications tab, Windows NT Task
    Manager, 162-163
applying
    feedback, 35-36
    snapshots, 260
    system policies, 336
architecture, total cost of ownership (TCO), 15
archive (copy) backups, 136
ASP. *See Active Server Pages*
assets, managing, 41-45
assigning
    drive letters, 142
    permissions, groups, 75
    resources, 187
    roaming user profiles, 328-329
    system policies, 333-336
AT command, 81
attacks, preventing, 108-109, 124-127
attributes, Hidden, 325
audit logs, viewing, 123
Audit Policy dialog box, Logon and Logoff
    option, 124
auditing
    external, 128
    Windows NT servers, 121-124
authentication, 107, 204, 221-222,
    238-239, 314-316
Automatic setting, services, 181

automatic state, 83
automating
    File Transfer Protocol (FTP)
        functions, 319-320
    software installations, 250-267

B

backups
    data, 134-151
    improvements, Windows 2000, 371
    operators group, 77
    policies, 65
    Registry, 325, 349
Balance setting, Server service, 180
batch files, creating, 80, 261-262
benchmarks, 176, 383
best practices, reducing total cost of owner-
    ship (TCO), 33-41, 43-50
Beverly Hills Software, 408
billing technical support, 54
bindings, protocols, 182-183
boot disks, creating, 250
boot files, fixing corruption, 148
bottlenecks
    finding, 101
    moving, 174
broadcasts
    controlling, 182
    effects on network traffic, 95
browsers
    authentication, 204
    opening File Transfer Protocol (FTP)
        sessions, 320-321
    World Wide Web, 276-277, 283
buffer sizes, restricting, 167
business cases, defining solutions for,
    34-35
Business Research Group, 22
Bypass File Security for Backing Up Files,
    granting, 134

C

C2 level of security, 115
caches
    displaying names, 100
    managing passwords, 129

caching data, 175

calculating paging file settings, 177

calculators, 28-30

calendaring, Outlook Web Access (OWA), 294

call-back verification, Remote Access Service (RAS), 222-223

capturing data, Network Monitor Agent, 200

card, video, 186

carrier sense media access/collision detection (CSMA/CD), 183

cartridges, 136

case sensitivity
command-line prompts, 79
user names, 120
VBScript, 356

case studies, evaluating, 6

cataloging backups, 138

CD-ROM (compact discs), 136

central processing units (CPU)
column headings, Windows NT Task Manager, 164
upgrading, 185-186

CEO (chief executive officers), 13

Certificate Server, 399

Certified Professional Magazine, 408

CGI (Common Gateway Interface), 277

Challenge-Handshake Authentication protocol (CHAP), 221

change management procedures, 63-65

changing
drive letters, 142
group priorities, 336-337
options
ping command-line tool, 98
startup, 181
physical disk locations, 178-179
profiles, Windows 95/98, 331-332
protocol bindings, 182-183
Registry, 256, 325, 349
services, 82, 180
settings
paging files, 178
roaming user profiles, 330-331
security, Internet Service Manager, 202-203
system policies, 336
unattend.txt, 254
update frequency, Windows NT Task Manager, 162

CHAP (Challenge-Handshake Authentication Protocol), 221

charge backs, technical support, 54

Chart of Accounts, 25-26

Chart view, Windows NT Performance Monitor, 158

chief executive officers (CEO), 13

choosing
authentication levels, File Transfer Protocol (FTP), 314-316
backup hardware, 135
databases, 295
files to back up, 139
home directories, File Transfer Protocol (FTP) service, 312
options, auditing, 122
roaming user profiles, 328-329
scripting languages, 350-351
user permissions, Log On As setting, 181

CIM (Common Information Model), 206

classes, Microsoft, 406-407

Client-Based Network Administration Tools, installing, 198

client/server architecture, total cost of ownership (TCO), 15

clients
configuring, 223, 234-240
managing, 368-369
setup, Outlook Web Access (OWA), 293-294
thin, 210-212

cloud icons, 91

clustering, 145

CNet's News.Com, 408

collisions, detecting, 183

column headings, Windows NT Task Manager, 163-164

COM (Component Object Model), 282

command line
opening File Transfer Protocol (FTP) sessions, 319-320
tools, 78-81, 256

commands, 79-81, 96-100, 148, 325, 355

comments, receiving and applying, 35-36

Commit Charge value, Windows NT Task Manager, 165

Common Gateway Interface (CGI), 277

Common Information Model (CIM), 206
communication, 48-49, 54-57, 59-62
compact discs (CD-ROM), 136
companies
    managing access to information, 65
    posting news, 304
compatibility, Transmission Control
    Protocol/Internet Protocol (TCP/IP)
    commands, 100-101
compilers, Java Virtual Machine, 277
Component Object Model (COM), 282
components, interactions among
    hardware, 174-176
compressing data, 77
computing, distributed, 15
configuring
    Alert methods, Windows NT Performance
        Monitor, 160
    clients, 223, 234-240
    File Transfer Protocol (FTP), 311-313
    logs, File Transfer Protocol (FTP),
        317-318
    modems, Remote Access Service (RAS),
        217-223
    Outlook Web Access (OWA), 292
    policies for changing, 63-65
    protocols, Remote Access Service (RAS),
        218-219
    scopes, Dynamic Host Configuration
        Protocol (DHCP), 104-106
    servers, 216, 234-240
    Windows Internet Naming Service
        (WINS), 95
connections
    creating
        Open Database Connectivity (ODBC),
            296-298
        Dial-Up Networking (DUN), 223
    machines with friendly names,
        troubleshooting, 101
    polling, 288
    verifying, 98
    virtual private network (VPN), 240
consoles, Microsoft Management,
    311-312, 367, 399
consulting, 13-14, 391
contacting remote users,
    Server Manager, 194
controllers, domain, 74, 330

controlling
    broadcasts, 182
    resources, 65-66
controls, ActiveX, 279
converting
    partitions, 77
    profiles, 329
copying
    data, Redundant Array of Independent
        Disks (RAID), 141-143
    directories, 85
    profiles, 329-330
costs, 7
counters
    Windows 95/98 System Monitor, 169
    Windows NT Performance Monitor,
        155-157
CPU. See central processing units
creating
    Active Server Pages (ASP), 298-302
    boot disks, 250
    connections
        Dial-Up Networking (DUN), 223
        Open Database Connectivity (ODBC),
            296-298
    databases, 295-296
    files
        answer, 251-256
        batch, 80, 261-262
    forms, Outlook Web Access
        (OWA), 294
    policies, 134-135, 333-337
    profiles, 328, 332, 337
    shares, Server Manager, 195
    shortcuts, 356-358
    snapshots, 256-257
    special-purpose directories, File Transfer
        Protocol (FTP), 316
    static addresses, Dynamic Host
        Configuration Protocol (DHCP)
        Manager, 104
    templates, 75-76
    warning messages, File Transfer Protocol
        (FTP), 317
    Web platforms, Windows NT,
        282-284
criticism, receiving and applying, 35-36
Cscript command, 355
CSMA/CD (Carrier sense media access/
    collision detection), 183

D

daily backups, 136

data
accessing, 279-280
backing up, 134-151
caching, 175
capturing, Network Monitor
Agent, 200
compressing, 77
encryption
Internet Protocol (IP)-based, 110
Remote Access Service (RAS), 222
recovering, 147-148
replicating, Redundant Array of
Independent Disks (RAID), 141-143
restoring, 134
security, Secure Sockets Layer
(SSL), 318
transporting, costs, 7

Data Link layer, 91

databases
creating, 295-296
inconsistencies, causes of, 95
object linking and embedding, 279
publishing to Web, 295-297, 300-303
querying and registering, Windows
Internet Naming Service
(WINS), 182
Registry, 201-202, 256, 324-325, 348-350
Security Accounts Manager (SAM), backing up, 144
tools, 283

DCOM (Distributed Component Object
Model), 282

Default User directory, 326

default views, adding counters, 155

defining
functions, information technology (IT)
departments, 54
scope options, Dynamic Host
Configuration Protocol (DHCP),
105-106
solutions to technical projects, 34-35
system policies, 333-335

defragmenting disks, 187-188

DejaNews, 409

deleting accounts, 76

Deloitte & Touche, 5, 22

denial of service attack, 108

Desktop Management Task Force (DTMF),
Common Information Model (CIM), 206

Desktop TCO & ROI Calculator, 28-29

desktops, creating shortcuts, 357-358

destinations
host unreachable message,
troubleshooting, 101
packets, monitoring, 183

detecting
collisions, 183
modems, Remote Access Service (RAS),
217

developers, responsibilities, 13

devices, upgrading drivers, 186

DFS. *See Distributed File System*

DHCP. *See Dynamic Host Configuration
Protocol*

DHTML (dynamic hypertext markup language), 280

dial-in permissions, granting, 220

Dial-Up Adapter counter, Windows 95/98
System Monitor, 169

Dial-Up Networking (DUN), 223, 225

dialing, Remote Access Service
(RAS), 224

dialing location settings, Remote Access
Service (RAS), 225

dialog boxes, Audit Policy, 124

Difference detectors, 263

difference files, generating, 258-259

differential backups, 136

dir /a command, 325

directories
creating, 316
managing, File Transfer Protocol (FTP)
service, 312-313
replicating, 85
snapshot, excluding, 258
user profiles, 326-327

directors, information technology (IT)
departments, 13

Disabled setting, services, 181

disabled state, 83

disabling
accounts, 76
unnecessary services, 180-182

disconnect, idle, 225

Disk Administrator, backing up data,
141-142

Disk duplicators, 263

disks
    boot, creating, 250
    defragmenting, 187-188
    emergency repair, 144
    mirroring, 142
    physical, changing locations, 178-179
    striping, 142
    throughput, optimizing, 176
    tracking, Windows NT Disk
        Administrator, 142
Display Logo When Scripts Executed in
    MS-DOS property, 353
displaying
    audit logs, Event Viewer, 123
    drive mappings, 358-359
    event logs
        Event Viewer, 123-124
        Web-Based Administrator
        (WBA), 205
    files, Registry, 325
    logging information, Windows NT
        Performance Monitor, 161
    names, network caches, 100
    network statistics, Windows NT
        Diagnostics, 200
    options, File Transfer Protocol (FTP) log
        configuration, 317
    services, 82
    text files, command output, 97
    values, Windows NT Performance
        Monitor, 161
Distributed Component Object Model
    (DCOM), 282
distributed computing, 15
Distributed File System (DFS),
    Windows 2000, 375
DNS. *See Domain Name System*
documenting
    backups, 138
    network settings, 97
Domain Name System (DNS), 93-94,
    99, 374
domains
    collision, 183
    controllers, copying profiles, 330
    described, 74
    limitations, Active Directory service,
        372-373
    resolving names, 92-96
downloading updates, 401
downtime, costs, 7

drivers
    troubleshooting, 72
    upgrading, 186
drives
    assigning letters, partitions, 142
    displaying mappings, 358-359
    logical, 175
    physical, 175
    speed, 136
    storage capacities, 135-136
DTMF. *See Desktop Management Task Force*
dumb terminals, 211
DUN. *See Dial-Up Networking*
duplicating
    data, Redundant Array of Independent
        Disks (RAID), 141-143
    directories, 85
    dynamic address allocation, 103
    profiles, 329-330
Dynamic Host Configuration Protocol
    (DHCP)
    allocating network addresses, 102-106
    managing Internet Protocol (IP) addresses,
        184
Dynamic Host Configuration Protocol
    (DHCP) Agent, 106
Dynamic Host Configuration Protocol
    (DHCP) Manager, creating static addresses,
    104
dynamic hypertext markup language
    (DHTML), 280
dynamic volume management, 372

E

e-commerce, 387-388
editing
    drive letters, 142
    group priorities, 336-337
    options
        ping command-line tool, 98
        startup, 181
    physical disk locations, 178-179
    profiles, Windows 95/98, 331-332
    protocol bindings, 182-183
    Registry, 256, 325, 349
    services, 82, 180

settings
  paging files, 178
  roaming user profiles, 330-331
  security, Internet Service Manager,
    202-203
  system policies, 336
  unattend.txt, 254
  update frequency, Windows NT Task
    Manager, 162
editors, dynamic Web page, 276
education
  classes offered through Microsoft,
    406-407
  costs, 7
  employees, 48-49
  information technology (IT) staff, 14-15
  users, security, 117
  Web-based, 305
email, usage policies, 60-62
emergency repair disks (ERD), 144
employees, managing, 45-49
enabling
  auditing, 122
  Logon and Logoff option, Audit Policy
    dialog box, 124
  physical security, 127
  Remote Administration, 201
encapsulation, 223
encryption, 110, 222, 238-239, 242
enforcing
  stronger passwords, 120-121
  system policies, 324-344
enhancing communications, 54-55
Entire Network option, 218
erasing accounts, 76
ERD (emergency repair disks), 144
Ethernet, 183
evaluating
  case studies, 6
  hardware, 43-45
  security risks, 115
  service-level agreements, 57
  total cost of ownership (TCO), 8
event logs, 70-72, 123-124, 205
Event Viewer, 70-72, 123-124
event-driven languages, 278
Exchange Server, backing up data, 146
excluding snapshot directories, 258

expectations from users, 55-56
extensions, 399

F

failed message, troubleshooting, 101
FAT. *See File Allocation Table*
fault-tolerance, Redundant Array of
  Independent Disks (RAID), 141-143
feedback, receiving and applying, 35-36
File Allocation Table (FAT)
  converting, 77
  restoring data, 134
  security, 117
File System counter, Windows 95/98 System
  Monitor, 169
File Transfer Protocol (FTP), 90,
  310-322
files
  boot, fixing corruption, 148
  creating
    answer, 251-256
    batch, 80, 261-262
  difference, generating, 258-259
  HOSTS, resolving domain names, 92
  .ini, 349
  initialization, 324
  paging, optimizing memory settings,
    177-178
  Password Filter DLL, enforcing stronger
    passwords, 121
  Registry, viewing, 325
  selecting for backup, 139
  sharing, File Transfer Protocol (FTP),
    310-322
  storage, 77
  swap, optimizing memory settings,
    178-179
  templates, system policies, 332-333
  text, 97
  unattend.ext, 254
filtering, packets, 107-109, 236-238
filters, setting, 71
finding
  bottlenecks, 101
  feedback, 35-36
  information about Internet Protocol (IP)
    addresses, 96-97

Setup Manager, 251
solutions to technical projects, 34-35
firewalls
described, 107-108
Point-to-Point Tunneling Protocol (PPTP),
238
preventing network attacks, 125-126
fixing corrupt boot files, 148
folders. *See directories*
forms
automated, 305
creating, Outlook Web Access (OWA),
294
freedom of information, 392
friendly names, troubleshooting
connections, 101
FrontPage 98, 399
FTP. *See File Transfer Protocol*
full (normal) backups, 136
future of total cost of ownership (TCO),
382-394

G

GartnerGroup, 21, 25-28. *See also Interpose,*
Inc.
gateways, 91
gathering information about Internet Protocol
(IP) addresses, 96-97
general best practices, reducing total cost of
ownership (TCO), 5-10, 33-50
generating
audit trails, 121-124
difference files, 258-259
granting
Bypass File Security for Backing up Files,
134
permissions, dial-in, 220

H

hardware
backup, selecting, 135
costs, 7
dumb terminals, 211
evaluating, 43-45
interactions among components, 174-176

replacing, 185-186
standardizing, 58-59
support, Windows 2000, 366
tuning, 184-186
upgrading, 185-186
headings, columns, 163-164
help desks
improving communications, 54-55
managing, 36-38
procedures, 39-40
responsibilities of technicians, 12
setting goals and metrics, 38-41
Hidden attribute, Registry, 325
Hide When Minimized setting, Windows NT
Task Manager, 162
hierarchical naming system, 93
Hierarchical Storage Management (HSM),
370
HKEY_CLASSES_ROOT, 348
HKEY_CURRENT_USER, 348
HKEY_LOCAL_MACHINE, 348
HKEY_SOFTWARE, 348
home directories, choosing, 312
host names, 99, 101
hosts, 207
HOSTS files, resolving domain names, 92
hotfixes, 400
HSM (Hierarchical Storage Management), 370
Hypertext Transfer Protocol (HTTP)
protocol, 90

I

ICMP (Internet Control Messaging Protocol),
90
icons, clouds, 91
identifiers, security, 76
idle disconnect, Remote Access Service (RAS),
225
IETF (Internet Engineering), 216
Task Force
IIS. *See Internet Information Server*
Image Name column heading, Windows NT
Task Manager, 164
implementing total cost of ownership (TCO),
9-10

improving communications, 54-55

Incoming directory, 316

inconsistencies, databases, 95

incremental backups, 136

indexes, multimedia demonstrations, 414,
    416-418

information, freedom of, 392

information technology (IT) departments
    functions and goals, 10-15, 33-36, 54,
        389-391
    policies and procedures, 54-67

.ini files, 349

initialization files, 324

Inspect options, WINNT /ox
    command, 148

installing
    applications, 368, 250-267
    Client-Based Network Administration
        Tools, 198
    Dynamic Host Configuration Protocol
        (DHCP), 104-106
    Outlook Web Access (OWA), 292
    Point-to-Point Tunneling Protocol (PPTP),
        235
    Remote Access Service (RAS), 217-218
    Web-Based Administrator (WBA), 205
    Windows Internet Naming Service
        (WINS), 94
    Windows NT Network Monitor, 166
    Windows NT Zero Administration Kit
        (ZAK), 339-340

IntelliMirror, 369

Internet
    browsers, 276-277, 283, 320-321
    cloud icons, 91
    data security, Secure Sockets Layer (SSL),
        318
    managing Web servers, 202-206
    pages
        adding security, 303
        dynamic editors, 276
    protocols
        bindings, managing, 182-183
        Challenge-Handshake Authentication,
            221
        configuring, Remote Access Service
            (RAS), 218-219
        Dynamic Host Configuration,
            102-106, 184
        File Transfer, 90, 310-322
        Hypertext Transfer, 90
        Internet, 90, 96-97, 106, 110, 184,
            285

        Internet Control Messaging, 90
        IPSecure(IPSec), 242
        IPX/SPX, 90
        Layer 2 Forwarding, 242
        NetBEUI, 90
        NETBIOS, 90
        Network News Transfer, 408
        Password Authentication, 221
        Point-to-Point, 90
        Point-to-Point Tunneling, 234-235,
            238, 241
        Simple Mail Transfer, 90
        Telnet, 90
        Transmission Control/Internet,
            90-112, 126
        User Datagram, 90
        virtual private networks
            (VPN), 241

publishing Web databases, 295-297,
    300-303

reliability, 240

remote networks, 107

resources
    Beverly Hills Software, 408
    CNet's News.Com, 408
    Microsoft Certified Professional
        Magazine, 408
    Microsoft classroom training, 407
    Microsoft Knowledge Base, 405
    Microsoft online seminars, 406
    Microsoft online support, 405
    Microsoft Security Advisor Program
        site, 400
    Microsoft TechNet, 404
    Microsoft telephone support, 406
    newsgroups, 408-409
    NT Security.Net, 408
    search engines, 411
    Ultimate Collection of Windows
        Shareware, The (TUCOWS), 408
    Whatis.com, 408
    Winfiles.com, 408
    Ziff-Davis Anchordesk, 408

scripts, 360-361

servers, managing, 202-206

services, 240

sites
    measuring performance, 99
    Security Advisor Program, 400

support, Windows 2000, 379

technologies, 270-297, 300, 303-308

total cost of ownership (TCO), 16

training, 305

usage policies, 59-60

Internet Connection Services for Remote
    Access Service (RAS), 225, 399
Internet Control Messaging Protocol (ICMP)
    protocol, 90
Internet Engineering Task Force
    (IETF), 216
Internet Information Server (IIS),
    126-127, 282, 399
Internet layer, 91
Internet Protocol (IP) Address Reservation,
    creating, 104
Internet Service Manager, managing Web
    servers, 202
Interpose, Inc., Desktop TCO & ROI
    Calculator, 28-29. *See also GartnerGroup*
Intranet, 274, 310-322
intruders, thinking like, 116
IP. *See protocols, Internet*
ipconfig commands, 96-97
ipconfig utility, 96, 101
IPSec. *See protocols, IPSecure*
IPv6. *See protocols, Internet*
IPX/SPX protocol, advantages and
    disadvantages, 90
isolating
    network traffic, 183-184
    ping problems, Windows NT Network
        Monitor, 167
IT. *See information technology departments*

J-K

Java Virtual Machine, 277
JavaScript, 277-278
JScript, 277-278
Kernel counter, Windows 95/98 System
    Monitor, 169
Kernel Memory value, Windows NT Task
    Manager, 165
keys, Registry, 348
Knowledge Base, 405

L

L2TP (Layer 2 Forwarding protocol), 242
LAN. *See local area networks*
languages
    scripting, 277-280, 350-352, 356
    support, Windows 2000, 378
launching
    applications from servers, 341
    File Transfer Protocol (FTP), 311,
        319-321
    Internet Service Manager, 202
    Lotus ScreenCam, 414
    Repair Disk utility, 144
    Server Manager, 199
    Windows 95/98 System Monitor, 168
    Windows NT
        Backup, from command line, 140-141
        Disk Administrator, 141
        Performance Monitor, 155
        setup, 254
        Task Manager, 162
    winipcfg command, 97
    WinPopUp utility, 202
Layer 2 Forwarding protocol (L2TP), 242
License Management Service, 85
licenses
    managing, 43, 83-85
    network applications, 264
    service-level, 57
local area networks (LAN),
    Ethernet, 183
local user profiles, 328
locking workstations, 129
Log On As setting
    options, 83
    specifying user permissions, 181
Log view, Windows NT Performance
    Monitor, 158-161
logging
    saving and viewing information, 160-161
    transactions, 134
Logical Disk counter, Windows NT
    Performance Monitor, 156
logical drives, 175
logins, scripts, 86

Logon and Logoff option, Audit Policy dialog box, 124

Logon dialing, Remote Access Service (RAS), 224

logons, setting restrictions, 76

logs
audit, 123
configuring, File Transfer Protocol (FTP), 317-318
event, 70-72, 123-124, 205

Lotus ScreenCam, running, 414

lowering total cost of ownership (TCO), 5-10, 33-50

Lycos, 411

M

machine-specific settings, 255

Macmillan Knowledge Base, 418-419

magazines, *Microsoft Certified Professional*, 408

maintaining
policies, 56
profile permissions, 330

management state, 288

managers, information technology (IT) departments, 13

managing
access, company information, 65
accounts, 73-77
Active Directory service, 374
assets, 41-45
audit trails, 121-124
clients, 368-369
costs, 7
directories, File Transfer Protocol (FTP) service, 312-313
employees, 45-49
group policies, 369
hardware, 43-45
help desks, 36-38
information technology (IT) departments, 33-36
Internet Protocol (IP) addresses, 184
licenses, 43, 83-85
networks, 70-88, 383-386
permissions
administrators, 118
users, 117-121
profiles, 324-332

protocols
bindings, 182-183
Transmission Control/Internet (TCP/IP), 90-112
resources, 62-66
security, 114-131, 314
servers, 193-214
services, 82-83
sites, File Transfer Protocol (FTP) service, 312-313
storage, 370-372
users, 73-77, 200-202, 324-332
volumes, 372
Windows NT File System (NTFS), 77
workstations, 200-202, 207-208, 211-212

mandatory profiles, 328-329, 332

Manual setting, services, 181

manual state, 83

mappings
causes of errors, 95
drives, displaying, 358-359

masks, subnet, 91

measuring
security risks, 115
success of help desks, 38-41
total cost of ownership (TCO), 3-18

media
backup, storage capacities, 135-136
streaming, 303-304

Mem Usage column heading, Windows NT Task Manager, 164

memory
optimizing settings, 177-182
upgrading, 185

Memory counter, Windows NT Performance Monitor, 156

Memory Manager counter, Windows 95/98 System Monitor, 169

MetaCrawler, 411

metrics, help desks, 38-41

Microsoft
classes, 406-407
comments on studies, 22
future of Windows operating system, 393
Knowledge Base, 405
Security Advisor Program Web site, 400
software. *See software*
TechNet, 21, 404
technical support, 405-406
Windows Management Interface (WMI), 206

Mimimize Memory Used setting, 180
Mimimize Throughput for File Sharing
    setting, 180
Mimimize Throughput for Network
    Applications setting, 180
minidrivers, 186
mirroring disks, 142
modems, configuring, 217-223
modes, Windows NT Zero Administration
    Kit (ZAK), 338-339
modifying
    drive letters, 142
    group priorities, 336-337
    options
        ping command-line tool, 98
        startup, 181
    physical disk locations, 178-179
    profiles, Windows 95/98, 331-332
    protocol bindings, 182-183
    Registry, 256, 325, 349
    services, 82, 180
    settings
        paging files, 178
        roaming user profiles, 330-331
        security, Internet Service Manager,
            202-203
        system policies, 336
    unattend.txt, 254
    update frequency, Windows NT Task
        Manager, 162
monitoring
    packet destinations, 183
    performance, 154-171
moving bottlenecks, 174
multicasting, Internet Protocol (IP), 285
multilanguage support,
    Windows 2000, 378
Multilink, Remote Access Service (RAS), 225
multimedia demonstrations, 414-418
multiuser support, Windows 2000, 378

N

Name Server Lookup (nslookup) utility, 99
NAT. *See network address translation*
nbtstat -r command, 100

nbtstat utility. *See NetBIOS Over TCP/IP
    Statistics utility*
NET commands, 79-80
NetBEUI protocol, advantages and
    disadvantages, 90
NetBIOS Over TCP/IP Statistics
    (nbtstat) utility, 100
NETBIOS protocol, advantages and
    disadvantages, 90
Netscape Navigator, browser
    authentication, 204
NetShow, 304
netstat utility, 100
NetWatch, 209
network address translation (NAT), 107, 125
network administrators,
    responsibilities, 12
network analyzers, 116
Network Client Administrator, 72
network diagrams, cloud icons, 91
Network interface layer, 91
Network layer, 91
Network Monitor, 166-167
Network Monitor Agent,
    capturing data, 200
Network News Transfer Protocol
    (NNTP), 408
Network Segment counter, Windows NT
    Performance Monitor, 156
news, posting, 304
newsgroups, 294, 408-409
NNTP (Network News Transfer Protocol), 408
normal backups, 136
notifying remote users,
    Server Manager, 194
NSA (United States National Security
    Agency), 115
nslookup utility (Name Server Lookup utility),
    99
NT Security.Net, 408
NTFS. *See Windows NT, File System*

O

object linking and embedding for databases (OLEDB), 279

objects
ActiveX Data, 279
Windows NT Performance Monitor, 155-157
WScript, 352

obtaining information about Internet Protocol (IP) addresses, 96-97

ODBC. *See Open database connectivity*

Office 97, network installations, 264

OLEDB. *See object linking and embedding for databases*

online seminars and support, Microsoft, 405-406

Open database connectivity (ODBC), 279, 296-298

Open Systems Interconnection (OSI) model, 91

opening
applications from servers, 341
File Transfer Protocol (FTP), 311, 319-321
Internet Service Manager, 202
Lotus ScreenCam, 414
Repair Disk utility, 144
Server Manager, 199
Windows 95/98 System Monitor, 168
Windows NT
Backup, from command line, 140-141
Disk Administrator, 141
Performance Monitor, 155
setup, 254
Task Manager, 162
winipcfg command, 97
WinPopUp utility, 202

optimizing performance, 174-190

options
accounts, 83, 119
auditing, selecting, 122
changing
ping command-line tool, 98
startup, 181
Entire Network, 218
Log On As setting, 83
Logon and Logoff, Audit Policy dialog box, 124
packs, Windows NT, 398-400
Remote Access Service (RAS) authentication, 222

setting
scope, Dynamic Host Configuration Protocol (DHCP), 105-106
scripts, WScript, 353
This Computer Only, 218
viewing, File Transfer Protocol (FTP) log configuration, 317
WINNT /ox command, 148

Orange Book security, 115

OSI model (Open Systems Interconnection model), 91

outages, networks, 57

Outlook Web Access (OWA), 292-294

output commands, saving and viewing, 97

outsourcing, 13-14, 243, 391

overriding system policy settings, 336

OWA (Outlook Web Access), 292-294

P

packages, 263

packaging, Windows 2000, 366

packets
filtering, 107-109, 236-238
monitoring destinations, 183
tracking paths, 99

packs, option, 398-400

paging files, optimizing memory settings, 177-178

PAP (Password Authentication Protocol), 221

parameters, Internet Protocol (IP), 106

partitions
assigning drive letters, 142
converting, 77
described, 175

partners, push and pull, 95

Password Authentication Protocol (PAP), 221

Password Filter DLL file, enforcing stronger passwords, 121

passwords, 119-121, 129

patches security, 400

Paused state, 83, 181

PDC (primary domain controller), 74

performance
drives, 136
monitoring, 154-171
optimizing, 174-190
Web sites, measuring, 99

Performance Monitor, 72, 155-161

Performance tab, Windows NT Task Manager, 162, 165-166

permissions
  granting
    Bypass File Security for Backing Up Files, 134
    groups, 75
    Remote Access Service (RAS), 220
  users
    managing, 117-121
    profiles, 330, 332
    specifying, Log On As setting, 181

Personal Fax Server, 227

Physical Disk counter, Windows NT Performance Monitor, 156

physical disks, changing locations, 178-179

physical drives, 175

Physical layer, 91

Physical Memory value, Windows NT Task Manager, 165

physical security, enabling, 127

PID. *See Process ID column heading*

ping utility
  commands, 98
  isolating problems, Windows NT Network Monitor, 167
  troubleshooting network problems, 101

ping-based traffic, preventing entry into networks, 108

planning
  security, 114-131
  technology refreshes, 59
  total cost of ownership (TCO), 8-9

platforms, building, 282-284

Point-to-Point (PPP) Multilink, Remote Access Service (RAS), 225

Point-to-Point Protocol (PPP), 90, 215-216

Point-to-Point Tunneling Protocol (PPTP), 234-235, 238, 241

policy groups, creating, 336-337

polling, connection, 288

posting company news, 304

PPP. *See Point-to-Point Protocol*

PPTP. *See Point-to-Point Tunneling Protocol*

Presentation layer, 91

preventing network attacks, 108-109, 124-127

primary domain controller (PDC), 74

printing text files, 97

Process ID (PID) column heading, Windows NT Task Manager, 164

Processes tab, Windows NT Task Manager, 162-164

processing transactions, 287

profiles, users, 324-332

Profiles directory, 326

programmer responsibilities, 13

programs
  administrative, wizards, 70
  Client-Based Network Administration Tools, installing, 198
  command-line
    management, 78-81
    Regini, 256
    Transmission Control Protocol/Internet Protocol (TCP/IP), 96-102
  database, 283
  Difference detectors, 263
  Disk Administrator, 77
  Disk duplicators, 263
  Event Viewer, 70-72
  installing, 250-267, 368
  Internet Connection Services for Microsoft RAS, 399
  Internet Information Server (IIS), 282, 399
  Internet Service Manager, 202
  licensing, 43, 57, 83-85, 264
  Lotus ScreenCam, 414
  logs, 70
  Microsoft Exchange Server, backing up data, 146
  Microsoft FrontPage, 98, 282
  Microsoft Message Queue Server (MSMQ), 288, 399
  Microsoft Script Debugger, 399
  Microsoft Site Server Express, 399
  Microsoft SQL Server, backing up data, 146
  Microsoft Transaction Server (MTS), 287-288, 399
  Microsoft Visual InterDev, 282
  NetWatch, 209
  Network Client Administrator, 72
  Network Monitor Agent, capturing data, 200
  Office 97, network installations, 264
  Outlook Web Access (OWA), 292-294
  password-breaking, 116
  Performance Monitor, 72
  ping, isolating problems, 167
  public key encryption, 242
  Remote Access Administrator, 220

Remote Administration, accessing
Registry, 201-202
Remote Command Client (rcmd), 209
remote control, managing servers and
workstations, 207-208
Remote Execute (rexec), 209
remote management, Windows NT
Resource Kit, 209-210
Remote Registry Service, 209
Remote Scripting Host (RSH), 361
Remote Shell (rsh), 209
Repair Disk utility (RDISK), backing up
data, 144
running from servers, 341
Secure Sockets Layer (SSL), 242
Security Configuration Manager, 128
Server Manager, 70, 194-195, 199
Server Service (rcmdsvc), 209
Service Monitor Configuration, 209
Setup Manager
combining with SysDiff, 260-261
creating answer files, 251-256
Shutdown Manager, 209
SNMP Monitor, 209
standardizing, 58-59
Synchronization Manager, 377
System Policy Editor, 333-337
Systems Management Server (SMS), 263
testing, 302
third-party
authentication, 242
backing up data, 146
total cost of ownership (TCO), 19-32
uninstalling, 368
User Manager, 73-77
Visual InterDev Rapid Application
Deployment Components, 399
Web-based, 270-297, 300, 303-308
Web-Based Administrator (WBA),
managing Web servers, 204-206
WinBench, 176
Windows 95/98 System Monitor, 168-169
Windows 2000, 366-380
Windows NT Backup, 139-140
Windows NT Diagnostics, 73, 200
Windows NT Disk Administrator, backing
up data, 141-142
Windows NT Network Monitor, 166-167
Windows NT Performance Monitor,
155-161
Windows NT Task Manager, 162-166
Windows NT Terminal Server (WTS),
managing remote workstations and
servers, 210

Windows NT Zero Administration Kit
(ZAK), restricting access on computers,
339-340
Windows Scripting Host (WSH), 347-348,
353-359
WinPopUp utility, sending and
receiving messages, 201

prompts, command, 79

properties, WScript, 353

protecting
company information, 65
data, 134-151

protocols
bindings, managing, 182-183
Challenge-Handshake
Authentication (CHAP), 221
configuring, Remote Access Service (RAS),
218-219
Dynamic Host Configuration (DHCP),
102-106, 184
File Transfer (FTP), 90, 310-322
Hypertext Transfer (HTTP), 90
Internet Control Messaging (ICMP), 90
Internet (IP), 90, 96-97, 106, 110, 184,
285
IPSecure (IPSec), 242
IPX/SPX, 90
Layer 2 Forwarding, 242
NetBEUI, 90
NETBIOS, 90
Network News Transfer (NNTP), 408
Password Authentication (PAP), 21
Point-to-Point (PPP), 90, 215-216
Point-to-Point Tunneling (PPTP), 234-235,
238, 241
Simple Mail Transfer Protocol (SMTP), 90
Telnet, 90
Transmission Control/Internet,
managing (TCP/IP), 90-112
User Datagram (UDP), 90
virtual private networks (VPN), 241

proxy servers, function of, 109

**public folders, Outlook Web Access (OWA),
294**

public key encryption, 242

publishing, Web databases, 295-297, 300-303

push and pull partners, 95

push technology, 286-287

Q-R

querying databases, Windows Internet Naming Service (WINS), 182

RAID. *See Redundant Array of Independent Disks*

RAM. *See Random Access Memory*

Random Access Memory (RAM), optimizing settings, 177-182

RAS. *See Remote Access Service*

rcmd (Remote Command Client), 209

rcmdsvc. *See Server Service*

RDISK. *See Repair Disk utility*

reassigning resources, 187

receiving
feedback, 35-36
messages, WinPopUp utility, 201

recovering data, 147-148

Redirector counter, Windows NT Performance Monitor, 156

reducing total cost of ownership (TCO), 5-10, 33-50

Redundant Array of Independent Disks (RAID), replicating data, 141-143

refreshes, technology, 45, 59

Regini, 256

registering databases, 182

Registry, 201-202, 256, 324-325, 348-350

reliability of Internet, 240

Remote Access Administrator, 220

Remote Access Service (RAS), 215-229, 232-235, 399

Remote Administration, accessing Registry, 201-202

Remote Command Client (rcmd), 209

remote control applications, managing servers and workstations, 207-208

Remote Execute (rexec), 209

remote networks, 107

Remote Registry Service, 209

Remote Registry service, changing policy settings, 336

Remote Scripting Host (RSH), 361

remote server management, 194-214

Remote Shell (rsh), 209

remote shutdowns, 210

removing accounts, 76

Repair Disk utility (RDISK), backing up data, 144

repairing corrupt boot files, 148

replacing hardware, 185-186

replicating
data, Redundant Array of Independent Disks (RAID), 141-143
directories, 85
profiles, 329-330

reply time, 98

Report view, Windows NT Performance Monitor, 158, 161

Require Encrypted Authentication option, 222

Require Microsoft Encrypted Authentication option, 222

response time, 98

restartable file copy, Remote Access Service (RAS), 225

restoring, data, 134

restricting
buffer sizes, Windows NT Network Monitor, 167
computer access, Windows NT Zero Administration Kit (ZAK), 339-340

restrictions, logons, 76

return on investment (ROI), 4

reviewing total cost of ownership (TCO), 10

rexec (Remote Execute), 209

rights
granting
Bypass File Security for Backing Up Files, 134
groups, 75
Remote Access Service (RAS), 220
users
managing, 117-121
profiles, 330, 332
specifying, Log On As setting, 181

roaming user profiles, 328-332

ROI (return on investment), 4

routers, 91, 99

Routing and Remote Access Service (RRAS) Update, 226, 241, 398

RRAS. *See Routing and Remote Access Service Update*

RSH (Remote Scripting Host), 361

rsh (Remote Shell), 209

running
applications from servers, 341
File Transfer Protocol (FTP), 311,
319-321
Internet Service Manager, 202
Lotus ScreenCam, 414
Repair Disk utility, 144
Server Manager, 199
Windows 95/98 System Monitor, 168
Windows NT
Backup, from command line,
140-141
Disk Administrator, 141
Performance Monitor, 155
setup, 254
Task Manager, 162
winipcfg command, 97
WinPopUp utility, 202
runtime compilers, Java Virtual Machine, 277

S

saving
command output to text file, 97
logging information, Windows NT
Performance Monitor, 160
scalability, Active Directory service, 373
Schedule Service, 82-83
scheduling
backups, 136-137
Outlook Web Access, 294
resource-intensive tasks, 187
tasks, 81
scopes, Dynamic Host Configuration Protocol
(DHCP), 104, 106
scripting, 277-280, 346-351, 354-362
scripts
login, 86
Web-based, 360-361
search engines, 411
searching
bottlenecks, 101
feedback, 35-36
information about Internet Protocol (IP)
addresses, 96-97
Setup Manager, 251
solutions to technical projects, 34-35
Secure Sockets Layer (SSL), 242, 318
security
adding to Web pages, 303
company information, 65

data, Secure Sockets Layer (SSL), 318
firewalls, 107-108
logs, 71
patches, 400
physical, enabling, 127
planning, 114-131
policies, 62-63
protocols
File Transfe (FTP), 310-322
Transmission Control Protocol/
Internet (TCP/IP), 107-110, 126
servers, 235-239
settings, changing, 202-203
system policies, 338
Web-based, 284
Security Accounts Manager (SAM)
database, backing up, 144
Security Advisor Program Web site, 400
Security Configuration Manager, 128
security identifier (SID), 76
segmenting networks, 183-184
selecting
authentication levels, File Transfer
Protocol (FTP), 314-316
backup hardware, 135
databases, 295
files to back up, 139
home directories, File Transfer Protocol
(FTP) service, 312
options, auditing, 122
roaming user profiles, 328-329
scripting languages, 350-351
user permissions, Log On As
setting, 181
seminars, Microsoft, 406-407
sending messages
network outages, 57
WinPopUp utility, 201
sensitivity, case
command-line prompts, 79
VBScript, 356
Server counter, Windows NT Performance
Monitor, 156
Server Manager, 70, 194-195, 199
server operators group, 77
Server Service (rcmdsvc), 179-180, 209
Server TCO Calculator 1.0, 30
servers
backing up data, 146
configuring, 216, 234-240
connections, virtual private network
(VPN), 240

Domain Name System (DNS),
    resolving host names, 99
extensions, 399
Internet Information, 126-127, 282
managing, 193-199
Microsoft Transaction, 287-288
Personal Fax, 227
proxy, function of, 109
remote management, 194-214
running applications, 341
security, 235-239
steps in full recovery, 147
UNIX, compared to Windows NT, 22
Web, managing, 202-206
Windows 2000, 366
Windows Internet Naming Service
    (WINS), 95
Windows NT
    auditing, 121-124
    compared to UNIX, 22
    NetShow, 304

Service Monitor Configuration, 209

service-level agreements (SLA), 57, 387

services
    Active Directory, 372-374
    changing, 82, 180
    Dynamic Host Configuration Protocol
        (DHCP), installing, 104-106
    File Transfer Protocol (FTP), configuring,
        311-313
    Internet, 240
    Internet Connection for Remote Access,
        225
    License Management, 85
    managing, 82-83
    Microsoft Connection Manager for
        Remote Access, 225
    NetShow, 304
    packs, Windows NT, 398
    remote, managing, 194-195
    Remote Access, 215-229, 232-235, 399
    Remote Administration, accessing
        Registry, 201-202
    Remote Registry, changing policy
        settings, 336
    Routing and Remote Access Update, 226,
        398
    Schedule, 82-83
    Server, optimizing memory settings,
        179-180
    specifying user permissions, Log On As
        setting, 181
    startup options and settings, 181
    states, 83
    troubleshooting, 72

unnecessary, shutting down, 180-182
viewing, 82
Windows Internet Naming,
    broadcasts, 182

Session layer, 91

sessions, File Transfer Protocol (FTP), 319-321

setting
    authentication levels, File Transfer
        Protocol (FTP), 314-316
    filters, 71
    goals
        help desks, 38-41
        technical projects, 34-35
    logon restrictions, 76
    options
        *scope, Dynamic Host Configuration
            Protocol (DHCP), 105-106*
        script, WScript, 353
    threshold values, Windows NT
        Performance Monitor, 159

settings
    changing
        paging files, 178
        policies, 336
        roaming user profiles, 330-331
        *security, Internet Service Manager,
            202-203*
    dialing location, Remote Access Service
        (RAS), 225
    Entire Network, 218
    Log On As
        options, 83
        specifying user permissions, 181
    machine-specific, 255
    memory, optimizing, 177-182
    networks, documenting, 97
    paging files, calculating, 177
    services, 180-181
    SysDiff, 258
    This Computer Only, 218
    Windows NT Task Manager, 162

setup
    clients, Outlook Web Access (OWA),
        293-294
    Windows NT, running, 254

Setup Manager, 251-256, 260-261

shares, Server Manager, 195

sharing files, security, 310-322

shortcuts, creating, 356-358

Shutdown Manager, 209

shutdowns, remote, 210

shutting down unnecessary services, 180-182

SID (security identifier), 76

Simple Mail Transfer Protocol (SMTP) protocol, 90

Simple Network Monitor Protocol (SNMP Monitor), 209

SLA. *See service-level agreements*

SMP. *See symmetric multiprocessing*

SMS (Systems Management Server), 263

snapshots, 256-258, 260

sniffers, 116

SNMP Monitor, 209

software
   administrative, wizards, 70
   Client-Based Network Administration Tools, installing, 198
   command-line
      management, 78-81
      Regini, 256
      Transmission Control Protocol/Internet Protocol (TCP/IP), 96-102
   database, 283
   Difference detectors, 263
   Disk Administrator, 77
   Disk duplicators, 263
   Event Viewer, 70-72
   installing, 250-267, 368
   Internet Connection Services for Microsoft RAS, 399
   Internet Information Server (IIS), 282, 399
   Internet Service Manager, 202
   licensing, 43, 57, 83-85, 264
   logs, 70
   Lotus ScreenCam, 414
   Microsoft Exchange Server, backing up data, 146
   Microsoft FrontPage, 98, 282
   Microsoft Message Queue Server (MSMQ), 288, 399
   Microsoft Script Debugger, 399
   Microsoft Site Server Express, 399
   Microsoft SQL Server, backing up data, 146
   Microsoft Transaction Server (MTS), 287-288, 399
   Microsoft Visual InterDev, 282
   NetWatch, 209
   Network Client Administrator, 72
   Network Monitor Agent, capturing data, 200
   Office 97, network installations, 264
   Outlook Web Access (OWA), 292-294
   password-breaking, 116
   Performance Monitor, 72
   ping, isolating problems, 167
   public key encryption, 242

Remote Access Administrator, 220
Remote Administration, accessing Registry, 201-202
Remote Command Client (rcmd), 209
remote control, managing servers and workstations, 207-208
Remote Execute (rexec), 209
remote management, Windows NT Resource Kit, 209-210
Remote Registry Service, 209
Remote Scripting Host (RSH), 361
Remote Shell (rsh), 209
Repair Disk utility (RDISK), backing up data, 144
running from servers, 341
Secure Sockets Layer (SSL), 242
Security Configuration Manager, 128
Server Manager, 70, 194-195, 199
Server Service (rcmdsvc), 209
Service Monitor Configuration, 209
Setup Manager
   combining with SysDiff, 260-261
   creating answer files, 251-256
Shutdown Manager, 209
SNMP Monitor, 209
standardizing, 58-59
Synchronization Manager, 377
System Policy Editor, 333-337
Systems Management Server (SMS), 263
testing, 302
third-party
   authentication, 242
   backing up data, 146
total cost of ownership (TCO), 19-32
uninstalling, 368
User Manager, 73-77
Visual InterDev Rapid Application Deployment Components, 399
Web-based, 270-297, 300, 303-308
Web-Based Administrator (WBA), managing Web servers, 204-206
WinBench, 176
Windows 95/98 System Monitor, 168-169
Windows 2000, 366-380
Windows NT Backup, 139-140
Windows NT Diagnostics, 73, 200
Windows NT Disk Administrator, backing up data, 141-142
Windows NT Network Monitor, 166-167
Windows NT Performance Monitor, 155-161
Windows NT Task Manager, 162-166
Windows NT Terminal Server (WTS), managing remote workstations and servers, 210

Windows NT Zero Administration Kit (ZAK), restricting access on computers, 339-340

Windows Scripting Host (WSH), 347-348, 353-359

WinPopUp utility, sending and receiving messages, 201

special-purpose directories, creating, 316

specific account option, 83

specifying
    authentication levels, 314-316
    home directories, 312
    user permissions, Log On As setting, 181

speed
    drives, 136
    monitoring, 154-171
    optimizing, 174-190
    Web sites, measuring, 99

SQL Server, backing up data, 146

SSL. *See Secure Sockets Layer*

staffing, information technology (IT) departments, 390-391

standardizing, hardware and software, 58-59

Started state, 83, 181

starting
    applications from servers, 341
    File Transfer Protocol (FTP), 311, 319-321
    Internet Service Manager, 202
    Lotus ScreenCam, 414
    Repair Disk utility, 144
    Server Manager, 199
    Windows 95/98 System Monitor, 168
    Windows NT
        Backup, from command line, 140-141
        Disk Administrator, 141
        Performance Monitor, 155
        setup, 254
        Task Manager, 162
    winipcfg command, 97
    WinPopUp utility, 202

startup settings, services, 181

state management, 288

states
    managing, 288
    services, 83, 181

static addresses, creating, 104

statistics, network, 200

Stop Scripts After Specified Number of Seconds property, 353

Stopped state, 83, 181

stopping

network attacks, 108-109, 124-127

unnecessary services, 180-182

storage
    drive capacities, 135-136
    files, 77
    managing, 370-372
    profiles, 324-325, 327
    Registry scripts, 348-350

streaming media, 303-304

strength of passwords, enforcing, 120-121

striping disks, 142

subdirectories, user profiles, 326-327

subnet masks, 91

success, help desks, 38-41

suggestions, receiving and applying, 35-36

Sun Microsystems, 277

swap files, optimizing memory settings, 178-179

symmetric multiprocessing (SMP), upgrading central processing units (CPU), 186

Synchronization Manager, 377

SysDiff, 256-261

system account option, 83

system log, 70-72

System Monitor, 168-169

system policies, enforcing, 324-344

System Policy Editor, 333-337

system settings, SysDiff, 258

systems administrators, responsibilities, 12

Systems Management Server (SMS), 263

T

tables, file allocation
    converting, 77
    restoring data, 134
    security, 117

tabs, Windows NT Task Manager, 162-166

tape backups, storage capacities, 135-136

Task Manager, monitoring performance, 162-166

Task Station mode, Windows NT Zero Administration Kit (ZAK), 338

TCO & ROI Calculator, 28-29

TCO Manager, 26-28

TCO. *See total cost of ownership*

TechNet, 404

technical projects, defining solutions for, 34-35

technical support
    charge backs, 54
    Microsoft, 405-406

technical training, Microsoft, 406-407

technicians, help desk, 12

technologies
    push, 286-287
    Web-based, 270-297, 300, 303-308

technology refreshes, 45, 59

telephone support, Microsoft, 406

Telnet protocol, 90

templates
    creating, 75-76
    system policies, 332-333

terminals, dumb, 211

testing
    applications, 302
    backups, 147-148

text files, saving command output to, 97

thin clients, 210-212

thinking like intruders, 116

third-party authentication, 242

third-party software,
  backing up data, 146

This Computer Only option, 218

threshold values, setting, 159

throughput, disks, 176

tightening account policies, 119

time reply, 98

times, access, 175

tools
    administrative, wizards, 70
    Client-Based Network Administration,
      installing, 198
    command-line
      management, 78-81
      Regini, 256
      Transmission Control Protocol/Internet
      Protocol (TCP/IP), 96-102
    database, 283
    Difference detectors, 263
    Disk Administrator, 77
    Disk duplicators, 263
    Event Viewer, 70-72
    installing, 250-267, 368
    Internet Connection Services for Microsoft
      RAS, 399
    Internet Information Server (IIS), 282, 399
    Internet Service Manager, 202

licensing, 43, 57, 83-85, 264

logs, 70

Lotus ScreenCam, 414

Microsoft Exchange Server, backing up
  data, 146

Microsoft Message Queue Server
  (MSMQ), 288, 399

Microsoft Script Debugger, 399

Microsoft Site Server Express, 399

Microsoft SQL Server, backing up data,
  146

Microsoft Transaction Server (MTS),
  287-288, 399

Microsoft Visual InterDev, 282

NetWatch, 209

Network Client Administrator, 72

Network Monitor Agent, capturing data,
  200

Outlook Web Access (OWA), 292-294

password-breaking, 116

Performance Monitor, 72

ping, isolating problems, 167

public key encryption, 242

Remote Access Administrator, 220

Remote Administration, accessing
  Registry, 201-202

Remote Command Client (rcmd), 209

remote control, managing servers and
  workstations, 207-208

Remote Execute (rexec), 209

remote management, Windows NT
  Resource Kit, 209-210

Remote Registry Service, 209

Remote Scripting Host (RSH), 361

Remote Shell (rsh), 209

Repair Disk utility (RDISK), backing up
  data, 144

running from servers, 341

Secure Sockets Layer (SSL), 242

Security Configuration Manager, 128

Server Manager, 70, 194-195, 199

Server Service (rcmdsvc), 209

Service Monitor Configuration, 209

Setup Manager
    combining with SysDiff, 260-261
    creating answer files, 251-256

Shutdown Manager, 209

SNMP Monitor, 209

standardizing, 58-59

Synchronization Manager, 377

System Policy Editor, 333-337

Systems Management Server (SMS), 263

testing, 302

third-party
  authentication, 242
  backing up data, 146
total cost of ownership (TCO), 19-32
uninstalling, 368
User Manager, 73-77
Visual InterDev Rapid Application
  Deployment Components, 399
Web-based, 270-297, 300, 303-308
Web-Based Administrator (WBA),
  managing Web servers, 204-206
WinBench, 176
Windows 95/98 System Monitor, 168-169
Windows 2000, 366-380
Windows NT Backup, 139-140
Windows NT Diagnostics, 73, 200
Windows NT Disk Administrator, backing
  up data, 141-142
Windows NT Network Monitor, 166-167
Windows NT Performance Monitor,
  155-161
Windows NT Task Manager, 162-166
Windows NT Terminal Server (WTS),
  managing remote workstations and
  servers, 210
Windows NT Zero Administration Kit
  (ZAK), restricting access on computers,
  339-340
Windows Scripting Host (WSH),
  347-348, 353-359
WinPopUp utility, sending and
  receiving messages, 201
topology, Ethernet, 183
total cost of ownership (TCO)
  evaluating, 8
  future of, 382-394
  implementing, 9-10
  measuring, 3-18
  planning, 8-9
  reducing, 5-10, 33-50
  reviewing, 10
  studies, 19-32
  tools, 19-32
  Windows 2000, 366-380
Total Cost of Ownership Distributed
  Computing Chart of Accounts, 25-26
Totals value, Windows NT Task Manager, 165
TPC-C (Transactional Processing Performance
  Council), 383
tracert utility, 99, 101
tracking
  disks, Windows NT Disk Administrator,
  142

paths, packets, 99
performance, 154-171
traffic
  allowed, 107
  networks
    effects of broadcasts upon, 95
    isolating, 183-184
  ping-based, 108
training
  classes offered through Microsoft,
  406-407
  costs, 7
  employees, 48-49
  information technology (IT) staff, 14-15
  users, security, 117
  Web-based, 305
transactions
  logging, 134
  processing, 287
Transactional Processing Performance Council
  (TPC-C), 383
translation, network addresses, 125
Transmission Control Protocol/Internet
  Protocol (TCP/IP), 90-112, 126
Transport layer, 91
transporting data, costs, 7
troubleshooting
  corrupt boot files, 148
  drivers, 72
  modem detection, Remote Access Service
  (RAS), 217
  services, 72
  Transmission Control Protocol/Internet
  Protocol (TCP/IP) commands, 96-102
TUCOWS (Ultimate Collection of Windows
  Shareware, The), 408
tuning hardware, 184-186

U

UDP (User Datagram Protocol), 90
Ultimate Collection of Windows Shareware,
  The (TUCOWS), 408
unattend.txt, 254
unidrivers, 186
uninstalling applications, 368
uninterruptible power supplies (UPS), 146
United States National Security Agency
  (NSA), 115

UNIX servers and workstations, 22-23
updates
changing frequency, Windows NT Task
Manager, 162
downloading, 401
Routing and Remote Access Service
(RRAS), 398
Windows operating system, 401
upgrades
automatic, 264
hardware, 185-186
Windows 2000, 368
Upload directory, 316
UPS (uninterruptible power supplies), 146
User Datagram Protocol (UDP)
protocol, 90
User Manager, 73-77
users
accounts, 73-77
applying system policies, 336
communications, 55-57
managing, 200-202
names, case sensitivity, 120
permissions
managing, 117-121
specifying, Log On As setting, 181
profiles, 324-332
remote, notifying, 194
security, training, 117
support, Windows 2000, 378
utilities
administrative, wizards, 70
Client-Based Network Administration
Tools, installing, 198
command-line
management, 78-81
Regini, 256
Transmission Control Protocol/Internet
Protocol (TCP/IP), 96-102
database, 283
Difference detectors, 263
Disk Administrator, 77
Disk duplicators, 263
Event Viewer, 70-72
installing, 250-267, 368
Internet Connection Services for Microsoft
RAS, 399
Internet Information Server (IIS), 282, 399
Internet Service Manager, 202
licensing, 43, 57, 83-85, 264
logs, 70
Lotus ScreenCam, 414
Microsoft Exchange Server, backing up
data, 146

Microsoft Message Queue Server
(MSMQ), 288, 399
Microsoft Script Debugger, 399
Microsoft Site Server Express, 399
Microsoft SQL Server, backing up data,
146
Microsoft Transaction Server (MTS),
287-288, 399
Microsoft Visual InterDev, 282
NetWatch, 209
Network Client Administrator, 72
Network Monitor Agent, capturing data,
200
Outlook Web Access (OWA), 292-294
password-breaking, 116
Performance Monitor, 72
ping, isolating problems, 167
public key encryption, 242
Remote Access Administrator, 220
Remote Administration, accessing
Registry, 201-202
Remote Command Client (rcmd), 209
remote control, managing servers and
workstations, 207-208
Remote Execute (rexec), 209
remote management, Windows NT
Resource Kit, 209-210
Remote Registry Service, 209
Remote Scripting Host (RSH), 361
Remote Shell (rsh), 209
Repair Disk (RDISK), backing up data,
144
running from servers, 341
Secure Sockets Layer (SSL), 242
Security Configuration Manager, 128
Server Manager, 70, 194-195, 199
Server Service (rcmdsvc), 209
Service Monitor Configuration, 209
Setup Manager
combining with SysDiff, 260-261
creating answer files, 251-256
Shutdown Manager, 209
SNMP Monitor, 209
standardizing, 58-59
Synchronization Manager, 377
System Policy Editor, 333-337
Systems Management Server (SMS), 263
testing, 302
third-party
authentication, 242
backing up data, 146
total cost of ownership (TCO), 19-32
uninstalling, 368
User Manager, 73-77
Visual InterDev Rapid Application
Deployment Components, 399

Web-based, 270-297, 300, 303-308
Web-Based Administrator (WBA),
   managing Web servers, 204-206
WinBench, 176
Windows 95/98 System Monitor, 168-169
Windows 2000, 366-380
Windows NT Backup, 139-140
Windows NT Diagnostics, 73, 200
Windows NT Disk Administrator, backing
   up data, 141-142
Windows NT Network Monitor, 166-167
Windows NT Performance Monitor,
   155-161
Windows NT Task Manager, 162-166
Windows NT Terminal Server (WTS),
   managing remote workstations and
   servers, 210
Windows NT Zero Administration Kit
   (ZAK), restricting access on computers,
   339-340
Windows Scripting Host (WSH), 347-348,
   353-359
WinPopUp, sending and receiving
   messages, 201

files
   Registry, 325
   text, command output, 97
names, network caches, 100
network statistics, Windows NT
   Diagnostics, 200
options, File Transfer Protocol (FTP) log
   configuration, 317
services, 82
values, Windows NT Performance
   Monitor, 161
views
   default, 155
   Windows NT Performance Monitor,
      158-161
virtual memory, swap files, 178-179
virtual private networks, 231-247
Visual Basic Script (VBScript), 352, 356
Visual Basic, Scripting Edition (VBScript), 278
Visual InterDev Rapid Application
   Deployment Components, 399
voice over IP, 285
volumes
   described, 175
   managing, 372

V

values
   Performance tab, Windows NT Task
      Manager, 165
   subnet masks, 91
   threshold, setting, 159
   viewing, Windows NT Performance
      Monitor, 161
VBScript. *See Visual Basic, Scripting Edition*
verification, call-back, 222-223
Verify Windows NT System Files option,
   WINNT /ox command, 148
verifying
   backups, 147-148
   network connectivity, 98
video cards, upgrading, 186
videoconferencing, 285
viewing
   drive mappings, 358-359
   logs
      Event Viewer, 123-124
      Web-Based Administrator (WBA), 205
      Windows NT Performance Monitor,
         161

W

WAN. *See wide area networks*
warning messages, File Transfer Protocol
   (FTP), 317
WBA. *See Web-Based Administrator*
WBEM (Web-based enterprise
   management), 206
WDM (Windows Driver Model), 206
Web-Based Administrator (WBA),
   managing Web servers, 204-206
Web-based enterprise management
   (WBEM), 206
Whatis.com, 408
wide area networks (WAN), adapters, 217
Windows Driver Model (WDM), 206
Windows Internet Naming Service (WINS)
   broadcasts, 182
   resolving domain names, 94-96
Windows Management Interface
   (WMI), 206

Windows NT
  Backup, 139-140
  building Web platforms, 282-284
  Diagnostics, 73, 200
  Disk Administrator, backing up data,
    141-142
  Network Monitor, 166-167
  NT File System (NTFS), 77, 116, 134
  option packs, 398-400
  Performance Monitor, 155-161
  Resource Kit, 209-210
  Server, 304, 398
  servers, compared to UNIX, 22
  service packs, 398
  Services, states, 181
  setup, running, 254
  Task Manager, 162-166
  Terminal Server, 210
  total cost of ownership (TCO), 16-17
  workstations, compared to UNIX, 22-23
  Zero Administration Kit (ZAK), 339-340
Windows operating system
  95/98
    automating installation, 262
    monitoring performance, 168-169
    profiles, 331-332, 337
  2000, total cost of ownership (TCO),
    366-380
  Device Manager, updating
    drivers, 186
  future of, 393
  updates, 401
Windows Scripting Host (WSH), 347-348,
  353-359
Windows Update, 186
Winfiles.com, 408
winipcfg command, 97
WINNT /ox command, 148
WinPopUp utility, sending and receiving
  messages, 201
WINS. See Windows Internet Naming Service
wizards
  administrative, 70
  Dial-Up Networking (DUN) setup,
    Remote Access Service (RAS), 225
WMI. See Windows Management Interface
workflow policies, 62-66
workstations
  automating installations, 250-256
  locking, 129
  managing, 200-202, 207-208,
    211-212
  UNIX and Windows NT compared, 22-23

World Wide Web
  browsers, 276-277, 283, 320-321
  cloud icons, 91
  data security, Secure Sockets Layer (SSL),
    318
  managing Web servers, 202-206
  pages
    adding security, 303
    dynamic editors, 276
  protocols
    bindings, managing, 182-183
    Challenge-Handshake Authentication,
      221
    configuring, Remote Access Service
      (RAS), 218-219
    Dynamic Host Configuration,
      102-106, 184
    File Transfer, 90, 310-322
    Hypertext Transfer, 90
    Internet Control Messaging, 90
    Internet, 90, 96-97, 106, 110, 184,
      285
    IPSecure (IPSec), 242
    IPX/SPX, 90
    Layer 2 Forwarding, 242
    NetBEUI, 90
    NETBIOS, 90
    Network News Transfer, 408
    Password Authentication, 221
    Point-to-Point, 90
    Point-to-Point Tunneling, 234-235,
      238, 241
    Simple Mail Transfer, 90
    Telnet, 90
    Transmission Control/Internet,
      90-112, 126
    User Datagram, 90
    virtual private networks
      (VPN), 241
  publishing Web databases, 295-297,
    300-303
  reliability, 240
  remote networks, 107
  resources
    Beverly Hills Software, 408
    CNet's News.Com, 408
    Microsoft Certified Professional
      Magazine, 408
    Microsoft classroom training, 407
    Microsoft Knowledge Base, 405
    Microsoft online seminars, 406
    Microsoft online support, 405
    Microsoft Security Advisor Program
      site, 400
    Microsoft TechNet, 404
    Microsoft telephone support, 406

newsgroups, 408-409
NT Security.Net, 408
search engines, 411
Ultimate Collection of Windows
  Shareware, The (TUCOWS), 408
Whatis.com, 408
Winfiles.com, 408
Ziff-Davis Anchordesk, 408
scripts, 360-361
servers, managing, 202-206
services, 240
sites
  measuring performance, 99
  Security Advisor Program, 400
support, Windows 2000, 379
technologies, 270-297, 300, 303-308
total cost of ownership (TCO), 16
training, 305
usage policies, 59-60
World Wide Web Publishing Service, 204
WScript, 352-355

WSH. *See Windows Scripting Host*
WshArguments object, 352
WshEnvironment object, 352
WshShell object, 352
WshShortcut object, 352
WshSpecialFolders object, 352
WshURLShortcut object, 352
WTS. *See Windows NT, Terminal Server*

X-Z

Yahoo!, 411
ZAK. *See Zero Administration Kit*
Zero Administration Kit (ZAK),
  restricting access on computers, 339-340
Ziff-Davis
  Anchordesk, 408
  benchmarking software, 176

Windows NT TCP/IP
By Karanjit Siyan
1st Edition
480 pages, $29.99
ISBN: 1-56205-887-8

If you're still looking for good documentation on Microsoft TCP/IP, then look no further—this is your book. *Windows NT TCP/IP* cuts through the complexities and provides the most informative and complete reference book on Windows-based TCP/IP. Concepts essential to TCP/IP administration are explained thoroughly, then related to the practical use of Microsoft TCP/IP in a real-world networking environment. The book begins by covering TCP/IP architecture, advanced installation, and configuration issues, then moves on to routing with TCP/IP, DHCP Management, and WINS/DNS Name Resolution.

Windows NT DNS
By Michael Masterson, Herman L. Knief, Scott Vinick, and Eric Roul
1st Edition
340 pages, $29.99
ISBN: 1-56205-943-2

Have you ever opened a Windows NT book looking for detailed information about DNS only to discover that it doesn't even begin to scratch the surface? DNS is probably one of the most complicated subjects for NT administrators, and there are few books on the market that really address it in detail. This book answers your most complex DNS questions, focusing on the implementation of the Domain Name Service within Windows NT, treating it thoroughly from the viewpoint of an experienced Windows NT professional. Many detailed, real-world examples illustrate further the understanding of the material throughout. The book covers the details of how DNS functions within NT, then explores specific interactions with critical network components. Finally, proven procedures to design and set up DNS are demonstrated. You'll also find coverage of related topics, such as maintenance, security, and troubleshooting.

Windows NT Registry
By Sandra Osborne
1st Edition
564 pages, $29.99
ISBN: 1-56205-941-6

The NT Registry can be a very powerful tool for those capable of using it wisely. Unfortunately, there is very little information regarding the NT Registry, due to Microsoft's insistence that their source code be kept secret. If you're looking to optimize your use of the Registry, you're usually forced to search the Web for bits of information. This book is your resource. It covers critical issues and settings used for configuring network protocols, including NWLink, PTP, TCP/IP, and DHCP. This book approaches the material from a unique point of view, discussing the problems related to a particular component, and then discussing settings, which are the actual changes necessary for implementing robust solutions. There is also a comprehensive reference of Registry settings and commands, making this the perfect addition to your technical bookshelf.

Windows NT Performance Monitoring, Benchmarking, and Tuning

By Mark Edmead and Paul Hinsberg
1st Edition
288 pages, $29.99
ISBN: 1-56205-942-4

Performance monitoring is a little like preventative medicine for the administrator: no one enjoys a checkup, but it's a good thing to do on a regular basis. This book helps you focus on the critical aspects of improving the performance of your NT system, showing you how to monitor the system, implement benchmarking, and tune your network. The book is organized by resource components, which makes it easy to use as a reference tool.

Windows NT Terminal Server

By Ted Harwood
1st Edition
416 pages, $29.99
ISBN: 1-56205-944-0

It's no surprise that most administration headaches revolve around integration with other networks and clients. This book addresses these types of real-world issues on a case-by-case basis, giving tools

and advice on solving each problem. The author also offers the real nuts and bolts of thin client administration on multiple systems, covering such relevant issues as installation, configuration, network connection, management, and application distribution.

Windows NT Security

By Richard Puckett
1st Edition Summer 1999
600 pages, $29.99
ISBN: 1-56205-945-9

Swiss cheese. That's what some people say Windows NT security is like. And they may be right, because they only know what the NT documentation says about implementing security. Who has the time to research alternatives; play around with the features, service packs, hotfixes, and add-on tools; and figure out what makes NT rock solid? Well, Richard Puckett does. He has been researching Windows NT Security for the University of Virginia for a while now, and he's got pretty good news. He's going to show you how to make NT secure in your environment, and we mean really secure.

MCSE Core NT Exams Essential Reference
By Matthew Shepker
1st Edition
256 pages, $19.99
ISBN: 0-7357-0006-0

You're sitting in the first session of your Networking Essentials class and the instructor starts talking about RAS and you have no idea what that means. You think about raising your hand to ask about RAS, but you reconsider—you'd feel pretty foolish asking a question in front of all these people. You turn to your handy *MCSE Core NT Exams Essential Reference* and find a quick summary on Remote Access Services. Question answered. It's a couple months later and you're taking your Networking Essentials exam the next day. You're reviewing practice tests and you keep forgetting the maximum lengths for the various commonly used cable types. Once again, you turn to the *MCSE Core NT Exams Essential Reference* and find a table on cables, including all of the characteristics you need to memorize in order to pass the test.

Back Office Titles

Implementing Exchange Server
By Doug Hauger, Marywynne Leon, and William C. Wade III
1st Edition
400 pages, $29.99
ISBN: 1-56205-931-9

If you're interested in connectivity and maintenance issues for Exchange Server, then this book is for you. Exchange's power lies in its ability to be connected to multiple email subsystems to create a "universal email backbone." It's not unusual to have several different and complex systems all connected via email gateways, including Lotus Notes or cc:Mail, Microsoft Mail, legacy mainframe systems, and Internet mail. This book covers all the problems and issues associated with getting an integrated system running smoothly, and addresses troubleshooting and diagnosis of email problems with an eye toward prevention and best practices.

Other Books By New Riders Press

Certification

A+ Certification TestPrep
1562058924
A+ Certification Top Score Software
0735700176
A+ Certification Training Guide
1562058967
A+ Certifiction Fast Track
0735700281
A+ Complete v 1.1
0735700451
A+ Fast Track: DOS/Windows
0735700206
CLP Training Guide: Lotus Notes
0789715058
MCSD Fast Track: Visual Basic 6
Exam 70-176 0735700192
MCSD TestPrep: Visual Basic 6
073570032X
MCSD TestPrep: Visual Basic 6
Exam 70-176 0735700370
MCSD Training Guide: Visual
Basic 5 1562058509
MCSD Training Guide: Visual Basic
6 Exam 70-176 0735700311
MCSE + Internet Complete Version
1.2 0735700729
MCSE Essential Reference: Core
NT Exams 0735700060
MCSE Fast Track: 6-in-1 Bundle
1562059092
MCSE Fast Track: Internet
Information Server 4 156205936X
MCSE Fast Track: Networking
Essentials 1562059394
MCSE Fast Track: TCP/IP
1562059378
MCSE Fast Track: Visual Basic 6,
Exam 70-175 0735700184
MCSE Fast Track: Windows 98
0735700168
MCSE Fast Track: Windows NT
Server 4 1562059351
MCSE Fast Track: Windows NT
Server 4 Enterprise 1562059408
MCSE Fast Track: Windows NT
Workstation 4 1562059386
MCSE Simulation Guide: Windows
NT Server & Enterprise 4
1562059149
MCSE Simulation Guide: Windows
NT Workstation 4 1562059254
MCSE TestPrep Software: Elective
Exams 1562059009
MCSE TestPrep: Core Exams
0735700303

MCSE TestPrep: Exchange Server
5.5 0789716119
MCSE TestPrep: Internet Explorer 4
0789716542
MCSE TestPrep: Networking
Essentials, Second Edition
0735700109
MCSE TestPrep: SQL Server 6.5
Design & Implementation
1562059157
MCSE TestPrep: TCP/IP, Second
Edition 0735700257
MCSE TestPrep: Windows 95,
Second Edition 0735700117
MCSE TestPrep: Windows 98
156205922X
MCSE TestPrep: Windows NT
Server 4 Enterprise, Second Edition
0735700095
MCSE TestPrep: Windows NT
Server 4, Second Edition
0735700125
MCSE TestPrep: Windows NT
Workstation 4, Second Edition
0735700087
MCSE Top Score Software: Core
Exams 0735700338
MCSE Training Guide: Core Exams,
Second Edition 1562059262
MCSE Training Guide: Internet
Explorer 4.0 1562058894
MCSE Training Guide: Internet
Information Server 4 1562058231
MCSE Training Guide: Internet
Specialist Exams 1562058797
MCSE Training Guide: Microsoft
Exchange Server 5.5 1562058991
MCSE Training Guide: Networking
Essentials, Second Edition
156205919X
MCSE Training Guide: TCP/IP,
Second Edition 1562059203
MCSE Training Guide: Windows 95,
Second Edition 1562058800
MCSE Training Guide: Windows 98
1562058908
MCSE Training Guide: Windows
NT Server 4, Second Edition
1562059165
MCSE Training Guide: Windows
NT Server Enterprise, Second
Edition 1562059173
MCSE Training Guide: Windows
NT Workstation 4, Second Edition
1562059181

OCP Training Guide: Oracle DBA
1562058916
Scott Mueller's Ultimate A+
Certification Kit 0735700710

Graphics

3D Studio MAX 2 Effects Magic
1562058835
Dynamic HTML Web Magic
1568304218
HTML Artistry: More Than Code
1568304544
HTML Web Magic, 2nd Edition
1568304757
Inside 3D Studio Max 2, Volume I
1562058576
Inside 3D Studio Max 2, Volume II:
Modeling & Materials
1562058649
Inside 3D Studio Max 2, Volume III:
Animation 1562058657
Inside Adobe Photoshop 5
1562058843
Inside Adobe Photoshop 5, Limited
Edition 1562059513
Inside AutoCAD 14, Limited
Edition 1562058983
Inside Softimage 3D 1562058851
Inside trueSpace 4 1562059572
Net Results: Web Marketing that
Works 1568304145
Photoshop 5 Artistry 1562058959
Photoshop 5 Type Magic
156830465X
Photoshop 5 Web Magic
1562059130

Internet

New Rider's Official World Wide
Web Yellow Pages 0735700052
New Rider's Official World Wide
Web Yellow Pages, 7E 1562058746

Networking

Cisco Router Configuration and
Troubleshooting 0735700249
Networking with Microsoft TCP/IP,
3E 0735700141

Open Source

Developing Linux Applications
0735700214

Windows Technologies

Inside Windows 98 156205788X
Windows 98 Professional Reference
1562057863

We Want to Know What You Think

To better serve you, we would like your opinion on the content and quality of this book. Please complete this card and mail it to us or fax it to 317-581-4663.

Name _____

Address _____

City_____State_____Zip _____

Phone _____

Email Address _____

Occupation _____

Operating System(s) that you use_____

What influenced your purchase of this book?
- ❏ Recommendation
- ❏ Table of Contents
- ❏ Magazine Review
- ❏ New Riders' Reputation
- ❏ Cover Design
- ❏ Index
- ❏ Advertisement
- ❏ Author Name

How would you rate the contents of this book?
- ❏ Excellent
- ❏ Good
- ❏ Below Average
- ❏ Very Good
- ❏ Fair
- ❏ Poor

How do you plan to use this book?
- ❏ Quick reference
- ❏ Classroom
- ❏ Self-training
- ❏ Other

What do you like most about this book?
Check all that apply.
- ❏ Content
- ❏ Accuracy
- ❏ Listings
- ❏ Index
- ❏ Price
- ❏ Writing Style
- ❏ Examples
- ❏ Design
- ❏ Page Count
- ❏ Illustrations

What do you like least about this book?
Check all that apply.
- ❏ Content
- ❏ Accuracy
- ❏ Listings
- ❏ Index
- ❏ Price
- ❏ Writing Style
- ❏ Examples
- ❏ Design
- ❏ Page Count
- ❏ Illustrations

What would be a useful follow-up book to this one for you?_____

Where did you purchase this book? _____

_____

Can you name a similar book that you like better than this one, or one that is as good? Why?

_____

_____

How many New Riders books do you own? _____

What are your favorite computer books?_____

_____

What other titles would you like to see us develop? _____

_____

Any comments for us? _____

_____

_____

_____

Windows NT Network Management, 1-56205-946-7

www.newriders.com • Fax 317-581-4663

Fold here and tape to mail

New Riders Publishing
201 W. 103rd St.
Indianapolis, IN 46290

New Riders How to Contact Us

Visit Our Web Site

`www.newriders.com`

On our Web site you'll find information about our other books, authors, tables of contents, indexes, and book errata. You can also place orders for books through our Web site.

Email Us

Contact us at this address:

`editors@newriders.com`

- If you have comments or questions about this book
- To report errors that you have found in this book
- If you have a book proposal to submit or are interested in writing for New Riders
- If you would like to have an author kit sent to you
- If you are an expert in a computer topic or technology and are interested in being a technical editor who reviews manuscripts for technical accuracy

`sales@newriders.com`

- To find a distributor in your area, please contact our international department at the address above.

`pr@newriders.com`

- For instructors from educational institutions who wish to preview New Riders books for classroom use. Email should include your name, title, school, department, address, phone number, office days/hours, text in use, and enrollment in the body of your text along with your request for desk/examination copies and/or additional information.

Write to Us

New Riders Publishing
201 W. 103rd St.
Indianapolis, IN 46290-1097

Call Us

Toll-free (800) 571-5840 + 9 + 4557
If outside U.S. (317) 581-3500. Ask for New Riders.

Fax Us

(317) 581-4663